CHILD HOMICIDE

Parents Who Kill

Lita Linzer Schwartz
and
Natalie K. Isser

CRC is an imprint of the Taylor & Francis Group,
an informa business

CRC Press
Taylor & Francis Group
6000 Broken Sound Parkway NW, Suite 300
Boca Raton, FL 33487-2742

Printed in the United States of America on acid-free paper
10 9 8 7 6 5 4 3 2 1

International Standard Book Number-10: 0-8493-9366-3 (Hardcover)
International Standard Book Number-13: 978-0-8493-9366-2 (Hardcover)

Library of Congress Cataloging-in-Publication Data

Schwartz, Lita Linzer.
Child homicide : parents who kill / by Lita Linzer Schwartz and Natalie K. Isser.
p. cm.
Includes bibliographical references and index.
ISBN 0-8493-9366-3 (alk. paper)
1. Filicide. 2. Infanticide. 3. Homicide. 4. Children—Crimes against. I. Isser, Natalie. II. Title.

HV6542.S39 2006
364.152—dc22 2006044035

Visit the Taylor & Francis Web site at
http://www.taylorandfrancis.com

and the CRC Press Web site at
http://www.crcpress.com

Preface

Drought, plague, and flood are some of Mother Nature's means of population control. Tens of thousands can die in any of these, as we have seen in the tsunamis of 2004 and the hurricanes of 2005. Countries and subcultures often control population growth by war, with thousands killed or starved to death on each side. Societies whose economy cannot support a growing population enact population-limiting laws or simply practice wholesale neonaticide when families grow too large or the newborn is the "wrong" gender (i.e., female). All cultures' moral codes are constituted within the exigencies of survival.

Although infanticide is generally abhorred, a case can be made for its appearance in societies that lack the resources to feed all the children who are born (Posner, 1998). Scheper-Hughes (1989) noted that, in the "impoverished Third World today, women had had to give birth and to nurture children under ecological conditions and social arrangements hostile to child survival, as well as to their own well-being" (p. 14). Under these adverse conditions, women purposely allow weak and infirm infants to die or neglect them as part of their efforts to ensure the well-being and survival of the rest of their families.

Although we are more aware today, early in the 21st century, of instances of child homicide, this crime is not a modern phenomenon. Despite universal reprobation, neonaticide and infanticide have been practiced on every continent and by people on every level of cultural complexity, from hunters and gatherers to those in "higher" civilizations, including our ancestors and contemporaries. "Rather than being the exception, it has been the rule" (Williamson, 1978, p. 61). People are horrified when parents kill their children, and the media focus much attention on such crimes. It is likely that we are more aware of such events today simply because modern communications carry these news items farther and faster than they did even a few decades ago. This may also provoke "copycat" cases as less mentally stable or less capable parents see killing their children as a solution to their problems.

Today, most societies deplore child homicide and many, including ours, debate the right to have an abortion. Population problems, though, continue to exist. In a sense, those who commit child homicide are also practicing population control, but after the fact instead of before conception. These individuals and their acts against their children are our objects of study. Child killing within the family can be divided into three categories based on the age of the victim: neonaticide, infanticide, or filicide. The murderer in these cases is usually one of the child's parents; occasionally, it is someone acting *in loco parentis*. Most of the books available focus on mothers who kill their children of any age; they seriously underestimate the number of father figures who commit infanticide and filicide. Their role in child homicides is amply demonstrated in the pages that follow.

To begin, we must provide a context for the crime by looking at the roles of neonaticide, infanticide, and filicide in history. To do this, we will discuss these crimes as they occurred in Biblical and ancient times, up to our modern era. Apart from historical research, we know that they were also the core of much literature, from *Medea* (Euripedes, 431 B.C.) to the contemporary novel (e.g., *The Angel of Darkness* by Carr, 1991). Such crimes were certainly evident in many of the folk and fairy tales still read to children today. They also often have a cultural endorsement that we in the United States and in most Westernized cultures do not quite comprehend.

Here, we will focus on neonaticide that is not a culturally supported matter, but rather an individual one; we will also keep this crime distinct from infanticide and filicide, which occur under different circumstances. An abundance of questions arises from each of these crimes. These questions inevitably lead to discussion of the politics and semiotics involved in contraception, abortion, and sex education (although such a discussion is not a major focus of this work). Depending upon the circumstances of the individual case and, to a lesser extent, the community in which a child homicide case occurs, how much media attention is given to the specific case? What is the effect of media focus on the crime and its perpetrator? Does media publicity affect the penalty to be paid by the murdering parent or parents?

In some cases, the mother of an abandoned neonate may not be found, as often happens in large cities. How does she live with herself afterward, even if she is not punished by the courts? If she is found, should she be regarded as legally insane at the time of the crime or as guilty of manslaughter or first- or second-degree murder? To what extent should her age or circumstances be considered in weighing the charge and, if she confesses or is found guilty, the penalty? Is imprisonment the appropriate penalty? These questions lead to examining the crime from the perspective of therapeutic jurisprudence.

If the baby's father was involved in the neonaticide, does that change the legal perspective? If he was not involved, should he be permitted to escape any penalty for his role in the pregnancy that led to the crime? The law varies among communities, as well as among states and nations; it has changed over the centuries and even over recent decades. Awareness of these variations is necessary to the construction of any new policies.

Many of these questions arise in cases of infanticide and filicide as well, with others added to the list. In an era when births are shown in almost complete detail in televised soap operas or "family" shows, there seems to be little excuse for anyone to be uninformed about infantile crying and bodily functions. What psychological factors operate to repress such knowledge in the minds of those who kill an infant for crying too long, too often, or at the "wrong" time? Social welfare agencies exist in virtually every community in the United States, so why are some parents so overwhelmed by child care that they murder a child rather than seek outside help? In cases in which parents separate, why does one parent kill their offspring rather than provide child support or permit the other parent to have visitation or shared custody? Why are children the victims of their parents' inability to cope with life? Does postpartum depression or postpartum psychosis play a role in these crimes?

The issues of sex education, contraception, abortion, and euthanasia are related to some of the proposals to cope with these dilemmas; however, they are fraught with sharp political nuances and insuperable divisions of opinion, passion, and, sometimes, religion. In the following chapters, we will try to treat these questions with objectivity. We will also provide sociobiological, historical, and literary perspectives on these child homicide crimes, as well as seek to answer the many psychological questions that arise from these perspectives. In short, we will examine the mothers and fathers in terms of background and motives; the role, if any, of mental illness; the response of the legal system in terms of charges and penalties; and future directions in terms of preventive measures.

Natalie K. Isser

Lita Linzer Schwartz

The Authors

Natalie K. Isser, Ph.D., is a graduate of the University of Pennsylvania and professor emerita of The Pennsylvania State University, Abington College. She has written on French anti-Semitism, human rights, and French public opinion and diplomacy during the Second Empire. Dr. Isser teaches part-time and has continued research on a variety of topics, such as American melodrama, movies, and history and the social and cultural roots of American populism.

Lita Linzer Schwartz, Ph.D., is a graduate of Vassar College, Temple University, and Bryn Mawr College. She is distinguished professor emerita of The Pennsylvania State University, where she taught at the Abington College (née Ogontz campus). A licensed psychologist in Pennsylvania, she also holds a diplomate in forensic psychology from the American Board of Professional Psychology. Dr. Schwartz is a fellow of the American Psychological Association and the American Academy of Forensic Psychologists, as well as a member of the International Council of Psychologists and the Association of

Family and Conciliation Courts. She is actively involved in a number of writing projects on topics as varied as adoptive and surrogate parenting, cults and sects, media violence and its impact, gifted children, and female artists and photographers.

Child Homicide is the fourth book coauthored by this interdisciplinary team. They have written more than 20 articles and conference presentations together, in addition to developing and coteaching a course in "cultural pluralism." Their first book, *The American School and the Melting Pot*, was named an "outstanding academic book, 1986–1987" by *Choice*, a publication of the American Library Association.

Acknowledgments

We are most appreciative of the help provided by Jeannette Ullrich and Binh Le, members of the Penn State Abington College Library staff. They located sources when we could not and enhanced our computer search skills, without which our research would have been much more difficult. We are also appreciative of Steve Isser's input with respect to legal sources.

Table of Contents

1 Children: An Endangered Species throughout History

The first two chapters in this book emphasize the historical, cultural, literary, and sociobiological connections of neonaticide, infanticide, and filicide. Including these aspects provides a context for understanding not only these homicidal acts, but also why our horror at them is affected to a greater or lesser degree. This background also reveals attitudes toward women that permeate societies and indeed are taught to little children in fairy tales that feature wicked figures (wolves, ogres, and others) who kill children, as well as stepmothers who abuse them.

Those who are familiar with the Bible of Western religions are also familiar with the story of Moses, the infant who was abandoned in a basket that floated on the Nile. They are aware that first-born children were slain when Moses, long rescued and grown to manhood, sought to lead his people out of Egypt, although it was not the parents who killed them. The implication is that this divine act was in the cause of a greater good—convincing Pharaoh to release the Hebrews from slavery. This biblical tale has been replicated in the New Testament and in other religions, indicating the universality of religious themes that often employ the metaphor of abandonment or murder of the first-born male.

It will quickly become apparent from the historical and cultural surveys that poverty, whether of the individual or of the society, plays a significant role in whether or not children are allowed to live. When it comes to literature, however, emotions dominate the motives—anger, jealousy, shame, revenge—and these tend to reflect the era and culture in which they were written. Literature is also the vehicle by which the artist explains gender, power, and moral relationships between individuals and society.

Resnick (1970) was the first to define neonaticide as the killing of an infant at or within hours of its birth; infanticide was the murder of a child up to the age of 1 year and filicide was the murder of a son or daughter older than 1 year. These crimes were regarded as unnatural acts because women especially were supposed to love and nurture children. These unnatural acts were ranked in the past with witchcraft, heresy, parricide, sodomy, and murder—acts that challenged the established order and stability of society as well as the social order of the family. At all times and in all places, child homicide was also a constant reminder of the fragility of the prevailing moral order.

In the past, killing newborn infants occurred for a variety of reasons: sacrifice, primitive birth control, eugenics, shame, and fear of punishment for adultery or illegitimacy. Jimmerson, for example, wrote of classical Chinese texts from as early as 2000 B.C. telling of cases of infanticide and infant abandonment (1990). References to direct infanticide can be found in later texts. Jimmerson gave the example of the legalist philosopher Han Fei, writing in the third century B.C., who noted that parents' attitudes to a child vary by the child's gender. "Both come from the parents' love, but they congratulate each other when it is a boy and kill it if it is a girl because they are considering their later convenience and calculating their long-term interests" (p. 39). Other evidence shows that the practice continued in China: the Han dynasty (205 B.C. to 220 A.D.) cases include punishment for infanticidal parents. Beginning in the 12th century, the government began to set up foundling homes for abandoned children, first in Fujian province, where female infanticide was particularly prevalent, and later in other central southern provinces (Jimmerson, 1990).

Culture and primitive superstitions also played a large role, with common customs and perspectives that transcended time and society, indicating a persistent thread of behavior and values. These cultural similarities are still prevalent today.

Gender and Child Homicide

Gender relationships have also played a large role in the analysis of child homicides. Women were and are often the victims of crime, abuse, battering, and rape, and only women can bear children. Thus, women in illicit relationships, whether they were actively participating or seduced or raped, were forced to bear the stigma of the relationship if they became pregnant. They bore it alone if the man involved did not wish to acknowledge his responsibility. The women also had to endure the abortion or the burden of an unwanted child.

Throughout history, prosecutions of and convictions for neonaticides and infanticides have been, on the whole, more merciful than those of other kinds of homicides. Most contemporary societies have also refused to punish neonaticide as they do other homicides. Customs and laws often treat child murderers in a selective and targeted manner. For example, it has been alleged that men are generally punished more severely than mothers (Resnick, 1970). This might be because gender stereotypes and cultural images of women produce responses that affect public sympathy and attitudes when they kill their offspring. (The truth of Resnick's allegation will be discussed in Chapter 5.) Women have been perceived as the "mother" (chaste and pure) or as Eve (the wanton temptress). The word "mother" brought to mind the symbol of the warm nurturer, and if reality failed this expectation, a cultural disappointment was evoked, frequently abetted by individual experience.

Cultural assumptions were that mothers were self-sacrificing, compassionate, caring, and, above all, loving. The notion of "good mother" was often confused with that of the "good woman" (Neal, 1995). Thus, one of the commonly held assumptions was that women were not criminals and that any illegal activity on their part was therefore pathological. Mothers who killed their infants were unnatural and considered to be "mad" or evil sociopaths ("bad") (Wilczynski, 1991, p. 72). When tried for crimes, women were too often judged not only on the basis of their legal infractions, "but also for their compliance or variance with stereotypically female behavior" (Wilczynski, p. 72). If the female had not conformed to assumed gender characteristics, she was perceived as "bad." This was especially true in cases of neonaticide and infanticide because these crimes contradicted the concepts of motherhood and femininity that involved nurturing, selflessness, and the projection of the child's role in the family (Knelman, 1998).

Stereotypes affected the way in which society characterized and punished women. This often led to confused and ambiguous laws. The accused were good women who were victims or they were unnatural and wicked. Because women *could not* kill their children if they were normal women, there must have been mitigating circumstances, such as mental aberrations. The arguments based on mental disturbance were frequently used to create sympathy and leniency for mothers, based on the belief that reproduction and lactation produced emotional disturbance. "This concept could appear to legitimate the notion that women are inherently unstable because of their biology, which, of course, had implications for the integration of women into spheres outside the domestic" (Lansdowne, 1990, p. 41).

This behavioral pattern seems to have been derived from a combination of sympathy for the defendants, based on an awareness of the social environment that was so unfriendly to women, and on the difficulty of distinguishing between murder and natural infant mortality. All peoples, however, even those that practiced child sacrifice and exposure, as we shall demonstrate, abhorred child homicide.

The Literary Legacy

Infanticide came to possess enormous symbolic significance as evidenced by its treatment in mythology and other literature. The myths are the reflection and creation of cultures. For example, in the Medea story and fairy tales, they are reconstituted and reordered at different times and places to help us grasp the essential values of our cultures. Often they are integrated into the popular culture and become the arbiters of taste and an integral part of the political dialogue. Literature, art, and popular culture, with their symbols, analogies, and, sometimes, simplifications, enable us to grasp some of the moral ambiguities inherent in all discussion of child homicide.

The problems of child homicide involve not only the crime, but also the social and economic environments that spawn the despair and insensitivity that make such acts possible. The codes of the communities that involve shame, disgrace, or punishment for transgressing sexual behavior dicta also push young women to commit such evil acts. Psychological and sociological analysis (to be discussed later) can help to understand these factors that shape the way in which we regard and treat those who commit child homicide in practice and in law. However, literature, stories, and popular tales also provide rich insights.

Legacies of Ancient Cultures

In ancient Greece, exposure of newborns to the elements was permitted and, in some cases, especially in Sparta, enforced by law. Weak or deformed infants were destroyed because of their imperfections or for fear that they would become wards of and cost to the state. Plato called for eradication of babies "begotten by inferior parents," and Aristotle felt exposure was the best method of controlling overpopulation (Langer, 1974). Hellenist Greece's sex ratios favoring males indicated that exposure remained the choice of family and sex selection (Pomeroy, 1993).

The Romans continued this practice. Under the doctrine of *Pater Potestas*, only the father could choose to put his child to death (Lagaipa, 1990; Mays, 1993). The mother could not expose the baby without his authorization, but divorced fathers who denied paternity and fathers of illegitimate infants had no rights (Lee, 1994).

Greek mythology and literature refer to this common method of population control. Many of the infants exposed in the Greek stories—Zeus, Poseidon, Hephaistus, Asclepius, and Oedipus—were the product of illicit relationships between the gods and mortal women (Bennett, 1922). The founders of Rome, Romulus and Remus, were raised by wolves. Although the Greeks did abandon newborns as their best form of birth control, they nevertheless loved their children; indeed, they chose exposure or abandonment in the hope that some childless couple might adopt and save the child—another common thread in the myths.

Unlike in the classical world, Judaism, developing in the Middle East, renounced any form of neonaticide and condemned all practices that smacked of child sacrifice or exposure. Old Testament stories firmly negated any form of child homicide. These traditions were incorporated into Christian doctrines and firmly embedded into the canon law of Catholic, and later Protestant, churches. During the Middle Ages, infanticide was firmly denounced, although it was difficult to detect because children died from "overlaying," neglect, and disease (Langer, 1974). When child murder was detected, the church issued harsh penalties (horrible deaths) if the child was unbaptized or illegitimate. In contrast, married women who killed their children were treated more leniently—generally, a public humiliation with public penances for a number of years (Kellum, 1973). Child homicide was regarded with severity, although infant mortality was very high. Literature and fairy tales thus contain matter-of-fact stories of child abuse and neglect. Yet, even these myths and tales revealed a consistent horror of child murder in the ancient world.

Mythologies

Mythologies of all cultures contain tales of gods, goddesses, and heroes of great deeds, wars, and catastrophes that reveal much of the morality and values of the cultures that created them. Ancient myths were also part of religious and moral traditions and contained a variety of metaphors to describe an incomprehensible and often inimical environment. Graves (1988) claimed that the study of myths should begin with archaeology, history, and religion, rather than psychology, and these old stories do indeed, by their analogies, reveal much early history. Dundes stressed the importance of folklore as "an autobiographical ethnography of a people, which makes implicit worldview principles and themes … explicit" (Bendix & Zumwalt, 1995, p. 20).

Fairy Tales

Fairy tales illustrate the poverty and difficulties of peasant life in preindustrial societies—worlds of stepmothers, orphans, excruciating toil, life at a bare subsistence level, and overt unrepressed emotions. Peasant life was brutish, short, and mean, and fairy tales illustrated this well. Hansel and Gretel and "le petit poucet" were representative of the abandonment of children in hard times. Other forms of infanticide and child abuse occurred frequently in these stories. Parents turned their children out to become beggars; often they sold their offspring to the devil or the parents ran away, abandoning their children (Darnton, 1985).

Mothers in these fairy tales often adhered to the stereotypical image of the mother described earlier, and it is the stepmothers who were cruel in the tales of Snow White, Cinderella, and Hansel and Gretel. In other cultures of the Middle East, Africa, and India, the myths often speak of the "great earth mother goddesses" of fertility and procreation, some of whom are also responsible for death. "The good mother and the evil mother of European folk tales were often seen to coexist in one unpredictable goddess of birth and death in mythologies throughout much of the world" (Amighi, 1990, p. 132).

Child Homicide in Literature and Opera

One of the most notable plays in the Western literary canon is Sophocles' *Oedipus*, in which the father, Laius, exposed his infant son because of a fateful prophecy on Mount Citharon. Laius wounded his son's ankles to justify his abandonment, but the infant was rescued by a shepherd. Oedipus lived to fulfill his awful destiny despite his father's attempt at filicide. However, it is the story of Medea, based on ancient mythology and recreated by Euripedes, that permeates our culture and symbolizes the inherent weakness of all societies.

Medea

Euripedes' play *Medea* has been shown on the stage with regularity. It vividly uses the act of filicide to engage our emotions with the destiny of Medea and rivets the audience's outrage about her crimes. It is a complicated and emotional portrait that gains our sympathy even as it moves us to horror and anger at the protagonist's final act of revenge.

Medea was a witch, a feminist, and a powerful woman. She was a woman obsessed by love who betrayed her father and killed her brother to help her lover, Jason, obtain the Golden Fleece. In return, he pledged marriage, protection, and love. She left her home to go to a strange land, Corinth, where she was regarded as an outsider and a barbarian. She was plagued by feelings of guilt, loneliness, rejection, and passionate love, all of which are recognized and pitied by the chorus in the opening scenes. Despite his debt to Medea, her husband abandoned her for another woman—Creon's daughter, the princess of Corinth. Betrayed, Medea sought to avenge her honor. She vowed revenge and used her occult powers to kill Princess Glauce and Creon, and then wreaked final vengeance on Jason by killing their sons. In committing these unspeakable murders, Medea overstepped the bounds of revenge and honor and was abandoned by the chorus.

Euripedes' drama is especially effective because Medea and Jason are archetypes; she is the overly passionate and erotic female who turns to violence and he is the callous husband who, with sophist rationalization, can dismiss his wife and children and assume that, as long as he supports them, he is justified (Ashe, 1992). So important is this story that contemporary writers have characterized infanticide and filicide as the Medea syndrome (Crouch, 1987). Indeed, much of the legal and psychiatric literature has used Euripedes' *Medea* as the paradigm of child homicide (Ashe, 1992; Reid, 1997).

The drama was based on earlier Greek myths that the audience of ancient times recognized and knew very well. In one older version, Medea was partially a victim as Creon avenged Medea's murder of his daughter by killing 13 of Medea's 14 children and placing their bodies on display in the Agora, or marketplace (Graves, 1988). The Corinthians felt that this story was a stain on their reputation and, according to legend, commissioned Euripedes to write a play in which he absolved Creon of child homicide, made Medea the "barbarian" as the perpetrator of filicide, and heightened the dramatic effect by reducing the number of children to two (Graves, 1988). Other versions of the original myth involved the gods Zeus, Hera, Aphrodite, and Eros.

Another explanation for the change and revision of the original myth by Euripedes was laid to political events. Athens, the so-called center of Greek civilization, had repressed a rebellion against its domination by the Island of Melus and committed innumerable atrocities unworthy of a humane people. Euripedes wanted his play to expose the fragility of civilization and its moral code (Hornblower, 1983). For the Athenians, theater was their "school," so he used the characters of Medea and Jason to reveal the qualities of intermingled good and evil, reason and emotion. He used the heinous crime of filicide as the metaphor for the inhumanity of the Athenians, but carefully kept the analogy more palatable to the Greeks by making Medea a sorceress and barbarian (Barlow, 1989; Vasillopoulos, 1994).

The play still strikes a resonant chord with us. The relationships are familiar in their primitive emotions of obsession and erotic love. What gives the play such power is that Medea is not all evil. She is not lovable, but she is a powerful voice for women's rights, although that voice is muted by her terrible crime. The complexity of the characters and meanings of the filicide, honor, and duty still command our interest.

Faust

One of the other legends that revealed the same ambiguity about neonaticide was that of Dr. Faustus. This legend, a part of folklore and literature, was the tale of men who sold their souls to the devil in return for riches, pleasure, youth, knowledge, or power. The fable permeated popular and literate culture, and, like the Medea syndrome, the cliché "Faustian bargain" has become part of our language.

The legend arose from the tales of a real person, Dr. Johannes Faust, who was born in Knittlingen and died about 1540. He was probably a traveling doctor and con-artist with old "magical" potions and cures. His notoriety led Martin Luther to denounce him as the "devil's brother-in-law" and Philipp Melanchthon to characterize him as full of devils (Brenton, 1996). The story was so good that it gradually became a part of early German legends and, in 1587, appeared in a collection by J. Spies (Grim, 1988). It was so well liked that it became a part of popular culture and frequently was performed as part of puppet shows and plays at local fairs. A variety of widely distributed pamphlets and prints also circulated the story.

The reoccurrences of neonaticide received renewed attention in the literature of the 18th century, especially in Germany of the 1760s to late 1870s (Werner, 1960). Horror and sympathy for these unnatural crimes, based upon a sense of the callousness of seducers and rigidity of the law, pervaded the general literature. That was probably the reason that Goethe included this theme in his work.

Goethe reconstituted the old legend into a powerful story that captured the inner fears of men about aging, death, and the search for knowledge. *His* Faust made a pact with the devil to regain his youth and happiness. Part one of Goethe's long poem rested on the debates between Faust and Mephistopheles, in which Faust was regaled with song and wine in various fun-making establishments and had an illicit relationship with a young girl named Gretchen (a/k/a/ Marguerite). In the course of this ugly seduction, her brother was killed trying to defend her honor and her mother died from a poisoned draught under mysterious circumstances, possibly at her daughter's hand. Gretchen bore an illegitimate child and, in her maddened and grief-stricken condition, committed neonaticide.

She was captured and condemned to death for the double murders. On the eve of her execution, Faust commanded Mephistopheles to help him rescue her. They came to rescue Gretchen/Marguerite riding on the backs of magic horses, but she was frightened by Mephistopheles and prayed to God. She paid the full penalty of decapitation. However, God was merciful because she had repented of her sins, and her soul eluded Mephistopheles, as did Faust who also repented and was saved. Goethe added the sordid story of

Gretchen to the plot of the original legends, but hers is the minor story (Goethe, 1808/1950).

In this tale, the neonaticide was not the center of the metaphor; rather, Gretchen suffered for failure to avoid temptation and her lapse of moral scruples even though she was perceived as a victim of Faust and his evil companion's seduction. The story reflected, as our study will show, the concept that women who kill babies are unnatural and must suffer from some form of dementia. Goethe also revealed the shame and humiliation that would befall her in the anger and contempt her brother expressed (Piers, 1978). She was punished by death for two murders. This was made more acceptable to readers because she had been suspected in the death of her mother.

The Faust story as adapted by Goethe appealed to an avant-garde culture, but its attraction was also felt by opera composers and their librettists. The two best known are the operas by Berlioz and Gounod. The *Damnation of Faust* by Berlioz was truer to the Goethe poem than Gounod's libretto. In the Berlioz drama, Faust was placed in Hungary, and the seduction of Marguerite occurred through the magic of Mephistopheles. Marguerite was condemned, but Mephistopheles made a pact with Faust: In return for his soul, the girl was delivered. She repented her sins and was saved.

The love story in Berlioz's opera was minor and only significant in explaining Faust's damnation. In contrast, the Gounod opera libretto in its story line revealed the problems of shame and abandonment that often led young women to deny their pregnancies and commit murder. This version focused on the love story between Faust and the young woman and was meant to appeal to a wider, more popular audience than the one by Berlioz.

"Popular culture in much of Europe allowed a degree of sexual contact during courtship and bridal pregnancy was common" (Wrightson, 1982, p. 7). If the girl or woman was abandoned or misled, however, the disapprobation became disproportionate to the dilemma and the young woman became a victim. Gounod's opera, although based on the Faust legend, placed the love story in this latter context. After Faust made his pact with the devil, he saw Marguerite and set out to woo her. She was a young and foolish woman led astray by the blandishments of the more sophisticated Faust (beautifully shown in the famous "Jewel Song") and was lured into an illicit relationship. Her brother, Valentine, tried to defend her honor, but was killed by Faust who, with Mephistopheles, was forced to flee. Subsequently, Marguerite had her baby, but in her shame lost her mind and committed neonaticide. She was condemned to die and was executed, despite Faust's attempts to save her.

Jenufa

A modern variation of this latter theme was powerfully portrayed in the opera *Jenufa* by Leon Janacek, first performed in 1916. In his libretto, based on a story by Gabriella Preissova, the heroine, Jenufa, is in love with young Steva and has an affair with him. He then abandons her in favor of the mayor's daughter. Jenufa has a child, but her former suitor, Laca, is unwilling to assume the care of his rival's child. Jenufa's stepmother, fearing that Laca's proposal was Jenufa's last chance for marriage, secretly kills the baby but assures Jenufa that it died of natural causes. Jenufa agrees to marry Laca, but, on the day of her wedding, the baby's body is found and the stepmother confesses to the murder. She is arrested and although there is widespread revulsion at her crime, Jenufa forgives her because the motive had been to make her happy. The opera ends with Jenufa and Laca gaining maturity and with their love enhanced through suffering (Kobbé, 1919/1987).*

The power of the music and the story is augmented by the libretto, which used the theme of infanticide to illustrate the complexity and diversity of human motives and emotions. Moreover, by maintaining feminine stereotypes, the librettist kept the heroine's purity fresh by making her the loving mother; even the stepmother who committed the unspeakable crime acted out of love for her stepchild. The ambiguity of moral behavior in this opera again illustrates problems of the mitigating circumstances so often cited in cases of child homicide, as will be seen in the following chapters.

An Historical Note

During the Middle Ages and even up to early periods in modern times, there was great credulity. Belief in witchcraft was widespread. Sometimes, the midwife or wet nurse would be accused of witchcraft, or women accused of neonaticide or infanticide would claim that they were possessed by the devil. More common than actual murder was the abandonment of infants. The living newborn was left in a public place, sometimes on the steps of a church or convent, in the hope that the child would be cared for by others.

If in the past it was difficult to discern a viable living infant, the law often used the legal fiction of concealment to punish mothers who could not be detected as having murdered their infants or to mitigate the sentences of mothers who were convicted of the murder.

* Life imitates art as two legal cases illustrate. In 1923, a mother was convicted of manslaughter for the murder of her daughter's newborn. The appellate court reversed the conviction because of insufficient evidence (*People v. Kirby*, 1923). Another mother took her 16-year-old daughter's newborn and left it in a nearby garage where it died from neglect. The baby, she claimed, would have caused trouble for her daughter and herself. She also killed the newborns of her two other daughters who had delivered out of wedlock (*People v. Westfall*, 1961).

> From its inception as a sex-specific crime in 1623, infanticide has been concerned with theories about women. The initial object of the law was to punish single women for becoming pregnant and for refusing to live with their sin. Thus the crime was created to affect moral and social behavior (O'Donovan, 1984, p. 264).

The law referred to was passed in England in 1623 and was an act to prevent destroying or murdering bastard children, on the presumption that a woman who concealed the death of her illegitimate child was guilty of murder. The law was designed to regulate illicit sexual conduct. Because mothers could easily dispose of or hide the murdered infant, the law, which was also aimed at illegitimacy, was passed against concealed pregnancies. The rate of conviction rose, but, despite the penalties, neonaticide remained commonplace (Oberman, 1996). The only way to rebuff the supposition of neonaticide was the testimony of another person that a child had been born dead, "even if the woman could prove that the child had been alive and then died of natural causes" (Lansdowne, 1990, p. 43). The law was never applied rigorously and by the 18th century it had fallen into disuse. The legal effort, however, did serve a role in later literature.

The Heart of Midlothian

Sir Walter Scott's *The Heart of Midlothian*, an historical novel set in 17th century Scotland, was based upon a Scottish law of 1690 that was almost the same as the earlier English one. The principal themes were justice, rebellion, and social order. The parts of the plot that centered on the act of concealment of pregnancy were based on an anonymous account heard by Scott of an incident that had occurred 80 years before. Helen Walker, a country woman, had refused to lie in court to save her sister's life and then had walked to London to seek a reprieve for her (Scott, 1830/1994).

The principal themes of the novel included the conflicts between English and Scottish cultures and between the emerging commercial urban development and traditional rural values. Scott also observed the problems of authority, social order, rebellion, and justice. Trained as a lawyer, he attacked the legal system as rigid and corrupt, but necessary for the maintenance of social stability (see Murphy, 1994).

In the novel, the heroine was Jeanie Deans, whose sister, Effie, a young Puritan girl, was seduced by George Staunton, a leader of the Porteous Riot (an actual historical event). He was the black sheep of a prosperous family and was reckless, dissipated, and irresponsible. Forced into hiding because of his role in the riot, he was unable to help Effie. Effie gave birth to a baby boy in the woods, helped by an evil midwife named Meg Murdockson, who disappeared and took the newborn with her. Effie lost consciousness and, upon wakening, discovered that her infant was gone. She was accused of neonaticide because she had concealed her pregnancy and the baby had disappeared.

Her sister Jeanie refused to lie under oath that she knew of the pregnancy, and Effie was convicted of neonaticide and condemned to hang. Even though she was pressured to do so, Jeanie felt she could not lie as a matter of honor (Cohen, 1993). However, she was determined to save her sister and walked to London to try to obtain a pardon from the queen. Effie was granted clemency and sentenced to 2 years in exile. She then married Staunton, who had resumed his role as a gentleman, and she became a lady.

In true Victorian fashion, however, Scott needed to make the couple pay for their transgression. After all, Effie had borne a child out of wedlock and, though she had not murdered her baby, she had broken society's rules. Her stolen son, called "The Whistler," had been reared by ruffians and smugglers. When his father, Staunton, learned of his existence and attempted to find him, the boy killed him unknowingly during a fracas and robbery attempt. The lad subsequently escaped and went to America to live with the Indians. Effie later retired to a convent. Scott reminded his readers of the great truth: "that guilt though it may attain temporal splendor, can never confer real happiness; that the evil consequences of our crimes long survive their commission" (1830 [1994], pp. 531–532).

The novel, though overly long and weakened by too many plot lines, possessed one element pertinent to this study. Scott captured the problem still extant even in more enlightened times: that so many young women refuse to acknowledge their pregnancies and manage to keep them a secret. Many even give birth alone and unaided. Although Scott based his partly realistic plot on the *Law of 1690* (which was replaced in his time by more lenient legislation), the reader is confronted by the gender discrimination of the law and society that seemed to be applicable to women only, as if they conceived and bore illegitimate children with no males involved. Scott also used the theme of illegitimacy and infanticide, as Ledwon (1996) pointed out, to emphasize the power of the mother in society:

> The mother holds the power of life or death over the newborn infant, particularly if she conceals her pregnancy from society. The threat of the murderous mother is the threat that maternity … no less than of paternity, may be only a legal fiction. (p. 16)

Popular culture of the 17th and 18th centuries reflected the same interest in the fallen women that Scott later recaptured in his novel. Scottish ballads recalled tales of seduced girls and their babies. The best known and most realistic was a song entitled "Mary Hamilton," which was revised and sung for almost a century. In the song, Mary Hamilton bravely announces that she killed her newborn and mounts the scaffold almost in defiance of a society that denigrated women's sexual and emotional needs:

> Sae, weep na mair for me, ladies,
> Weep no mair for me;
> The mither that kills ain bairn
> Deserves weel for to dee. (Symonds, 1997, p. 57)

Adam Bede

One of the most widespread themes in the didactic novels of the 19th century was that of innocent, humble country girls who, after coming to the city, were seduced by predatory upper-class men and then abandoned to their terrible fate (Gillis, 1983). The purpose of these novels was not only to exhort young women to avoid temptation for moral reasons, but also to illustrate vividly the very realistic consequences of shame and despair that befell women who did not protect their virtue. George Eliot (1859/1981) played upon this theme in *Adam Bede*. Her narrative was based on her aunt's experience with respect to a young woman who had been convicted of infanticide and was to be executed.

The novel portrayed the interplay of class, gender, and communal mores in the development of the tragedy of neonaticide. The story was centered in the village of Hayslope, where Adam Bede, a young carpenter, fell in love with Hetty Sorel, the young ward of tenant farmers (the Poysers). However, Hetty became involved in a secret liaison with Arthur Donnithorne, the local squire's grandson and heir, which resulted in her pregnancy. Overwhelmed with apprehension, she left the village, delivered her baby in another town, and then abandoned it to die. She was arrested for neonaticide and condemned to hang, although her sentence was later commuted to transportation—a terrible exile where she died alone. Arthur, her lover, filled with remorse, served 10 years in the army and then came home to resume his role as the local landlord and squire. Meanwhile, Adam Bede, suffering from Hetty's betrayal and her tragic fate, developed greater tolerance and patience for human frailties. He subsequently married Dinah, the local evangelical Methodist minister.

Eliot's novel depicted real people: rural tenant farmers and artisans as they struggled to earn a living and establish communal relationships. It was a "shame" society in which there were rigorous mores and social codes that Arthur and Hetty broke. Ever the Victorian moralist, Eliot was, nonetheless, sympathetic and accurate in creating portraits that illustrated the complexity of motives and behavior. She used the story of neonaticide to demonstrate that even decent people, driven by inner weaknesses, could commit the most horrible crimes. Neonaticide in this case was never condoned, but the idea of mitigating circumstances, or clemency, became more acceptable, even though Eliot punished her characters for their moral lapses (Allen, 1993).

Beloved

The novels and plays already discussed treated the case of women who had been seduced, lured, or driven by erotic desires. They were complicit in their victimization in that they had yielded to temptation and defied their communal mores. They paid a great price for their moral frailties, far greater than their male counterparts (a matter to which we will return later), but the men and women shared the blame for their victimization. There were other women, however, who were not willing partners in their predicament of unwanted pregnancy. They were truly victims of the social system because they were slaves or lived in harsh patriarchal societies.

Under the institution of slavery, the master claimed the woman's maternal history and her identity as a mother. She was subjected to sexual exploitation and to his will, with no choice in the matter (Tobin, 1993). The slavery system had a particularly deleterious effect on mother and child. The mother was separated from her children and was usually so enervated by hard work that she could do very little for them anyway. In some cases slave women offered resistance to that institution by refusing to bear children (i.e., sexual abstinence). Others used primitive contraceptives and abortifacient drugs and, in a few cases, practiced infanticide. Still other slave women attempted escape, but some abandoned their babies knowing that the master and other women would take care of them (Fox-Genovese, 1988).

Toni Morrison (1988) used filicide as a technique to force us to confront the nightmares of slavery in her novel *Beloved*. In her book, Morrison, like Eliot, based some of her plot on real episodes in history and intertwined them with African-American myths. The plot is set in the period immediately after the Civil War. It tells the story of Sethe, a slave woman, who killed her second oldest daughter, Beloved, to spare her the dehumanization of slavery. Morrison used infanticide and filicide to illustrate the brutalization and spiritual degradation brought to fruition in slavery and the subsequent caste system in the South.

Sethe's mother had been raped, after which she abandoned her babies and attempted to escape. She was branded and hung. Sethe had married and given birth to three daughters. After the death of her good master, Sethe and her children escaped to freedom, but she was caught while nursing her youngest. Fearing for her daughters at the hand of the new, harsh master, she committed the one filicide, but was stopped before she could commit the other two. Sethe was tried for filicide, but was defended by a White abolitionist lawyer who turned her case into an attack on the institution of slavery. She served 3 months in prison and then returned to her surviving children at the home of her mother-in-law in Ohio.

Haunted by the ghost of her murdered child, Sethe was ostracized by the community, which regarded her as evil, whatever her motives had been. The book raises questions about the motives that haunt and drive people—especially those arising from brutal and degrading environments such as slavery and poverty. These murders also forced the reader to rethink what good and evil are. Sethe's deed, reprehensible as it was, represented "individual defiance to the oppression of slavery and the beginnings of claiming and defining the self, of breaking the physical and psychological boundaries of oppression" (Jones, 1993, p. 625).

The character of Sethe was based upon the life of Margaret Garner, a slave mother who committed filicide in 1856. She had attempted to escape with her family and when faced with recapture by her master, killed one child and wounded two others to spare them the travails of slavery (Weisenburger, 1998). In 2005, Morrison recreated the tragedy in an opera entitled *Margaret Garner* with music by Richard Danielpour. Its world premiere was held in Cincinnati, Ohio, with performances to follow in Philadelphia in 2006. The music—eclectic in style, combining lyrical melodies, jazz, and folk spirituals—and the poetic libretto recreated the passion, degradation, and terrible pain of slavery and its human victims.

Woman Warrior: Memoirs of a Girlhood among Ghosts

Just as Toni Morrison was involved with the psychological effect of slavery upon women's lives, Maxine Hong Kingston is a writer concerned with gender relationships and women's adjustments to the larger community. Her book, *Woman Warrior: Memoirs of a Girlhood among Ghosts* (1989), is somewhat autobiographical and speaks of the woman caught between two cultures. Kingston is an ethnic Chinese in the United States writing in the English language, but part of a family literate in Chinese. Kingston mixes family stories and Chinese myths in a fascinating tapestry.

Her book opens with the tale of the author's aunt, No-Name. It is a cautionary story for young people who would presume to defy the mores and bounds of the community. No-Name is so named because she disgraced her family and is therefore denied her identity and personhood. No-Name becomes pregnant out of wedlock in a society that tolerates no deviance and in which illegitimacy is the ultimate shame. On the night she gives birth, the villagers, furious at her sin, punish her by raiding her family's home, destroying the furnishings, and killing the livestock. Humiliated and guilt stricken, the young woman drowns herself and her baby in a well.

The lesson was clear. Women were carefully monitored and their conduct scrutinized. Any deviation from established codes would not be tolerated, and any disgrace would also involve her family. The woman's role was clearly defined: to be subordinate as wife and mother to the will of man, but clearly not to be defiled outside marriage.

Alan's Wife

At the end of the 19th century (1894 to 1914), feminists used drama to express their visions of motherhood. Women began to protest their subordinate roles in family and community. In examining their roles, they perceived women's function as serving their husbands or their children or both. *Her* needs, desires, and aspirations must be suppressed in order to best serve the interests and needs of her family. She, therefore, could not exist for herself (Fitzsimmons & Gardner, 1991, p. xii). *Alan's Wife,* written by Florence Bell and Elizabeth Robins at the turn of the century (1901), was a protest against their culture's assumptions.

The heroine, Jean Creyke, kills her handicapped son. She does this because her husband is dead, and she fears that if and when she is unable to care for the child, he will be placed in harm's way. She characterizes her deed as one of love and in the last act unflinchingly accepts her death sentence. Even this gesture is part of the feminist dialogue, for Jean can escape the death penalty for infanticide if she claims she was insane when she acted. Jean refuses, hoping to be reunited with her husband in death (Wiley, 1990). The play is essentially an "indictment of an uncaring society" in which Jean takes complete control and responsibility (Bell & Robins, 1901). It is not a very good play and fortunately has not been revived. Though it is ostensibly about women's place in society, the unresolved problem is that of euthanasia—a topic that has preoccupied political debate and will be discussed later.

Saved

In the 20th century, especially in the idealistic period of the 1960s and 1970s, many became critical of a society besieged by a new technocracy and unsettled by cultural change and its instability. Child homicide became the vehicle by which one playwright criticized this society. In his play *Saved,* Edward Bond (1966) was not interested in gender relationships. His drama, produced in England in 1965, reflected his anger at a society corrupted by materialism and greed, which he considered to be the outgrowth of an evil capitalist system. He uses the murder of a child as a metaphoric device to engage our attention as to how the bottom stratum of the community behaves in a "consumer-based and technologically driven society" (Hay & Roberts, 1980, p. 39).

The play is centered on a casual but lusty affair between two disreputable characters who consummate their affair in a careless and loveless fashion.

The child who is the consequence of their sexual attachment is later murdered for no apparent reason other than as part of a meaningless whim. The horrible scene of men stoning a baby on the stage evokes the audience's visceral dismay, partly because the audience believes that children are meant to be protected because they are totally vulnerable. Bond's use of overt filicide called attention to the "cultural and emotional deprivation of our children that makes them dead even before they are assaulted" (Hay & Roberts, 1980, p. 51). The use of child homicide made this play very controversial, and it has provoked enormous emotional and angry reactions.

Summary

It is apparent that neonaticide, infanticide, and filicide have provided themes and plots for literature from ancient times to the present. The literary imagination offers an incisive illumination of the various past and contemporary cultural attitudes regarding women and maternity. Novels, dramas, popular songs, and narratives involve us in the various socioeconomic, psychological, and emotional environments that led to child homicides. Through analogy and metaphor, the artist depicts the ambivalence of the one who commits neonaticide—the intensity of despair and abhorrence coupled with sympathy for the mothers and their victims.

Often, the message conveyed is that society not only affirms the female's proper role, but also decrees what happens when she deviates from it. In other words, it is the society that is condemned through the act of a parent murdering a child. That the act was not simply the product of the author's mind is evident when one examines historical and cultural patterns regarding these crimes, as will be done in the following chapter.

2 Neonaticide in Theory and in History: Who Are the Perpetrators?

Because child homicide has always occurred, social scientists and other professionals mystified by such unnatural behavior have long searched for a variety of answers. They have perceived nature as a benign force and life among other species as utopian. The search has been in varied, sometimes overlapping, fields, including sociobiology, cultural anthropology, and history.

Sociobiological Perspectives

As biologists and anthropologists advanced their knowledge of genetics, they extended their observations to other species, using newer scientific models based on closer scrutiny. These examinations of social and instinctive behaviors were more subtle and sophisticated, exemplified by the insect studies of William Hamilton in the 1960s, and then followed by the works of George Williams, Robert Trivera, Richard Alexander, and Edward O. Wilson, who carried on the studies of altruism and mating selection among animals.

This newer form of analysis, known as evolutionary biology or sociobiology, is a systematic study of the biological basis of all forms of social behavior including sexual and parental conduct for all living things. Destruction is not uniquely human; it occurs in living organisms among plants and animals and other mammals, including primates. Most sociobiologists were more interested in animals than plants and were primarily zoologists. Older notions of animals' lack of cruelty, hierarchy, and even murder had to be discarded as sociobiologists observed animal behavior more closely.

Hrdy (1992) studied primates (langur apes) very closely and discovered numerous examples of infanticide. Males killed babies that were not theirs in order to pair with their mothers. He also perceived animal species as seeking to maximize their reproductive needs and cooperating only to enhance their genetic interests (Hrdy, 1992). Reports of infanticides and cannibalism among nonhuman primates were noted (but not necessarily as a regular practice). "What is distinctive in human species is selective removal on the basis of conscious intent" (Dickemann, 1975, p. 1008).

Anthropologists discovered evidence of instances of human groups such as the Ache hunter–gatherers in Paraguay that permit infanticide on the grounds of infidelity and fatherless children (Wright, 1994). Ache hunters are very cooperative and the society seemed benign, but if a father dies, the chances of a child being killed increase fourfold. "It's not uncommon for orphaned children to be thrown into their father's grave" (Zimmer, 1996, p. 73).

In the mid-1970s, studies of the genetic basis for some human behavior presented new ideas about evolution. Wilson's book (1980) was widely discussed and his theories gained some acceptance. He examined the behaviors of insect and animal life and began to discuss the integration of neo-Darwinian explanations of genetic and animal behavior as pertinent to human development and behavior. He spoke of attempting to create data on the widespread incest taboo, infanticide, mental retardation, and schizophrenia, thus merging the efforts of biology with those of psychology, anthropology, and sociology to create a broad-based social science effort. Sociobiology became the analysis of social behavior as it emerged from organic evolution. The research devolved on two levels: an abstract method, which depended upon mathematical models of genetics, ecology, and demography, and the concrete, which analyzed specific problems of the species and their physical and social evolution.

Research, observations, and statistical analysis concluded that species' behavioral patterns, including humans, generally adapted to the best outcome for reproduction or the genetic continuation of future generations. Therefore, cooperation within a family, tribe, pride, or den is achieved as a means to bring about the desired goal of reproduction; according to Daly and Wilson (1988), this idea has been "abundantly confirmed by recent research on nonhuman animals, and there is a growing body of empirical studies indicating its applicability to human society, too" (p. 520). Sociobiology thus became concerned with the complexity of social organization based upon demography, ecology, genetics, and other components of behavior in societies.

Some of these explanations are based on studies of altruism, aggression, and cooperation accompanied by the use of Darwinian natural selection.

Mutations that occur as a result of natural and environmental adaptation are included in these theories (Dawkins, 1976). Thus, sociobiology has created a model that makes evolution a part of social behavior as well. The models established among animals are clear and decisive, but when they were extrapolated to human behavior they were not as precise and, moreover, they aroused emotional distress among many scholars and thinkers (Lumsden & Wilson, 1983). These concepts were difficult to accept because of the belief that sociobiology implied genetic determinism to human growth. Thus, the propagation of these studies could only result in the preservation of racism and sexism. The propensity toward aggression or dominance could lead to acceptance of destructive human traits.

Political ideology colored the emotional content of the debates (Montagu, 1980). Some scholars felt sociobiology was based on questionable speculation that would support the dominance of patriarchal society and a laissez faire attitude toward social problems. There were others who criticized sociobiology on a sounder basis. They argued that while biological imperatives were sound in the evaluation of insect and animal behavior, they cannot be relevant to what is essentially the essence of humanity: the products of human consciousness, art, music, and philosophy.

They conceded that some human tendencies can be elucidated by zoological theory such as kin relationships and the incest taboo, as well as some sexual practices; however, the critics stressed that human beings have created a variety of social institutions and communities because they have free will and creativity. It is this mental agility that leads to culture beyond the descriptions of biology (Gould, 1980). Quadagno (1979, p. 109) asserted that "in terms of logic and method, sociobiology cannot be applied to the analysis of complex human social behavior." Others questioned the accuracy and validity of the models and scientific data (Williams, 1981). In contrast, Peter Singer noted:

> The account of ethics [that] sociobiologists offer is incomplete and therefore misleading. Nevertheless, sociobiology provides the basis for a new understanding of ethics. It enables us to see ethics as a mode of human reasoning which develops in a group context, building on more limited, biologically based forms of altruism. (1981, p. 149)

In response to its many criticisms and as a result of continued empirically based and scientifically rigorous research, sociobiologists advanced insightful descriptions of the reproductive behavior of humans as well as animals. They also became more circumspect about the dominance of genes and began to explore the cultural contributions to human development (Durham, 1990).

Scientists began to carry research even further afield and began to conceptualize evolutionary theories about the mind and human intelligence.

Man was a product of his genes and his culture (which included history, economics, and environment)—"unique and remarkable properties of the human mind resulting in a tight linkage between genetic evolution and cultural history," according to Lumsden and Wilson (1983, p. 20). Genes and culture are inextricably linked in circular fashion: genes provide the means of development and learning to absorb the culture, which is consequently altered to adapt to change. This causes some people to function more adroitly in the modified society, and they then reproduce their altered genes.

"In sum," according to Lumsden and Wilson, "culture is and shaped by biological processes while the biological processes are simultaneously altered in response to cultural change" (1983, p. 118). They began to elucidate a more ambitious program that sought to unite the biological and social sciences even more closely. They conceived of a theory of gene culture as coevolution, which was a further extension of sociobiology and what they considered a further push to integrate the social and physical sciences. They hoped to forge new links among biology, economics, and even history. They further established three criteria by which sociobiology could be judged:

> It must create rigorous explanations that have been speculative tenets of the social sciences.
>
> It must be testable and should be predictive (which at the present is not true for any of the social sciences).
>
> It should give rise to new questions as well as "identify previously unknown parameters and laws to be woven into a network of verifiable explanations from genes through the mind to culture." (Lumsden & Wilson, 1981, p. 346)

Wilson's more recent work, *Consilience*, has continued that search for the unity of human knowledge (1998).

Richard Alexander attempted to relate morality to biology by showing that "evolved human nature and morality are compatible, and … the great value of evolutionary understanding lies in its guidance, in developing appropriate and useful ideas and hypotheses about human activities and tendencies" (1987, p. 10).

Evolutionary psychology developed from the works of sociobiology as psychologists began to explore the mind in the same way that biologists were examining genetic human behavior (Buss, 1999). According to these thinkers, the brain must have evolved according to the same evolutionary process as other organs. Pinker (1997b) claimed that the mind resembles the computer modules designed to perform certain tasks. Therefore, these modules are pushed by their genetic instincts to love, cherish, and take care of children and parents.

The interest in the relationship between genetics and culture created a new attention to how the mind works (Pinker, 1997b), which has been described as "the investigation and characterization of the innate psychological mechanisms that generate and regulate behavior" (Durham, 1990, p. 193). There was hope that the new psychology would help connect the new sociobiology and human behavior even more closely. The result was the belief that man's need to adapt to an ever changing and hostile physical environment necessitated genetic tendencies that fostered free will in order to be able to meet the challenges (Pinker).

As research increased and became more refined, many scholars began to attribute new significance and value to the studies even if they still were uncertain of some conclusions. Wright (1994) has argued that many ethical judgments may have biological origins and, if we want to develop a meaningful morality, we need to continue to learn more about our basic psychological drives. Continuing in this vein, Wright discussed the reasons that homicides occur.

Primitive societies also decried neonaticide, but those who carried it out as a social policy did so only for the following reasons. Unhealthy or handicapped infants were killed, as were those children born under difficult or threatening circumstances (i.e., the mother had younger children or no husband or in the case of twins). The population controls among primitive peoples are consciously limited by abortion, infanticide, or prolonged abstinence. It was duly noted that, among nomadic peoples, restriction of population was necessary to fulfill nursing obligations and mobility of the group. There was evidence of widespread abandonment of "deformed infants," and in many communities, there was frequency of female infanticide. These practices were believed to have dated from Upper Paleolithic times (Carr-Saunders, 1922, p. 113).

The conflict between environmental demands of a nomadic society and fertility needs were illustrated by the Australian aborigines. Women on the move had to carry their children and goods and they could carry only one child. To facilitate the group's mobility, efforts were made to control fertility by prolonging nursing periods for as long as 3 or 4 years. Primitive abortion was tried and if that failed, neonaticide was practiced. Deformed children were smothered, and if the mother died in childbirth or while nursing, the child was also killed (Hughes, 1987).

These circumstances do not exist in developed or modern societies. Certainly there is ample food and medicine, and today even single parenthood is acceptable. However, the studies of Daly and Wilson (1988) show that a large percentage of child homicides in Canada are the murders of stepchildren. Furthermore, Wright suggests that some crimes are "committed by the natural fathers who have begun to doubt—consciously or unconsciously—that they are" (1994, p. 390).

Despite approbation and acceptance by some scholars, others still feel uneasy about the implications of these biological studies. There is the fear that human nature is being reduced to biological or genetic tendencies that limit chances for the amelioration of injustice and the ability to recreate our societies (Rothstein, 1998). The speculations of sociobiology caused some to question whether laws should be modified to include genetic factors. Jones claimed that while evolutionary biology revealed its influence upon some responses, men were still capable of rational behavior and free will. However, he continued, "the law should orient itself to take into account the evolutionary influences that can help generate new legal strategies for regulating human behavior" (Jones, 1997, p. 1125).

Part of the new synthesis in the evolving work of the evolutionary biologist was the incorporation of anthropology and what came to be known as cultural evolution (Durham, 1990). As noted, anthropologists have long studied ancient and modern primitive societies. Carr-Saunders (1922), cited a few paragraphs earlier, was the first to show evidence of infanticide on a worldwide basis and consequent studies have not abrogated much of his evidence.

Some sociobiologists claim that "all organisms, including people, are products of the historical process of differential survival and reproduction … " (Daly & Wilson, 1984, p. 487). Although that factor may be appropriate for primitive peoples in hostile environments where there is a lack of sustainable food and shelter, it is inapplicable in modern societies where other psychological and cultural behaviors prevail under conditions of relative plenty. Factors such as illegitimacy, youth of the mother, stepparent households, or mental illness of the parent are more predictive of neonaticide and infanticide than mere survival needs today (Daly & Wilson, 1984).

Killing of offspring was also observed across diverse cultures. These homicides were linked to the enhancement of the status and welfare of the family and were best illustrated by the case of Rajputs and other castes of northern India. Dickemann's study (1979) tried to explain the killing of daughters. Based on sociobiological analysis, she claimed,

> Lineage needed wealth and high social status in order not to perish in bad times. The great cost of dowries hampered the accumulation of wealth; therefore higher-caste families often killed their female infants … because of the nature of the marriage system. (p. 350)

If this practice is so widespread and neonaticide persists even in the most technologically advanced societies where the notion is abhorred, then is this crime a part of evolutionary process and sociobiological in its origin? Pinker claimed that neonaticide was a way of conserving the family by sacrificing the infants in a harsh and unforgiving environment and that women's brains led them to these sacrifices (Pinker, 1997a). Sociobiologists point out the significant argument that nature provides bonding between mother and infant via the nursing process and leaves a gap of a day or two before the mother can nurse; during this gap the maternal instinct is not aroused. It enables the mothers and society to provide a space in which the infant can be abandoned or exposed. Thus, they claim that "both biology and cultural tradition seemed designed to permit mothers, for a brief period, to practice infanticide" (Hrdy, 1984, p. 50).

Granzberg (1973) claimed that twin homicide was more likely to occur in societies that lacked sufficient facilities to enable mothers to properly rear two children simultaneously while tending to necessary chores for survival. His findings have been challenged by others who contend that twin homicide occurs more often in aggressive societies or those in which women have inferior status (Lester, 1986). Ball and Hill (1996) supported Granzberg's thesis by more rigorous analysis and concluded:

> Infants who are twins may be subjected to infanticide not because they are twins per se but because by virtue of being twins they manifest attributes that would cause them to fall into one of several categories under which any infant, singleton or twin, would be killed (p. 863).

The prevalence of this behavior, however, gives some credence to Pinker's assertions.

Despite the belief that neonaticide is part of "human nature," anthropologists also declare that primitive societies often display contradictory attitudes toward infanticide "that [are] both universally practiced and universally condemned" (Carr-Saunders, 1922, p. 115). Abortion and infanticide were practiced occasionally, but they were considered socially undesirable and, therefore, subjected to strict social regulation. Infanticide and neonaticide may be allowed only if they occur before the baby has been named and accepted as a bona fide member of its society (Carr-Saunders, 1922). The less eligible a child is for membership in the group, the less seriously the act of killing the child is viewed. The fact that societies create sanctions against unrestricted infanticide suggests that mothers, though loving and nurturing, do kill unwanted infants (especially if they have borne and reared a number of children) (Carr-Saunders, 1922). Scholars should also be cognizant of the high mortality rate caused by natural causes in primitive societies.

Evolutionary social scientists deduce therefore that teenagers, faced by the birth of a child and desperate at their condition, will resort to established genetic patterns of behavior (Pinker, 1997a). Similarly, the findings of Daly and Wilson have statistically illustrated that infants in Canada and Great Britain are 60 to 70 or more times more likely to die at the hands of a stepparent than a natural parent, confirming evolutionary biologic analysis that stepparent homicide is the pattern observed in other creatures such as insects, birds, primates, and other mammals (1988, 1994, 2001). Thus, these scholars suggest that another facet of selective infanticide has been observed in nature and among men. (Note: This will be discussed at greater length in Chapter 8.)

Despite this evidence, the conclusions are still highly speculative. Neonaticide is not widespread, although we are more aware today, early in the 21st century, of instances of child-killing. This crime has never been prevalent or acceptable. Since the Middle Ages neonaticide has not been a culturally supported matter, but rather an individual one. As already noted, all child homicide was condemned by Judaism, Christianity, and Islam. Yet, the historical tradition records a continual account of instances of child abandonment and neonaticide. Amighi (1990) hypothesized that, given the difficult lives of average persons in unsophisticated cultures, "the infanticidal mother is expressing resentment against the new infant who is adding to her burdens or that an emotional detachment is evoked to permit her to abandon or kill her infant" (p. 135).

Cross-Cultural Perspectives

A Brief Look at Asian Cultures

Neonaticide or abandonment of baby girls was part of a long Chinese tradition based, as it was in India, on custom and economic necessity (sons were the only support for aged parents); girls needed dowries that reverted to the new family. This made daughters a burden unless their marriage could provide upward social mobility by creating alliances with more powerful families. Opposition to this custom coexisted with the practice (Waltner, 1995).

By the end of the 19th century there were attempts to bring relief to Chinese children through the creation of hospices and attempts to suppress some neonaticide (Leung, 1995). The 20th century Chinese Revolution and its rush to modernization led to the adoption of a one-child-per-family policy for many years that is only now being eased. Nevertheless, it is believed that many girls may have been killed and their bodies hidden or neglected so that they died from disease, especially in the poorer rural districts, with none of these deaths recorded as infanticides. As in India, new technology, when available, allows for gender-directed abortions, although they are discouraged by the government (Hull, 1990; Johansson & Nygren, 1991; Li, 1991).

The urban populace have mostly cooperated and accepted the stringent regulations for child bearing. Contraception and sterilization are the preferred methods of fertility control, and women are sometimes coerced into having abortions although physical force is no longer used. Penalties such as fines and loss of privileges are used to enforce birth control policies. A sex imbalance that favored male babies over female seemed to suggest continuing female sex selection and neonaticide as well as female adoptions. The opposition expected in the countryside led the government to acknowledge parental preference for boys by allowing a couple, after a 5-year wait, to try for a second child if the first was a girl. In some areas, as the government moderated its policy, it even allowed a try for a second child if the first birth had been a male. In some underpopulated areas, even third and fourth children are sometimes permitted. The government's relaxation of its regulations, plus strict statutes against infanticide and antenatal sex selection, seems to have reduced lop-sided gender ratios (Hesketh & Zhu, 1997).

Even in those societies in parts of China and India where daughters were perceived as a drain on their family's assets and were frequently abandoned, present day changes have been dramatic. The Indian government has sought to restrict population growth and to deter the sex selection that became possible with the availability of ultrasound in some locations, with mothers opting for abortion early in pregnancy if the fetus was female. As in China, the efforts to limit family size have been more successful than the efforts to limit sex selection.

In Japan it was long believed that the peasant population suffered economic distress and accordingly limited the size of their families. However, more recent studies have shown that the limit was adopted not because of economic distress, but rather to increase their standard of living. The way to limit families in earlier centuries was believed to have been by abortion and neonaticide. Even that view is questioned by newer demographic studies that indicate that child homicides did exist, especially in premodern times (Hanley, 1983), but in relatively small numbers. Japanese fertility was controlled by the custom of long nursing, mobility, primitive contraception, and a high infant mortality rate from disease (Cornell, 1996).

Cultural Causes in the West

Homicidal mothers come from varying social classes and differing locales: rural, suburban, and urban. Studies in the past and the present indicate that although the neonaticidal and infanticidal actions are similar in end result, psychological and environmental circumstances vary widely, as do the periods in which the crimes occurred.

In medieval times, infanticide and neonaticide were viewed with horror along with parricide, heresy, witchcraft, and murder as crimes challenging the established order. Whenever there was clear evidence of neonaticide in the records throughout late medieval and early modern Europe, it seemed there was a preponderance of illegitimate children killed by single girls or widows. What made the crime even worse in the eyes of many was the fact that these newborns had not been baptized (Riet, 1986). For most women, such pregnancies were socially disastrous and the woman and her family were disgraced (Ruggiero, 1992; Wilson, 1988). They were even more fearful of the public humiliation imposed by church authorities, loss of livelihood, and the certainty of social isolation and poverty (Shorter, 1975; Wrightson, 1982).

The Church was more concerned that neonaticide was evidence of extramarital affairs, adultery, or illegitimacy (which was rarer then) than in the crime of murder. The absence of effective birth control devices meant that options were few for couples in and outside marriage. One factor that has remained stable throughout history is the "association between infanticide and illegitimacy" (Kellet, 1992, p. 2).

What was more common in medieval times than actual murder was what could be considered homicidal neglect—for example, children drowning in wells or falling into ditches, scalding deaths in boiling pots of water, wandering away outside. Parents toiled long and hard and such neglect "would have been a fairly efficient means of ridding oneself of unwanted and demanding burdens but also the death would be acceptably accidental, at least by secular law standards" (Damme, 1978, p. 7). Another common cause of death of the young infant was "overlaying." It was the custom in poor families for infants to sleep with parents, and in many cases death of the child was probably deliberate, or so it seemed, especially because so many more female babies died than males (Damme, 1978; Kellum, 1973; Sauer, 1978).

One of the more heinous superstitions used when encountering a dead child was the belief that Jews had killed him or her for use of the blood in rituals, rather than seeking the perpetrators of neonaticide or infanticide. These latter beliefs persisted into modern times, as attested to by the Fokhancy affair in Rumania in 1859 and the Beiless affair in Russia in 1913.

> Christians lose their children and the enemies of the Jews charge the latter with having kidnapped or killed them in order to use their hearts and blood for sacrifice .... These things happen under the completely false pretence that children were abducted and murdered by Jews .... (Schultz, 1991, p. 282)

In these ritual murder accusations, "the motivations ascribed to the Jews' 'crimes' were either to mock the Easter celebrations or to celebrate the Passover" (Kellum, 1973, p. 378). There were even a number of instances of poor Christian parents offering to sell their children to Jews to be killed, and as late as 1699, a poor woman offered to sell her baby for that purpose to Meier Goldschmidt, court jeweler to the king of Denmark (Trachtenberg, 1943). Parents were so harried that they were willing to sell their children for what they thought were nefarious purposes.

An Historical Perspective

Neonaticide between the 15th and the 19th centuries was relatively rare. The penalties were often given great publicity. In the period of the 16th and 17th centuries, infanticide was considered ungodly and legislators were anxious to suppress it. Of all kinds of homicide, neonaticide was easiest to conceal in spite of the fact that there was little privacy in the villages and communities. Women of the village kept a wary eye open for suspicious behavior on the part of young women, especially those who were considered more vulnerable to seduction: single women (virgins or widows). Domestic servants most frequently became pregnant and had illegitimate children during the *ancien regime* because they were most vulnerable (Riet, 1986).

As Shorter (1975) cogently observed, people in much of Europe and some of colonial New England were densely grouped in villages and hamlets, rather than in the rural farms of the northern United States. In those areas, surveillance and community controls were far stricter because privacy was difficult to maintain. There was relatively little social and physical mobility, and the local courting customs were enforced in order to prevent illegitimacy and other social ills (Shorter, 1975). Nevertheless, when pregnancy occurred, it was often hidden and denied if the woman was unable to get married. When babies' bodies were discovered, it was even more difficult to determine how they died. Thus, laws were passed against the concealment of pregnancy in order to attenuate the problem of neonaticide and reduce the instances of illegitimacy (Wrightson, 1982).

English courts of the 17th and 18th centuries revealed the same motives and the same denials of pregnancy (Hufton, 1974). Most instances of abandonment and child murder occurred in instances of bastardy, which by the 17th century was considered a matter of social disgrace (Illick, 1974; Francus, 1997). Hoffer and Hull (1981) speculated that, for many women, "neonaticide was a deliberate form of delayed abortion. It involved concealment, and probably was the most common among poor, unwed mothers" (p. 157). Before the last part of the 19th century, abortion was perilous and sometimes ineffective, so delivering the baby and killing it by neglect or force at birth (sometimes *in utero*) seemed more prudent. In these cases women sometimes had the assistance of friends, lovers, and, especially, midwives (Illick, 1974).

A study of neonaticide in Bavaria in the 19th century, based on a series of police dossiers, revealed data about the women that parallels modern problems for some pregnant women and reinforces the knowledge of the universality of this type of homicide. Servant girls faced no shame, no censure—their problems were to keep their jobs, and the majority did work up to the very moment of birth. Thus, these girls made no preparation for the births or even the babies. Their motivation for killing did not derive from extreme conditions. Generally, it was because the father denied paternity or would not give them support. There was usually no prospect of marriage, and for some, extreme poverty made another mouth to feed difficult. Typically, the accused showed few feelings of sorrow or guilt; she probably regarded it as a late abortion.

Schulte (1984) speculated that the lack of remorse was tied to the prevalent attitudes in poor, peasant Bavaria, where there was great fertility and even greater infant mortality. Survival of children in large families depended upon the will of their parents. The parents generally felt that killing the baby was little different from the frequent killing of barnyard animals for food.

A similar analysis of neonaticide and child abandonment in 19th century Corsica revealed cultural differences. In Southern Mediterranean society, factors of honor and shame played a paramount role in the motivations of the behavior of Corsican women. "Sanctions deriving from notions of female honor were thus the usual cause of neonaticide, overriding economic necessity or any feeling towards children as such" (Wilson, 1988, pp. 764–765). The law of 1810 was harsh toward the crime; the punishment was death, although other homicides carried the penalty of life imprisonment. However, judges and prosecutors lessened the punishment by allowing for extenuating circumstances or convictions on lesser charges (Wilson, 1988).

As to the characteristics of the mothers prosecuted for neonaticide, they resembled women of other countries. The overwhelming number were unmarried; a few were widows and a few were married women living apart from their husbands. The major difference was that in Corsica there were few servants and farm workers; most women lived at home with their parents. Poverty in these cases was not the major cause of homicide, and in many instances the babies were killed by accomplices—the lover or the woman's mother. The primary motive was the wish to avoid dishonor and shame (Wilson, 1988). In Belgium, too, "living honor was strong and the social pressure also more unbearable" (Leboutte, 1991, p. 182).

A factor that further promoted despair in Catholic countries was a strong patriarchal culture that allowed fathers to avoid legal responsibility for the support of their illegitimate children. In addition, fathers were legally protected from any attempt to identify them as the parent (Kertzer, 1993). There was a high rate of neonaticide among servant girls vulnerable to seduction, on the one hand, and the overt attempt to use the sexual encounter to capture the commitment of marriage on the other. Once pregnant, the woman faced shame and dismissal; to avoid such a fate, the young girl concealed the pregnancy and destroyed the baby. In France and England, household servants formed the largest proportion of such women (McBride, 1976).

The increased number of unwed women's pregnancies in Victorian Europe was partly the result of the urbanization and modernization occurring in Western Europe. The sudden influx of people into the cities, with their inherent anonymity and poor living conditions, made the seduction of young women easy. Squalid social and economic conditions in domestic and factory labor led to deplorable behavior. Children were left unsupervised and, in the earlier part of the century, child labor also led to premature sexual experimentation (Edwards, 1981). Young women were victimized and harassed in their homes and the factories where they worked, with pregnancy resulting in the loss of their job as well as shame and blame. Sometimes the young women became involved in hope of or because of the promise of marriage. The men could disappear, leaving the women to bear the consequences of their amorous dalliance (Tilly, Scott, & Cohen, 1976). (This has not changed too much over the decades.)

Since girls who were pregnant would be raising illegitimate children, they frequently felt their only choices were neonaticide or abandonment. On the other hand, the more protected upper-class young women could always be sent abroad if they became pregnant, and they did not have to face the same consequences as their poorer sisters. (This, too, is still true in many situations.)

The passage of the *Poor Law of 1834* in Victorian England and its cruel treatment of the indigent also contributed to the rising number of neonaticides. The single mother could no longer receive aid from her local parish. She had to keep her child in an institution called "the poor house," where the poor were sequestered and separated by sex. The law also relieved the father of responsibility because the sole purpose of the law "was to make girls realize the harsh consequences of sexual delinquency so they would guard their chastity and bastardy would decline" (Sauer, 1978, p. 27).

The *Poor Law* was especially cruel because most of the time it prohibited financial aid to women with illegitimate children. Even so-called deserving women with children (widows or deserted married women with children) received piddling welfare payments (Thane, 1979). The harsh bastardy provisions against unmarried women eventually turned public opinion against the law because many began to realize that the woman was an innocent victim of seduction (Henriques, 1967; Thane, 1979). "The larger proportion of neonaticides was attributable to the women of limited resources who, through isolation and desperation, often concealed the birth of their child, killing the infant within the first twenty four hours through exposure or other means" (Barlow & Clayton, 1996, p. 215).

After the 1870s, the decline in the birth rate in industrialized societies became the norm as information about contraception and abortion was disseminated in the middle classes. Contemporaries viewed neonaticide as a crime of unmarried women (usually seduced and abandoned mothers), despite the fact that there was a decline of illegitimacy later in the century. The reality of continuing neonaticide rested on bad socioeconomic conditions—the punitive bastardy legislation embodied in the *Poor Law* with its refusal of "outdoor" relief, the difficulty of getting fathers to support their children, and the inability of women to find work. Many thought that the *Poor Laws* forced more neonaticide and abandonment (Behlmer, 1979).

Chances of adoption for infants were slim. Foundling hospitals accepted few of the children. Neonaticide thus appeared to be an appropriate response to the economic pressures for many mothers. As family planning spread at the end of the century and abortion became more common, there appeared to be a decline in neonaticide (Behlmer, 1979). Imperial Germany's statistics on abandonment, neonaticide, and abortion reflected many of the same tendencies seen elsewhere. Neonaticide declined as convictions for abortions rose precipitously (Richter, 1998; Sauer, 1974).

Poverty rather than shame was the primary motivation for neonaticide in the 19th century United States. In Philadelphia, hundreds of dead infants were found in cesspools and streets; 483 were found in one 4-year period and 41 cases of homicide went to trial between 1860 and 1900 (Friedman, 1991; Lane, 1986). Friedman claimed that infanticide was also a crime of immobility; abortion as an alternative was more commonly practiced in the United States (Friedman, 1991; Mohr, 1978). The United States, as a more mobile society, had many men who moved frequently, seeking opportunity on the frontier. However, the new cities developing in the West also gave many women a chance to change identities and conceal their single parenthood, although poor women locked in urban slums had little choice. It was here that more neonaticide occurred. Infanticide was rarer in the West than in the East or South. "There were no prosecutions for infanticide in Alameda County, California between 1870 and 1910 and no newspaper accounts of such crimes. In Oakland, California this was an exceptionally rare crime" (Friedman, 1991). Records of infanticides in 19th century Ohio corroborate findings that we noted in early Europe. In insular communities bounded by common values, language, and snoopy neighbors, social behaviors that inhibited infanticide were enforced (Wheeler, 1997).

Death rates for girls in colonial America, and even later, for girls under age 9, were sometimes twice those for boys. Sheila Johnson, a demographer, claimed that the growth of modernization in the 19th century meant that boys' labor contributed to the cash crop economy while daughters' work had no monetary value. Girls, therefore, were overworked and underfed in poor rural areas, leading to a higher death rate than for boys. In urban settings where girls could find employment in factories, they and their brothers died at more equal rates (Burke, 1984).

Abandonment

Examining a cross-cultural group of myths, folk tales, and rituals, Amighi (1990) found that stories of "maternal or parental abandonment of children are very common and found in many cultures. They may express ambivalence toward children" (p. 135). In addition, given the difficult life of the average person in many unsophisticated cultures, Amighi hypothesized that "the infanticidal mother is expressing resentment against the new infant who is adding to her burdens or that an emotional detachment is evoked to permit her to abandon or kill her infant" (p. 138). Either feeling could lead to neonaticide or abandonment, even in more sophisticated societies.

Abandonment was far more frequent in the past than murder. Some mothers were hesitant to kill their newborns outright, and they often nursed the hope that their babies would be cared for by compassionate strangers. Infant abandonment became prevalent throughout Europe during the late Middle Ages from southern Europe to Russia as an alternative to neonaticide and filicide. Parents abandoned babies when unable to support them because of poverty, shame, illegitimacy, or incestuous relationships, or when inheritance or other resources might be compromised. Most abandoned babies in the early Middle Ages were rescued and brought up as adopted members of the household or as laborers.

European society as a whole did not place serious sanctions against the practice, but rather tolerated or regulated it. The sale of children had been common in ancient and medieval Europe (Boswell, 1988). As illegitimacy rose in the 15th, 16th, and 17th centuries, so did the number of abandoned babies. The causes of this phenomenon varied, as did the causes of neonaticide. Poverty brought about by seasonal change, bad economic conditions, and the inadequacy of fertility control plagued the family's welfare. Sometimes, parents abandoned their babies and hoped that they could reclaim them later (Kertzer, 1993). In periods of catastrophe or crisis, more male children were left, but generally there were more abandoned girls (Gavitt, 1994; Trexler, 1973).

The number of abandonments increased so dramatically that governments were forced to create foundling homes. By the time of the Reformation, foundling homes had become part of the architectural landscape of urban northern Italy and they had been established in France, Spain, and Portugal. By establishing a locus, these institutions gathered all of the troubling aspects of child abandonment in one place, hiding the babies from the public eye. At first, they were additions to hospitals, and then they became "substantial institutions generally run by lay boards in close consultation with the Church" (Boswell, 1988, p. 418). The creation of these institutions made abandonment quite common in Catholic Europe, but it was not as widely practiced in northern Protestant areas where there were no foundling homes.

When the Catholic Church of the counter-Reformation era imposed the strict definition of legitimate sexual relations as those only engaged in after a religious ceremony, infant abandonment became more frequent. Unwed mothers raising their children was seen as encouraging sinful behavior, but many desperate mothers, and their families, wanted to protect their babies. The foundling hospitals continued to increase throughout the 18th and 19th centuries as the state began to supervise the welfare of poor mothers and children and regulate families, reproduction, and sexuality (Tilly et al., 1976).

One of the devices that made abandonment easier because it provided anonymity while lessening guilt was the rotating wheel called *ruota* in Italy, *la tour* in France, and *roda* in Portugal. This was a

> revolving cylinder with an opening on one side of its revolving surface; its closed side faced the street. An outside bell was placed nearby. When a woman wanted to abandon a newborn child, she merely had to alert the person on duty by ringing the bell and straight way the cylinder, revolving on its axis, would present its open side to the exterior. It would then receive the infant and continuing the motion, convey the child inside the hospital. (Donzelot, 1979, p. 26)

Abandonment existed on a large scale in France, and the many foundling hospitals there facilitated this practice as opposed to just leaving the baby on a doorstep. Most babies were born in public institutions and many were brought into hospitals by midwives or were "delivered anonymously at hospital gates" (Wrightson, 1982, p. 13). The abandoned children were sent to the country to be nursed because bottle feeding was not really available until the late 19th century and wet nursing was the cheapest way of caring for babies. The practice was especially prevalent among poor women who had to work in factories, mines, or domestic service. The mortality rates were appallingly high (Fuchs, 1984, 1992; Sussman, 1975). "Institutional neglect by well-intentioned but overburdened and under-financed charitable institutions made what was probably the largest contribution to infanticide in modern Europe" (Rose, 1986, p. 14).

In Britain, the national mortality rate for infants was 15 to 16%, but babies left with baby farmers reached a 90% rate. Most deaths were probably unintentional, occurring because poor rural women lived under appallingly squalid conditions and were ignorant of any notion of cleanliness. However, parents often took out burial insurance on their children and, to increase benefits, often insured children in several clubs, making a profit on their death (McKee, 1984; Sauer, 1978).

Baby farms were also a prominent feature of the working class in many 19th century American cities. It was a way for neighborhood women to pool their resources to care for their babies, enabling them to work and also "in its worst abuses a latent system for the disposal of unwanted babies" (Broder, 1988, p. 130). Mothers who wished to abandon babies they could not afford would simply leave them at a baby farm and disappear. "In this way, baby farmers often served as unwilling agents in the process of abandonment" (p. 139). The economic dislocations caused by the Civil War and Reconstruction, plus the South's postbellum industrialization, produced suffering and poverty, resulting in a marked increase in the number of infant abandonments and homicides (Green, 1999).

The Basque country was the one area of Europe that had unusually low rates of abandonment in the 18th and early 19th centuries. Despite a high illegitimacy rate—one-fourth to one-third of all newborns—there were few problems. In this society, no shame was attached to single mothers because a large number of babies were born in concubinage relationships (often involving priests). The extended family was the prevalent model and thus they were able to sustain and integrate the illegitimate children. Unlike Mediterranean Europe and even northern Europe, there were no institutions that could care for foundlings. Instead, the laws required the fathers to assume responsibility for their children, and often mothers relinquished their children to the fathers' families (Valverde, 1994).

As the country modernized its laws and customs to be more in conformity with the rest of Europe, the number of abandonments also began to rise sharply. The Church enforced its ban against sex as sinful, insisted that priests become more celibate, and declared unmarried motherhood unacceptable. As in the rest of Europe, the extended family declined, fathers were no longer required to support their children, and the increase in poverty contributed to factors that were inimical to the welfare of lower-class newborns (Valverde, 1994).

In France, admissions of abandoned babies rose from 40,000 a year in 1784 to 138,000 in 1822. By 1830 there were 270 revolving boxes in use throughout France, with 336,297 infants legally abandoned during the period from 1824 to 1833. Between 80 and 90% of the babies died within the first year of life (Harris, 1977). By 1874 in France, French legislators regulated the wet nursing "industry" to ease the high infant mortality rate. They also hoped to discourage mothers from working outside the home and considered regulations to protect children and women's labor (Cole, 1996).

The *tours* were closed, and mothers could no longer anonymously leave their newborns. Instead, the mothers were taken to a government bureau where they were interviewed and their inability to care for the babies was reviewed before they were admitted to the hospitals. Mothers felt encouraged to keep their children, even when they were illegitimate, because the government provided assistance. The result was a drop in abandonment because the women preferred help that enabled them to keep their children (Litchfield & Gordon, 1980).

Penalties of the Past

Whenever there was clear evidence of neonaticide in the records throughout the late medieval period and early modern Europe, it seemed a preponderance of illegitimate children had been killed by single girls or widows. One factor that has remained stable throughout history is the "association between infanticide and illegitimacy" (Kellet, 1992, p. 2). The Church worried that an unbaptized infant's soul would be damned to eternal punishment, and retribution for that crime was heavy (15 years' public penance rather than 7 years), but punishments were often mitigated (to 7 years) if the guilty women were poor (Kellum, 1973). What was most clear in the penalties prescribed by ecclesiastics was that they were addressed to females only, never to men or even to parents. Illegitimacy was not condoned. However, Damme (1978) points out, as do many others, that church punishments were moderate because "it was merely a recognition by the church of a method of population control by the poor that may have been necessary, in many cases, for survival" (p. 4).

As the Middle Ages waned into the Renaissance and the 16th and 17th centuries, jurisdiction over crimes passed to the secular courts as the emergence of the modern state diminished the power of Catholic and Protestant churches. Gradually, the church authorities became more determined to regulate the sexual and social behavior of their members, and the acceptance of unwed motherhood became intolerable.

The war against illicit sexual relations and their products—illegitimate babies—became most intensive in the 16th century, a time of profound religious rivalries and a fear of witchcraft. Because social and economic pressures did not abate for the poor, neonaticides continued. In addition, court records show that most of the reported neonaticides were illegitimate babies, indicating the significance of the stigma of bastardy (Damme, 1978).

The criminal statutes became brutally severe in these cases, allegedly because of the difficulty of enforcing the laws and, therefore, the greater need to instill fear as a deterrent for these crimes. Princes, hampered by lack of police and modern methods of detection, compensated by providing a "fiercely retributive character to punishment" (Ransel, 1988, p. 13). Hanging was not enough; the punishment had to be *awful.*

The penalties prescribed for the crimes were appalling: in late medieval France, guilty mothers were burned or buried alive after torture. The codes of the Holy Roman Empire, as issued in 1332, followed medieval German precedent and included live burial, drowning in a sack, or impaling. These sentences were replaced in the 17th century by torture and decapitation, The punishments varied from country to country, ranging from simple beheading to burning or burial alive. After the witchcraft hysteria of the 17th century subsided, the harsh persecution of women began to abate, and there were fewer indictments and executions in England and France, and then the rest of Europe.

However, inadequate forensic and scientific techniques, faulty diagnosis, and cover-ups made child homicide difficult to assess. To satisfy the need to promote order and to legislate "proper" sexual behavior, states began to pass laws creating a presumption of murder in cases in which the unmarried woman was alone at the time of birth and the baby was later found dead. This was written into French law in 1156, 1586, and again in 1708. Unless the woman could prove that the child was stillborn or died naturally, she could be convicted of infanticide. Similar laws, in which failure to declare a pregnancy could result in the charge of infanticide if the baby was not found alive, appeared in England in 1624, Sweden in 1627, Wurttemburg in 1658, Scotland in 1690, and Bavaria as late as 1751. The single mother became a social pariah, reduced to prostitution or other socially denounced means to stay alive. These pressures often led her to hide her pregnancy and to kill the newborn (Symonds, 1997).

Similar laws were also passed during the colonial period in the United States—notably in New England and Pennsylvania—and as late as 1855 in New Jersey (Rowe, 1991; Wheeler, 1997; Zimmer, 1996). The laws in the United States varied widely, but reflected their roots in the English common law. "The aim was to punish 'Jews and dissolute women' who produced 'bastard children' but lacked enough 'natural affection' to keep them alive" (Friedman, 1991, p. 654). Similar laws were passed in Canada beginning in 1758, and legal records indicated that the vast majority of women charged with this crime were unmarried (Saunders, 1989).

The rate of conviction rose for a short time, but, despite the penalties, neonaticide remained commonplace (Oberman, 1996). When babies' bodies were discovered, it was difficult to determine how they had died. Forensic medicine did not exist and it was impossible to differentiate a stillbirth from a murder (Wrightson, 1982). The only way to rebuff a supposition of neonaticide was the testimony from another person that a child had been born dead, "even if the woman could prove that the child had been born alive and then died of natural causes" (Lansdowne, 1990, p. 43). The law was never applied rigorously and, by the 18th century, fell into disuse.

Gradually, because the crime was perceived as so "unnatural," it came to be regarded as a result of mental disturbance. As early as the 15th century in France, mercy might be granted on this ground, although only after a long imprisonment; in many German states by the 18th century, sympathy for the mother was reflected by acquittal or reduced sentences (Kord, 1982). In England, the same defense was used and in many cases it was successful, even if some women who were clearly deranged were executed.

Attitudes in England and Scotland gradually became more humane and clemency was given more often. In England, the law of 1624 was repealed, but the law of 1803, although less severe than the earlier law, still provided capital punishment for women who killed their newborns. The final clause declared that single women acquitted of murder, but who had concealed their pregnancy, could be imprisoned for 2 years (even if the child had been stillborn) (Jackson, 1996). The same easing of the law's severity occurred in Scotland. It became more and more difficult to convict women of infanticide. From 1799 to 1809, 26 women were accused of infanticide, but there were no convictions. In 1809, a new law that reduced the penalties to 2-year imprisonment made convictions rise again (Symonds, 1997).

Sympathy for women increased during the nineteenth century, based partly on a more compassionate view of young women's suffering as a result of being victims of seduction and sexual exploitation. That, plus the belief that puerperal insanity was a legitimate defense in cases of neonaticide, led judges and prosecutors to reduce the punishment by allowing for extenuating circumstances or by convicting them on lesser charges (Showalter, 1980; Wilson, 1988). Juries, too, acquitted large numbers of women indicted for similar reasons. By the 19th century, in some jurisdictions, the treatment for women involved in child homicide differed from other murder cases by using the rubric of extenuating circumstances to reduce the severity of punishments (Fuchs, 1992).

From its inception as a sex-specific crime in 1623, infanticide has been concerned with theories about women. The initial object of the laws of secret pregnancy of 1623 (and later) in England, Europe, and the United States was to punish single women for becoming pregnant and for refusing to live with their sin. Thus, "the crime was created to affect moral and social behavior" (O'Donovan, 1984, p. 264). In the 19th century, attitudes changed toward women; people became more ambivalent and sympathetic. As ideology altered the feminine role to perceive women as more dependent and weak, but also as mistresses of morality and culture in the home, any deviation from the ongoing standards of motherhood meant that the female was obviously mentally ill. Her problems were caused by her gender and biological destiny, and thus she was more vulnerable, requiring protection and avoidance of the world outside the domestic sphere.

Summary

Combining the contemporary studies of sociobiologists with a survey of the perception of child homicide over many centuries in Western Europe and, to a lesser extent, the United States provides a vital context for regarding the same crime today. We continue to have religious influences, social disapproval of illegitimacy *and* unwed motherhood, and conflicts about how to deal with those who kill infants. However, we come to study the crime with the recognition that it is not something "new" in this world and that many of the pressures that caused young women to kill their newborns in the past still exist, as do the difficulties of knowing how to handle them.

3 Motives for Murder

As we have shown, cultural mores, economic development, and technical and medical progress have created communities that can provide more favorable and more nurturing environments for families. Yet the problem of child homicide remains, though on a smaller scale than in the past. Women's status and rights have been firmly established on more equal terms in Western societies. They have gained the vote and, in general, have access to more control of their reproductive functions. Young people enjoy more freedom from adult supervision, have greater economic opportunities, and have a far longer adolescence than formerly.

The rising divorce rate and the earlier physical maturation of youngsters have abetted earlier sexual activity. The pressure to engage in sexual intercourse is substantial. This has led to a dramatic increase in teenage pregnancy that has just begun to slide in the past few years. When a boy urges a girl to have intercourse—"everyone does it!"—what alternatives does she have? (She *could* say "no," but may be weighing this against the consequences in terms of future dates, peer popularity, or other factors.) If she "does it" and becomes pregnant, again what alternatives does she have? Homicide is one tragic option: neonaticide by a panic-stricken mother at the time of birth, infanticide by an ill-prepared parent in the child's first year of life, or filicide even later.

What are the salient characteristics of homicidal mothers? They differ in socioeconomic background, community, and education. Though different in these instances, they do possess other similarities. The women are usually young and single. The majority of them live with parents, guardians, or relatives. They are often, but not always, poor. Most are not married or do not have committed relationships. They keep themselves isolated and are unwilling to admit even to themselves that they are pregnant. Yet past and present studies indicate that, although the actions (neonaticide or infanticide) are similar in behavior, psychological and environmental circumstances vary widely.

Why Murder?

Why are children the victims of their parents' inability to cope with life? Are children expendable? What can stir a parent to kill a child, especially a newborn? People are horrified when parents kill their children, and the media focus varying amounts of attention on such crimes. Professionals and the lay public need to understand why these incidents occur and what family, medical, public agency, educational, and legislative actions can and should be undertaken to reduce them. (We believe that it is too much to hope that such cases can be totally eliminated.)

In 1984, Christoffel wrote that homicide warranted review as "the only leading cause of death of children under age 15 to have increased in incidence in the last 30 years … " (p. 68). Several other studies published in the 1980s and later sought the risk factors involved in neonaticide, infanticide, and child homicide (Cummings, Theis, Mueller, & Riveraet, 1994; Emerick, Foster, & Campbell, 1986; Palermo, 2002; Siegel et al., 1996; Wilkey, Pearn, Petrie, & Nixon, 1982; Winpisinger, Hopkins, Indian, & Hostetler, 1991). They tended to agree that these factors included young, usually teen-aged, unmarried women from poor, often non-White backgrounds, with less than a high school education, and who had had little or no prenatal care. Data from the National Center for Health Statistics, however, show that the birth rate for unmarried women by age declined for teenagers from 1980 to 2003, while it increased for almost all other groups (Figure 3.1).

Of course, not all of those who commit neonaticide or infanticide are teenagers; some are chronologically mature women who may have other motives for their actions. Furthermore, many of the recent cases we have found involve young women from middle-class, White backgrounds, often college students. The one factor that our sample appears to have in common with those cited is the lack of prenatal care (Figure 3.2).

As we indicated earlier, child homicide can be divided by the age of the victim into neonaticide, infanticide, and filicide. Child killing can also be divided by murderers. In neonaticide, the perpetrator is most often the new mother, who has usually given birth unattended (Kunz & Bahr, 1996; Smithey, 1998). Occasionally, she has the child's father with her, as in the Grossberg-Peterson and Sims cases. The murderer in infanticide and filicide is more frequently male, usually one of the victim's parents and more rarely both parents. Occasionally in these cases, the murderer may be a nonparent, often male, who is acting *in loco parentis*. Kunz and Bahr (1996) found that

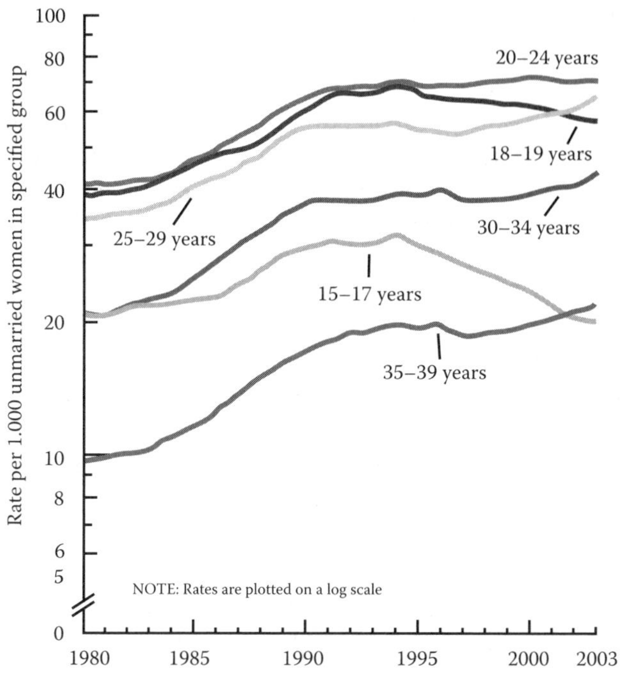

Figure 3.1 Births per 1,000 unmarried women by age of mother, 1980–2003.

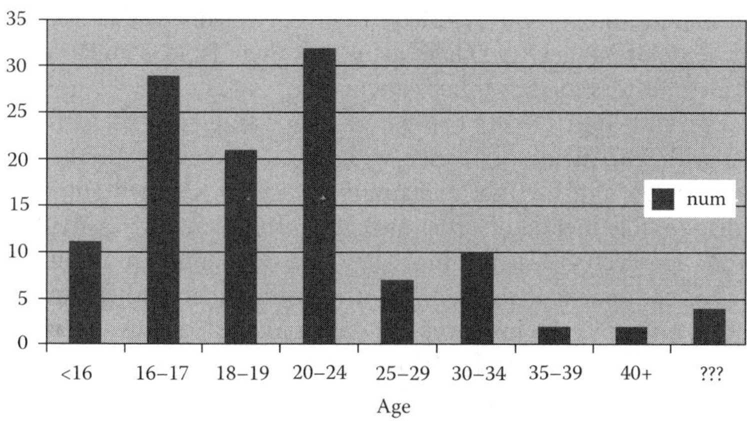

Figure 3.2 Neonaticide cases 1990–2005 by age of alleged perpetrator (N = 118).

U.S. government and other data "suggest that children are at greater risk when they and their parents are young" (p. 349), but age is not the only criterion for victims or perpetrators.

Overpeck and her colleagues studied linked birth and death certificates for children born in 1983 to 1991 and found 2,776 cases of infant homicide for which they were able to identify a number of risk factors (Overpeck, Brenner, Trumble, Tripletti, & Berendes, 1998). They were not, however, able to find birth certificates for 2.0 to 2.8% of the deaths in that period and found that this was more common "for infants who were less than 28 days old when they died than for those who were older" (p. 1212). They concluded that the strongest risk factors for newborns "were a maternal age of less than 17 years, a second or subsequent birth for a mother 19 years old or younger, and no prenatal care" (p. 1213). Having completed fewer than 12 years of education, especially those mothers over age 19, was also a high risk factor. (It should be noted that 18 years is the usual age for completion of high school education (grade 12), so this is not always indicative of being a high school dropout.) As we read reports of neonaticides and infanticides, there was ample graphic support for these conclusions.

The most recent available data from the National Center for Health Statistics of the Centers for Disease Control and Prevention indicated that "infant mortality rates were higher for mothers who began prenatal care after the first trimester or not at all" (MacDoman & Atkinson, 1999, p. 5), with an infant mortality rate of 35.6 per 1,000 live births in 1997 for those who had no prenatal care at all (MacDoman & Atkinson, Table 1, p. 10). The highest frequency of infant mortality by age of mother was for the group aged under 20 years; by years of education for the mother it was in the 9 to 11 years of education group, as noted earlier. Early neonatal deaths (< 7 days) were at a rate of 3.8 per 1,000 live births, but there is no correlational tie of any of these factors to each other conclusively.

McKee and Shea (1998) compared their sample of 20 adult women charged with infanticide or filicide with those studied by Resnick (1970), d'Orban (1979), and Bourget and Bradford (1990). Of their subjects, 80% had a diagnosable mental disorder and 35% were mentally retarded or with borderline intellectual functioning. They were also much more likely to be categorized as "low income" than was true in the other studies, and most of them were unemployed. Just over 20% were in adult abusive relationships. Given a detailed background, McKee and Shea found that "These women lacked adequate resources with which to cope with the stressors preceding the children's deaths" (p. 685). Furthermore,

> [The] great majority of these killings were apparently not due to impaired judgments from intoxication but, rather, were the result of distorted reality contact or were impulsive, unplanned acts evolving from extreme levels of situational stress, frustration, anger, depression, or a combination of these. (p. 685)

They rarely used weapons.

The motives for these crimes may vary considerably from one case to another, and especially with the age of the victim. In some cases, denial is operative; in others, uglier motives surface, like revenge against a third party. As to method, suffocation or drowning of neonates, horrible as it is, does not carry the sadistic quality seen in many of the child abuse cases that end up as infanticides and filicides.

Neonaticide

What sets the stage for a parent—usually the mother as already noted—to kill a newborn or to abandon it to almost certain death? Many questions evolve from this one. For example, does she acknowledge or deny, even to herself, the fact that she is pregnant? What are her resources? What are the (typically young) woman's relationships with her parents? What is the role of a young woman's religious training? *Is* neonaticide a belated alternative to abortion, or is abortion, as some claim, early neonaticide? Do attitudes and laws regarding abortion have any relation to neonaticide? What is the role of the social climate of a particular era with respect to out-of-wedlock motherhood? What alternatives to neonaticide exist in a given society at a particular point in time? In short, what are the social, political, and sexist ramifications of neonaticide in addition to the criminal nature of the act?

Resnick's classic study of neonaticide (1970) suggested several motives. In considering them, however, we must remember that abortion was not legally an option in the United States at the time at which he wrote (*Roe v. Wade* was not decided until 1973) and that the perception of illegitimacy changed markedly between the late 1960s and the late 1990s. Furthermore, his reasoning was based on the 37 neonaticides that he found in a review of world literature in the period from 1751 to 1968—hardly a sizable sample for that expanse of time. These reminders do not negate his work; they simply sharpen our interpretation of his findings.

Although Resnick found that 83% of the neonaticide reports he located were motivated by the baby being an "unwanted child," he asserted that "illegitimacy, with its social stigma, is the most common motive" (1970, p. 1419). One would need to question that today because unwed motherhood is not seen in quite the same negative terms at all levels of society as was true 30 or more years ago. For some young mothers, shame and guilt may still be primary motives for doing away with the unwanted baby in some way; for many others, these feelings are not part of the picture, although they may still have other motives for neonaticide.

On the other hand, Resnick also included as a motive denial of the pregnancy by the "mother" to herself, with the apparent expectation that the child will be stillborn or somehow magically disappear. When neither of these occurs, the young mother does away with the neonate. In many other cases, he found that the girl felt she could not reveal her pregnancy to *her* mother, fearing anger, punishment, or rejection. These situations are still prominent as motives for neonaticide. They raise the question of the nature of the relationship between the girl and her parent(s). On the one hand, there may be little communication between them; on the other hand, mother and daughter may be close, but daughter may be aware that her parents view her behavior as a reflection of themselves. This would increase the daughter's denial or inability to cope because of the shame it might bring.

Resnick also mentioned rape or extramarital pregnancy as motives for neonaticide. However, if the rape is reported to the authorities, abortion of the fetus would be permitted in many jurisdictions. This depends, also, on the point in the pregnancy at which the rape is reported. A case in Michigan was reported (Philadelphia: channel 6, 7/17/98, 5:30 P.M. news) in which the court would not allow an abortion of a 12-year-old's pregnancy because she was in her 27th week and Michigan law prohibits abortion after the 24th week except to save the mother's life. In this case, apparently the girl's parents were not aware of her condition until she was in her 26th week. At her age, irregular menses are quite common and would not have raised the possibility of pregnancy if other symptoms were absent. (Note: The abortion was finally allowed in her 29th week.) She had been impregnated by her 17-year-old brother, who was subsequently indicted for rape, pleaded guilty to fourth-degree criminal sexual conduct, and hoped to avoid deportation for his felony (Associated Press, 1998).

Extramarital pregnancy is another matter because a married woman has more options available to her and presumably would be more active in resolving her situation than a passive teenager. She could conceivably pass off the pregnancy as one originating in her marriage, although this may be risky if the resulting child looks too much like the biological father or if her husband had been absent for 10 or more months. She might be able to obtain an abortion on the grounds of risk to her mental health. She could also, of course, commit neonaticide.

Scrimshaw (1978) alleged that "mortality may sometimes be a response to high fertility instead of a stimulus to it" (p. 383). This may involve "under-investment" in unwanted children in terms of their care, feeding, and response to their illnesses. It happens in terms of gender, a child born in fewer than 3 years after birth of the next oldest child, and twins, and " … it is possible that sex preferences and the sex composition of the 'ideal' family can significantly affect morality within the family" (p. 389).

To most people, the murder of one's newborn or infant is beyond contemplation or comprehension. Indeed, it is most often unpremeditated even by those who commit neonaticide or infanticide. That being the case, we must look beyond simple intent in our attempt to understand why these crimes occur. Oberman (1996) put the case well:

> Neonaticide is not so much about a lack of economic resources as it is about a lack of communication and community. As is the case with infanticide, neonaticide is not merely an individual problem; it is a reflection of an atomized society that places little value on the mental and physical well-being of its most vulnerable constituents. Those who would prevent neonaticide must begin by identifying and remedying girls' vulnerability long before they become pregnant. (p. 73; reprinted with permission of the publisher, Georgetown University and American Criminal Law Review. © 1996.)

Part of that vulnerability is simple naiveté; these young women know little or nothing about contraception (although that may be due to religious teachings) and even less about the need for prenatal care if they do engage in intercourse and become pregnant. For those who deliver their babies and choose to raise them, they know frightfully little about child care or child development. (In our concluding chapters, we will review what is being taught in the schools and a number of programs that appear to have greater effectiveness than traditional health education courses.)

Psychological Explanations

One can look at the psychological aspects of neonaticide from the viewpoint of the individual alone or recognize that the individual is also a member of a family and a community. "At the individual level, the girls involved in neonaticide cases possess so little self-esteem that they are incapable of acting to protect themselves. Their insecurity almost certainly contributes to their becoming pregnant in the first place, and it leads to their paralysis once pregnant" (Oberman, 1996, p. 71). In addition, many of the girls fear that they will be excluded from their families when they are found to have had sex and to be pregnant. In Oberman's opinion, their fear may be justified. She found that many neonaticide cases

> show evidence of families that are remarkably disinterested in their children's lives. Those who commit neonaticide lack relationships with open, caring, reliable adults--, adults who will recognize the signs of pregnancy, confront the girls about their situations, and

> initiate the difficult conversations about the alternative resolutions to pregnancy, including motherhood. This isolation from loved ones, even within the home, clearly constitutes a structural factor that contributes to neonaticide. (1996, p. 71; reprinted with permission of the publisher, Georgetown University and American Criminal Law Review © 1996.)

Such isolation is not always the case. The fear of being rejected may be real, but is based on recognition by the daughter that her parents think she is perfect and her knowledge that her pregnancy is "letting them down."

With young women, unintended pregnancy does not necessarily lead to marriage. The prospect of single parenthood with all of its physical and emotional responsibilities, perhaps to dropping out of school and the abandonment of hopes and plans for the future can also consciously or unconsciously propel an adolescent to neonaticide. Mapanga (1997) has addressed several of these problems with respect to adolescents, but they also hold true for unmarried young adult women.

The Role of Shame

As Massaro (1997) has suggested, "*shame* has become in the 1990s what *self-esteem* was in the 1980s … The shameworthy ones are usually Others—typically, general categories of others unlikely to pen a response: unwed mothers, deadbeat dads, urban youths … " (p. 646). It is interesting which group leads the list. She adds that shame is potentially destructive rather than reintegrative, principally because it is a call for *humiliation* of offenders. Shame is not a new way of dealing with pregnancy among the unwed; it has been used by parents, the clergy, and others for centuries to keep (or try to keep) unmarried girls from having sexual relations or, failing that, from having babies.

With respect to neonaticide particularly, what is the role of shame? Does the girl deny her pregnancy, even to herself, out of shame at her sexual behavior because pregnancy was an admission of having had sex and indeed would provoke feelings of shame (Ehrenreich, 1998)?

Shaming will clearly promote one end: it communicates the shamer's disgust for the offender and the offense. Plainly, it is cheaper than imprisonment; for some, however, it may evoke greater rebellion and more outrageous and maladaptive behavior. In the latter type of situation, it may be that the young woman remains in a state of denial of the "crime" she has committed, or, at the other extreme, she assumes the attitude that "if I've got the name, I'll play the game."

An example of the influence of religious background is found in a case presented by Green and Manohar (1990). The patient was an only daughter among six children of a family that practiced a strict Protestant faith, lived in a socially isolated community, and avoided contemporary ways of living, which were regarded as sinful. After a severe beating by her father, one of many over the years, she left home at age 18 and subsequently entered into a common-law relationship. At age 23, unmarried, she delivered her baby alone and it drowned in the lavatory bowl. She was initially charged with second-degree murder, which was subsequently changed to infanticide, and admitted to a psychiatric hospital.

The dynamics of the case appeared clear. From the perspective of her religious cultural background, to be pregnant out of wedlock was considered a major sin. Obtaining an abortion would have been considered an even greater sin. The young woman had moved away from her parents' home, although not their attitudes, in an attempt to live more independently. "Before the birth of the baby she had never been able to inform her parents that she was living in a common-law relationship" (Green & Manohar, 1990, p. 123). When hospitalized, she claimed to have no memory of having pregnancy tests or of having been pregnant, and she said that she did not realize she was in labor until the baby appeared. As Green and Manohar pointed out, the fact that she had seen a physician and been told she was pregnant is quite unusual in cases of neonaticide, but they caution that, when physicians diagnose pregnancy in unmarried women, they should also explore "the impact of pregnancy on the mother's psychosocial status" (1990, p. 123).

A team of psychiatrists (Silva et al., 1998) has made a strong case for considering the impact of the individual's cultural background in evaluating those who commit neonaticide. In the case on which their article was focused, the young woman's family was opposed to out-of-wedlock sexual activity, birth control methods as alternatives to abstinence, and abortion. She was not in denial of the pregnancy as many other 18-year-olds have been, but thought about seeking abortifacent herbs in Mexico or leaving her baby at a church. Unfortunately, the pregnancy had continued long past the time when the herbs might have been effective, and the baby arrived before she could abandon it safely.

Another case illustrates the lingering power of shame that still exists in our secular, free-wheeling society. An 18-year-old college student (Aldridge) became pregnant and concealed it from her boyfriend, family, and friends. While staying with her male companion, she went into labor and delivered the baby in the bathroom without awakening him. After the delivery, she tied off the umbilical cord and bathed the baby in the tub. She claimed the baby slipped under the water. Aldridge attempted to revive the infant by thumping on its chest, but the baby died. She wrapped the baby in towels and placed it in her book bag and then transferred it to a trunk that she then took to a storage unit.

Later, when she went to a hospital for care of vaginal bleeding, she admitted giving birth but claimed that she gave the baby up for adoption. Only after 3 months, when the storage unit was opened for an inventory analysis, was the decomposed body found and eventually traced to her. During the interrogations, Aldridge confessed that she felt submerging the baby was the best method of handling the problem because her parents would be ashamed of her and others would hate her. She was convicted of first-degree murder with malicious intent (*Kuturah Aldridge v. Comm. of Va*, 2004, 44 Va. App 618, 606 S.E. 2dd 539). This case, like others cited, also illustrates the immaturity and the emotional instability that accompany the thoughtless and rash behavior of these young women.

Denial of Pregnancy

In the past as well as the present, the most mysterious and yet most common trait exhibited in neonaticide is the denial of pregnancy. An interesting phenomenon is that, in most cases, families and friends also deny it. The girl or woman gains little weight compared to most pregnant women and is able to disguise that with boxy blouses or sweaters. If she misses her menstrual period, she attributes that to some other cause. When she delivers the baby, often in a restroom, she says that she felt the need to defecate and was totally shocked when a baby appeared. It is not only a matter of *saying* this; she actually believes it. "That discomfort I felt down below must be a premenstrual cramp or a little constipation." Alone, possibly frightened but often in total denial, the girl or woman delivers a newborn baby whose very evolution she has denied for as long as 8 or 9 months.

The delivery is relatively easy and brief, or the young woman exerts monumental self-control in not making a sound during contractions or even during the delivery. The existence of this child is so threatening to her and her way of life that she suffocates or drowns or shakes the life out of the newborn. "Denial and rationalization of symptoms and denial of pregnancy may result in inadequate responses at the time of childbirth, and this may result in the death of the newborn" (Finnegan, McKinstry, & Robinson, 1982, p. 674). Even those delivered in a hospital, however, had come seeking aid for stomach pains, flu, or other sources of pain, not for delivery of a baby whose existence *in utero* they and those close to them denied.

This denial behavior is not a contemporary phenomenon. Records of English courts of the 17th and 18th centuries revealed similar denials of pregnancy, and this had been observed also in France and in the American colonies (Hufton, 1974). Court records in Victorian England indicated the isolation, denial, and concealment of pregnancy (Higginbotham, 1989). Most of the servant girls in 19th-century Bavaria had their babies in the privy and treated the births as evacuations that did not affect the rhythm of their work.

They denied the pregnancy and "subsequently told the judge that they had not known they were pregnant. They had certainly lost 'something'; they did not know it was a child" (Schulte, 1984, p. 85).

Our contemporary society has seen similar behavior. Although motives may differ, social and economic circumstances may be disparate, and even the ambience may be different, young women seem to react to their dilemma in the same way. Women in the past and present who commit neonaticide generally have made no plans for the birth or care of their children. Massive denial of the gravid state is a prominent feature of this clinical situation, with the denial so powerful that it affects not only the young woman's perceptions, but also those of her family, friends, teachers, employers, and even physician.

Five cases in Iowa reported in 1987 exemplify this pattern of behavior (Saunders, 1989):

In February 1987, a 19-year-old college freshman drowned her 9-lb. baby boy in a college dormitory toilet after denying and concealing her pregnancy. She pleaded guilty to a charge of child endangerment and was sentenced to 10 years in prison.

A 14-year-old girl gave birth to a living baby girl whom she hid in a closet, where the infant died of exposure. She was tried in juvenile court for endangering the life of a child; her sentence was withheld from the press.

A $4^1/_2$-lb. baby girl was found in a ditch, dead from exposure. Her mother, a 17-year-old, was subsequently found and charged with murder. Her sentence was also withheld.

A 28-year-old claimed that she did not realize she was pregnant until her newborn was found dead in a toilet. She was sentenced to 20 years for endangerment and neglect of a baby.

Another 28-year-old was discovered dead from blood loss after delivering a 5-lb. baby who was found dead from exposure. No one knew she was pregnant.

These cases echo the scenario played out in the past: the mothers denied or concealed their pregnancy.

Other studies provide additional evidence. In Oberman's (1996) study, of her 47 cases of neonaticide, 19 denied the pregnancy to themselves, 10 concealed it from others, and 43 delivered without assistance, which is consistent with other studies. Similarly, in the study by Overpeck et al. (1998), " … 95 percent of infants killed during the first day of life were not born in a hospital as compared with 8 percent of all infants killed during the first year of life … ." (p. 1214)

Denial of pregnancy can also contribute to prenatal conditions that render the newborn underweight, ill at birth, or possibly mentally retarded. This is because the young woman has not had any prenatal care and generally is not following a diet or physical regime that would be helpful to the pregnancy and developing baby. A 17-year-old high school senior in eastern Pennsylvania was raped twice, saw the school nurse periodically for what were noted as menstrual cramps and spotting, bled profusely midway through her pregnancy, thought it was a miscarriage due to the second rape, and gained only 10 lbs. throughout her whole pregnancy.

"While these circumstances seem hard to believe, it is important to bear in mind that Lisa was a naïve, 17-year-old girl who felt ashamed and afraid and who confided in no one" (Atkins, Grimes, Joseph, & Liebman, 1999, p. 7). She delivered a full-term baby girl who was not breathing, hid her in an overnight bag at her hosts' home in New Jersey, and then in a garage at her own home. Taken to the hospital shortly thereafter, the doctors found signs of the delivery and "Lisa" admitted to what had happened.

Wheelwright (1998) related the case of a 21-year-old in Manchester, England, who endured 17 hours of labor alone that ended in a breech delivery. In another case, a young 20-year-old at a local community college had a premature infant alone at home, refusing to summon the aid of her sleeping family. She had a long, difficult labor and was discovered hemorrhaging in the bathroom the next morning. She was taken to the emergency room where medical intervention saved her life. The doctor's testimony indicated that the problems of her self-delivery could induce shock. Her premature baby later died (*State v. Maurico*, 1987).

In a study done in Dade County, Florida, Crittenden and Craig (1990) noted a high number of spontaneous births and subsequent drownings of newborns in toilets, echoing results found by Mitchell and Davis (1984), who had conducted an earlier study in the same county. The new mother commits neonaticide and will deny that, too, as ever having happened. Whether in cases of drowning or other birth settings, often the girl or woman throws the little body, wrapped in a trash bag, into a trash can. "Out of sight, out of mind!" Clearly, the baby never existed.

One of the more sensationalized cases was that of Melissa Drexler, the so-called "Prom Mom," who arrived at the site of her high school prom, excused herself to go to the ladies' room, and shortly thereafter came out and allegedly danced at her prom (Hanley, 1997). She was arrested when a maintenance worker found the infant's body while the prom was still on and Drexler was dancing and enjoying herself. One friend was quoted as saying that, to her knowledge, Drexler did not know she was pregnant; the mother of another friend commented that she certainly did not look $8^1/_2$ months pregnant when shopping for a prom dress a few weeks before the event (Goodnough & Weber, 1997).

In a less publicized incident, a 20-year-old college student gave birth alone during the night (3 a.m.), wrapped the baby in a blanket, and took it to the basement, placing it in a wood-burning stove. She took a bath, retrieved the baby's remains, placed the bundle in her car's trunk for later disposal, and then attended her college classes the next morning as if nothing had happened (*State v. McGuire*, 1997). This echoes the view of Brozovsky and Falit (1971), who suggested that the denial can be so potent that it affects not only the pregnant young woman, but also all of those who know her.

Denial was not even mentioned by Nadeau (1997) in her discussion of a revised typology of filicide; nor was neonaticide mentioned in the work of Resnick (1992) on the alternatives available to a pregnant girl (abortion, mothering, adoption). Yet, a number of psychologists, psychiatrists, and obstetricians have written about the hysterical denial of the young girl and the more psychotically based denial of a young woman who suffers from a chronic mental illness. The difference is clarified by Spielvogel and Hohenor (1995):

> It is common for primaparous women who are unfamiliar with symptoms of pregnancy and for those who are ambivalent about being pregnant not to recognize their pregnancy until the second trimester. When pregnancy is denied throughout most or all of gestation, significant risk to the infant and mother may result, such as … neonaticide. Persistent denial can occur in women with otherwise intact reality testing (nonpsychotic denial) and in those with a thinking disorder and general deficits in cognitive functioning or reality testing (psychotic denial). (pp. 220–221; courtesy of Blackwell Science)

Additional reasons for nonpsychotic denial may include young age, anger toward the baby's father, rejection of the fetus, childhood psychological and sexual traumas, and "conflicted or inhibited sexuality in response to strict religious or parental prohibitions of premarital sex" (Spielvogel & Hohenor, 1995, p. 221). Separation from the partner or stress arising from other interpersonal problems may also precipitate a denial of pregnancy (Brezinka, Huter, Biebl, & Kinzl, 1994), as may social isolation (Finnegan, McKinstry, & Robinson, 1982). In the case of adolescents particularly, they may not reveal or discuss amenorrhea or other symptoms even if they visit their health caregivers, and thus they receive no prenatal care. They do not plan to do away with the baby after it is born; they simply refuse to think of it in any way at all, and "it" is what they perceive rather than a baby. Whether the neonate is killed as part of the denial or as a result of panic following the birth is often difficult to determine.

As previous cases illustrated, the denial of pregnancy and absence of prenatal care add to the risks of childbirth. The young woman not only risks her life, but also risks possibly severe damage to the baby in terms of brain damage, malnutrition, and a variety of defects. This may well have been the case with Amy Grossberg, who apparently had some bleeding during pregnancy and then had seizures and eclampsia following her unattended delivery (McCullogh, 1998; Most, 1999). According to testimony at the sentencing hearing reported on CNN's *Burden of Proof* (July 9, 1998), Brian Peterson, father of the baby-to-be, claimed to have asked Amy twice to have an abortion, which she refused to do for fear that her mother would find out, and to have neonatal care, which she also refused to do. She also wrote Brian letters in which she hoped that "it" would disappear (Most, 1999).

Margaret Spinelli, a psychiatrist at Columbia University who had worked with nine neonaticidal women, said that their denial could be linked to a dissociative disorder in which the pregnancy is denied so firmly that it is compartmentalized and separated from the conscious self (*ABC News*, 1997). She believed that there should be two psychiatric evaluations by specialists in perinatal psychiatry of these young women prior to their being handled by the legal system.

Psychological/Psychiatric Diagnoses

Psychotic denial of pregnancy may occur in women who are chronically mentally ill, possibly schizophrenic, and who may have lost custody of other children earlier. Another possibility is cognitive and ego impairment, allegedly occurring in connection with a close but ambivalent relation with the young woman's mother (Milden, Rosenthal, Winegardner, & Smith, 1985). Here, mother and daughter tend to be in denial of the pregnancy. Some young women believe that they are suffering from a blood clot or water retention that is contributing to an enlarged abdominal area or may misinterpret the symptoms of labor (Spielvogel & Hohenor, 1995). All of these young women need to be cared for during pregnancy and helped during delivery to avert postpartum emotional disturbances and fetal abuse or neonaticide (Miller, 1990; Spielvogel & Hohenor, 1995). One psychotic woman in her fourth pregnancy

> had a history of three consecutive unassisted home deliveries and subsequent neonatal deaths. Not knowing what to do, she placed two of her newborns in a garbage can and left the other unattended in her apartment. The woman was hospitalized in the psychiatric unit for her fourth delivery, and gave birth to a healthy infant

whom she gave up for adoption. (Spielvogel & Hohenor, 1995, p. 224; courtesy of Blackwell Science)

Defense attorneys for those who have committed neonaticide or infanticide frequently claim that the young woman was suffering from a reactive psychosis or a postpartum depression that made her commit the crime (she was mentally ill). Postpartum psychosis, sometimes mistakenly tied to neonaticide, may have applicability to infanticide—that is, murder of the infant after the first 24 hours but before age 1 year—but is not really a factor in neonaticide. This is because the onset of this condition as "baby blues" or as postpartum depression is usually a few days to a few weeks after childbirth (Schroeder, 1993). It has been mentioned in the *Diagnostic and Statistical Manual*, third edition (*DSM-III*) (American Psychiatric Association, 1980), but was considered an "atypical psychosis" rather than a discrete entity (Munoz, 1985). (Note: A fuller discussion of postpartum depression and psychosis, with more recent information, will be discussed in connection with infanticide and filicide in a later chapter.)

Whether there is a diagnosis incorporating denial as well a psychotic episode at the time of delivery resulting in the neonate's death and called "neonaticide syndrome" is debatable. Wolman's classic *Handbook of Clinical Psychology* (1965) refers to the psychoanalytic perception of denial as a defense against the perception of a painful reality (p. 322). Dealing with the content of the American Psychiatric Association's *DSM-III* (1987), Kaplan and Sadock (1996) have a similar definition of "denial" as a defense mechanism and briefly mention infanticide as one risk of untreated postpartum psychosis. There is no separate citation of "denial," "infanticide," or "neonaticide" in the APA's *DSM-IV* (1994) or the *DSM-IV-TR* (2000).

For an attorney to attempt to use "neonaticide syndrome" as a defense for one of the young women charged with neonaticide is difficult because it does not meet the *Frye* (1923) or *Daubert* (1993) tests of acceptability within the professional community. (This will be discussed at greater length in a later chapter.)

The confusion can be due to differing diagnoses, such as "neonaticide dissociative disorder" in one case and insanity with "acute stress disorder" in another, each offered as a defense to having committed neonaticide. An attorney who had been involved in cases using each of these no longer planned to present evidence that her client suffered from neonatal dissociative disorder because, she was quoted as saying, "that term is not generally recognized in the psychiatric community" (Illinois Report, 1998).

The existence of a neonaticide "syndrome" became a source of argument and appeal in the case of Stephanie Wernick, a college student who asphyxiated her newborn son, denied she had ever been pregnant, and was convicted of criminally negligent homicide (*People v. Wernick*, 1996). She had claimed insanity as a defense. Wernick's expert witnesses were allowed to testify that she had denied she was pregnant, that such denial occurs in almost all cases of neonaticide, that she may indeed not have known that she was pregnant, and that she suffered a brief reactive psychosis upon giving birth. They were not allowed to say that she suffered from the so-called neonaticide syndrome or to cite relevant clinical experience, and this decision of the lower court was upheld twice on appeal.

In two other cases of neonaticide in the Chicago area, one attorney was ready to present an insanity defense but the other was not. The one who chose not to raise this defense said that if the defense was used, (1) the defendant had to admit committing the crime; and (2) other defenses, such as having an alibi or alleging that someone else murdered the newborn, could not be used (Chen, 1998)

Going beyond neonaticide only, in a study of 60 women who had killed one or more of their children ($N = 76$) between 1870 and 1996, Lewis, Baranoski, Buchanan, and Benedek (1998) found that 52% "were found incompetent to stand trial and an even higher percentage found not guilty by reason of insanity (65%)" (p. 614). The victims ranged in age from birth to 26 years, with a median age of 2.50 years. Furthermore, it was found that "Although 25% of the total sample used a gun or a knife, 36% of the psychotic mothers used these weapons compared to only 5% of the nonpsychotic mothers" (p. 615); the children killed with these weapons were significantly older than those killed by other means (smothering, poisoning, drowning, beating, starvation, etc.). Although neonaticides were included in this sample, the use of a weapon to commit the crime was unlikely.

Reaction and Revenge

Depending upon the era in which a case occurred and the state, some homicides of pregnant women may be viewed as neonaticides; that is, the fetus, especially if viable, killed before birth is regarded as a newborn for the purposes of prosecutorial charges. These murders usually occur when the male does not want the child (if he is the father) or wants to punish his wife or girlfriend for becoming pregnant by another man, or even by him. Such an incident occurred in California when Larry Apodaca raped and assaulted his pregnant ex-wife, claiming that he would not permit her to bear anybody else's baby. After sustaining the beating, she delivered a dead fetus (about 22 to 24 weeks). The defendant was convicted of second-degree murder of a fetus, rape, and assault (*People v. Apodaca*, 1978). A similar incident involved another angry ex-husband who discovered that his ex-wife was pregnant and physically attacked her, causing a miscarriage (*People v. Keeler*, 1970).

Infanticide and Filicide

Infanticide, the killing of a child older than 24 hours up to 1 year of age, is the result of a different set of motives and perpetrators. Silverman and Kennedy (1988) asserted that immaturity and psychological stress were preeminent motives in infanticide. These can be understood to some degree when the age of many of the perpetrators is considered as well as the absence of proper preparation for parenting or the aid of a support system. Reaction to stress or family arguments or a desire for revenge against the child's other parent can lead to infanticide (rarely to neonaticide). The stress may be rooted in poverty, ill health, having too many children, or lack of a support system. It is taken out on the vulnerable baby who may be crying, have a wet diaper, or just be "there" and "in the way" as it were.

As we noted earlier, when births are shown in almost complete detail in televised soap operas or "family" shows and on the Internet, there seems to be little excuse for anyone to be uninformed about infantile behaviors and bodily functions. What psychological factors operate to repress such knowledge in the minds of homicidal caretakers? Child neglect, as in inadequate feeding, and child abuse, as in violent shaking of a baby, are often the basis of charges against the homicidal parent(s); infanticide does not have to result from drowning or stabbing, as can be seen in cases throughout the country. Why do these parents (or those serving in that role) batter and kill children who cannot control their behavior because they are too young to do so? When social welfare agencies exist in virtually every community in the United States, why are some parents so overwhelmed by child care that they can murder a child rather than seek outside help?

In cases in which the parents separate, one parent may kill their child or children rather than permit the other to have visitation or shared custody or, conversely, to avoid paying child support. Such a "revenge" motive, one of several postulated by Resnick (1970), is an example of warped thought processes and may lead to a defense at trial of mental illness. One might hypothesize that a parent against whom the other parent has secured a protection order (typically the father) is more likely to commit this crime as part of his crusade of revenge against the children's mother. However, it is difficult to secure accurate statistics to test this hypothesis.

Brody (1998) cited research by Daly and Wilson, evolutionary psychologists cited earlier, who found "the rate of infanticide was 60 times as high … in stepfamilies as in biologically related families" (p. F1). They and others who take the evolutionary perspective believe that the "underlying trigger" for abuse and conflict in stepfamilies "lies within inherently selfish genes, which are biologically driven to perpetuate themselves" (p. F1). This is seen in lower animal family groups, they assert, when a male that takes over an existing family typically kills offspring from the female's earlier matings.

It should be noted that stepparents have different motives and methods for infanticide and filicide than do genetic parents (Daly & Wilson, 1994; Weekes-Shackelford & Shackelford, 2004). In a replication of several studies focused on this issue, Weekes-Shackelford and Shackelford examined 3,925 cases of child homicide for the years from 1976 to 1994 in which a child under age 5 was killed by a (putative) genetic parent or a stepparent. Of these cases, they found (p. 77):

309 committed by stepfather
1,741 committed by genetic father
30 committed by stepmother
1,845 committed by genetic mother

They found that the stepparents were more likely to beat or bludgeon the child, while both of the genetic parents were more likely to asphyxiate or, for the fathers, to shoot the little one. Stepparents tended to be more resentful, bitter, and angry than the genetic parents.

Personal Gain

In at least some cases, beyond the ken of most people, babies are killed for the parents' financial gain. That is, the parents have taken out life insurance on the children and collect when the children die from "sudden infant death syndrome" (SIDS), drowning, arson, neglect, or some other cause. Several cases have been reported, usually after prolonged investigation, and tend to evoke sympathy in the minds of the public initially. In still another case, *Davidson v. State of Indiana*, the Supreme Court of Indiana upheld the conviction of Latine Davidson on two counts of murder of her children (*Latine Marie Gordon Davidson v. State of Indiana*, 1990).

Davidson had applied for AFDC welfare payments in June 1983 but her request was denied. A few weeks later, Davidson paid the premium due on her daughter's life insurance. The child died about 2 weeks later. In December 1983, Davidson received $5,000 in benefits from the policy. She gave birth to one son, Rodriguez, in October 1983 and a year later to another son. AFDC benefits were again denied to Davidson and her husband. In January 1985, Davidson secured a life insurance policy on the older boy. The next day, her husband found the 14-month-old boy dead in the bathtub.

It should be noted that murdering a child to collect on the child's insurance is not a modern phenomenon. In 18th- and 19th-century England, infants and young children died from burns, suffocation, drowning, excess medication, starvation, and indifference, just as happens today. "Under burial society rules a member, ordinarily a parent, received as beneficiary on the death of his or her insured child a payment from the society that considerably exceeded the combined cost of the insurance premium and the burial" (Forbes, 1986, p. 189). Some parents belonged to more than one burial society. It was very difficult to prosecute the parents in these burial society cases. Laws were passed in the 1889 to 1908 period, however, that made it a felony to benefit from the death of a child (Forbes, 1986).

There are also murders of babies that are initially labeled "crib" or SIDS deaths that, in cases where multiple instances occur in the same family, are subsequently labeled infanticide. The authorities may begin to suspect that they are dealing with a parent who enjoys the role of victim ("Poor woman!") even if there is no life insurance to collect. Whether the parent cannot cope with the stresses of parenting, seeks to collect insurance benefits, or is mentally ill differs in each situation.

Marie Noe and Waneta Hoyt are prime examples of such mothers. Their cases will be discussed in the chapter on syndromes. Another case very similar in context was that of Cheri Welch, who claimed that her 7-month-old baby had died of apnea reflex (similar to SIDS). Her 2-week-old boy was brought to the hospital bleeding and breathless. He was saved, but hospital personnel became suspicious of child abuse. Subsequent investigations revealed the death of another girl baby. At the same time, Welch claimed she was the victim of a rape. The authorities arrested her for the murder of two babies and attempted murder of the third. Psychological testing indicated that she suffered from borderline personality disorder or Munchausen syndrome by proxy (MSBP). She was convicted of first-degree murder and sentenced to life imprisonment (*U.S. v. Welch*, 1994). Welch's appeal of her confession as having been involuntary and in violation of her *Miranda* rights was denied by the U.S. Supreme Court in 1996 (*Welch v. United States*, 1995).

In these cases, the mother (unconsciously) seeks to gain sympathetic attention through her Munchausen syndrome by proxy activities. Here, the infant or child is repeatedly brought to the hospital suffering from shortness of breath, diarrhea, or some other symptom that has been falsified or induced in the child. A falsified history can create a damaging self-image in the child as being chronically ill, and the unnecessary medical tests to determine the cause of illness can do damage (Kahan & Yorker, 1991). While in the hospital, the child is fine and healthy; a few weeks at home, and the child is back at the hospital with new symptoms. After several such incidents, the child may die, with the death attributed to a respiratory or other illness unless someone checks his or her hospital records, as is normally done when child abuse is suspected. Artingstall (1998) provides a number of helpful clues to use in differentiating child abuse cases from those where the MSBP syndrome is the dominant factor.

It should be noted that fathers are rarely involved directly in MSBP cases, although it is suggested that they may be helpful in describing a child's symptoms (Kahan & Yorker, 1991). More likely, they will support the wife's sad tales. Controversy regarding MSBP has become so prolific in the courts and professional journals that a separate segment will be devoted to that later in this book.

Summary

These theories and motives relevant to killing one's child obviously cover a wide range of contexts and perspectives, as well as a range of children's ages. Apart from the socioculturally sanctioned motives, it is possible to find several of these motives operating within any society at a given point in time and, indeed, within the individual who commits the crime. In the following chapters, we will focus first on the unnatural deaths of newborns and then on those of infants and young children.

Neonaticide and Its Alternatives

4

Teen-aged girls today range from the truly naïve to the pseudosophisticated, from those who maintain their virginity to those vulnerable to peer pressure involving sexual relations to the promiscuous. They are exposed to sexually explicit films and song lyrics that almost assume that sexual relations among the young are the norm, while their parents debate with school boards as to whether there should be sex education in the schools and if there should, how much information and what kinds should be included. Surrounded by titillating stimuli, but with insufficient factual information to help them cope with it, preadolescents and adolescents alike are often ill prepared to prevent pregnancy or to deal with it.

As Pipher (1994) has pointed out,

> Girls are scared of many things. They are worried that they will be judged harshly for their bodies and lack of experience. They are worried about getting caught by their parents or going to hell. They fear pregnancy and STDs. They worry about getting a bad reputation, rejection and pleasing their partners. They have seen sex associated with female degradation and humiliation, and they have heard ugly words describing sex, words that have more to do with aggression than love. So they are fearful of being emotionally and physically hurt. For the most part, girls keep their anxiety to themselves. It's not sophisticated to be fearful. (p. 207)

Add to this confused picture the fact that many girls also live in a stressful family environment where their psychological, and perhaps other, needs are not being met, and a situation exists in which these girls become highly vulnerable to sexual activity. They are often afraid that if they refuse to have

Table 4.1 What Are the Options?

No sexual intercourse
Sexual intercourse with contraceptives
versus
Sexual intercourse without contraceptives
Pregnancy occurs:
Abortion
versus
Carry to term:
Mother the child
versus
Place for adoption
versus
Abandon
versus
Commit neonaticide

intercourse with a boy, they will be rejected, and they want desperately to be loved by someone. Indeed, some girls in this situation seek to become pregnant because they believe that at least the baby will love them unconditionally. Unfortunately, they seem to be unaware of the time and care needed by, and the demands of, infants. This can lead later to infanticide by unprepared caretakers of either gender.

If the girl or woman elects not to have intercourse, obviously there will be no pregnancy. If she chooses to have intercourse, but only with the use of contraceptives, there will be no pregnancy as long as the contraceptive is effective. If no contraception is used, there is the risk of pregnancy, and then there are other choices to be made, as seen in Table 4.1.

The adolescent girls who become pregnant are considered to have immature cognitive development in that they take risks without weighing the potential outcomes of their behavior. According to Stoiber, Anderson, and Schowalter (1998), several studies have shown that the bent toward risk behavior plus situational factors such as educational disadvantage, school failure or school dropout status, and strong peer pressure to have sex contribute strongly toward adolescent pregnancy. In addition, they reported that parents did not discuss sexually transmitted diseases, pregnancy, conception, or contraception with their children.

Strong peer pressure, in the form of higher scores on the "powerful other" locus of control subscale in terms of health decision-making, was also a significant finding in Morgan's study (1995) of sexually active suburban, middle-class adolescent girls and pregnancy. She hypothesized that they might be more susceptible to peer pressure than others, and this might place them at a higher risk for unintended pregnancy than more self-reliant peers. On the other hand, the ability to control impulses and delay gratification requires a sense that there are choices to be made and consequences of choices. A third perspective, that of Stevens-Simon and McAnarney (1994), suggests that childhood physical or sexual abuse is a common antecedent of adolescent pregnancy and is tied as well to the birth of smaller and less mature infants.

Although the birth rate for teenagers has been declining in recent years, according to the National Center for Health Statistics (Ventura, 1984; Ventura, Mathews, & Curtin, 1999b; Ventura, Hamilton, & Sutton, 2003), a different estimate shows that about 11% of girls aged 15 to 19 years get pregnant each year, or approximately 1 million pregnancies (Benoit, 1997). The Alan Guttmacher Institute reported, in 1998, that the rate of adolescent pregnancy was declining, with 101 pregnancies per 1,000 girls aged 15 to 19 years in 1995 as compared with 117 per 1,000 in 1990 (Lewin, 1998).

These figures may be incomplete and a slight underestimate according to Henshaw (1997), who analyzed 1992 data for the institute. None of the sets of data accounts for all of the pregnancies because they have excluded pregnancies among even younger girls or because of unregistered births (and deaths, such as neonaticides). The National Center for Health Statistics does, however, show that the number of births per 1,000 for girls aged 10 to 14 years has declined from a high of 1.4 in 1990 to 1994 to a low of 0.8 in 2001 (Ventura et al., 2003) and lower still in 2002 (0.7) and 2003 (0.6) (Martin et al., 2005, Table A) as seen in Figure 4.1.

Not all of those who commit neonaticide, however, are teenagers (or younger). This is apparent if we examine data from available studies as well as that which we have collected. In the cases we found with mother's age reported between 1990 and late 2005 ($N = 118$), 61 were aged 10 to 19 years and 53 were 20 years of age or older (plus 4 of unknown age), with a median age of 18 to 19 years. In Oberman's study (1996), the median age of those who committed neonaticide was 17 years, but this means, obviously, that half of her sample of 47 were older than 17 years.

Adler (1984) pointed out that several studies of adolescents indicated that both males and females lacked appropriate information about contraceptives, and that when the youths *were* cognizant of the need for contraception, it was the girl who was expected to handle this, not the boy. However, if the girl did use a contraceptive method or sought information about preventing pregnancy, this was admitting to herself (and perhaps others) that she planned to have intercourse. The use of contraceptives was also often seen as violating religious instruction. Either of these reasons provoked feelings of guilt in the girl.

Vance (1985) similarly commented on the ignorance and naiveté of many teenage girls: their "lack of motivation to take responsibility to prevent pregnancy; … fear of asking for help in preventing pregnancy; and inner feelings

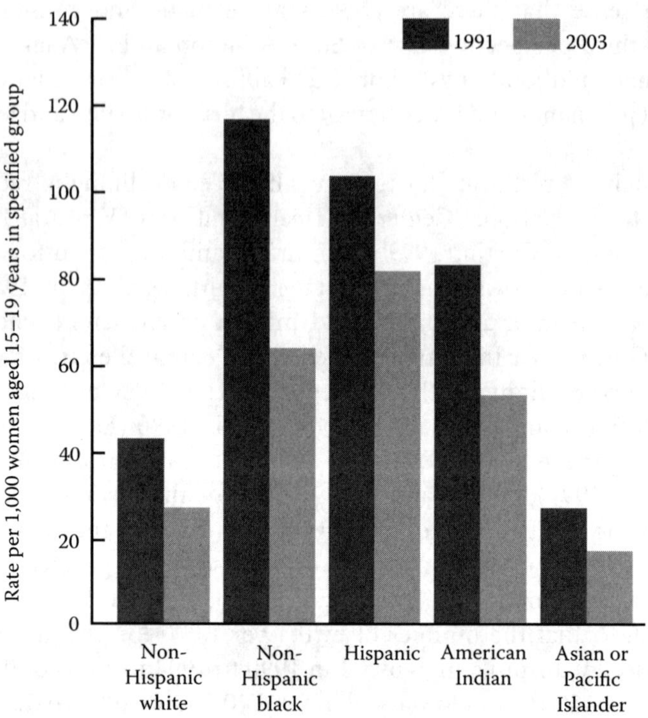

Figure 4.1 Neonaticide by ethnic background.

of denial based on false assumptions that 'it can never happen to me'" (p. 274). Given the thousands of entries on the Internet under the heading of "adolescent pregnancy," however, there is little excuse for girls not to learn about contraceptives or sources of help if they become pregnant.

If pregnancy does occur, a more frequent outcome than the youths anticipate, denial tends to persist throughout most of the pregnancy, if not through the delivery. Prenatal care and abortion are typically avoided because either of these would be an admission to the self, and others, that the girl was pregnant (Bluestein & Routledge, 1992).

The denial may be the result of paranoid schizophrenia, borderline or inadequate personality disorder, or a kind of hysterical amnesia designed to avoid admitting to the moralistic self even that the girl had participated in sexual intercourse (Milden, Winegardner, & Smith, 1985; cf. Brozovsky & Falit, 1971):

> What happens to the babies, secretly growing inside the mothers who are unaware, and by extension, unable to make any antepartum decisions—to terminate or continue the pregnancy, to seek

prenatal care, to plan to relinquish the babies for adoption or to raise them in their own families?" (Milden et al., p. 256)

Options in Pregnancy

As shown in Table 4.1, if the girl admits to herself, even briefly, that she is pregnant, she has two principal options: abortion or to continue the pregnancy. If she chooses the former, she enters an arena full of conflicts; if she chooses the latter, she then has other decisions to make.

Abortion

Even to contemplate an abortion means that the female has admitted to herself that she is pregnant. That is not a universal truth among women of child-bearing age. Should the woman do so, termination of an unwanted pregnancy is an option for many girls and women, although not in good conscience for those who are Roman Catholics or followers of several other faiths. In the United States, abortion *is* legal in the first trimester, subsequent to the *Roe v. Wade* decision in 1973, and in some jurisdictions even during the second trimester. Whether the pregnant woman is a teenager or an adult, access to abortion must be available if she is to exercise this option. Such access may depend on her age, the state in which she lives, her socioeconomic status, and the dangers that may exist in her community relative to abortion. (The many factors affecting availability are discussed more fully in a later chapter.)

Adler (1992) identified five types of pregnancy and found that each provoked a different type of response following an abortion. "A woman's responses following abortion are likely to be a function both of her desire for pregnancy and of her feelings about abortion" (p. 20), with those least desirous of pregnancy and least antagonistic toward abortion obviously having the most benign responses. There are differences between unplanned and unintended pregnancies; between those that are premarital and those that are extramarital; between those of adolescents and those of adult women; and between knowledge or ignorance of the pregnancy within the female's family. All of these lead to varying perceptions of and responses to abortion.

There is also her initial admission that she is pregnant, rather than being in denial, which would lead to the pregnancy being carried to term. Studies suggest that those adolescents who choose to have an early abortion do so because they recognize their immaturity as potential parents, and that they face far fewer physical risks from the abortion than from pregnancy, as well as fewer adverse psychological effects (Adler, Smith, & Tschann, 1998).

The Committee on Psychiatry and Law of the Group for the Advancement of Psychiatry (GAP) considered the right to abortion in the pre-*Roe v. Wade* era (1969) and averred that the effects of being unwanted (for the child) and having an unwanted child (for the mother) were highly negative for both. Furthermore, they suggested that "Those who believe abortion is murder need not avail themselves of it. On the other hand, we do not believe that such conviction should limit the freedom of those not bound by identical religious conviction" (1969, p. 219).

They cited Erikson's consideration (1950) that the mutilation of a child's spirit by being an unwanted child is the most deadly of all possible sins and forced motherhood as being equally bad for a woman. Erikson's view is still valid some decades later, although this should not be seen as advocating abortion, but rather as recognizing the roots of negative self-esteem, child abuse, and other undesirable outcomes. David's longitudinal study (1992) of unwanted children born to mothers who had been denied an abortion similarly found negative effects on their psychosocial development that were apparent in adulthood.

However, young women who choose to seek an abortion contrary to their religious tradition may face severe psychological consequences. The Roman Catholic position that asserts that life begins at the moment of conception means that termination of pregnancy is murder. This means that the young woman must abandon or challenge her moral underpinnings. Guilt can become a massive burden for her. Abortion is a difficult ethical, complex, emotional decision for any woman and requires maturity to accept the challenge of this choice.

An extreme case involving abortion and religion is one in which a 10-year-old girl in Brazil was raped. When she was 3 months pregnant, she applied for an abortion, which is permitted in Brazil in rape cases, and was supported at the time by her father. The judge withheld his ruling for several weeks, awaiting information of possible harm to the girl if the abortion were performed. The health minister supported the girl's application, but some Catholic clergy opposed it, with one priest asking, "What crime has that child [the fetus] committed?" (Reuters, 1997). (The dispute as to which life is the more "valuable" is also seen in Islamic writings, as will be discussed later. Abortion is forbidden, although it *may* be justified in cases of rape when the woman has reported the rape and sought immediate medical attention.)

Apparently a retired obstetrician and a priest persuaded the Brazilian father to reverse his stand and he withdrew his approval of the procedure (Mathis, 1997). An angry editorial writer saw this turn of events as a clear-cut case of child abuse from a mental health as well as physical health perspective. The right to life of the as yet unborn child is certainly a matter for reasonable debate, he agreed—most of the time. In this case, however, "there is another innocent child and, when it comes down to the value of life, hers has supremacy. How dare the father, the doctor and priest seek their own satisfaction and soothe their own consciences at her expense" (Mathis, 1997).

Ebrahim was inclined to support abortion in rape cases, but then asked " ... would that be just? After all, the fetus has committed no crime. How then could its life be terminated?" (1991, p. 85). Islamic law has five permanent and unchangeable axioms, among them "life," "morality," and "progeny." "Pregnancy outside the bond of marriage violates the purpose of morality. Abortion, child abuse and neglect violate the purpose of life ... . 'Unwanted pregnancy' and 'unwanted birth' violate the purpose of progeny" (Kasule, 2003, p. 50). Abortion *is* permitted by the law if the mother's life is endangered by continuation of the pregnancy because if she dies, so does the fetus. This creates a choice between saving one life or losing two, and abortion is the lesser of two evils in such a situation. (Note: Neonaticide and infanticide are also forbidden under the law.)

Judaism, in general, opposes "abortion on demand" or in cases of unwanted pregnancy, but supports it if the mother's life is in serious physical danger or, more rarely, if it would endanger the mother's psychological health (this would be considered a valid reason for an abortion) (Werblowsky & Wigoder, 1965). The emphasis on the mother, the "most proximate life," as more than one rabbi has put it, obviously differs from that of anti-abortion groups that place the fetus' "life" above that of the prospective mother. Full human rights, in Jewish law, are extended only to a *born and viable* being.

Carrying the Pregnancy to Term

If abortion is ruled out and the pregnancy continues to delivery, the young woman who has not denied her pregnancy is confronted with choices again: mother the child, place it for adoption, abandon it alive at a location where someone will find it (possibly a designated "safe haven"), or kill it. The term "it" is used advisedly, for most of these young women do not regard the entity they are carrying as a baby even when it is born. The problem is described clearly by Resnick (1970). "[W[omen who seek abortions are activists who recognize reality early and promptly attack the danger. In contrast, women who commit neonaticide often deny that they are pregnant or assume that the child will be stillborn" (p. 1416).

These women neither prepare for the newborn nor plan for its demise. The denial usually means that the girl has no prenatal care, even when problems arise, for she denies to her doctor any relationship between symptoms such as nausea or weight gain and a pregnancy. A very busy doctor may take her at her word. The lack of prenatal care that results in damage to or the death of the fetus may be cause, in some jurisdictions, for the state to charge the woman with manslaughter or "depraved indifference" to the welfare of another.

Mothering

For some young women, perhaps who are "love children" raised by unwed mothers, the choice is to keep the children. Perhaps they simply consider this a normal life pattern, and it may be so in their community, or perhaps they think of what might have been their lot in life had their mother not raised them. As one 14-year-old mother put it, she decided to keep her baby "for selfish reasons. I wanted someone who I knew would love me" ("So You're Going to Be a Mother," 1999, p. 24).

What some of them may not realize is the tremendous change in daily routine, as well as lifestyle, that occurs as soon as the baby is born. For many new mothers, the sudden loss of control of one's use of time is not only a shock, but also an emotional and possibly a physical strain. There is also a loss of privacy and possibly loss of physical, emotional, and financial support. According to Ogle, Maier-Katkin, and Bernard (1995), achieving the status of being regarded as a "good mother" requires nurturing ability, willingness to make great sacrifices, and some kind of "inherent knowledge" that not only causes great stress for the mother, but may be especially remote experientially for the younger mother.

Psychiatrists, psychologists, and social workers in the 1950s viewed unwed mothers as mentally ill. "They remarked frequently that unmarried mothers got pregnant easily, had few miscarriages, little nausea, no food fads, no moods, and no delivery complications; and exhibited an unusual degree of contentment" (Solinger, 1990, p. 46). These were generally, however, young women already admitted to maternity homes and well past their first trimesters when seen.

The fact that the girl had not prevented or terminated her pregnancy was seen as conclusive proof of psychological disturbance by psychiatrists in the pre-*Roe v. Wade* era (1945–1965). No one referred to the legal obstacles in the way of contraception and abortion at that time. "Displaying surprising willingness to expect criminality in girls and women, they were willing, as well, to deepen their blame of the victim by using her law-abiding behavior to justify the diagnosis of mental illness" (Solinger, 1990, p. 47). Why did they become pregnant even though they were single?

> Girls and women were driven into sex and pregnancy, professionals determined, as a result of both gender dysfunctions and family dysfunctions … . The most typical patterns appeared to be a weak father and a hypochondriacal and controlling mother, or a strong but neglectful father and a frustrated mother. (p. 47)

Mothers got the most blame for the daughter's pregnancy—that is, the daughter allegedly felt unloved by her mother. As recently as 1988, a Pennsylvania couple was charged with endangering the welfare of their child because they allowed a young man to visit her in their home although they were aware that he and their daughter (age 13 years) were having intercourse; as a result the girl became pregnant. Although the jury voted to convict, they were found not guilty of neglect by the trial court (*Commonwealth v. Campbell*, 1990). The perspectives of that pre-*Roe* era are interesting to consider a few decades later:

> White girls and women who were illegitimately pregnant before *Roe* could only anticipate rehabilitation and ultimately a "normal" life if they relinquished the baby for adoption.
>
> If a White girl or woman had a sex life or a baby before marriage at that time, she was considered by those in the psychiatric mainstream to be "sick." Any evaluation of her sex life could only be done *after* marriage.
>
> White unwed mothers suffered in that earlier period because they had no legal basis to control their lives. "The application of psychiatric theory to single pregnancy further legitimated the use of science to punish women for their unsanctioned sexual experience and to limit their control over their own bodies and their own children." (Solinger, 1990, p. 52)

Although many adolescent girls in earlier periods and today choose to mother their children, it is too often a case of poorly prepared and poorly informed "children raising children." This usually serves neither of them well because the young mother has no time to develop her individuation, educational potential, or even physical health; her lack of parenting skills, as well as the earlier lack of prenatal care, can affect her child's physical and cognitive development negatively (Coley & Chase-Lansdale, 1998). Although the health risks to these children are cause for concern, so are the increased risks of abuse and involvement with law enforcement (Corcoran, 1998).

Milden at al. (1995) compared nine cases of denied pregnancy in the literature with eight cases of denial that they had seen in their university hospital. Five of the nine women gave birth at home; three of them committed neonaticide. In the hospital sample, seven of the eight young women kept their babies. The latter group was principally from low socioeconomic status, Black, single-parent families, but the patients were very involved with their mothers. Their decision to mother the baby was not typical of what is found in the professional literature.

Sometimes the adolescent mother continues to live with her family and has help from *her* parents, but it takes substantial internal resources and external support for her to mature successfully and to rear her child responsibly. The headline on one newspaper article says it all: "The secret of motherhood: Birth may come naturally, sometimes unexpectedly, but nurturing must be learned" (Straight, 1998). Arnoldi (1999), who became a mother at age 17, raised her daughter, worked, sent the daughter through college although she herself had not graduated from high school, and now shares her story with adolescents, especially those in high school equivalency programs. (A number of school districts, usually in large communities, have special programs for students who are parents that provide not only nursery care while the mother attends classes, but also parenting education. These will be discussed later.) The father, also usually adolescent, may feel a sense of having proved his manhood, but that does not necessarily extend to taking personal or financial responsibility for his child.

Relatively few studies have been focused primarily on a continuing involvement of the father with the adolescent mother and their baby. In a study of 105 adolescents aged 14 to 18 years—most of them from rural or small urban areas of lower socioeconomic status and pregnant with their first child—it was found that those who had a continuous involvement with the babies' fathers were less frequently the subjects of abuse or custody revocation investigations than the young women who were less involved (Cutrona, Hessling, Bacon, & Russell, 1998).

The father's support throughout the pregnancy and immediate postpartum period, especially when she was confronted with negative life events, appeared to enable the young mother to provide better parenting and a better child-rearing environment (as measured 6 months after delivery) than was true for her peers who did not have this significant relationship in operation. Many young parents unconsciously accept, even expect, a dependency on the government to provide for their basic needs and those of their children. As Benoit (1997) put it, "In other words, government can psychologically become the surrogate parent" (p. 409).

With changes in the welfare laws in the late 1990s and later, many dependent single mothers were no longer eligible for welfare checks. One of the difficulties, however, was that many of these women had inadequate preparation for any kind of job, let alone one that would pay for child care if their children were of preschool age or needed after-school care.

On the other hand, even if the fathers remain involved, there are risks if the father is an adolescent. There are conflicts arising between the roles of adolescent male and fatherhood, and there may well be unrealistic expectations of infant development and behavior (Robinson, 1988). This can lead to infanticide or filicide, as will be discussed later. Also, in an effort to provide financial support to his baby and its mother, the youth may drop out of school, leaving him in a negative competitive position in the labor market.

Clearly, not all of those who choose to mother the baby are adolescents or even unwed. It is still difficult in many locations for unmarried women to be accepted as mothers, although there are many more of them today than in the middle of the 20th century. One has to hope that they are mature enough emotionally to be nurturing mothers; regrettably, this is not always true and some of their children develop psychological problems or become victims of child abuse or homicide.

A Comment on "Illegitimacy"

The child born out of wedlock has never had an easy time in life. To begin, this child has been labeled illegitimate (one of the kinder terms), unfathered (impossible!), misbegotten, baseborn, or bastard. (Comment: Why the child must bear the brunt of one of these hostile descriptions when the child had nothing to do with its creation is unclear.) While the child is considered "unfathered," that simply reflects the fact that the mother does not know who he is or fails to identify him for reasons of her own, perhaps including fear of his anger. The Georgia General Assembly, in 1988, substituted the phrase "born out of wedlock" for the nastier terms to get rid of the stigma attached to the latter (Thompson, 1998).

The child is not acknowledged by or entitled, generally, to a parent's estate, especially not in the hierarchy-conscious British tradition, unless specific mention is made in a will. For all these reasons, the unwed young mother perceives this "thing" as less worthy or less legitimate than a baby born to a married couple. If that is the case, as Ehrenreich (1998) so aptly put it, the "thing" is trash and can be discarded as one throws out trash. As we know, this happens too frequently.

Having an out-of-wedlock baby and unmarried motherhood are not necessarily synonymous, and they are not as frowned upon today as used to be true. Many women who opted for careers before marriage and chose not to marry because they feared the possibility of divorce do want to be mothers. As they approach or pass age 40, they realize that their chances of achieving that goal are declining.

Those who can afford it may seek single motherhood through AID (artificial insemination by donor) rather than having to deal with an identified father who might make claims on the resulting child. There will, of course, be those who condemn the woman for her choice or later label the child negatively; others will cheer her on. Some of these women choose instead to adopt a child, often one from overseas. Not too many years ago, those wanted children would have been harshly labeled "bastards" like any others born to unwed mothers. Today, one must recognize the different faces of unwed motherhood that earlier generations chose not to recognize or accept.

Place for Adoption

In the United States from the beginning of the 20th century through the 1930s and 1940s, illegitimate babies were regarded as tainted, resulting from sins committed by the mother. Girls were expected to raise them by themselves or give them up for adoption. Legislators and caregivers, however, concerned over the new mothers' shame and desperation, often required mothers in maternity homes to breastfeed their babies for 3 months or more in order to create bonds that would prevent abandonment of the babies by their mothers (Solinger, 1992).

Society regarded unmarried pregnancy as shameful, as we have seen. Bridal virginity and conception only after marriage were vital elements of American culture. Hence, part of official and private policies was to encourage and facilitate adoption of illegitimate babies. Single motherhood was not an acceptable choice (at least not for most White women). Therefore, aided by a sizable number of White couples who wanted a child, adoption was encouraged and widespread. Often babies were taken from the mothers at birth and placed via adoption agencies or private intermediaries—lawyers, doctors, and nonprofessionals—who sometimes regarded the babies as commodities (Solinger, 1992).

Most Black women did not have the same support as their White peers, and there was less pressure put upon them to give up their babies. White women were perceived as sinners, but in the racial ambiance of the prewar years (and even later) prejudice labeled African American girls as irresponsible and amoral, but loving toward their babies. Social workers tended to ignore the plight of Black single mothers because they believed that these women would provide for their babies.

Those who perceived Black mothers in the same way as White mothers wanted them to place their babies for adoption, but few Black families were able or willing to cope with this option. Moreover, grandmothers occupied a nurturing role in African American culture and often helped to raise the babies. That suggested that single motherhood may have been more acceptable in that community. Some politicians viewed these women in a more punitive fashion, demanding that they be sterilized or removed from welfare rolls. As more young White women had babies and copied the African American pattern, the stigma was reduced (Solinger, 1992).

By the end of World War II, socioeconomic changes affected attitudes about sexual behavior. Breast-feeding regulations and other institutional policies became more and more difficult to sustain. The demographics of singles' pregnancies and new courtship mores had been altered by new methods of birth control and the nascent development of the women's movement—all of which led to growing sexual freedom. Increasingly, birth control methods and abortion were considered better alternatives to motherhood than adoption, especially after the development of birth control pills and the court decision in *Roe v. Wade* (1973).

For many young women, even today, mothering the baby is not seen as a viable choice; they recognize that they have neither the means nor the ability to be a mother or their families perceive that having a child out of wedlock is a disgrace. Placing the child for adoption means that the young woman must admit that she is pregnant not only to herself, but also to other parties because adoption takes advance planning as well as appropriate medical care. If she spends part of her pregnancy in a maternity residence, she is likely to receive counseling about her options, including adoption. At least one study (Mahler, 1997) indicates that although the adolescent mother may regret having placed her baby for adoption, she is not severely depressed. Rather, she more likely turned to education or employment than those who kept their babies. This finding was based on a study in the period from 1987 to 1992, when the rate of adoption was already dropping, as more recent statistics show.

Adoption was typically the response to an unwanted pregnancy through the 1960s. The National Center for Health Statistics reported in 1999 that "between 1989 and 1995, about 1% of babies born to never-married women were relinquished for adoption, down from 9% among such babies born before 1979" (Chandra, Abma, Maza, & Bachrach, 1999, p. 1). The decline in numbers is even more marked if only the babies of never-married White women are considered. "In the early 1980s, almost 20% of babies born to never-married White women were relinquished for adoption, compared with only 1.7% of such babies born in the first half of the 1990s" (Chandra et al., p. 9).

In the earlier period, as already noted, fewer children of never-married Black women were placed for adoption than babies of never-married White women, and that continues today. It is less often the option of choice today because of changes in the perception of adoption generally or, according to Demb (1991), in the Black community specifically because the babies available for adoption by nonfamily members are often the victims of their mothers' drug or alcohol addiction. (Note: Babies who are victims of fetal addictions are not, in fact, limited to the Black community.) Other problems may also be present in the infant that make the child less "adoptable" because medical science today can save so many fetuses and newborns who would have died a generation or more ago from assorted ailments.

Furthermore, some minority clients fear that the difficulty of finding an adoptive home for their child may doom the child to a life in foster or institutional care (Folkenburg, 1985). It should be noted, however, that interracial adoptions that *could* provide a home, for example, Caucasian parents adopting a Native American or African American child are often frowned upon, even fought, by members of the minority group (Schwartz, 2000). On the other hand, an organization called "Pact—an Adoption Alliance" seeks to place African American, Latino, Asian, and multiracial children in adoptive families (Pact, 1996).

Sobol and Daly (1992) cited data from a variety of studies showing that the estimated percentage of unmarried mothers who placed their babies for adoption dropped from 40% in 1963 to 14% in 1971, 7% in 1982, and 3% in 1989. Some of this decline may reflect changing social attitudes in this period; some is due to the legalization of abortion and some to the increasing acceptance of unwed motherhood (Kalmuss, Nemerow, & Cushman, 1991). The decline may also be due to the option of adoption never being brought to the attention of the young women by family members, physicians, or counselors. In yet other cases, placing the child for adoption may be perceived as abandoning the child, although the opposite view would be "finding a family" for the child. Some research suggests that having a voice in choosing the adoptive parents is very helpful to the young birthmothers, regardless of the nature or amount of postadoption contact (Cushman, Kalmuss, & Nemerow, 1993).

Adoptions in the United States are arranged through social welfare agencies and through private parties, usually attorneys or physicians. It is perhaps easier for middle-class pregnant girls and women to work with the private intermediaries rather than social workers, while the opposite is true for the less affluent who may have had experience with welfare or other public agencies for other reasons. In either situation, the mother-to-be must first admit that she is pregnant and then to be willing to admit this to someone else who will now have a voice in how she fares during the pregnancy.

The practice may differ in other countries. For example, French law allows women total anonymity and cost-free delivery if they place their babies for adoption. Psychoanalytic interviews with 22 women, 18 of whom took advantage of this law, revealed earlier sexual and psychological traumas that contributed to their situation (Bonnet, 1993). In the other four cases, the women's denial was so total that they ended up committing neonaticide.

Contemporary adoption practice also has a controversy about the degree of contact, if any, that should exist after adoption between the biological mother and the child. This can provoke a variety of emotions, such as anxiety, guilt, or even resentment, in the mother and the adoptive parents, who may be uncomfortable with an "open" adoption on the one hand or in conflict about a "closed" arrangement on the other.

Appropriate counseling for the biological mother should include an explanation of all options with their respective advantages and disadvantages for all of the parties concerned (biological mother, child, adoptive parents). Even when there has been an open adoption, the girl may not have told her parents about the pregnancy or the placement and may suffer guilt feelings about denying them their grandparental role (Carrera, 1997). It should be noted that in most states today, the biological father may have to consent to the adoption as well as the mother (Schwartz, 2006).

Abandonment

As we noted earlier, Amighi (1990) found many references to abandonment as well as "justifications" for neonaticide in folk literature and social history (as did we). Feelings of resentment or emotional detachment could lead to neonaticide or abandonment even in more sophisticated societies. The ways in which the abandonment or neonaticide were carried out, discussed earlier, have certain similarities even with today's methods on the whole.

One unusual practice in such cases, however, has been the abandonment of neonates in coin-operated lockers in Japan (Kouno & Johnson, 1995). The baby might have been placed in the locker alive or dead and was not usually found until several weeks later, thus precluding finding the parents. An academic research committee in Japan studying infanticide found that mothers who kill their illegitimate newborns usually suffer from serious problems in coping with life's problems and requirements. They may change jobs frequently, for example. Their primary motives are poverty and fear of shame associated with having an illegitimate child. Mothers who kill their legitimate newborns, on the other hand, tend to be motivated primarily by already existing poverty that would be exacerbated by having more children (Bryant, 1990, p. 9). These findings do not differ significantly from those found in Western countries.

Abandonment of the neonate on church steps or near a hospital's emergency ward was another choice in the past and is still an option today, with a few additional locations now identified as "safe havens." In earlier times, as we have already shown, foundling hospitals and orphanages were also available for abandoned babies. The Salvation Army had group homes where the pregnant girl could stay until she delivered, and the New York Foundling Hospital, an arm of the Roman Catholic archdiocese in New York City, cared for newborns abandoned in that area. Neither of these options is as widely available in the early 21st century as was true a few decades ago.

Among the alternatives to neonaticide in different locations for dealing with an infant unwanted for various reasons are (Hrdy, 1992, pp. 413–414):

Exploitation of the infant as a resource, usually selling the infant
Abandonment of the infant (with the expectation that it will be found) with possible placement for adoption
Fostering out the infant to a relative or other person
Wet-nursing to release the mother for other roles
Oblation: child is placed with a religious institution
Reducing overall reproductive effort: delegating care to others
Reducing parental investment in particular children

The first of Hrdy's alternatives, selling the baby, is against the law virtually everywhere, although there is always someone willing to try that path (Schwartz, 2006). In some instances, an arrangement is made with adopting parents to pay for the mother's medical expenses related to the pregnancy and delivery, but almost any funds beyond those would be considered "selling" the baby and be illegal.

"From the perspective of reproductive strategies, abandonment of an infant should be default divestment strategy for parents terminating investment; infanticide would only be a last resort when this option is curtailed" (Hrdy, 1992, p. 415). The "safe haven" movement is a step in this direction.

Although the new mother cannot see herself rearing the child, she cannot bring herself to kill the newborn. She also cannot bring herself to admit to someone else that she has been pregnant and has delivered a baby, but she also recognizes that this *is* a baby and not an "it." Sometimes, the mother leaves the infant somewhere, wrapped in towels or a blanket and maybe with a note attached; in other cases, the baby is left on top of a trash bin or in a rest room. The use of trash cans or larger dumpsters for this purpose has led, in Italy, to the placement of signs on the bins that say "Not for babies" (Levene, 1998).

If the baby is found in time, there is a good chance for survival and, ultimately, adoption. The mothers are usually not located. Indeed, three of the cases that came to our attention between July and October 1997 were abandonments, with only one of the mothers identified (Vanessa Gomez). A girl in Pittsburgh left her 6-day-old infant, wrapped in a blanket, outside a hospital emergency room with a note that said she was "only 12 years old, and I can't take care of him" (Associated Press, 1997b). In another case, a woman walking her dog in suburban Los Angeles found a 6-hour-old baby boy in a shallow grave (Associated Press, 1997a). The newborn was subsequently placed in foster care. Earlier, a 19-year-old girl, herself the daughter of an unmarried mother, delivered herself and wrapped her unwanted baby in a paper bag that she placed on a trash can (Ratner, 1985). This was her second pregnancy, but neither her family nor her boyfriend's (with whom she was living) recognized that she was pregnant. Fortunately, the sorry story of this late adolescent's family history and self-deprecating image resulted in a plea bargain with a suspended sentence and a probationary period in which she was to have psychological counseling.

Not all cases of abandonment have the happy ending of the neonate surviving and gaining a home. Consider the situation in Oklahoma: "Fifteen abandoned newborns were found dead in Oklahoma between 1987 and 1997, according to a report by the University of Oklahoma Health Sciences Center. Just this month [February], three abandoned newborns were discovered. Two were dead" (Ruble, 1999). Whether the increase is factual, or simply a matter of better record-keeping, can be a matter of debate.

Neonaticide

The final option—one rarely mentioned in the literature on unwanted pregnancies—is neonaticide. According to several sources, approximately 250 neonaticide cases are reported to the Department of Justice annually, but the department has indicated that it does not keep separate records for such cases. The National Center for Health Statistics maintains data on infant deaths divided by "early neonatal" (< 7 days) and "late neonatal" (7 to 27 days), and as "28 days of age or less" and "1 year and under," depending on the table examined. However, it does keep data on neonaticide per se (i.e., age 24 hours or less and as a result of deliberate or inadvertent acts by the mother at or immediately following delivery). Separate records are not kept, and there is some question as to whether all cases are reported because some of the babies' bodies are never found.

As already noted, the girl or woman may have denied the pregnancy even to herself. She is convinced at the time of delivery, that she is having stomach cramps or needs to defecate. Delivery is unassisted. Frequently the baby is born as the mother sits on the toilet, and then the infant falls into the bowl and drowns. If the girl or woman is squatting on the floor, she may simply smother the newborn with her hand or a towel to prevent anyone hearing a baby's cry. Those who attempt to cut the umbilical cord use any handy tool—scissors, a razor blade, a nail file. The infant is then wrapped in something (a towel, plastic bags) and discarded. The blood is mopped up from the floor with rags or towels and the young woman goes on her way—to bed, to work, to school, or out with friends. It is extremely unusual for the father to be present at the time of delivery or immediately after. Indeed, he may not even be aware of the pregnancy or maintain his relationship with the mother-to-be if he is aware of it.

Brozovsky and Falit (1971) and others have characterized those who commit neonaticide as young women who deny and conceal their pregnancy so convincingly that those around them also deny it—a point made earlier. Furthermore, they determined that in 1967, 45.6% of the infants killed in the first year of life were victims of neonaticide. In Canada, the term "infanticide" was used to refer to what we call neonaticide, and in 45 cases reported from 1974 to 1983, 69% of the offenders were under age 21; 69.3% were single; and the most common occupation reported was "student" (Silverman & Kennedy, 1988). As many researchers have pointed out:

> Most neonaticides are the results of unwanted pregnancies and births. Mothers tend to be younger and unwed, and the inability of the girl to reveal her pregnancy to her mother, the stigma of having an illegitimate child, and the shame or fear of rejection are factors in many cases. (Bourget & Labelle, 1992, p. 668)

Comparable data are not available in the United States.

Green (1990) asserted that neonaticide is almost certainly underrepresented in official figures. Furthermore, he differentiated two groups of neonaticidal "mothers": (1) the emotionally immature who panic at the time of birth; and (2) the strong minded who premeditate the baby's death at birth.

A number of cases have involved college women and have thereby raised concerns at higher education institutions. The incidents "at colleges have raised questions not only about how well-acquainted students are with the medical services available to them, but also about the isolation that would allow a student to complete a full-term pregnancy in secret without being questioned by anyone on campus" (Geraghty, 1997, p. A49). Most colleges have facilities for confidential prenatal care; a few would require the pregnant student to move out of the dormitory. The need is recognized, however, to have faculty members and dormitory advisers better informed about where to refer a troubled, possibly pregnant, student for help.

Among married women, extramarital paternity is sufficient reason (in their minds) for neonaticide, although there may be other reasons. In one case in Milwaukee, a 30-year-old mother of two had been impregnated by a married man. He ignored her attempts to discuss the situation, so she ultimately decided to abandon (and asphyxiate) the newborn (Doege, 1998). An ignorant young mother may not intellectually calculate the pros and cons of infanticide. But she may consciously arrive at decisions that place the value of the infant lower than the perceived value of something else, such as more freedom (Reece, 1991, n. 30, pp. 704–705).

Sometimes the new baby is seen as "one child too many," and the overwhelmed mother commits neonaticide (Zurzola, 1998). In a few cases that we found, the woman was on cocaine or another drug when she delivered herself and killed the newborn. Deliberate neonaticide may also occur when the newborn is obviously handicapped. In this case, it is perceived by some as delayed abortion (Rue, 1985) or may even be seen as a "mercy killing," a topic to be discussed in Chapter 10. In any case, each of these mothers had a conscious reason, however warped, for killing her child.

Whether criminal charges of neonaticide or infanticide are to be filed against the mother often depends on the findings of an experienced pathologist. If such a charge is to be made, "then the pathologist must be certain that not only had the infant achieved separate existence but also that the cause of death was by a deliberate act or omission on the part of the mother" (Kellet, 1992, p. 13). Such acts might include failure to clear the baby's air passages (omission), failure to cut and tie the umbilical cord (omission), dropping the baby on a hard floor causing a skull fracture (deliberate), strangling the baby manually or by ligature (deliberate), smothering (deliberate), and drowning (deliberate). Concealment of the birth and abandonment after the birth have also been considered to be criminal acts and have been punished in various ways depending upon the laws in a given period and country (or state).

In 104 of the 119 cases that came to our attention through the media as having occurred from 1990 to 2005, the mothers were identified, charged, and, in many cases, tried or they pleaded guilty. (Only four of the fathers were also identified and charged.) Some of the babies were born alive and then killed, but at least 10 more were found alive and rushed to the neonatal care unit at a hospital. Although the laws dealing with neonaticide and infanticide make reference to postpartum depression as a mitigating circumstance in these cases, the condition is not present in neonaticide because the clinically defined onset for that condition is a matter of weeks after birth, not hours or minutes.

More often, the mother acts out of fear, shame, guilt, rejection, denial, or ignorance. This is not too surprising when one considers the youth of many of these "mothers." (For example, in the cases mentioned, 42 were 21 years of age or older, and the balance [72] were all in the age range of 12 to 20 years, with a few unknown.) That just over one third were aged 21 years or older, several of them having been pregnant previously, and they could still be in denial or claim ignorance of their condition does suggest, however, that committing neonaticide is not simply an adolescent reaction to an unpleasant or difficult situation.

Why Neonaticide?

As we have seen, a number of options are available to pregnant women. In most cases, the babies are wanted and the mothers have prenatal care, normal deliveries, and go on to raise their children. In cases in which the pregnancy is unwanted, the women have choices and decisions to make. Sometimes they cannot deal emotionally with the pregnancy and deny it right through the moment when they deliver the babies. This is most often the situation with neonaticide or, less frequently, abandonment. At the other extreme, some take measures to abort the fetus when they first discover their condition. Those who exercise neither extreme at the outset or the conclusion of pregnancy can still choose to raise the child or to place it for adoption.

Why some women choose the neonaticide option rather than selecting another option leads to a number of hypotheses. Some have been examined in this chapter, and others will be discussed in the next chapter when the neonaticidal woman has to present a defense in court.

Neonaticide and the Law

5

As we are aware from European and Latin American studies of neonaticide and infanticide, the popular perception is that only poor, uneducated, young, lower-class females commit these crimes. The American stereotype often adds non-Caucasian to the description and today has added middle-class and educated as well. Neonatal mortality is not always due to neonaticide, but Geronimus (1987) concurred with this later description, asserting that adolescent motherhood in the United States "occurs almost exclusively among socioeconomically-disadvantaged populations," and that a large percentage of these are from the Black population (p. 245).

A study of cases in Rio de Janeiro (1990 to 1995) also supported this perception of disadvantage plus minority ethnic origin as a basis for committing neonaticide (Mendlowicz, Rapaport, Mecler, Golshand, & Moraes, 1998). The mother simply does not have the means to raise a child, whether it is her first or her third. What became apparent in the 1990s and since, however, is that all four "traditional" descriptions may be too limiting and that the differences between the stereotype and reality may become critical issues in the prosecution of the young woman.

There is no question that, in most societies, women who kill their babies are regarded as having committed the ultimate sin. They have violated the stereotype of the loving, nurturing mother. As Reece (1991) points out, however, our criminal justice system also postulates that a person is only punishable for a crime for which he or she can be held morally responsible. The question then arises whether a woman who commits infanticide while suffering from a postpartum disorder can be held morally culpable. "If so, then she deserves punishment. But if she is not morally culpable, because she fell victim to something she could not control, punishment would be inappropriate" (Reece, pp. 747–748). Postpartum depression is not the issue in neonaticide, however, so the defense problems are quite different from those involved in other facets of child homicide.

Legal Ramifications

Throughout the literature, whether historical or contemporary, American or not, it is obvious that the crime of killing a newborn baby has resulted in a wide variety of charges. The discrepancies and inconsistencies in sentencing rest on the nature of state law and the rule of precedent. Judges are constrained by the exigencies of evidence and case law. In addition, the legal establishment makes no particular acknowledgment of the special circumstances of neonaticide. Prosecutors have therefore charged young women with a variety of crimes: murder in the first, second, or third degree; manslaughter; gross abuse of a corpse; and concealment of death (Bookwalter, 1998). Of the cases mentioned in the previous chapter, we were able to determine the charges in 101 cases, as can be seen in Table 5.1. The two most significant factors in determining the fate of the mothers are whether the babies were born alive and the mothers' intentions toward their newborns.

In both instances, the prosecutors must prove their case to the jury or the presiding judge. The state must show *beyond a reasonable doubt* that the baby was alive and that it had an independent circulation (*Shedd v. State*, 1934). The problem of determining whether the baby was alive is often difficult because, in most of the neonaticides, the only witness is the defendant, and the pathologist's evidence often is not conclusive or contains conflicts. Convictions in these cases vary widely and are affected by the lack of precision in determining how the baby died.

For instance, in one case, Stacy Myers delivered a baby in her friend's dorm room. After cutting the baby's cord with scissors, she wrapped it in a garbage bag and left it on a window sill outside her room. She had not

Table 5.1 Charges against Neonaticidal Mothers by Age and Charge (1990–2005)

	Age			
	< 18	18–19	20+	*N* =
Misdemeanor		1	1	2
Injury to child/child abuse	2		3	5
Manslaughter	9	7	8	24
Homicide	16	13	37	66
Other	3		1	4
Total	30	21	50	101

informed her friends of her pregnancy. She was convicted of second-degree murder and sentenced to 15 years. The appellate court reversed this decision, claiming that the prosecutors had not proved without a doubt how the baby died or even whether the baby had been born alive (*Myers v. Commonwealth*, 1994).

Similar cases such as that of Elizabeth Ehlert had the same outcome. Ehlert killed her newborn by wrapping it in a garbage bag and dropping it in a nearby lake. Despite strong circumstantial evidence and her prior history of two abortions, the pathologists' reports were unable to ascertain a "live birth." Though she was convicted of first-degree murder and sentenced to 58 years, the verdict was overturned by the appellate court, which overturned other convictions as well (*People v. Ehlert*, 1990; cf. *Lane v. Commonwealth*, 1978; *Singleton v. State*, 1948; *State v. Doyle*, 1978). In all of these cases, the young women escaped punishment.

If the prosecutor cannot sustain the charge of first-degree murder because it is impossible to prove whether or not the neonate was born alive and its death premeditated, the charge can always be reduced to "gross abuse of corpse" or "concealment of death." Manslaughter, which involves "unlawful killing without malice" (Ford, 1996, p. 531), may be subdivided as voluntary, involuntary, or aggravated, depending upon the jurisdiction in which the tragedy occurs, is another possible charge. Since murder, even second-degree, presupposes premeditation or planning of some kind, and manslaughter does not, the denial or psychological dissociation that accompanies many neonaticide cases would clearly make manslaughter the more appropriate charge (Bookwalter, 1998).

The divergence in charges and sentencing depends on the legislation of the various states, which often differs. Further complicating the legal decisions are the problems of evidence. Frequently the pathological analysis and physical evidence that give credence to the prosecutor's case determine the charges. Examiners and forensic pathologists are important figures in these cases because they are the professionals who can (usually) determine whether or not the baby was born alive (i.e., breathed on its own after birth).

Sometimes the experts disagree; even when a confession is freely given, there is very little physical evidence and the pathologists cannot prove whether the baby was alive at or after birth. This was even truer in the 19th and early 20th centuries, as we found in cases from that period. It was interesting that at least one of the techniques—trying to float the infant's lungs in water—was used more than a century ago and is still used (e.g., *Mary Harris v. State*, 1891; *John Josef v. State*, 1895; *Annie Cordes v. State*, 1908; Editorial Roundup, 1998).

Another factor influencing the disparity in the outcomes of neonaticide cases is that sympathy for the defendants often allows conviction for lesser crimes and consequently reduced sentences. The legal system has also been inconsistent in recognizing the psychological ramifications implicit in the crime and often ignores expert testimony in some cases (*People v. Wernick*, 1996). Barton (1998) concluded that "the same murder by the same mother could receive different treatment depending on the jurisdiction's laws, particular jury, or even the beliefs of a particular judge" (p. 619).

Variations in Charges and Sentencing

As is evident in the preceding quotation, the outcomes of trials for neonaticide vary widely. As one example, Rebecca Hopfer of Dayton, Ohio, was convicted of neonaticide and sentenced to serve 15 years to life in prison for her crime. Appeals for commutation of her sentence were made to the governor (*Ohio v. Hopfer*, 1996). Her family and supporters alleged that she was "victimized" as a White, suburban teenager—that is, no one could say she had been treated differently from a poor Black teenager who committed the same crime. The county coroner opposed any clemency action by the governor, saying no such appeals had been made to the governor on behalf of a poor Black woman who had committed the same crime (Editorial, 1998; France, 1997).

In contrast to this case, a high school senior (Anna) in suburban Chicago gave birth alone, left the baby in the toilet while she cleaned up the blood in the bathroom, then wrapped the dead newborn in a towel and hugged it against her body until she went to sleep. Later that day she told her best friend what had happened, and the friend told her father, who then contacted the police. Anna was arrested and charged with first-degree murder, but was found guilty of involuntary manslaughter by a jury. She was placed on probation and ordered to perform 1,000 hours of community service (Brienza, 1997).

Butterworth, a clinical psychologist in Los Angeles, is quoted as saying that the profile for these mothers is "a Caucasian under the age of 20 who comes from a middle- to upper-class home" (Puit, 1998). Examples that support his view in the mid- to late-1990s include Melissa Drexler, also known as the "Prom Mom," and Amy Greenberg and Brian Peterson, all of New Jersey, as well as several college students across the country, each of whom committed neonaticide.

In each case, the accused differ from the supposed traditional stereotype, and there was some feeling expressed in the press and elsewhere that "they should have known better" because they were better educated, middle or upper-middle class, had intact families, and had had more advantages than many other youths. If "they should have known better," there may be an implication that they should be more harshly treated under the law than if they had not had such advantages, as Hopfer claimed in her appeal. This is perhaps asserted even more when the woman is in her 20s or older or has had other children because the perception is that she is "old enough" to know better. Indeed, about one third of the cases we found involved women who were in the age range of 21 to 43 years; some had other children.

Bacilia Lucero, a 22-year-old illegal immigrant from Mexico who was living and working in northern New Jersey gave birth to a girl in January 1997. With the help of a male cousin, she threw the newborn out a third-floor window. The baby's body was found the next day and Lucero was subsequently arrested. The way in which her case was handled offers a sharp contrast to the treatment of Amy Grossberg and Brian Peterson, also residents of northern New Jersey. Their parents spent more than $1 million on their defense and their in-prison time was no greater than $2^1/_2$ years. No one interviewed Lucero about her motives or her problems.

> Neither young woman had wanted a baby, and neither was a danger to society, a threat to kill again, though Lucero was an illegal immigrant and possible flight risk. Yet after Lucero's arrest, her bail was set at $500,000 and when her family could not afford to pay it and her public defender lawyer could not get it reduced or raise any questions about the health of the baby, she was placed in a New Jersey mental institution. Her freedom was gone, and she would eventually plead guilty to aggravated manslaughter and be sentenced to 12 years in prison. (Most, 1999, p. 207)

As Most, an area reporter, pointed out, Lucero's case did not receive the media attention or public concern that the Grossberg-Peterson case did. In addition, this pair of cases shows sentencing markedly different from the sentences given Rebecca Hopfer and "Anna" mentioned previously.

> In order to accommodate neonaticide under modern murder codes, one must equate an unattended birth—the most commonplace and natural event in human history—with the pathological behavior of the depraved-heart murderer. So doing has the curious effect of criminalizing the birth process when it takes place without medical supervision. (Oberman, 1996, p. 80)

Of course, unsupervised births occur daily in many parts of the world, even today.

Some theorists look at a mother who kills as having violated her cultural image as life giving and other oriented and thus is not entitled to honor and deference. At the same time, she should, they feel, be punished more severely because she violated that image when she killed her baby.

The charge of first-degree murder generally requires premeditation—planning ahead of time. As we are aware from cases and studies in the psychological and legal literature and from contemporary cases in the headlines, the younger women rarely plan to kill their babies. Rather, the newborn's death seems to occur as a result of the young woman's *lack* of planning and *lack* of support, isolation, and hysterical denial of the pregnancy altogether.

Sadoff (1995), a well-known forensic psychiatrist, argues that neonaticide and infanticide occur more often from fear, depression, pain, or mental disorder than from cold premeditation. His opinion with reference to neonaticide is echoed in statements by other psychiatrists. A psychiatrist in Arizona, for example, said that the minds of some of the younger women in these cases "are so clouded with denial and fear, some don't understand they are having a baby" (Fimbres, 1998). "Although one might argue that the defendant was negligent in her failure to anticipate the impending birth of a child, and in her failure to take precautions to insure the baby's survival, this hardly can be seen as premeditated murder" (Oberman, 1996, p. 80). Nevertheless, 8 of 47 in Oberman's sample were so charged.

> At common law, manslaughter was broadly defined to govern unlawful killings that did not involve malice aforethought … . [I]nvoluntary manslaughter generally exists as a less severe offense than voluntary manslaughter or murder, and is applicable in circumstances where the defendant's conduct lacked a murderous intent, but involved a high degree of risk of death or serious bodily injury to the victim.
>
> This definition applies to neonaticide in that the pregnant woman who fails to acknowledge her condition and to plan for her impending delivery poses a distinct risk to her offspring's well-being. Even if her behavior prior to the birth is both legal and unintentional, it can be argued that, once the baby is born, the woman's failure to seek assistance is either criminally negligent or reckless because a parent has a legal duty to furnish medical care for her child. (Oberman, 1996, pp. 81–82)

The claim of "self-defense" has generally been rejected in involuntary manslaughter cases arising from neonaticide incidents, although in many cases, according to Oberman, the women could be seen as victims and their actions understood as almost inevitable responses to a hostile environment.

Manslaughter was the charge against eight of Oberman's neonaticide sample. Of the 101 cases that we have been able to track, 24 defendants were charged with or pleaded guilty to manslaughter. This was sometimes the result of plea bargaining down from a murder charge.

Should Neonaticide Be Punished? If So, How?

There is no question that neonaticide, in its most basic definition, is a crime. As a crime, it should normally be punished. A whole flock of questions arises from these simple statements.

Was the act premeditated? (If the mother denied the pregnancy throughout, can it be proved that she really knew that she was pregnant and planned to kill the newborn?)

Should the death of the newborn be equated with the murder of an older child or an adult? That is, are all homicides equal?

Is the accused a threat to herself (suicide) or to society (possible additional homicides)?

Although imprisonment will punish the individual guilty of homicide/manslaughter, what else will it accomplish (revenge? mental health treatment? mental health damage? deterrence of others?)?

If imprisonment is the decision, what term should the sentence be? (We have recorded widely varying sentences, ranging from community service and psychiatric care and probation in one New York case, to 25 years to life in another case. See Appendix A.)

Since many mental health *and* legal professionals recognize that neonaticide is often the result of disordered perceptions and thinking, it seems very strange that, in only 11 of the more than 115 cases we have tracked, was reference specifically made to psychiatric treatment or counseling as part of the sentence. Current practice seems to continue that reported by Resnick (1970), especially with regard to neonaticide: Hospitalization is more often recommended for mothers who have committed infanticide and possibly filicide, while mothers who committed neonaticide are sent to prison or placed on probation (not necessarily with therapy as a condition of the probation). Why is this so? Is part of the penalty in neonaticide cases punishment for the woman's (or girl's) sexual activity outside marriage?

Consider yet another case, this one involving a girl of 14 who cut her newborn's umbilical cord with scissors, wrapped the baby in a plastic bag that she then placed in a kitchen trash can, and claimed that she had not even known she was pregnant (*People v. Doss*, 1991). She was convicted of first-degree murder and sentenced to 20 years in prison; the conviction and the sentence were upheld on appeal. She had to have known that her behavior would kill the infant and that she was not in danger from the neonate, so technically she met the criteria for first-degree murder; however, in what ways will imprisonment for 20 years (or even less) rehabilitate her, help her to be a more effective adult, or even protect society?

Lisa, the midadolescent referred to in Chapter 3 (Atkins et al., 1999), eventually pleaded guilty to manslaughter and was sentenced to 4 years in prison, but she was paroled after 10 months. Prior to the trial, she suffered from post-traumatic stress disorder that involved nightmares, depression, overdependence on her parents, and suicidal thoughts. She and her parents were referred for therapeutic evaluation and counseling. Although this was all brought to the attention of the court at the time of sentencing, the state (New Jersey) argued that a prison sentence was necessary not only to punish Lisa and to deter others, but also to "send a message" at a time when there were several similar cases before the courts (Atkins et al., 1999). There is little or no evidence to support imprisonment as an effective deterrent in similar situations.

What defense can be offered in these cases? Frequently, the press reports pleas of innocence or "not guilty" by women accused of neonaticide. Typically, they would have denied the pregnancy and perceived that "things," not babies, emerged from their bodies. In other cases, they might appropriately enter pleas of "diminished capacity," although this appears to be underused in the cases we have followed.

Anglo-American Laws and Sentencing

There is a significant difference in perspective between British and American law when considering neonaticide, most of it stemming from statutory revision in the 20th century in the United Kingdom that moved away from the harshness of earlier legal views. Neonaticide is a crime that the law agrees is the killing of a newborn baby. American law does not recognize this as a separate category of crime, however, as the British and others do. "Neonaticide syndrome" is a legal construct rather than a psychiatric or psychological one, but it includes such elements as denial of pregnancy, concealment of pregnancy, and giving birth, usually alone, in an isolated setting. The denial aspect enables the prospective mother to avoid feelings of shame or guilt, and it also means that she does not premeditate the murder of the neonate.

British Law

Since the Infanticide Act 1922 (U.K.) and Infanticide Act 1938 (U.K.), British law has regarded postpartum psychosis as a means of reducing the charges for neonaticide and infanticide from murder to manslaughter, although in truth this condition is not applicable to neonaticide. In New South Wales (Australia), laws based on the Infanticide Act 1938 (U.K.) were adopted and enabled a judge to sentence a woman who had committed neonaticide or infanticide as if for manslaughter, which meant that a discretionary sentence could be given. This was considered to "offer a humane means of dealing with women who became temporarily deranged as a result of the aftereffects of childbirth" (New South Wales Law Reform, 1997, p. 102).

The New South Wales Law Reform Commission recognized that there may actually be different causes for neonaticide and infanticide, ranging from the hidden pregnancy of the single woman to the overwhelming socioeconomic stress of another child to raise, rather than only the postpartum psychosis possibly associated with infanticide. Accordingly, the commission recommended that the crime labeled "neonaticide" be abolished in New South Wales. They anticipated that such child killings would then be handled with a defense of diminished responsibility.

In England, the Criminal Law Revision Committee recommended altering the Infanticide Act 1938 to allow for environmental or other stresses, and it was entered into the Criminal Code Bill of 1989 as clause 64 (1) (Mackay, 1993). According to d'Orban (1979), changes in attitude, even before passage of these laws, resulted in shorter or suspended sentences, sometimes with mental health commitments, and with a small percentage serving short terms in prison.

Overall, British law and its derivatives in former colonies such as Canada and Australia tend to view neonaticide specifically and infanticide to a lesser degree as events due to psychological disorder that require treatment rather than punishment. As dreadful as the crime is, in truth the homicidal mother is more a threat to herself than to society—one of the principal reasons for incarcerating someone. The more recent laws also avoid the earlier legal connections to lactation and hormonal upsets as the basis for such tragic acts, which had an antifemale aura. In almost all cases of neonaticide, after all, the mother had not begun to breast-feed the newborn, so lactation was not a factor. Indeed, she had no emotional, let alone maternal, tie to the neonate, as we have indicated earlier. The baby is an "it," as Amy Grossberg and many others in her position have indicated. This leads to some interesting philosophical as well as legal questions.

Scottish law does not differentiate among neonaticide, infanticide, and other forms of homicide as English and Welsh laws do, but it does differentiate in practice between the sexes (Marks & Kumar, 1996). In 15 cases of infanticide committed by males, 12 of those convicted were remanded to custodial care; of the 8 women's cases, 2 were hospitalized (none of the men were), 2 were imprisoned, and the other 4 were placed on probation. In Marks and Kumar's earlier study in England and Wales (1993), they had found that 80% of the neonate cases were due to a nonviolent means (e.g., suffocation) or neglect, but in Scotland, they found more violence.

American Law

Iffy and Jacobovitz pointed out in 1992 that, as of that year, no American law required consideration of the mother's mental state when she committed neonaticide or infanticide, other than the usual concerns in homicide cases about the defendant's ability to "know" and "appreciate" the wrongfulness of her acts when she committed them.

Unlike the British pattern and others, each American state has its own laws for all imaginable infractions; in some categories, as is true here, there may not even be a federal law that acts as a guideline. "With such great diversity among jurisdictions, it does not seem likely that a uniform policy of humanitarian response to infanticides resulting from postpartum psychosis will soon emerge" (Katkin, 1992, p. 281). One could add that a uniform policy toward neonaticidal mothers is equally unlikely, although moves toward a "policy of humanitarian response" may be encouraged by the work of Wexler and Winick (1991) and others in the approach they have called therapeutic jurisprudence. In addition, laws sometimes remain on the books long after they are appropriate or relevant.

A third caveat is that there are situations in which federal law supersedes state law, as when certain crimes occur at a federal facility (*Assimilative Crimes Act*, 18 U.S.C. 13) or among Native Americans (*Major Crimes Act*, 18 U.S.C. 1111). Thus, few patterns can be found in the charges against the neonaticidal parent or the sentence imposed, as seen in Table 5.2.

Table 5.2 Sentences for Neonaticide (Fewest Years to Serve)

	Age						
	< 18	18–19	20s	30s	40s	Unknown	Total
No prison time	3	3	2				8
Under 1 year			3				3
1 to 4 years	7	7	7		1	1	23
5 to 14 years	4	4	4	1			13
15 years to life	3	1	8	6	1	1	20
N =	17	15	24	7	2	2	67

[a] *N* = 67. Includes three males and includes probation and prison terms.

Sentencing Alternatives

Imprisonment seems to be the first goal of prosecutors when confronted with cases of neonaticide. As we have seen, sentences of 10 years or more are not uncommon for the young woman convicted of some degree of manslaughter or murder. There is no provision for helping her understand or cope with her behavior, or even for educating her so that she can prevent a repetition of the behavior that landed her behind bars. As the murderer of her newborn, she is held in the lowest possible "esteem" by other women prisoners and may even be injured by them. Kaplan (1988) has reported on support group efforts to help these prisoners survive their incarceration without becoming more emotionally and psychologically damaged.

A second alternative, the one sometimes employed by British courts as noted earlier, is to hospitalize the girl or woman in a psychiatric facility where she can be treated for the condition that led to her crime or for the one that resulted from committing it. Once confronted with the outcome of her behavior in court, there is a strong likelihood that the young woman could become suicidal or severely depressed. Treatment in the psychiatric facility would, in essence, protect her from herself.

Related to this is a sentence of x number of years probation combined with mandatory psychotherapy or counseling. Realistic sex education might also be part of this treatment. Tied to the probation may be a condition of several hundred or a thousand hours of community service, often involved with educating younger students or perhaps working with babies and very young children who reside in orphanages or similar facilities.

Use of mental health treatment, whether in-patient or not—indeed, even in prison—is a viable alternative to allowing the neonaticidal woman to become a victim of her and others' most hostile emotions. It ties in very well with the therapeutic jurisprudence approach initially espoused by Wexler and Winick (1991) that we will discuss in the final chapter.

What about the Fathers?

> The adoption of the psychological explanation and a psychiatrically oriented cure for White single pregnancy [in the pre-*Roe* era] had a number of social functions. First, it spared the putative father from social opprobrium and responsibility—in fact, from professional attention of any kind. (Solinger, 1990, p. 51)

Rarely was the male identified, let alone punished, for impregnating a woman half a century ago, and he is not today, with the exception of rape cases (if the rapist is caught and convicted).

With rare exceptions, neonaticide is committed by the new mother who, as we have found, usually delivers the baby by herself. The fathers are nowhere to be found at the time, or even afterwards, in most cases. There *are* exceptions: two cases cited by Resnick (1970), two more cited by Kaye, Borenstein, and Donnelly (1990), the Murphy–Stockwell case (1995), the Grossberg–Peterson case in Delaware (where the murder took place), and possibly one in Wisconsin ("Eau Claire …," 1998).

In one of the cases that Kaye and his colleagues (1990) found, the man was from a wealthy family, had average intelligence, and was an alcoholic and psychopath who had impregnated a fellow inmate at a psychiatric center. He wrote a document in favor of infanticide and felt, after killing his newborn son in the mother's hospital room, that he had saved his social reputation and spared the woman a responsibility she could not handle. Found guilty of second-degree murder, he was sentenced to 25 years to life, but felt "cheated" in that he was not allowed to enter a defense of justifiable homicide and therefore present to the court his view of infanticide (Kaye et al., p. 137).

In their second case, the father was present at the delivery of his deformed and cyanotic son, who was also diagnosed as having genetic abnormalities associated with Trisomy 13 Syndrome, which is invariably fatal. After the baby was revived and the doctor was occupied with the mother, the man picked up his son, bent down, and smashed the baby's head on the floor, killing him instantly. He pleaded temporary insanity and was not convicted in either of his two trials. Kaye and his colleagues (1990) concluded that paternal neonaticide may be motivated by premeditation (for any one of several reasons), as was true in three of the cases they reported (two by Resnick and the first of their two), or by impulsivity, as happened in the last case summarized. Under these circumstances, the courts tend to be more punitive with men who premeditate the neonaticide and give them more severe sentences than they do to the mothers found guilty of the same crime (Kaye, Borenstein, & Donnelly, p. 138).

Asked what his most radical position might be, an Ohio newspaper editorial writer recalled the view of a radio talk-show host who would not allow male callers to comment on abortion. The writer agreed that it seemed unfair for males to walk away "unscrutinized, unscathed, and largely unknown," while their female partners were criticized for their sexual activity (Brewer, 1994, p. 6A). The same might be said when the woman commits neonaticide.

The Murphy–Stockwell case involved the burial of a newborn that was born alive by Lisa Murphy Stockwell, 17, and her husband Billy Stockwell,

22, in May 1995 in Tennessee. The charge against Lisa, seen as the "legal equivalent" of first-degree murder, was reduced because she was found to be under the domination of her husband. She was ultimately sentenced to 10 years in prison. Billy Stockwell was convicted of murder and sentenced to life (Donsky, 1997; Loggins, 1998).

In earlier cases the partners were involved in assisting the birth or in the destruction of the newborn. They are important, for all cases are based on precedents, and they were often cited. For example, a case in 1895 revolved around the conviction of John Campbell for neonaticide. He and the mother, Nancy Cook, were indicted, but he alone was tried and sentenced to 14 years. His conviction was based on the sole testimony of Cook, who insisted that she had not seen the baby but had delivered a live premature child. Campbell took the child and disposed of it. No body or remains were discovered.

The sentence was reversed by the appellate court on the grounds that the testimony of Nancy Cook required corroborative evidence. However, the judges said that neonaticide presented the greatest difficulties in identifying the corpus delicti (body of a murder victim) and each case must depend upon its own peculiar circumstances. The decision also stated that the baby's death could be established without direct proof, if the circumstantial evidence was cogent enough. This precedent also contributed to variations in indictments and sentencing (*People v. Campbell*, 1895).

Another similar episode involved a husband named Weaver, who was convicted of second-degree murder. He claimed the baby was born 40 minutes before he arrived home and he thought that it was stillborn. His wife (who had three children from a previous marriage) went into labor unexpectedly and had a rapid premature birth. Weak and exhausted, she was unable to attend the infant and lay alone for 40 minutes. When her husband returned, she told him that she had a miscarriage and gave him the baby wrapped in a blanket, which he placed in the toilet, and then called a doctor. The body was recovered, but pathologists could not agree on whether the baby died from neglect or had died shortly after birth. As in the Campbell case, the decision was reversed for lack of evidence (*Weaver v. State*, 1931). It should be noted that in both cases the mothers were not tried.

In contrast, the judge who sentenced Amy Grossberg and Brian Peterson made the opposite decision: he gave Peterson a slightly shorter prison term and 3 years less probation than Grossberg received (Dribben, 1998). Why? Peterson had plea-bargained and pleaded guilty to manslaughter before she did. If he had really been more "chivalrous," a term used by the prosecutor, he would have driven her to an emergency care facility rather than meeting her at a motel for the delivery and disposal of their baby. As one columnist put it:

> All is not fair in love and pregnancy. Since when does a boy worry about his reputation if he stumbles while drunk on the powerful cocktail of hormones and romance? How often do you read about a family disowning its son because he forgot to use a condom? (Dribben, 1998)

A case in Eau Claire, Wisconsin, involved a 13-year-old girl who was originally charged in adult court with the first-degree murder of her newborn ("Eau Claire ...," 1998). A few months later, the judge allowed her case to be transferred to juvenile court where she was found guilty of delinquency on a charge of first-degree reckless homicide. Her sentence, according to the newspaper report, could be as much as 5 years in a correctional facility. The 13-year-old boy who admitted sexually assaulting her and who may have been the father of the dead neonate was ordered to spend only 1 year in a group home—so much for equal responsibility!

"Dateline NBC" presented the neonaticide case of Audrey Iacona of Medina, Ohio, on March 16, 1999. The search of her parents' home for the dead neonate was shown in detail; the court presentations by attorneys and witnesses were shown; her parents were interviewed; and the judge's sentence, in abeyance while it was appealed, was pronounced. There was one very brief mention of a boyfriend whom she knew to be the father. He vanished into the landscape, while she was sentenced to 8 years in prison.

Each of these case illustrations contradicts the view of Resnick (1970) that the fathers are sentenced more severely for neonaticide and filicide than the mothers are, at least with respect to neonaticide. In the cases reported by Kaye, Borenstein, and Donnelly (1990) and in the Murphy–Stockwell case (1995), Resnick's statement holds true; however, more often, (1) the father is nowhere to be found; or (2) *he* gets a slap on the wrist and *she* is sent to prison. Parness (1993) argued for legislation that would provide for criminal prosecution of and penalties for biological fathers for prebirth damages, such as providing drugs to the expectant mother, physically abusing her, or lack of financial support during the pregnancy, which might contribute to malnutrition or lack of care. He also proposed that pregnant females be given information on the responsibilities of expectant fathers when they are given information about their prenatal care (assuming that they seek such care at all).

At the other extreme, a man sued his former girl friend for getting pregnant and thus causing him to be liable for child support (Ryan, 1998). He blamed her for not taking her birth control pills. As a columnist wrote, "Why didn't he take responsibility for birth control himself, either with condoms, a vasectomy, or, as crazy as it sounds, abstinence, until he was ready for fatherhood?" As is widely known, however, this is too rarely the practice with males.

Concluding Comments

It is apparent that much more is at stake in the matter of neonaticide than the "simple" murder, premeditated or not, of a newborn by his or her mother. The question of when the fetus legally becomes a "child" varies from state to state. Even feminist positions differ from each other, to some extent because of religious concerns. The role of the male in contributing to what is considered neonaticidal behavior (e.g., drug addiction or sexual intercourse when the doctor has advised against it) has too rarely been considered in the literature.

So many political/religious/philosophical positions are taken on these matters, with no one group willing to listen to the others, let alone compromising to reach some rational stance, that it is unlikely that reason will prevail in these cases. As to how to sentence or treat those who commit neonaticide, there are wide variations among the different jurisdictions in this country—much more than is true abroad. There are alternatives that appear to be underused here that will be discussed in a later chapter.

6 In Transition: From One Form of Child Homicide to Another

Moving from a focus on neonaticide to one on infanticide and filicide seems to be an appropriate point at which to deal with the concept of a "syndrome"—a term widely used in connection with all three types of child homicide, as well as in other situations. It occurs repeatedly with respect to child abuse or in an adult's defense. Too often, the term is overused, misapplied, or becomes a too convenient—if not legally appropriate—"shorthand." To illustrate the problem, consider the "syndromes" that follow:

Adopted child syndrome	Asperger's syndrome
Battered woman syndrome	"Black rage" syndrome
Down syndrome	Homosexual anxiety panic syndrome
Hostage syndrome	Munchausen syndrome
Munchausen syndrome by proxy (MSBP)	Neonaticide syndrome
Parental alienation syndrome	Post traumatic stress disorder syndrome
Rape trauma syndrome	Shaken baby syndrome
Sudden infant death syndrome (SIDS)	Tourette's syndrome

Some of those cited are clearly defined and "legitimate"—that is, accepted by the *DSM-IV* and the courts, or by the medical profession. Others are more controversial.

In the *DSM-IV*, a syndrome is defined as a group of "signs and symptoms, based on their frequent co-concurrence, that may suggest an underlying pathogenesis, course, familial pattern, or treatment selection" (American Psychiatric Association, 1994, p. 7). This type of classification system can enhance communication among professionals, but it can also:

Lead to a loss of information if it overlooks the uniqueness of the person being studied or treated
Stigmatize the individual thus classified
Ignore the continuity between normal and abnormal behavior by its "yes–no" approach
Bring into question inter-rater reliability of diagnoses
Be unable to determine the validity of the classification
Lead to severe consequences as a result of unreliable and invalid diagnoses (http://www2.hawaii.edu)

It is also necessary for clinicians to be alert to differences in culture and social status between the client/patient and the clinician. Cultural differences could include behaviors acceptable in the client's culture but not in the mainstream American culture, or vice versa, that might be labeled as part of a syndrome when they are not. Obviously, this can affect the responses to questions about symptoms and thus diagnosis of a syndrome. It might even play a role in an insanity defense.

Syndrome evidence is often presented at trial because it "allows a jury to understand why a defendant might act so differently from how a juror would expect himself or herself to act in a particular situation" (Wills, 2004, p. 1032). It may also help to override misconceptions or stereotypes. Whether the syndrome evidence is admissible depends on whether it meets the *Daubert* or *Frye* standards for evidence, and this may depend on the state in which the case is tried, as we will discuss elsewhere.

To illustrate the complexities of what constitutes a syndrome, we will discuss here four such clusters of behavior: neonaticide syndrome, shaken baby syndrome, sudden infant death syndrome (SIDS), and Munchausen syndrome by proxy (MSBP). Controversy is abundant with all of them.

Neonaticide Syndrome

Whether or not there *is* a neonaticide syndrome, it is generally recognized that the attributes in such a cluster are almost totally exhibited by females, except for the very few cases in which the newborn's father is present at delivery or within hours thereafter. Neonaticide is recognized as a "clinical entity," but it "has not yet been recognized as a syndrome or discrete psychiatric disorder in the *DSM-IV*" (Wills, 2004, p. 1033). Its most critical element is the denial of pregnancy that leads to the act of neonaticide. This is a very difficult thing for most jurors to understand. They will also need to know whether the subject had experienced psychotic breaks, dissociative states associated with the behavior, or command hallucinations.

In Stephanie Wernick's case (discussed in Chapter 8), "the court refused to hear evidence of 'neonaticide syndrome' because it had not yet been generally accepted in the field of psychiatry" (Spinelli, 2004, p. 147). Similarly, the attorneys for Carin Madden, a 20-year-old in Ohio, claimed that she suffered from "neonaticide syndrome," which led to her killing her newborn baby. Ohio law did not recognize the alleged syndrome as a defense. The attorneys said that concealing her pregnancy or failing to acknowledge it and giving birth in an isolated setting were symptoms of the syndrome (Kemme, 2000). However, this would not be admissible under a *Frye* hearing, as was the case here, because it has not been accepted by the scientific community as an "illness" (Welner, 1997).

Shaken Baby Syndrome/Shaking Impact Syndrome

What is "shaken baby syndrome (SBS)?" There are multiple answers to that question. In 1962, C. Henry Kempe published a paper that described symptoms caused by abuse rather than accident. These included outward physical indications of injury such as poor skin hygiene, multiple soft-tissue injuries, malnutrition, fractures (especially those of different ages indicating ongoing abuse), and "a history of previous episodes suggestive of parental neglect or trauma" (Lyons, 2003, p. 111). Among other symptoms mentioned was the frequent appearance of subdural hematoma.

Following up on Kempe's work, in 1972 and 1974, pediatric radiologist John Caffey described a constellation of clinical findings that were used to coin the term "whiplash shaken baby syndrome." Caffey's observations " … noted common injuries including retinal hemorrhages, subdural or sub-arachnoid hemorrhages, and minimal or absent signs of external cranial trauma" (Hatina, 1998, pp. 559–560; cf. Caffey, 1972, 1974). It is abusive head trauma resulting from shaking the baby, with or without impact (Lazoritz & Palusci, 2001; cf. Isser & Schwartz, in press).

Examination of the immense data available (about 1,000 or more articles and legal cases) reveals major controversies in the medical literature about SBS, especially about reaching agreement on useful and proven scientific evidence. Inadequate qualification of examiners, as well as lack of a profile of the social and familial risk factors that indicate guidelines on establishing the likelihood of abuse, is notably problematic. There is a need for a checklist or other diagnostic tools to assess suspicions of SBS and child abuse accurately (Donohoe, 2003). In some cases immaturity of the newborn infant may cause intracranial bleeding (Geddes, et al., 2003). Apnea, when the baby stops breathing, has also been the cause of brain damage (Lyons, 2003). Natural causes such as ruptured aneurysms, congenital bleeding, brittle-bone disease, water on the brain, and re-bleeding of a previous hematoma can also cause subdural and arachnoid hematomas. A few researchers have suggested that vaccine reactions could also cause these hematomas, although this is rare (Scheibner, 2001).

The courts, therefore, require evidence of retinal bleeding as further indication of SBS. Moreover, some experts believe that shaking alone cannot produce homicide; it must be accompanied by a trauma such as the impact of the head on a surface such as a pillow or bed (which would underlie the shaking impact syndrome). Such impact, whether from shaking or blunt cranial impact, can lead to serious injury or death of the baby (Hatina, 1998).

The victims of SBS or S-IS are rarely older than 2 years of age, with most less than 6 months of age. SBS is caused by the caretaker's violent shaking of an infant; this results in damage to the infant's brain and spinal cord because of the baby's undeveloped neck muscles. After the shaking, ruptured blood vessels and tears in the brain's tissues cause swelling and enormous pressure within the skull leading to severe injury or death. The signs and symptoms of SBS include a characteristic pattern of subdural hematomas, subarachnoid hemorrhages, and retinal hemorrhages, as Caffey suggested more than 30 years ago (Atwal, Rutty, Carter & Green, 1998; Case, et al., 2001), with an absence of signs of recent external trauma such as facial bruising (Alexander, Sato, Smith, & Bennett, 1990; Atwal et al., 1998; Saternus, Kernbach-Wighton & Oehmichen, 2000).

The mortality rate of SBS victims is extremely high. According to the Committee on Child Abuse and Neglect of the American Academy of Pediatrics, about 20 to 25% of children who were forcefully shaken or thrown die (2001b)—still too many innocents.

Given the intracranial injuries, symptoms of SBS in those who survive can include changes in behavior, lethargy, irritability, pale or bluish skin, vomiting, loss of consciousness, and convulsions (NINDS, n.d.) There may also be broken or dislocated bones or injuries to the neck and spine, although there are no external signs of injury (American Academy of Pediatrics Committee on Child Abuse and Neglect, 2001a). Survivors may also have lifelong problems including seizures, mental retardation, impaired vision or blindness, learning problems, or physical or emotional growth delays.

Shaken baby syndrome (SBS) has been widely accepted as child abuse or homicide and many caretakers and parents have been convicted of manslaughter or homicide because of shaking their babies. Hatina, however, also notes and warns that "the absence of retinal hemorrhages and the location of the optic nerve sheath hemorrhage [are] two important distinguishing features from classic shaken baby syndrome ... " (1998, p. 566). A respected forensic neuropathologist, Jan Leestma (2005), asserts that shaking alone cannot inflict mortal damage to the brain. There may be other causes of these symptoms, so it is imperative to obtain full and accurate information about the child's health history and for the attending clinician to conduct a thorough examination. Although a CT (computerized tomography) scan is apparently one of the best diagnostic tools now available, it is too often impractical or financially too expensive to use on every child brought to the ER (Semuels, 2005). The other key tool is a magnetic resonance imaging (MRI) test.

Infants have weak neck muscles and a brain in which brain tissue is not firm or fixed in place, so there is little to resist the rapid back-and-forth movement of being shaken. This contributes to the subdural hematoma and retinal hemorrhage, as well as other possible damage seen in SBS. According to Stuttaford (2005), the back-and-forward movement is more harmful than side-to-side shaking.

As the courts and police have become more aware of SBS, the presence of the two markers (subdural hematoma and retinal hemorrhage) usually leads to prosecution on the grounds of child abuse or homicide when applicable, even if there is no other suspicion of abuse. Unfortunately, there have been insufficient scientific underpinnings for this diagnosis, although shaking a baby is pernicious and may well be part of child abuse. Many of those accused, however, have been innocently prosecuted or convicted on the basis of flimsy evidence (cf. Uscinski, 2002).

In order to prevent false accusations that lead to injustice, expert medical evidence must have scientific validity, which is obviously often difficult to obtain. It is necessary to investigate cases very carefully, noting all the circumstances involved, so as to avoid conclusions based on one or two symptoms (Harding, Risdon, & Krous, 2004). The best way to achieve such a goal is to utilize a team of medical specialists that includes radiologists, ophthalmologists, biochemists, and pathologists (Kemp, 2002).*

According to specialists at the Children's Hospital of Philadelphia, the term "shaking impact syndrome" may be a more accurate description of the injuries sustained by babies from inflicted head injuries. They found that "It is the sudden angular deceleration experienced by the brain and cerebral vessels, not the specific contact forces applied to the surface of the head, that

* A particularly informative book in this area is *The Shaken Baby Syndrome: A Multidisciplinary Approach* (Lazoritz & Palusci, 2001), which includes chapters by pediatricians, psychologists, a radiologist, a neurosurgeon, law enforcement personnel and legal figures, a medical examiner, and a social worker. The majority of the chapters focus on the nature of the injuries and the potential outcomes from them, while a few discuss prevention of the most disastrous outcomes.

results in the intracranial injury" (Duhaime, Christian, Rorke, & Zimmerman, 1998, p. 1822). The resulting uncontrollable intracranial hypertension causes the infant's death. This team cautioned, however, that a few rare genetic or inherited conditions produce the same types of hematomas without child abuse; these can be detected by the use of MRIs, as well as checking the baby's and the family's medical histories.

A case in point is that of Alice and Miguel Velasquez. X-rays taken on a routine medical check-up revealed that their 4-month-old daughter had rib fractures. Though no other evidence existed of abuse or SBS, the father, principal caretaker of their daughter, was accused and arrested on charges of felony child abuse and their daughter was placed in foster care. Tests ordered by the defense revealed that the baby had a disease known as osteogenesis imperfecta (aka "brittle-bone" disease). Doctors on the case resisted the findings and authorities were reluctant to release the child until they were sure of her safety. Not until the appellate court reversed the conviction of the father did the parents get their daughter back. They subsequently sued the government and received $950,000 (Castaneda, 2005; cf. *Comm. v. Velasquez*, 2004).

Two other appellate cases illustrate conditions under which a baby is shaken hard or handled roughly, leading to the child's death. In Steven Galloway's case (*State of NJ v. Galloway*, 1993), he admitted shaking his girlfriend's infant son (also named Steven) hard several times, but claimed his diminished capacity kept him from intending to murder the child. On the date of the crime, his girlfriend's parents had already retired for the night, and she was out on an errand when little Steven started crying. Galloway picked the infant up, but he would not stop crying. Galloway "admitted to shaking the child hard to stop the crying. That shaking caused the child's head to bob back and forth rapidly, causing hemorrhaging of the blood vessels of the child's brain, commonly known as the 'shaken baby syndrome'" (p. 638).

When the mother returned from her errand, she became concerned about the baby's breathing and subsequently took him to the hospital. Hospital personnel, suspicious of the baby's injuries, alerted the police. They questioned Galloway a few times, informing him of his *Miranda* rights, and ultimately he admitted squeezing and shaking the baby very hard. His statement included a motive: he committed the offense "because his girlfriend had been raped and the baby was a product of the rape, and that he had always intended to do it" (p. 640). Ultimately, little Steven died from his injuries. The appellate division found that Galloway had a personality disorder, not "a mental disease or defect" and suffered a loss of impulse control. His sentence was upheld.

In a second case, that of Brian Smith (*Comm. of PA v. Smith*, 1996), the victim was a 5-month-old boy, Ryan. Smith and his live-in girlfriend, the baby's mother, went to visit a friend. The mother and her friend went to a bar, leaving Smith with the baby and the friend's four sleeping children. Apparently Smith played with the baby, then realized that something was wrong. He called the mother twice. She returned to find Ryan limp and not breathing. She called an ambulance, but at the hospital little Ryan was found to be brain dead and was removed from life support.

Smith was questioned at the hospital and, like Galloway, gave at least three different versions of what had happened. He finally admitted to having drunk eight beers and to have been tossing little Ryan up in the air when the baby was injured. The coroner, however, found six to ten blows to the head, administered over a more than 5-minute period. "The infliction of these injuries demonstrates a willful, premeditated, and deliberate killing," according to the coroner's finding (p. 233). Testimony during the trial showed that Smith had abused the baby many times before and had also physically and emotionally abused the baby's mother. Smith was known to have had mental health problems, including substance abuse and behavior control, for which he was supposedly taking medication.

The Smith case, unlike Galloway's, is one of severe child abuse that went far beyond shaking the baby. Little Ryan had numerous signs of external injuries to the cranium, eliminating shaken baby syndrome as the cause of his death.

As in other syndromes, there have been attempts to profile abusers in the hope of identifying and preventing future crimes. Unfortunately, as in other syndromes, there are similarities to be found, but researchers have not yet established a definitive profile. What has emerged from examining available databases is that in 1996 (based on U.S. Department of Health and Human Services statistics), 77% of the perpetrators were the parents and 11% were other relatives (cf. Hennes, Kiri, & Palusci, 2001). Our study, based on a database including only appellate court decisions assembled from Westlaw, confirms that parents (most often the fathers) were indeed the overwhelming majority of abusers, followed by live-in boyfriends, stepparents (more often stepfathers), other relatives, and babysitters or caretakers.

This study agrees in the main with the findings of Starling, Holden, and Jenny (1995), who investigated the medical charts of 151 infants who had suffered abusive head trauma. Their results questioned the assumption of many other researchers that mothers were the principal perpetrators of child abuse and homicide. Their conclusions showed that

Males outnumbered females 2.2:1
Fathers, stepfathers, and boyfriends committed 60% of the crimes
Babysitters (female) represented 17.3% of the perpetrators
Mothers were the abusers in only 12.6% of the cases

How can adults, or even teenagers, treat babies this way? What are the characteristics noted by researchers? Court records suggest lower family income levels, more single-parent households, and many more mothers with sleep-in boyfriends. However, the evidence is not very conclusive. The two main causes of abuse or shaking the baby seem to be persistent crying or perceived misbehavior.

The interaction between infant and caregivers that would lead to shaking incidents has not been thoroughly explored, but there are some indications that an unsatisfactory interrelationship triggers an abusive response. A colicky, fussy baby with an insensitive caretaker who does not respond leads to even more crying, ultimately producing a violent reaction by the caretaker, who may feel that the baby is rejecting him or her (Davies & Garwood, 2001).

Sudden Infant Death Syndrome

Sudden infant death syndrome (SIDS) "is defined as the sudden death of an infant younger than 1 year of age that remains unexplained after a complete autopsy, examination of the death scene, and a review of the clinical history" (Hunt, 2001, p. 346). Some of the risk factors associated with SIDS include the infant's face-down sleep position, soft bedding and blankets, impaired ventilatory and arousal responsiveness, maternal cigarette smoking, mild upper respiratory infection, and genetic susceptibility. Unfortunately, intentional suffocation "cannot be differentiated from SIDS by autopsy" (Hunt, p. 349).

As some experts have asserted, one SIDS death can be a tragedy; even two can be due to a tragic genetic flaw; but three or more certainly warrant investigation. The mothers tend to display frequent or bizarre symptoms of illness in the absence of real illness, labeled "Factitious Disorder by Proxy" in the *DSM-IV* and *DSM-IV-TR* (American Psychiatric Association, 1994, 2000). This latter behavior tends to be indicative of child abuse as well as parental illness. The relative risk for unexplained cause of death in the next sibling is greater than might be expected according to studies cited by Hunt, as is obstructive sleep apnea, which may have a genetic root. Again, if an accurate diagnosis or autopsy is to result, ER personnel and others must be aware of the child's and family's medical histories, as well as any prior episodes of sleep apnea or other respiratory problems. They also need to be alert to the possibility—and it *is* only a possibility—that the child's sleep problems may be induced *or imagined* by a parent who is behaving in accord with Munchausen syndrome by proxy (discussed in the next section).

It should be noted that some of the infants exhibiting frequent or prolonged apnea, impaired control of respiratory and heart rate, deficient arousal from sleep, and other abnormalities may be premature infants. They may also suffer in response to idiopathic apparent life-threatening events (ALTE), although this may also be caused by intentional suffocation (Hunt, 2001). Other studies suggest the possibility of genetic patterns contributing to SIDS deaths among some Amish infants, as well as unknown factors contributing to rates among African Americans and American Indians, that are two to three times the incidence of 0.55 deaths (of infants under 1 year of age) per 1,000 live births reported by the National Center for Health Statistics (Efrati, 2004). Some studies and law suits have also attempted to tie SIDS deaths to negative side effects of vaccinations given the infants a day or two earlier. However, repeated studies have not borne this out, as is shown in the sizable sample (N = 129,000+) examined by Griffin, Ray, Livengood, and Schaffner (1988) and echoed by smaller, more recent studies.

Confirmation of the potential interaction of minimal upper respiratory infection with subtle defects in the central nervous system or the sleep position and smoke exposure leading to SIDS was reported by Krous, Nadeau, Silva, and Blackstone (2003). On the other hand, Levene and Bacon (2004) cautioned that those examining the dead infant should be alert to the possibility of covert homicide, especially intentional suffocation as noted earlier.

Yet another cause of SIDS deaths, especially among those younger than 3 months of age, may be bed sharing or couch sharing with the infant's parents, with even higher risk if one or both parents smoke. Between half and three quarters of these infants were less than 11 weeks old (Tappin, Ecob, & Brooke, 2005).

As will be evident throughout the next several pages, SIDS deaths, or deaths diagnosed as due to SIDS because no other explanation could be found for them, sometimes turned out to be homicides committed by parents seeking sympathy or other forms of attention.

Munchausen Syndrome by Proxy (MSBP)

If a woman consults three or four doctors over a period of a few months with reference to persistent or recurring symptoms, is she truly ill with a rare disease with which few doctors are familiar, is she perhaps neurotically seeking sympathetic attention in the absence of family or friends, or might she be causing her symptoms to gain medical care because of Munchausen syndrome? Patients sometimes practice deception and distort their symptoms to gain medical care. They can produce infection by injecting themselves with bacteria, taking poisonous substances, or otherwise injuring themselves. They go from hospital to hospital, or doctor after doctor, subjecting themselves to dangerous and expensive diagnostic and surgical procedures. This kind of behavior has been categorized as evidence of Munchausen syndrome, a term introduced by Dr. Richard Asher more than 50 years ago (Asher, 1951).

If a mother brings her child to the emergency room or the pediatrician repeatedly, is she a truly concerned parent, or in need of attention, or guilty of child abuse in that she is causing symptoms in the child? Is she exhibiting Munchausen syndrome by proxy (MSBP)?

Although Munchausen syndrome wastes medical resources and adds to the ever increasing cost of medicine, the most pernicious form of this emotional disturbance occurs when parents deliberately and deceitfully injure their young and helpless children to procure unnecessary medical care for the children and to produce sympathy for their own apparent suffering. This bizarre and relatively rare behavior has been characterized as Munchausen syndrome by proxy (MSBP).

Munchausen syndrome by proxy, a form of child abuse that may lead to the child's death, was first identified under its present name by Roy Meadow, an Englishman (1977). In this syndrome, an adult, usually the child's mother, repeatedly creates and reports symptoms in a child that may, in some cases, lead to the child's death. Her complaints about the child's symptoms lead physicians to perform unnecessary diagnostic procedures that usually do not produce a specific diagnosis (Mason, 2004). The adult, however, gains a great deal of attention—often sympathy at what she is experiencing with such a sick child—and this may be what is indirectly sought. The child, usually an infant to a preschooler in age, allegedly (or sometimes really) displays one or more of a variety of symptoms, including rashes attributed to allergies, vomiting, bleeding, diarrhea, seizures, apnea, or fevers. It is rare for apnea, however, to occur in children older than 2 years, and more often it occurs in infants up to about 6 months old (Goldenberg, 1999).

The problem with the identification of the symptoms of MSBP in the current literature is that it is rather diffuse; very often, parents who are genuinely concerned about their children or are overinvolved in their children's development may be mistakenly identified as troubled individuals (cf. Anderegg, 2003; Smith, 2003). Other psychological explanations abound—for example, that perpetrators are trying to punish parental substitutes or to seek revenge for abuses of one kind or another in their own childhood. These theories are highly speculative and not at all validly predictive of the person's profile.

Enforced illnesses and treatment contribute to the mother or father's control because the child is forced into total dependence on the parent. The factitious disease is intractable and continuous. The parent keeps bringing the child back to the hospital for ongoing treatment of symptoms that never completely disappear. The child who is a victim of MSBP thus exhibits not only the physical effects of child abuse, but also psychological dysfunctions.

He or she displays behavior that is inappropriate for his or her age. The condition belies the symptoms and medical history described by the parents. Imperceptibly, the child colludes in the parent's deceit because he or she is too young and inarticulate to argue or very anxious to please and earn the parents' love and approbation (Flannery, 1999; cf. Gunter, 1998).

MSBP is a controversial diagnosis. "MSBP behavior manifests itself as violence against a child, and it thus constitutes criminal behavior" (Steelman, 2002, p. 275). If it is perceived in this way, then the medical testimony and the court must consider the violent effects of such behavior on the child. However, appellate decisions in Connecticut, New York, Ohio, Georgia, and the federal second circuit in the late 1990s showed "a growing acceptance of decisions by family court judges endorsing the reliability of MSBP diagnoses" (Prentice, 2001, p. 399).

The principal factors in cases of Munchausen syndrome by proxy are (Light & Sheridan, 1990; Meadow, 1977):

Illness in the child simulated or created by a parent (or someone acting in that role)
Repeated presentation of the child for evaluation and medical care
Denial of any contributing behavior by the parent
Quick disappearance of the symptoms when the child and parent are separated

The illness may be produced by poisoning, suffocation, or other means, as will be seen in the cases to be discussed here; in the case of genuine illnesses, it may be exacerbated or exaggerated by the presenting parent (Goldenberg, 1999). Meadow recently revised his criteria (2002) to read:

> The illness is fabricated (faked or induced) by the parent or someone in loco parentis.
> The child is presented to doctors, usually persistently; the perpetrator (initially) denies causing the child's illness.
> The illness goes when the child is separated from the perpetrator.
> The perpetrator is considered to be acting out of a need to assume the sick role by proxy or as another form of attention-seeking behavior. (p. 506)

The major change is the specific reference in the second criterion of the child's presentation to doctors, although the fourth criterion is also more explicit.

Clearly, because MSBP involves the welfare of children, it comes under the rubric of possible child abuse and is subject to investigation and prevention by state authorities. Even when symptoms seem suspicious, however, MSBP is hard to prove.

One of the early cases belatedly recognized as MSBP was that of Marie Noe, who had supposedly lost eight of her ten children to SIDS from 1949 to 1968 and also lost her remaining two children to death by natural causes. The loss of one child to SIDS, possibly a second as well, is regarded today as probably accidental, but more than two such deaths now arouse suspicions of MSBP and homicide. Noe was arrested in 1998 and charged with murder (Loyd, 1998). She was sentenced to 5 years of house arrest, probably because she was by then in her late 70s (Loyd, 1999). Waneta Hoyt, on the other hand, whose five children allegedly died of SIDS from 1965 to 1971, was prosecuted in 1994 and sentenced to 75 years to life. She did confess ultimately to smothering the children.

Noe and Hoyt experienced their multiple losses prior to the definition of MSBP. In apnea cases, in which the child has suddenly stopped breathing and is brought in for treatment, death is often attributed to SIDS, as in these early cases. The fact may be that the child was smothered or suffocated, as in the Noe and Hoyt cases. When, all those years later, the Noe and Hoyt cases were re-examined, it was because doubt had arisen that multiple SIDS deaths were due to genetics (Goldenberg, 1999). Indeed, in one of the cases to be discussed, the children involved had been adopted and were not related biologically, so the likelihood of all of them dying from SIDS became even less likely (Steelman, 2002).

The parent who displays MSBP behavior may originally bring the child for medical attention because of alleged apnea, for example, and the child will later succumb to supposed SIDS. If the child was hospitalized, typically the mother would be in constant attendance, hovering over the sick child and the attending medical personnel. Defendant mothers have claimed that incompetent medical personnel, who cannot explain the child's symptoms, have unfairly blamed them for creating or simulating the child's ailments (Steelman, 2002). They also question the validity of MSBP as a syndrome.

The American Psychiatric Association, however, has acknowledged MSBP in its *DSM-IV* as a "factitious disorder not otherwise specified" and as a category under consideration for further inclusion (Steelman, 2002). The criteria for factitious disorders include feigning physical or mental symptoms so as to be perceived as ill and having no other motive for their behavior (such as revenge, financial gain, or avoiding legal responsibility) (Morrison, 1995). It might be noted that other terms have also been used, such as "counterfeit illness" (Rosenberg, 1997) and, from a non-mental-health source, "fictitious" disorder as a play on words by Rod Liddle, a British journalist (2005).

In the case of MSBP, the mother, typically, creates these false signs in the child to gain attention. Some of the perpetrators are classified as "help-seekers" or as "doctor addicts" (also called "fabricators"); others are seen as "active inducers," who induce the child's symptoms through poisoning or smothering (Yorker, 1995; cf. Schreier & Libow, 1993). The inducers attempt to create the symptoms of illness through direct action (suffocation, use of poison, etc.). The addicts, on the other hand, seek treatment for nonexistent illnesses and use manipulative deception such as fake medical histories and false symptoms. Some parents are both. Some mothers who are inducers may not be patient or compliant. The child means less to these parents than being "an object to be used to manipulate an intensively ambivalent relationship with the physician" (Schreier & Libow, p. 11; cf. Feldman, Ford, & Reinholz, 1994).

The doctor addicts, some of them with a background or training in health care, are so aware of the child's medical history and possible appropriate procedures and treatment and so attentive to the medical staff that they may be allowed to perform some of the medical tasks related to the child's condition. This gives them access to medical equipment and medications. They are ultra-attentive, staying by the child's bedside almost around the clock. Light and Sheridan (1990) also indicated that MSBP mothers deny any knowledge of the etiology of the child's symptoms. The father may be emotionally or physically absent and is unaware of the mother's machinations. The mother with MSBP may only be "found out" when she is observed by hidden video surveillance or is kept away from the child's bedside and the youngster quickly becomes "miraculously" symptom free.

Often illnesses or death of other siblings in the family is part of the characteristics of MSBP and these medical histories often become factors in the initiation of investigation of the caretakers. "Filicide resulting from MSBP is uniquely recidivistic because the mother may come to thrive on the heightened attention she receives at the death of her child from a 'fatal illness'" (Steelman, 2002, p. 271). This condition has also been studied by the American Professional Society on the Abuse of Children, which has focused on the difficulties confronting diagnoses of MSBP in the criminal justice system (Goldman & Yorker, 1999).

It should be noted that some fathers *are* guilty of MSBP-type behavior. Meadow wrote

> Despite involvement with many cases of factitious illness abuse, I did not encounter a male perpetrator in the first 10 years of dealing with these families. However, in the last 10 years I have been involved with 15 cases involving male perpetrators. (1998, p. 211)

Of these 15 men, only 3 had no attention-getting physical disorders or symptoms of Munchausen's disease, but they all committed the child abuse of producing or inventing physical or psychological symptoms in their children. Their wives tended to be meek or, in some cases, ineffective child caretakers. Their passivity may have contributed to the abuse continuing longer without detection. Hospital staff personnel dealing with the children perceived the fathers to be overdemanding, overbearing, unreasonable, and often irritable. Unlike the mothers in MSBP cases, the fathers did not form close relationships with the hospital staff or parents of other children who were ill.

In Sheridan's review of 451 cases cited in the professional literature (2003), she found that 23.5% of the perpetrators were male, a marked increase from earlier perceptions. Furthermore, fathers were three times more likely to abuse their sons in this way than their daughters (p. 435).

As was mentioned earlier, the large number of deaths in the Noe, Hoyt, and similar cases initially suggested a genetic defect as the cause of the children's illnesses and deaths. However, two major cases argued against this diagnosis.

In one, Debbie Gedzius allegedly lost six children to SIDS between 1972 and 1987. The factor weighing against a genetic defect was the fact that there were three different fathers involved (Goldenberg, 1999). In the other case, Priscilla Phillips' two adopted Korean daughters suffered the same symptoms of vomiting, diarrhea, and seizures 2 years apart. The first child died; the second survived, doubtless due to the alertness of the pediatricians and their suspicions about nonbiological siblings exhibiting the same symptoms (Steelman, 2002). The second child's symptoms disappeared quickly when Phillips was forbidden to feed her in the hospital. The problem for the prosecutors was that they could not find a motive for this apparently bizarre behavior:

> In order to suggest a motive for appellant's alleged conduct, the prosecution, over the objections of defense counsel, presented evidence relating to the so-called "Munchausen's syndrome by proxy" through the testimony of Dr. Martin Blinder, a psychiatrist. However, Dr. Blinder had not examined the appellant, nor had he treated patients who displayed the syndrome which was the subject of his testimony. Rather, his testimony was based on various reports in professional journals, copies of which were made available to the jury. (*People v. Philips*, 1981, p. 72)

The California Court of Appeals upheld the lower court by affirming that the defendant's behavior was so unusual and inexplicable that the psychiatric testimony showed a possible motive. "The court further held that the psychiatric evidence was not inadmissible because the defendant did not make her mental state an issue" (*People v. Philips*, 1981, p. 89).

The Texas courts concurred with this view in *Reid v. State* (1998). In this case, the mother was convicted of the murder of one child and sentenced to 40 years' imprisonment. Her daughter, Morgan, had died from apnea episodes that she had experienced frequently, as did her brother Matthew. Matthew's episodes stopped after he was taken away from his mother. The case presented by the prosecutor was purely circumstantial, citing Matthew's medical history. MSBP was allowed as a reason for the mother's behavior.

In *Commonwealth v. Robinson*, a 19-year-old mother's 11-month-old son was rushed to the hospital. He was admitted and diagnosed as "failing to thrive." It was discovered that this was his third admission. Secretly, the mother had inserted sodium into his IV line. She told a friend, "He's not supposed to be dead. He is just supposed to be sick." After his death, she was convicted of involuntary manslaughter, even though testimony about MSBP was barred (*Commonwealth v. Robinson*, 1991).

The Kansas Supreme Court reversed a first-degree conviction for Diane Lumbrera. She was alleged to be a "sympathy junkie," but the expert was a pathologist who gave a broad definition of MSBP. The motive, Munchausen's syndrome, could not be established as a condition suffered by the defendant, although the state had presented a theory that Lumbrera acted out of desire for sympathy.

> The jury was instructed that statements, arguments, and remarks of counsel are not evidence and that if any statements are made that are not supported by the evidence, they should be disregarded. As previously noted, all evidence relative to Munchausen syndrome was stricken and the jury properly admonished in regard to same ... of reversible error. [MSBP was ruled out by the appellate court.] (*Kansas v. Lumbrera*, 1995, p. 68)

Other decisions reflected the ambiguity of how to determine the validity of the Munchausen evidence and how to evaluate its admittance in cases of child abuse. In a case over the termination of parental rights in a child custody case, the court allowed the introduction of expert testimony only after a hearing to determine the admissibility and scientific reliability of the experts' expected testimony on MSBP (*People v. Coulter*, New York, 1999). There was no doubt in the case of Aaron in New York that MSBP was accepted because the evidence was highly preponderant as to the factitious behavior of the mother inducing apnea episodes in her little son (*Matter of Aaron*, 1993).

A more disturbing story is that of Shauna, mother of 6-year-old Austynn, who desired that the custody of her son be restored to her. She had been accused of child neglect caused by her "mental disability" of MSBP. The court found that she had not been treated and had not even acknowledged her problem. Austynn was separated from his mother for 3 years, shuttled from one foster home to another. The mother argued that Austynn needed stability and love, especially since he had manifested severe behavioral dysfunction. The court denied Shauna's petition, for fear that Austynn would only be subject to more abuse (*re Austynn*, 2004).

Although the court in the case of *Aaron* accepted the MSBP profile, it was rejected in others. For instance, in the case of a contested adoption of a child taken from the mother for abuse and neglect, the evidence was clear from the expert testimony that the case raised "red flags," prompting the doctors to consider MSBP, but they did not rely on any profile evidence in establishing the diagnosis (*Adoption of Keefe*, 2000). In cases like *In re Haviland* (2003), the decision noted that "even without that testimony [MSBP], there is clear and convincing evidence that appellant mother subjected another child to egregious harm." In other cases, the appeal reversed the decisions of the family court because the mothers did not seem to have MSBP, and more significantly, the evidence of neglect was not proven conclusively

In July 2005, Stephanie McMullen was charged with trying to poison her 22-month-old son by injecting feces into his bloodstream. He had been removed from her custody 3 months earlier and was no longer exhibiting symptoms. Police alleged that McMullen was suffering from MSBP (CBS, 2005).

Clearly, whether the courts fully accepted the idea of MSBP, justice occurred and punishment was meted out when the evidence was clear and explicit. Mothers who were found guilty of murdering their children were sentenced to 40 years in prison (Lubbock, Texas), 45 years in prison (Tucson, Arizona), life in prison (Lewisburg, West Virginia), and life in prison without parole (Oklahoma City, Oklahoma). The two mothers who pled guilty to homicides received much lighter sentences: 10 years in prison followed by 12 years' probation (St. Petersburg, Florida) and 20 years' probation (Harrisburg, Pennsylvania) (Prentice, 2001).

Gaining Evidence

Doctors face daunting dilemmas in the handling of possible MSBP cases. Their ability to analyze and find cures for sick children depends somewhat upon their relationship with the patients' parents. This relies on trust and the truth about the nonverbal child's illness given by the parents. "Clinical practice is based on an assumption of truthfulness and a shared interest in the welfare of the child. Doctors are loathe to believe that mothers lie" (Barber & Davis, 2002, pp. 16–17). In MSBP cases, however, the relationship depends upon deceit and fabrication of symptoms. Under these circumstances, the doctor cannot adequately treat the patient. If he or she fails to discern MSBP, the patient cannot be cured. The doctor sometimes prescribes painful tests and thereby abets the parental abuse of the child. The doctor may be in a "no-win" situation no matter which way he or she goes.

On the other hand, the doctor is required by law in most states to report instances of child abuse to the proper authorities. MSBP *is* child abuse. If the doctor misdiagnoses the parent's flagrant attempts to induce illness, the physician is breaking the law. If, however, he or she overreacts to the parent's exaggerated concern and mistakenly calls it MSBP or reaches that conclusion because a solution to a child's rare medical problem cannot be found, he or she is liable for a lawsuit or perhaps sanctions by peers:

> Should a physician be able to evade liability simply by arguing that the parent caused a misdiagnosis as a result of MSBP? The law's ability to fashion a bright line for liability in MSBP cases further weakens when continuous deception intersects with murky medical treatment. (Perlman, 1998, p. 271)

The two methods of certain discovery are through the silent testimony of hidden cameras or separating the child from the mother. These techniques have been employed when MSBP was suspected. One is covert video surveillance in the hospital (CVS); the other is the use of apnea monitors at home (Steelman, 2002). Controversy is attached to both techniques. In the case of apnea monitors installed in the home, there is a question of how they may simply be ineffective preventive tools (Goldenberg, 1999).

In a study of these difficult cases, English physician David Southall began to use hidden cameras to observe mothers and to prevent and diagnose their aberrant behavior. However, CVS invoked many questions concerning the legality of its use.

Covert video surveillance has been used in hospitals to make clear and timely diagnoses of MSBP, with a means of proof acceptable to the courts (Hall, Eubank, Meyyazhagen, Kenney, & Johnson, 2000; Prentice, 2001). In the study reported by Hall and his colleagues, it is noted that the form given to patients' families on admission to the hospital contained the statement "Closed circuit monitoring of patient care may be used for educational or clinical purposes," and a sign at the hospital's entrance similarly indicated that hidden cameras monitored the facilities. Hospital security personnel were trained to monitor the cameras and caretaker activities around the clock in cases in which MSBP was suspected. Of 41 such cases in 1993 to 1997, 23 were classified as MSBP, with CVS evidence definitive in 13 of these, supportive in 5, and not needed in 5 others. Using CVS, it was also possible to determine whether parents were inducers or fabricators of symptoms. In four suspected instances, CVS monitoring showed the parents to be innocent of causing harm to their child.

Gaining eyewitness evidence of the perpetrator's behavior is difficult, but the use of CVS can be an effective tool to detect it. Southall and his colleagues wrote of the child protection benefits of such surveillance (Southall, Plunkett, Banks, Fakov, & Semuels, 1997), and Yorker (1995) cites several cases in which this has been true. Hall et al. (2000) reported that CVS was only begun after a multidisciplinary team agreed that its use was necessary to protect a child.

In one case, for example, hospital officials decided to put a video camera in the room of a 21-month-old child who was suffering from repeated infections that seemed suspicious to them. What they observed was the child's mother, Tracie Fleck, using a syringe to inject some substance into her daughter's IV tube (Associated Press, 2005a). Although Fleck subsequently admitted tampering with the IV tube, she denied that she had injected the fecal matter found by laboratory analysis into the tube, claiming that she had only introduced baby formula, water, and a drug used to treat her daughter's infections. She was sentenced to 6 years in prison. Nevertheless, there are protests about violation of Fourth Amendment rights to privacy when CVS is used, so the evidence (video tape) may not be allowed to be introduced as such.

Some commentators have argued, however, that CVS is unethical because it may potentially cause harm to the child and that it is unnecessary as well since other circumstantial evidence is available (Flannery, 1998). It is unclear in what ways CVS may harm the child. On the other hand, it is also debatable whether CVS is a violation of the individual's Fourth Amendment rights to privacy since its use in a patient's hospital room is designed to alert nurses to a change in the patient's condition.

Perhaps the morality of covert surveillance should not be the focal question. Rather, how do we protect children who are in danger from the aberrant behavior of their caretakers? Whose rights should we protect—those of the parent or those of the children? Whose welfare is more paramount? Mochow (1997) claims that a delicate balance must be achieved between the civil rights of the parents, especially against false accusations; the protection of the child from abuse and even possible homicide; "and the state's legitimate interests in protecting its workers from unnecessary harassment and litigation, via the qualified immunity doctrine" (p. 184).

Today, electronic surveillance occurs in a wide variety of locations, from the local bank or supermarket to restrooms in facilities open to employees and/or the public. Some may view this as an intrusion on their right to privacy in how they choose which brand of a product to buy or how long they spend in a restroom, and perhaps even what they do while there. It has been suggested that the legal controversy in the case of monitoring children's hospital rooms might be avoided by obtaining a warrant to use CVS in specific situations (Flannery, 1999; Yorker, 1995) or, as was the practice in the Atlanta hospital reported by Hall et al. (2000), have the use of CVS stated on the admission form that is to be signed by the parent or caretaker.

Studies of legal decisions found that many judges were not knowledgeable about psychological conditions and did not often consider them in sentencing. Moreover, they were not comfortable with or especially clear on the handling of the principles in the *Daubert* guidelines in assessing expert testimony. Most judges were more comfortable dealing with cases on a pre-*Daubert* level (Dahir, et al., 2005).

To make matters even more difficult, it should be noted that some syndromes do not meet the *Daubert* standards. Those guidelines cannot be applied to MSBP at present: Has the experts' testimony been tested? The literature is discursive, repetitive, and also anecdotal. Have the studies been subjected to peer review? Even if they have, many have questioned the validity of the studies or the reviews. Has the potential rate of error been assessed? It has not been for MSBP. Have standards and controls been established and maintained (Haywood-Brown, 2003)?

There are those who have documented cases of child abuse that meet the criteria for Munchausen syndrome by proxy, and others who assert that there is no such disorder or that, if it exists, it is overused. Meadow has written that the term is rarely heard in courts of the United Kingdom today (2003). It is a condition recognized in the *DSM-IV* as a "factitious disorder by proxy" (*American Psychiatric Association*, 2000, p. 781), although professional societies other than the American Psychiatric Association are still studying this particular form of child abuse and the development of guidelines with which to codify it. Complicating the controversy even more have been the decisions in mid-July 2005 to suspend Southall's medical license for 3 years and to void Meadow's medical license permanently (Jones, 2005).

It is apparent that there *are* parents who, because of their mental disorders, overplay the role of concerned and caring parent. Whether they put the child at risk by smothering, putting poisonous substances in food or medication, or imagine and exaggerate symptoms, they are guilty of a form of child abuse. In a number of such instances, the child dies. In some cases, more than one child may succumb to the ministrations of a seemingly "exemplary" parent. Although the numbers of deaths, or even cases, may be relatively small when compared to other child homicides, there is a need for emergency room and other health-care personnel to be alert for possible Munchausen syndrome by proxy cases to prevent further damage to a child.

There are other areas in which MSBP occurs, especially in allegations of sexual abuse. These include conflicts over child custody in acrimonious divorce cases (Barker & Howell, 1994) and accusations of molestation in nursery school and child-care centers. Making unfounded accusations of sexual abuse to gain the upper hand in a divorce case is as damaging to the child as to the adult accused, not to mention dishonest.

Conclusion

Although much of this chapter has been devoted to Munchausen syndrome by proxy because of the many controversies surrounding this topic, the other syndromes discussed are also very important. Moreover, shaken baby syndrome and SIDS will be more in evidence as we present examples of cases in the chapters to come on infanticide and filicide. All three syndromes have been discussed at length in numerous law review and journal articles and frequently in the press because of the difficult legal issues, as well as the difficulties prosecutors may have in obtaining definitive evidence that the homicidal parent is suffering from one of them.

The other highly controversial issue in parental homicides is the role of postpartum depression and psychosis in these tragedies. This is the focus of our next chapter.

Postpartum Depression Disorders

7

According to an article published in 1999, more than 10,000 children had died in the previous decade at the hands of their parents or caretakers (Liang & Macfarlane, 1999). These tragedies were variously attributed to child abuse, of which deliberate child homicide would certainly be a segment. The focus here is on a subsection of that segment: homicides committed as a result of the mother's postpartum depression or postpartum psychosis.

Differentiating the Disorders

In speaking of postpartum depression, the primary problem is not a question of the mother developing (or not developing) a relationship with her infant as much as it is the depression that occurs, from "depression generally, including genetic factors, a previous tendency to depression, adverse events, disturbed relationships, lack of support and social isolation" (Brockington, 2004, p. 91). The mother's mood can obviously affect her relationships not only with the infant, but also with her other children and members of her family.

Despite their pain, not all postpartum depressed women see a psychiatrist, as has been noted by a number of professionals. "Several therapists say they see depression in a group they find surprising: take-charge, controlling women with a history of caretaking. They are good at masking their pain and have a hard time asking for help" (Burling, 2005a, p. F12). These are women who take care of themselves, but in the most severe cases are unable to control their emotions.

One such woman, Mary Jo Codey, an elementary school teacher, spoke in 1993 of her experience with the disorder a decade earlier. In mid-2005, wife of the acting governor of New Jersey, Codey led the state-sponsored campaign to increase people's awareness of postpartum depression feelings and treatment, appearing on television ads speaking in English and Spanish, and also in radio ads. In addition, the state's campaign has a Website and a 24-hour toll-free hot line (Scheier, 2005). In addition to reaching the women, their doctors should be alerted to the possibility of their patients' problems in this area.

Although 60 to 80% of new mothers experience "baby blues" in the first 2 weeks after delivery, 10 to 25% experience the more severe postpartum depression that may last up to a year or two, and an additional one to four women per thousand suffer from postpartum psychosis (Kelly, 2002). Those who have postpartum depression may have symptoms such as mild chest pains, feelings of despair and inadequacy, hallucinations, new fears or phobias, an inability to cope, loss of normal interests, bizarre thoughts, nightmares, and general difficulty in performing regular daily activities.

Women suffering from postpartum psychosis may lose touch with reality for extended periods of time and experience delusions, hallucinations, and rapid mood swings (Bienstock, 2003; Dobson & Sales, 2000; Kelly, 2002). Some of the psychotic women had auditory hallucinations that told them to kill their children so that the little ones would be safe with God. They might confess to their crime and even recognize that murder is wrong, "but were also likely to believe the homicide was justified, because of delusional thinking" (Lewis & Bunce, 2003, p. 467).

"The two factors most indicative of a woman's risk for future postpartum depressive disorders are whether she suffered previously from a postpartum depressive disorder, and whether she suffered a previous depression not related to pregnancy" (Kelly, 2002, p. 254). Her risk may be increased by the preceding factors. According to the American Psychiatric Association, "Once a woman has had a postpartum episode with psychotic features, the risk of recurrence with each subsequent delivery is between 30% and 50%" (2000, p. 423).

Swendsen and Mazure (2000) summarized the findings of six retrospective studies and two prospective case-control studies focused on the relationship between stressful life events and clinical diagnoses of depression. The timing of the stress assessments in some of these studies included pregnancy as well as the first few months following delivery of a baby. Among the key factors found related to postpartum depression were the mother's psychiatric history, the presence or absence of social support (including that of the husband), and whether the mother had coping strategies for dealing with stressors. Perhaps further investigation is needed to discover whether sufficient attention is paid to these factors by family members, doctors, and others to prevent the mother from becoming homicidal and possibly suicidal.

Another relevant study, at Michigan's Center for Forensic Psychiatry, focused on 55 filicidal mothers referred for evaluation from 1974 to 1996 (Lewis & Bunce, 2003). The evaluations were based on referrals by attorneys who raised the issues of competency and criminal responsibility. Determination of the presence of psychosis was based on whether the woman had experienced delusions, hallucinations, and disorganization of thinking and behavior at the time of the filicide (p. 352).

The 29 women in the psychotic group, as compared with the 26 in the nonpsychotic group, were found to be older, more likely to have been married, better educated, to have a history of psychiatric hospitalization or outpatient treatment, and to have reported prior homicidal ideation toward their children. The psychotic women were also more likely to have made suicide attempts, killed multiple victims, and voiced concerns about their children to family members or their psychiatrists less than 2 weeks before the homicide.

Case Examples

The media have reported many cases of child homicide reflecting postpartum depression or postpartum psychosis. Constance Fisher of Maine drowned her first three children in the bathtub in 1954. She was committed to Augusta (Maine) State Hospital, but was released 5 years later as recovered. In 1968, she drowned three more of her children, was found innocent as a result of mental illness, and was recommitted (*Houston Chronicle*, 2001).

Maria Isabella Amaya of Port Chester (New York) stabbed her four children to death and then attempted suicide, unsuccessfully. She was under psychiatric care at the time. Found competent to stand trial, Amaya entered a plea of not guilty by reason of mental defect. The plea was accepted, and she has been hospitalized or under supervised care since (*Houston Chronicle*, 2001; O'Malley, 2004).

At least one infanticidal mother "discovered" postpartum depression belatedly—that is, some 4 years after her conviction for murdering two infant daughters in 1986 and 1989. Paula Sims then tried to have her sentence set aside on the grounds that her counsel had not entered an insanity plea. The Appellate Court of Illinois, Fifth District, ruled in 2001 that her counsel had not been ineffective and upheld her life imprisonment (*People v. Sims*, 2001).

On the other hand, Dawn March, age 17 when she threw her 6-month-old daughter into the Housatonic River in 1989, was the first person in Connecticut to be acquitted of infanticide on the grounds of suffering from postpartum psychosis (Owens, 2005). "Despite hypnosis and years of psychiatric treatment, March has been unable to remember putting Shawna into the river. Doctors diagnosed her as having a single occurrence of major depressive disorder, along with a dissociative episode that led to her daughter's death" (p. 87). At the time of the infanticide, she had said that demonic voices told her to throw the child into the river. She was subsequently confined to a state psychiatric hospital for several years, then was released conditionally under state supervision and was released from that supervision in mid-2005.

The Andrea Yates Case

The most notable example in recent years is doubtless that of Andrea Yates, a Texas woman who killed her five children by drowning them in May 2001. In the 2 years prior to the murders, she had been hospitalized four times for depression, attempted suicide twice, and been on medications to control her depression, hallucinations, and other symptoms (Manchester, 2003; O'Malley, 2004). Actually, she had a lengthy family history of mental illness, mostly cases of depression; almost everyone in her family had been diagnosed with some form of depression (Liu, 2002). In the opinion of perinatal psychiatrist Deborah Sichel, however, it is likely that Andrea suffered from bipolar I disorder (manic-depressive), possibly with schizoaffective disorder, and she was given inappropriate medication, which aggravated her situation (O'Malley, 2004).

It should be noted that, in July 2005, the Federal Drug Administration warned that adults who were prescribed antidepressants

> should be closely monitored for warning signs of suicide, especially when they first start the pills or change a dose … . [T]here are concerns that antidepressants may cause agitation, anxiety, and hostility in a subset of patients who may be unusually prone to rare side effects. (Associated Press, 2005a)

How much awareness Andrea's psychiatrists may have had of these possible side effects is, of course, unknown. Consider her situation in the years of her marriage—particularly in the years just prior to the filicides (Denno, 2003; Liu, 2002; Michalopoulos, 2003; O'Malley, 2004):

Husband Rusty's (and her own) determination to have as large a family as possible (until they changed their minds when she became ill again after daughter Mary's birth)

Lived in a converted Greyhound bus with husband and the first four children; husband bought a new home after her second suicide attempt

Postpartum psychosis following birth of her first child (with later relapses)

Hallucinations, voices heard, at least two suicide attempts

Feeling that she was possessed by Satan and heard him speak to her
Sole caretaker of her children (husband allegedly never changed a diaper)
Home-schooled her children
Caretaker of her father, who suffered from Alzheimer's disease and other serious conditions until he died in March 2001 (2 months before she killed her children)*
Birth of fifth child despite doctor's advice not to have any more children after the fourth was born and her symptoms returned
Catatonic, sleepless, deeply depressed within a few weeks after the last birth

Earlier, Andrea and Rusty had come under the influence of an itinerant, definitely nontraditional, preacher, Michael Woroniecki, after Noah's birth; this had resulted in the home-schooling and her feelings of inadequacy and wrongdoing. Among other views that he espoused was one that encouraged couples to have as many children as possible. After the tragedy, Woroniecki claimed that Andrea had told him she hated Rusty and that she was intoxicated by the drugs that Rusty had obtained for her with sinister motives on his part (O'Malley, 2004, pp. 97–98). Woroniecki's perceptions and resulting "guidance" appear at minimum to have contributed to Andrea's depression and other problems.

Spinelli (2004) has considered the situation from a different perspective—that of prevention. She looked at possible precipitants of the tragedy overlooked in Yates' case (and others) but which might, if recognized, have prevented Yates' homicides. Some of these were mentioned in the personal history just presented; others may still be overlooked in this and similar cases:

Personal and family histories of psychiatric illness
Difficult childbearing history
Denial, lack of awareness, fear of stigma
Psychiatric treatment with (or without in Yates' case) family intervention
Inadequate psychoeducation
Inadequate medical education about postpartum disorders and poor medical management of them
Lack of formal *DSM-IV* diagnostic criteria for postpartum disorders (which are essential for appropriate defense representation under the law)

* As a result of a prenatal prevention study by Herz (1992), one of the specific recommendations to new parents was that the new mother *not* be a nurse to relatives or others in late pregnancy or in the months following delivery.

Yates' behavior on the day she killed her children was allegedly "composed" (Denno, 2003), which the prosecution used effectively in its case against her. She was clearly aware that she had done something wrong, since she called the police to report that she needed police help. She also called her husband to come home, but he had not arrived before the police officer to whom she calmly said, "I just killed my kids" (O'Malley, 2004, p. 4).

Testifying on behalf of Andrea Yates was Dr. Philip Resnick, who had studied child homicide for three decades (O'Malley, 2004). Dr. Park Dietz, a psychiatrist, stressed Andrea's statement to the police in his testimony as a prosecution witness. It should be noted, however, that Dietz supposedly had "no expertise in postpartum depression or psychosis" (Denno, 2003). Dietz also testified that Yates had gotten her idea of how to commit the homicides from a "Law and Order" program shown shortly before she killed her children. He later had to admit that there had been no such program. [It should be noted that, in February 2006, a story was published that included an area citizen's report to authorities that the program *L.A. Law* had presented such a story, but there was no way to prove that Yates had watched it (O'Hare, 2006).] This led the Court of Appeals (First District of Texas) to conclude that "his false testimony could have affected the judgment of the jury. We further conclude that Dr. Dietz's false testimony affected the substantial rights of appellant. Therefore, the trial court abused its discretion in denying appellant's motion for mistrial" (*Andrea Pia Yates, Appellant,* 2005, January 6).

The Court of Appeals reversed the trial court's judgment and remanded the case for further proceedings. In May 2005, "Harris County prosecutors asked the Texas Court of Criminal Appeals to reverse a lower court's decision to overturn the conviction of Andrea Yates for drowning her children in a bathtub in 2001" (Easton, 2005b). This objection to being reversed is not too surprising given that Harris County is regarded as one of the most punitive jurisdictions in the Western world (Denno, 2003). Yates' attorneys, of course, filed a response to the court in July 2005, saying that the jury's decision to overturn the conviction should stand (Associated Press, 2005b).

If one considers, however, Yates' view of herself as a "Satanic mother" who deserved to be punished (O'Malley, 2004), then her sanity at that time and at the time of trial needs to be questioned. One of her explanations for the homicides was that she was saving the children from Satan (Michalopoulos, 2003). Other testimony reflected her abnormal behavior (catatonic periods, hallucinations) in the last few days before the murders. All of these behaviors, in addition to those she exhibited over the previous several years, exemplify a case of postpartum psychosis. When she called the police immediately afterward, though, she did not mention Satan, that she was an evil person, or the need to save her children from some fate worse (than death) if they lived (Michalopoulos, 2003). This latter behavior seemed to point to sanity in the eyes of jurors.

Where was Rusty Yates while Andrea took care of the children and suffered her emotional ailments? He was at work as an engineer for NASA, earning money for the family's basic needs, but apparently neither contributing to the care of the large family he created nor considering the doctor's strong advice, after the fourth child was born, that he and Andrea forego having more children. He was, however, extremely concerned about her depressed states and about treatment she did (or did not) receive (O'Malley, 2004). Although, according to a news report, Rusty visits Andrea at the psychiatric prison where she is confined, he filed for divorce, in part, at least, so that he could rebuild his life. The divorce was finalized on March 17, 2005 (Easton, 2005a).

Capital murder charges had been filed against Andrea Yates, to which she pled not guilty by reason of insanity (NGRI). "Under Texas law, a defendant can be found not guilty by reason of insanity if it is determined that, because of a mental defect or disease, she did not know the difference between right and wrong at the time the crime was committed" (Michalopoulos, 2003, p. 384). That Andrea knew enough to call the police after the drownings convinced many that she did, indeed, know that she had done wrong, especially since she made no mention at the time of Satan's involvement or any other such pressures. Psychologists and psychiatrists were called to testify by the defense and the prosecution. As noted previously, apparently Dr. Dietz's testimony (for the prosecution) was the most convincing, even though part of it was later shown to be in error. That error resulted in a reversal of Yates' conviction. The Texas Court of Appeals upheld the reversal on November 9, 2005, which means that she will be afforded a new trial or, as the district attorney indicated, be allowed a plea bargain (CNN.com, 2005b). A retrial was scheduled for March 20, 2006, but was postponed until June 2006. Meanwhile, Rusty Yates remarried on March 18, 2006 (*ABC 7 News*, 2006).

Other Cases

Two other cases in Texas in 2003 also involved child homicide and mothers who claimed they were not guilty by reason of insanity, although postpartum depression/psychosis was not mentioned in their cases. They are mentioned here because their outcomes differed from that in the Yates case and demonstrate some of the difficulty in applying the Texas Penal Code's language, especially the words "know" and "wrong" (Whitley, 2005). There is also a conflict between the penal code and the Mental Health Code in Texas, for the latter includes references to postpartum psychosis as neurobiological in nature and treatable (Liu, 2002).

Deanna Laney, who bashed in the heads of her 8- and 6-year-old sons, but spared her 2-year-old son (claiming that God would have to finish the job), was found not guilty by reason of insanity. Whereas Yates said she knew that her acts would be seen as wrong by God and society as well as her husband, "Laney believed God commanded her actions and that they were not, therefore, wrong" (Morris, 2004). This is the key, under the Texas Penal Code, for the accused to be able to prevail with an insanity defense, as Laney did.

Four months later, Lisa Diaz drowned her 6- and 3-year-old daughters. Over a 17-month period immediately preceding the filicides, she had visited doctors 90 times, convinced that she had lupus, "mad cow" disease, tuberculosis, multiple sclerosis, internal worms, ringworm, and other diseases. She would even wash her hands 10 times an hour, do the family linens daily, and spray Lysol on everything her children touched because she thought her daughters had ringworm (Whitley, 2005). Her husband had wanted her to see a psychiatrist, and a physician also recommended this, but she never went. After her arrest, a Dallas psychologist interviewed her on videotape, capturing much of her mental state before antipsychotic medication took effect.

Unlike Yates, Diaz was acquitted, deemed not guilty by reason of insanity. Although Diaz had not had psychotherapy prior to the murders, six experts agreed that she was delusional and psychotic prior to them. She believed that people were watching her and that there were evil spirits in her home; she heard voices telling her that she and her daughters were going to experience a slow and painful death (Whitley, 2005).

Eerily similar to the Andrea Yates' case is that of Lashaun Harris in California (Marshall, 2005). Harris, a poor, 23-year-old mother of three, heard voices telling her to feed her children to the sharks, so she threw them into San Francisco Bay. Family members had been concerned about her mental instability, and she apparently wanted to get help, but had been refused admission to a mental health facility because she did not have health insurance. One relative thought she had been taking medication for her emotional problems, but she had apparently not taken it for several months (CNN.com, 2005a).

In yet another case that relates in a strange way to that of Andrea Yates, Helen Kirk strangled her 3-year-old son Justin in March 2005 because she claimed he was the devil. The "strange" element is, as she wrote in court papers, that in 2002, 3 years before her crime, her "husband accused her of being 'crazy' and likened her to Andrea Yates" (Eshbacher, 2005). Joseph Kirk confirmed this comparison (McGee, 2005). Helen had had psychotherapy in the years prior to the filicide. Whether she had been suffering from postpartum depression or psychosis could not be ascertained. However, given her husband's characterization of her, one must wonder if he could have arranged more support for her or more protection for their son.

In all of these cases, with Kirk's to a slightly lesser extent, the father ignored warnings about his wife's mental health and its effect on the safety of their children as a passive bystander or acted contrary to those warnings. Why were none of the fathers questioned more closely about their contribution to the ensuing tragedy?

What Can Be Done

When there is a past history of depression, as in the cases just described, there is now increasing movement toward prescribing antidepression medication in subsequent pregnancies and immediately after those babies are delivered (Burling, 2005a). The American College of Obstetricians and Gynecologists and the American Psychiatric Association endorse treatment with medication and psychotherapy. However, the Federal Drug Administration warning noted a few pages earlier should be observed by anyone prescribing such medication.

Early Diagnosis

Unless a woman's doctor is completely familiar with her past difficulties, he or she may not be aware that the patient is having a serious postpartum disorder. During her postpartum checkup a month or 6 weeks after delivery, if she responds to a simple "How are you doing?" with statements of fatigue or fear that she will not be able to care for her infant, the caregiver's usual answer to her may be that that is "normal" or "to be expected." Unfortunately, the caregiver may not pursue the issue further.

It might be more appropriate to give her the Edinburgh Postnatal Depression Scale, a 10-item, 3-minute screening instrument for such disorders (Cox, Holden, & Sagovsky, 1987; cf. ACOG, 2002, Spinelli, 2004). She is asked to underline the response to each item that most closely resembles how she has felt in the preceding week. In practice, Wisner and colleagues "found that a score greater than 10 on the EPDS was a strong and consistent indicator that women had postpartum depression—a finding similar to those from studies in Europe ... " (Wisner, Gracious, Piontek, Peindl, & Percl, 2003, p. 54).

Edinburgh Postnatal Depression Scale

1. I have been able to laugh and see the funny side of things.
   a. As much as I always could
   b. Not quite so much now

   c. Definitely not so much now
   d. Not at all
2. I have looked forward with enjoyment to things.
   a. As much as I ever did
   b. Rather less than I used to
   c. Definitely less than I used to
   d. Hardly at all
3. I have blamed myself unnecessarily when things went wrong.*
   a. Yes, most of the time
   b. Yes, some of the time
   c. Not very often
   d. No, never
4. I have been anxious or worried for no good reason.
   a. No, not at all
   b. Hardly ever
   c. Yes, sometimes
   d. Yes, very often
5. I have felt scared or panicky for no very good reason.*
   a. Yes, quite a lot
   b. Yes, sometimes
   c. No, not much
   d. No, not at all
6. Things have been getting on top of me.*
   a. Yes, most of the time I haven't been able to cope at all
   b. Yes, sometimes I haven't been coping as well as usual
   c. No, most of the time I have coped quite well
   d. No, I have been coping as well as ever
7. I have been so unhappy that I have had difficulty sleeping.*
   a. Yes, most of the time
   b. Yes, sometimes
   c. Not very often
   d. No, not at all
8. I have felt sad or miserable.*
   a. Yes, most of the time
   b. Yes, quite often
   c. Not very often
   d. No, not at all
9. I have been so unhappy that I have been crying.*
   a. Yes, most of the time
   b. Yes, quite often
   c. Only occasionally
   d. No, never

10. The thought of harming myself has occurred to me.*
    a. Yes, quite often
    b. Sometimes
    c. Hardly ever
    d. Never

Response categories are scored 0, 1, 2, and 3 according to increased severity of the symptoms. Items marked with an asterisk are reverse coded (i.e., 3, 2, 1, and 0). The total score is calculated by adding together the scores for each of the ten items.

Cox, Holden, and Sagovsky (1987) cautioned that the Scale identifies depressive illness only, and not anxiety neuroses, phobias, or other personality disorders; that it may be repeated after 2 weeks to verify the initial responses; and that the scale's score should not override clinical judgment. Its advantage, obviously, is that it can put the woman's doctor on alert, which is ultimately to her advantage.

Another instrument that may alert a clinician to a woman at risk for committing child homicide is the Maternal Filicide Risk Matrix, developed by McKee (2006). It can be completed at five different stages of the woman's life: prepregnancy; pregnancy; early post partum (to age 6 months); late post partum (6 months to 1 year); and postinfancy (age 1 year and older). The risk and protective factors affecting her are studied in three "domains": individual, family of origin, and situational.

McKee evaluates many areas as "risks" or potential stressors, as well as possible "protective" factors: age, level of education, family relationships, marital status, ability to attach emotionally, resources (or lack of them), experience with psychotherapy or social agencies, and so on. He also attempts to determine "risk intervention points" (RIPs)—what Spinelli has termed "missed opportunities" (2005)—that, if acted upon in a timely fashion, might prevent a homicide.

Although the Risk Matrix is based on McKee's work with homicidal mothers, an alert clinician could use it with a depressed patient, or one who is allegedly abusive to her children. Even being familiar with the instrument and the factors it considers would enhance a nurse's or social worker's alertness to a woman's potential for acting on her depressed feelings.

Indeed, concern about postpartum disorders and their possible tragic outcomes moved legislators in the Pennsylvania House in 2005 to pass the Prenatal and Postnatal Counseling Act requiring doctors or midwives to inform pregnant women about the symptoms of each of the levels of postpartum disorders and where counseling is available if they have these symptoms (Burling, 2005b; OLPA). At the federal level, in 2003, H. R. 846 was introduced by Rep. Bobby L. Rush (D-IL) and S. 450 was introduced by

Sen. Richard J. Durbin (D-IL). These bills were called the Melanie Blocker-Stokes Postpartum Depression Research and Care Act in memory of a Chicago woman who committed suicide as a result of postpartum psychosis. There was no further action on either bill in the 108th Congress (OLPA). In May 2005, Rep. Rush reintroduced the Blocker-Stokes Bill (H. R. 1940), citing the need for public awareness and appropriate treatment for this condition (Rush, 2005).

Legal Controversies

In the United States, several tests are used to determine legal insanity: "the M'Naghten test, the 'irresistible impulse' test, the 'product' or Durham test, the American Law Institute's Model Penal Code or the federal statutory definition test" (Kelly, 2002, p. 261). The M'Naghten test is considered by some to be an inappropriate standard to use today because of its passage in the Victorian era, when women's status was different from what it is now, and because of more modern knowledge about the human brain's functions than was then available (Quinlan, 2003/2004). The Model Penal Code, section 4.01(1) provides that

> A person is not responsible for her criminal conduct if, at the time of the conduct, as a result of mental disease or defect, she lacks substantial capacity to (1) appreciate the criminality of her conduct or (2) conform her conduct to the requirements of the law. (Kadish & Schulhofer, 1995, p. 954)

It should be noted, though, that some states have abolished the insanity defense altogether. Passage of an "American Infanticide Act," effective nationwide and somewhat similar to the law in Britain, is considered unlikely due to disparate views about postpartum disorders, as already noted, and the desire for retribution by some people against mothers who betray the popular conception of mother love (Gordan, 1998). As Meyer and Oberman (2001) have noted,

> In general, society views women as innate nurturers who are expected to remain joyful and happy during their pregnancy and throughout motherhood. Consequently, when new mothers … experience negative emotions they often suffer in silence, coping with the shame and guilt that often accompany such feelings. (p. 79)

"Due to the lack of nationwide uniformity, infanticidal mothers who assert postpartum psychosis in their defense experience vastly disparate results" (Kelly, 2002, p. 249). Expert witnesses, such as psychiatrists or psychologists in these cases, may testify at the woman's trial, but the admissibility (and acceptance) of their testimony is determined by the trier of fact—that is, the judge or jury (*Daubert,* 1993). The outcomes of a number of cases reflect the difficulty that the triers of fact may have in determining which testimony of two or more expert witnesses they should accept. Again, this was seen in the Yates and other cases cited here.

There is a need to recognize that pretrial publicity in the media may inform prospective jurors or reinforce their existing views regarding crime or people's behavior. Some of this influence may depend on the nature of the media to which the potential juror is usually exposed—neoconservative, liberal, or somewhere in between—or other potential sources of bias. As Kovera (2002) pointed out, warnings to prospective jurors to disregard abundant pretrial publicity about a case may simply increase their curiosity about it or may alter the standards by which they judge a defendant's behavior patterns that increases the availability of prejudicial information to prospective jurors.

When it comes to a jury trial involving a postpartum depression defense, Dobson and Sales (2000) asserted that while most lay people may be experienced with depression in others or themselves, they are unlikely to be familiar with the most severe forms of the disorder. This could then predispose them to "picture depressives as not psychotic, as able to tell right from wrong, and as able to control their impulses and actions to comport with the law—thereby precluding a successful claim of madness" (Finkel, Burke, & Chavez, 2000, p. 1120). This presumption may also be emphasized in media portrayals of child homicide cases.

If the woman fails to convince the triers of fact that postpartum depression or psychosis makes her "not guilty by reason of insanity," there is a question of how she should be punished. Should she be imprisoned or sent for psychiatric treatment? We have already indicated that in Britain, mothers who kill a child aged 1 year or younger are typically sent for psychiatric treatment, but that is not necessarily the policy in this country. Indeed, in most of the media-reported cases that we have been able to follow to sentencing, the woman has been sentenced to prison and psychiatric treatment is rarely mentioned (see appendix A and appendix B).

Unfortunately, the most recent editions of the American Psychiatric Association's *Diagnostic and Statistical Manual of Mental Disorders* (1994; 2000) still do not define postpartum depression or postpartum psychosis as a specific mental disease; this does not help the defendant. On the other hand, feminists are concerned about the ramifications of using postpartum psychosis as a defense or as a mitigating factor. It might promote sexism as well as "detract attention from other real events in women's lives and further the notion that women should not be accorded full responsibility for their actions" (Lentz, 1989, p. 543).

Spinelli (2004) deplores this state of affairs as promoting "disparate treatment" under the law and clearly ignoring the fact that a homicidal mother with either condition needs psychiatric treatment rather than a long prison sentence or the death penalty. Extrapolating from Supreme Court and other appeals court decisions, Bard (2005) has asserted that such treatment is part of the medical care for which the state is responsible under the Eighth Amendment. Unfortunately, psychiatric hospitals have been closed down in appreciable numbers, and prisons have few resources for psychotherapy (Bard, 2005).

On the other hand, there *are* cases in which a postpartum disorder is not at the root of the infanticide or filicide. Although these perpetrators may also need psychiatric treatment, it may be added on to whatever prison sentence they are given—if they are fortunate enough to have a judge attuned to their need for it.

8 Infanticide and Filicide by Parents and Their Surrogates

What may have been acceptable in one location or at one period in history, modern or otherwise, in terms of caring for children or disciplining them, may not be socially acceptable or legally permissible in another place or at another time. Whipping children or socking them with a fist, considered by some to be almost a parental "prerogative," is now perceived as child abuse. Not taking a child for medical care or starving a child is neglect and is regarded as a criminal offense.

This was not always the case. A child who was beaten and woefully neglected in New York in the 1870s was removed from the abusive family only because, according to legend, the founder of the Society for the Prevention of Cruelty to Animals intervened on her behalf "and persuaded the courts to accept the case because she was a member of the animal kingdom" (Gelles, 1995, p. 10). The legend is just that, but it served to demonstrate the need for child protective services and ultimately led to the founding of the Society for the Prevention of Cruelty to Children in December 1874 (Gelles, 1997). This is an interesting commentary on people's priorities—one that has not changed for some people in more than a century.

What begins as child abuse—whether by malnutrition, shaking, beating, or other means—too often becomes infanticide or filicide, whether committed by the child's parent or by a parent surrogate such as a live-in partner, nanny, or someone else allegedly caring for the child. When the killer of an infant is the mother, the cause of her action is often attributed to postpartum depression by her attorney and may well be, as we showed earlier. There are other motives as well, whether the killer is the mother, father, or someone else. Another cause of infanticide and filicide—Munchausen syndrome by proxy—has also been discussed. In this chapter, we examine some of the other motives for child abuse that ends as child homicide.

According to National Vital Statistics Reports, thousands of children through the age of 14 years are victims of homicide every year (Anderson & Smith, 2005; Hoyert, Kung, & Smith, 2005). These data typically do not include information on who killed these children or the method of assault, but do provide a source of concern.

Motives

There have been some suggestions as to the psychological characteristics of the perpetrators of child abuse, but these are only suggestions. More research is needed to confirm or to clarify more details. To review such factors, mentioned earlier, the perpetrators

- May have been abused as children
- May have some psychiatric disorder, such as depression
- May suffer from low self-esteem, making them unable to endure the stress of caring for an infant, especially if the baby is colicky or chronically ill
- May lack information about child-rearing and parental expectations and responsibilities

Substance abuse, such as alcohol or drugs, may be a contributing factor. Domestic abuse may also be a factor in some of the mistreatment of small children (D'Amico, 2001).

What is the situation, for example, when a young mother (age 20) kills her 9-week-old baby? Renee Beth Smith's husband, serving with the U.S. Navy, left 1 day after their daughter's birth to take a 14-week course in Texas, leaving mother and baby in Hawaii alone (Matsuoka, 1997). Did the young woman smother the baby deliberately in anger at the Navy for ordering her husband away and at her husband for obeying those orders (displaced aggression)? Was she under undue stress at trying to deal with the care of the infant alone and therefore guilty of killing without malice? Was she suffering from postpartum depression? If found guilty of murder, she was liable for life imprisonment without parole (Accused baby killer, 1998). (She did, in fact, plead guilty to murder to escape incarceration "without possibilities," a reference to minimum sentences [Hall, 1999].)

Gartner (1991), using data from the World Health Organization, found that

> Infants living in nations with a high proportion of teen births face significantly higher risks of homicide, as predicted … . Nations with higher rates of illegitimate births, teen births, and divorce have higher child homicide rates. For both age groups [younger than 1 year, 1 to 4 years], the family characteristic most strongly associated with homicide is teen births (p. 236).

In a review of studies from industrialized nations published in English-language, peer-reviewed journals since 1980, Friedman, Horwitz, and Resnick (2005) found, however, that "There were virtually no distinguishing features to suggest which young, poor, and undereducated women with poor prenatal care were at risk for neonaticide" (p. 1582). Nor did the studies include "calculations of relative risks for filicide in women with specific disorders or maternal characteristics associated with filicide" (p. 1583).

What Kind of Parent … ?

Before looking at the defenses raised in the Smith case and others, we should examine the motives of those who murder children, usually their own. Wilczynski (1997a), in her book *Child Homicide*, listed ten categories of motives, some of which we have already touched on:

1. Retaliating killings (those in which one parent murders the children to get back at the other parent, usually an ex-spouse at the time)
2. Jealousy of or rejection by the victim (usually the father commits the homicide)
3. Unwanted child (the most common basis of neonaticide)
4. Discipline (overzealous corporal punishment of the child for crying or disobedience)
5. Altruistic
    a. Primary (usually "mercy killing" of very ill/retarded child)
    b. Secondary (possible postpartum depression, lack of support in parenting)
6. Psychotic parent (delusions about child)
7. Munchausen syndrome by proxy (direct physical actions of parent that lead to invasive medical investigations of child)
8. Secondary to sexual or ritual abuse
9. No intent to kill or injure (neglect in the absence of criminal intent)
10. Not known

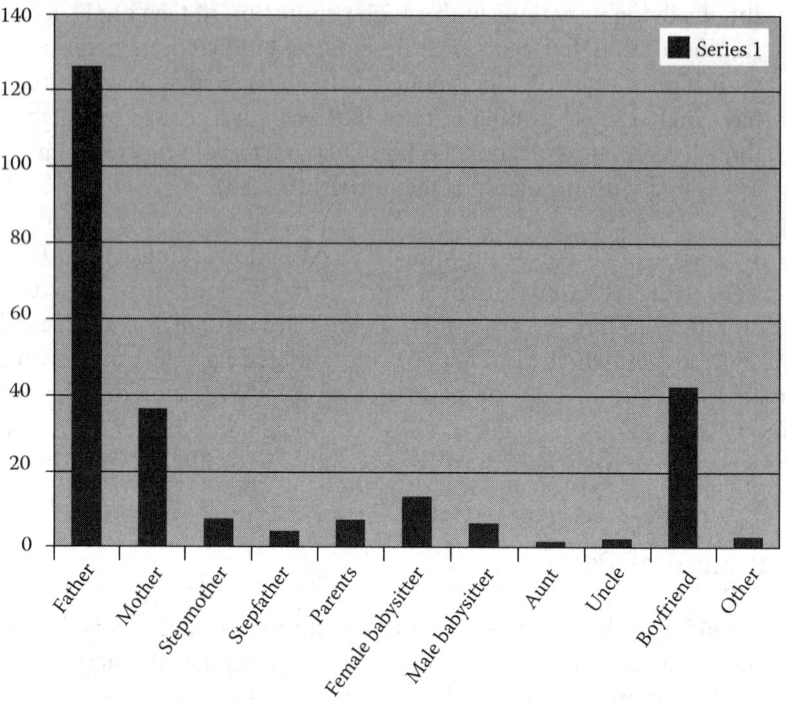

Figure 8.1 Who commits infanticide?

The motive most critical to our study of neonaticide, of course, is the "unwanted child" category. Figure 8.1 shows the alleged perpetrators of neonaticide according to their relationship to the child. When it comes to infanticide and filicide, discipline is a cause associated more with fathers, stepfathers, or other males, than with mothers. Secondary altruistic infanticides are at the root of many of the defenses to be discussed in the next section. Retaliation filicides are most often seen in cases of very hostile divorces in which the more bitter parent, frequently the father, will kill the children rather than let the other parent have custody of them, or to avoid paying child support. Wilczynski (1997a) does not include the child homicides involving cultural pressures discussed elsewhere in this work, such as killing one twin from a set or killing a female child in China or India. She does, however, hypothesize different meanings of child homicide by gender of the assailant:

> For men, filicide is more likely to be an expression of instrumental concerns and their desire to exert power and control within their family. For women, on the other hand, filicide reflects their simultaneous position of power and powerlessness, and expressive concerns are more likely to dominate. (p. 65)

She sees infanticide and filicide, therefore, as an extreme enactment of traditional gender roles.

In 1995, the U.S. Advisory Board on Child Abuse and Neglect presented its report to Congress: "A Nation's Shame: Fatal Child Abuse and Neglect in the United States." Like Wilczynski (1997a), it distinguished between the parents by gender

> Enraged or extremely stressed fathers and other male caretakers are the perpetrators in most abuse fatalities, although most parenting and child abuse prevention programs target women. (Women are most often held responsible for child deaths from bathtub drowning, fires started by unsupervised children, dehydration and starvation.) (Cavaliere, 1995, p. 34)

Women who kill their children, according to d'Orban (1979), may be found in six categories:

1. The battering mother: sudden impulsive killing; explosive temper; or because of a stimulus arising in the child
2. Mentally ill mothers: perpetrators have a diagnosis of psychosis or major depression
3. Neonaticidal mothers: kill the infant within 24 hours of birth
4. Retaliating women: aggression against the child was displaced from the spouse
5. Mothers of unwanted children: killed by omission or commission
6. Mercy killers: cases of true suffering to the victim and no gain for the mother

In the McKee and Shea study (1998) mentioned in Chapter 3, the authors attempted to define characteristics common to women who murder their children. They found several characteristics that appeared to span not only national borders among the English-speaking subjects, but also many decades. The pattern suggested includes these factors: "nonaddicted, acting alone and without weapons, kills only one of her children, likely of preschool age" (p. 686). McKee and Shea pointed out that the rate of mental illness in their subjects and those of d'Orban (1979) and Bourget and Bradford (1990) far exceeds that in cases in which the insanity defense has been used.

An example illustrative of the preceding description is that of Barbara Avery, who was sentenced to 20 to 30 years for the murder of her 38-day-old infant, whom she dropped down the garbage chute. Unable to find a babysitter, she disposed of the infant and then reported that the baby had been kidnapped. Upon being interrogated by the police, she finally confessed. The only defense witness at her trial was the psychiatrist who testified that she was of marginal intelligence with a mild mental deficiency. He also noted that she had a personality disorder, though it was not a major psychosis (*People v. Avery*, 1980).

In a study of 42 women imprisoned for murdering a child, Crimmins, Langley, Brownstein, and Spunt (1997) found that many of them had experienced inadequate mothering, lack of protection as children, years of frustration, and the use of violence as a means of "settling" disputes. They had such poor self-esteem and lack of a sense of self that they were unable to form emotional attachments to *their* children. Ostracized within the prison system, they expressed a need for some program to help them deal with the loss of their children, as well as programs related to domestic violence and to parenting. (It is interesting to note that a support group for women convicted of infanticide was set up at the Bedford Hills women's prison in New York State in the mid-1980s and has continued [France, 1997].) McQuaide and Ehrenreich (1998) also asserted the need for more psychological support systems in women's prisons, with awareness of ethnic differences built in, in part to assist women in developing more positive relationships with their children.

Seven of nine women imprisoned for fatally abusing their children similarly had suffered physical or emotional abuse in *their* childhoods (Korbin, 1986). Like the men to be described next, the women in this sample suffered from additional problems, including neglect as children, poverty, spousal abuse, lack of effective support networks, and other risk factors.

What is wrong with the men who commit infanticide or filicide? Although men have been found to be the principal abusers of young children, as we will discuss later, there has been very little attention paid to their role in books on the subject of child homicide.

In one small study ($N = 12$), it was found that "Most of the filicidal men grew up with multiple developmental stressors: exposure to violence, parental abuse, separation from parents, parental death … . As adults, most lived in poverty and isolation from social supports" (Campion, Cravens, & Covan, 1988, p. 1143). Most of them also had neurological or psychological problems that increased their vulnerability to these experiences; in addition, substance abuse contributed to impulsive behavior in at least half of the sample.

Marleau, Poulin, Webanck, Roy, and Laporte (1999) similarly found that the majority of their subjects (eight of ten) had personality disorders that, when combined with situational factors such as financial or domestic stress, contributed to committing the filicide for which the subjects were hospitalized in Montreal in the period from 1982 to 1994. Four of the subjects were psychotic at the time of the filicide; four others were under the influence of psychoactive substances at the time; and six of them had tried to commit suicide following the filicide. None of the subjects had been in therapy prior to the murder. Several of the cases involved an extended suicide plan ("in which a person develops a suicide plan but cannot leave 1 or more significant persons behind" (Marleau et al., 1999, p. 59) or was seen as altruistic homicide in which the person was killed for the victim's own good (in the eyes of the perpetrator). Only one case was seen as motivated by revenge against a separated spouse, although a second case resulted in accidental filicide when the real target was the murderer's spouse.

What becomes apparent from these and other studies is that the homicidal father tends to be poorly educated (i.e., not a high school graduate), unemployed and receiving welfare assistance or in a low-paying job, relatively isolated from social supports, and psychologically disturbed. It has been suggested that if a parent is evaluated and there is any possibility of suicidal or homicidal ideation, the evaluator ask questions about the parent's children—parent–child relationship, children's caretaker, parental responsibility—in an effort to pick up any possible threats to the children's well-being (Marleau et al., 1999; cf. Guterman & Lee, 2005).

It should be noted that stepparents have different motives and methods for infanticide than do genetic parents (Daly & Wilson, 1994, 2001; Hofferth & Anderson, 2003; Weekes-Shackelford & Shackelford, 2004). In this era of increasing divorces with subsequent remarriage or cohabitation with a new partner, the number of children living with a stepparent or someone in that role has increased markedly. Schnitzer and Ewigman (2005) found in their study that children living in such households were nearly 50 times as likely to die from injuries resulting from abuse than children living with both of their biological parents. In some cases, the new family is enlarged by the birth of children to the new couple, so there are biological *and* stepchildren living in the same household (aka *blended* families). Most often, the children are living with their mother and her new partner rather than with their father and his new partner. This explains, at least in part, why there are so many more child homicides committed by stepfathers than stepmothers.

As background, one might consider Hofferth and Anderson's study (2003) of more than 2,500 children living with both biological parents (married or cohabiting), or one biological parent and one stepparent (married or cohabiting), and with or without additional children born of the latter relationship. They found that the earlier in the child's life that the new relationship began, the better it was for the child. However, there also had to be consideration of whether the new parent had obligations from prior marriages or relationships that impinged on his ability to provide support to the nonbiological child, emotional as well as financial. As they point out, the role of the biological father in the child's life also affects the stepfather's role. From what is essentially a positive perspective in this study, we now turn to seriously negative cases that arise in part from poor reasons for selection of the new spouse.

Daly and Wilson have documented that "there is a large overrepresentation of stepchildren among child abuse victims, especially those violently slain, and the evidence to date suggests that step relationship *per se* is the relevant risk factor, rather than some correlate thereof" (2001, p. 288). Their earlier studies in the United States, Canada, and Britain (1988, 1994) found not only substantial differences in the ratio of young children murdered by a stepparent to those murdered by a genetic parent, but also differences in the kind of lethal abuse perpetrated. Stepfathers were more likely to beat a child than to shoot or asphyxiate one. (They did not study stepmothers because young children rarely reside with them, as already noted.) They found that young children were 70 to 100 times more at risk of death at the hands of stepparents than those of genetic parents.

Other Motives

Infanticide may also reflect maternal inadequacy rather than a postpartum disorder. That is, the mother (usually) is simply overwhelmed by the mechanics and responsibility of infant and child care and sees doing away with the infant as her only solution. That may have been the case of the young Navy wife in Hawaii, as well as a number of other cases we have seen reported.

The mother may be depressed for some other reason, or be otherwise mentally ill. That is, her act has no criminal intent *per se*, but reflects her psychological state. Too often, her condition is minimized or shrugged off, with tragic results. This may have been the situation with Susan Smith's drowning of her two young sons. As Gottlieb, a psychologist, observed (1996), if a woman with children is diagnosed as having a major affective ailment such as depression, then an investigation into the well-being and safety of her children is justified. If she is suicidal, there is a real risk that she might commit filicide so that her children will not be left alone and uncared for when she dies.

A study of neonaticidal women adjudged not guilty by reason of insanity (NGRI) by Holden, Burland, and Lemmen (1996) supports this conclusion. Furthermore, Holden and colleagues found that the crimes of these women did not appear "to have been committed because the child was unwanted, by accident in the course of a beating, or as a means of revenge toward a spouse" (p. 33). Lack of appropriate diagnosis is a critical factor here.

There is often an attempt to claim that the woman who commits neonaticide or other child homicide was emotionally disturbed to some degree at the time. In the Wernick case (1996) mentioned earlier, for example, the defense asserted that she had suffered from a brief reactive psychosis. The prosecution's forensic psychologist, on the other hand, did extensive psychological evaluation and found Wernick to be a very self-centered and manipulative young woman, who was highly resilient, with impressive ego strength and an unusual capacity to face ordeals (Kirwin, 1997). As Kirwin testified at the original trial, Wernick did not meet the criteria for a brief reactive psychosis as defined in the *DSM-III-R* (American Psychiatric Association, 1987), which included rapid emotional shifts, inarticulate speech, and overwhelming confusion. (Note: A battle of the experts, as occurred here, is not uncommon when there is a psychiatric defense.)

Other motives for killing a baby or a child include the parent's belief at one extreme that the child will suffer more by continuing to live than by dying and, at another extreme, a mercenary aim. That is, in the first case, the child may have a severe, possibly terminal illness and the parent sees himself or herself doing a "mercy killing" to spare the child continued pain (DePalma, 1997; Rue, 1985). This may be accomplished by giving an overdose of prescribed medicine, suffocation, carbon monoxide poisoning, or some other method. So-called mercy killings are also done by parents under severe wartime conditions when infants and young children might otherwise be tortured by the enemy. Two instances of this motive would be at Masada in the first century and in Bosnia in the late 20th century (Nadeau, 1997).

The mercenary aim would involve collecting insurance taken out on the child's life. This was apparently the motive of Susan and Billy G. Mitchell, mentioned in chapter 3 (Bridis, 1997), and Ellen Baker Boehm, also mentioned earlier (Costen, 1995). Yet a third case involved a woman, Dina Abdelhaq, who insured her children's lives, killed them, and attempted to use the insurance funds to pay off her gambling debts (Chase, 1999; Simpson, 1999). She was convicted on federal insurance fraud charges after state prosecutors determined that murder would be difficult to prove.

There are also cases in which the deaths of the children are attributed to the mother's drug abuse, as in the Charlene Wise case in Philadelphia in 1997. Wise had punished her 5-year-old daughter by putting her in the basement for several weeks and providing minimal food and water, until the malnourished child died. (She had punished her 8-year-old son in the same way, but to a lesser extent, and he survived.) Wise blamed her actions on her use of cocaine and other substances. As an interesting (and depressing) side note, the city's Department of Human Services had closed its file on the family 2 months before the little girl's death (Loyd, 1999).

Faith Healing

A particularly difficult type of case to prosecute involves neglect of a child's medical needs by parents who are members of a religious sect (or a cult) that prohibits medical intervention. These tragedies are more passive in nature and, indeed, are not aggressive maltreatment in the eyes of the perpetrators' church, although they may be considered so in the eyes of the law in some states (Hughes, 1990; *Long v. Texas*, 1979). The difficulty arises because of the Constitution's separation of church and state and the alleged infringement on the parents' religious freedom of choice if the court forces them to obtain medical care for their child. One interpretation of *Prince v. Comm. of Mass.* (1944) is that parents may not force their religious beliefs on their children to the detriment of the children's welfare.

On the other hand, the courts "balance the parents' fundamental freedom of religion and rights of privacy protected by the Constitution against the state's compelling interest in the preservation of the lives of its citizens" (Damme, 1978, p. 21). Some states, however, apparently exempt faith-healing parents from manslaughter or murder charges (Michaud, 2001; Van Biema, 1998).

In a study of the Faith Assembly, founded in 1963, Hughes (1990) reported investigation by and findings of the Indiana State Board of Health with regard to an unusually high rate of perinatal and maternal mortality within the group. Hobart E. Freeman, the founder and leader of the group, believed and preached that demons lived in medical drugs, that three quarters of physical illnesses had psychosomatic origins, that medicines failed to heal, and that hospitals failed to cure illness. On the other hand, if a child died even though the parents had not consulted doctors, Freeman said that the reason was that their faith was not strong enough for the child to be healed. The state began to prosecute members of the group for causing their children's deaths in 1984.

Members of the First Church of Christ Scientist ("Christian Scientists") prefer spiritual healing to medical attention, as do members of the Followers of Christ church and similar sects. Children, who cannot determine their own therapeutic needs, are often allowed to die rather than have life-saving medication or surgery. Neighbors or extended family members may report cases of such apparent parental neglect to local welfare or police authorities in hopes of preventing a death, but whether the child is then treated depends on state law. In a Minnesota case, for example, an 11-year-old boy, son of Christian Scientists, was treated by spiritual healing methods, but died of a complication of diabetes mellitus that was treatable by conventional medicine. The state indicted the mother and stepfather on charges of child neglect and second-degree manslaughter, but the indictments were ruled to be in violation of constitutional guarantees and had to be dismissed (*State v. McKown*, 1991).

In another case, Lorie and Dennis Nixon were tried on charges of involuntary manslaughter in the death of their daughter, Shannon. The

16-year-old died of a heart attack as a result of her untreated diabetes. The Nixons, members of the Faith Tabernacle Church (a faith-healing denomination), had also lost a son, aged 7, to an untreated inner-ear infection some years earlier. They had eight surviving children when Shannon died in 1996, and Mrs. Nixon was pregnant with her 11th child when the new case went to trial the following year (Combs, 1997). In June 1997, the Nixons were convicted of involuntary manslaughter and child endangerment. They were sentenced to $2^1/_2$ to 5 years in state prison (*News in Brief*, 1997).

The Nixons appealed to the state supreme court, which upheld their conviction (*Comm. v. Nixon*, 1998). Ultimately, they appealed to the U.S. Supreme Court, which declined to hear the case or to have it retried at the state level (Anonymous, 2001; *Nixon v. PA*, 2001). The Nixons claimed that Shannon chose to follow her religious beliefs. The Pennsylvania Supreme Court had ruled that "although Shannon, as a mature minor, had a right to refuse medical treatment pursuant to her constitutional right to privacy, this right does not discharge her parents' duty to override her decision when her life is in immediate danger" (*Comm. v. Nixon*, 1998).

Asser and Swan (2000) examined child fatalities that occurred 1975 to 1995, mostly from the files of a nonprofit organization—CHILD (*C*hildren's *H*ealth Care *I*s a *L*egal *D*uty). The cases were classified according to their expected outcomes with preventive or remedial medical care. Diagnoses in 113 cases indicated that only 2 cases would not have benefited from treatment. Of 59 prenatal and perinatal deaths, all "but 1 of the newborns would have had a good to excellent expected outcome with medical care" (p. 8). The high proportions of fatalities resulted from lack of such care because of religious beliefs of the parents. As of 2000, such religious exemptions were *not* allowed in only five states (Massachusetts, Maryland, Nebraska, North Carolina, and Hawaii).

In addition to Christian Scientists and members of the Faith Tabernacle Church, other denominations allow only very limited bases for medical intervention, including Jehovah's Witnesses, the No-Name Fellowship, and the General Assembly and Church of the First Born (Michaud, 2001). Dewayne and Maleta Schmidt, members of the last-named group, lost their newborn, Rhianna Rose, in May 2005 from an infection usually treated with antibiotics, less than 2 days after her birth. Their church "advocates prayer and faith healing over medical intervention but does not require members to shun medical care" (Associated Press, 2005c).

The Schmidts said they would continue to abide by their beliefs should a similar situation arise again, but the judge in the case appointed a guardian to ensure that their other children received medical care. They were sentenced to 6-year sentences, but most of that was suspended to about 1 year each at a work release facility, with each of them serving two 6-month terms alternately so that one parent could be at home caring for their other children (Associated Press, 2005d).

As noted earlier, in *Prince v. Comm. of Mass.* (1944), the court said that although parents had autonomy and a right to free exercise of religion, the life of a child was above these rights. Stanfield then concluded:

> State legislatures should be pressured to closely examine and repeal their current exemption laws in order to protect the lives of the children who are dying. Children are dying because no necessary medical treatment is being provided on account of their parents' religion. (2000, p. 86)

At the other extreme, Vaillant (2000), a district attorney, wrote that he could never prosecute the parents in such cases. He believed that they had suffered enough in losing their child. The conflict remains unresolved in most states.

Cultural Differences

In some occurrences, the different cultural values of the defendants are threatened by events in their new environment. The consequent cognitive dissonance can lead to what appears to be irrational behavior, possibly involving suicide attempts, infanticide, or filicide. Kunst and Reed (1999), for example, presented the case of a Mexican-American woman who committed infanticide, but was found NGRI. According to these researchers, her cultural background apparently contributed to her emotional state.

As another example, Fumiko Kimura, a Japanese immigrant living in California, discovered that her husband had had an extramarital affair for 3 years. The shame of it for her and the potential of a social stigma for their young children led her to attempt *oya-ko shimju*, an "almost ceremonial crime of parent–child suicide" ritually committed in response to a man disgracing his family (Matsumoto, 1995, cf. Kim, 1997). Apparently mentally disturbed by her husband's behavior and responding in a traditional Japanese way to it, Kimura carried her infant daughter and 4-year-old son into the Pacific Ocean from the beach at Santa Monica. The children drowned despite the rescue efforts of two college students, although they managed to save Kimura.

In yet another instance, Khoua Her, a Hmong refugee living in Minnesota, strangled her six children, possibly as the result of mental illness (Lavilla, 1998). She had had her first child at age 13, after an arranged marriage, but apparently was reluctant to care for him. Her husband's mother took care of that baby and the five children born later. There had been many calls to the police for intervention in domestic violence incidents in the home between Her and her estranged husband, at which times he often said that she had threatened him with a gun. Elders in the Hmong community tried twice to help the couple through mid-1997, but were no longer counseling them in 1998. After staying elsewhere with her mother for a few months, Her returned to Minnesota, obtained a restraining order against her husband, and even rejected food for the children that his parents tried to bring to the home.

The Hmong community, traditionally an isolated group in Laos, typically tries to resolve marital conflicts through mediation led by the elders, rather than turning to the courts, but failed to do so in this case. At least some of the couple's difficulties, and perhaps especially Her's problems, are attributed by some to "the poverty, the cultural gap between parents and kids, the American pull to be an individual versus the Hmong orientation of putting the group first … " (Lavilla, 1998). The cultural gap is difficult, however, to use as a sole defense in filicide.

Paternal Homicide

As we have noted, neonaticide committed by fathers is very rare, but father figures are more often the guilty parties in infanticide or filicide in later childhood. "Fathers" include men who live with the mother of the children as her husband and the children's biological father, as stepfather, or as live-in lover or boyfriend. They may displace their anger or lack of patience with a crying child or suffer from a personality disorder (Scott, 1973). They may become homicidal because of intoxication or substance abuse (Campion et al., 1988). Resnick (1969) found that the method used by a parent to kill a child varies by gender: mothers tended to drown, gas, or strangle a child, while fathers stabbed, squeezed, struck, or banged the head of the child.

Palermo (2002) offered case examples that included shaken baby syndrome, battered child syndrome, head trauma, stabbing, or drowning. Some of the father figures involved were psychotic; others were unable to control their destructive emotions. In a study by Herman-Giddens and colleagues (1999), it was found that almost two thirds of child maltreatment fatalities were at the hands of the children's biological parents. They also found that most of the time (65.5%), the killer was male: father, stepfather, or mother's boyfriend. Other studies place the percentage even higher, as noted in Chapter 6. The data collected in our Westlaw research concerning perpetrators of filicide are shown in Table 8.1 and corroborate these other findings.

Such crimes are found in many cultures. For example, a small-scale study of paternal filicide in Fiji, a nonindustrialized society, suggests that many of the motives are similar to those in the West, as are the homicidal techniques (Adinkrah, 2003). Physical punishment is common as a disciplinary method in Fiji, as is wife abuse; both are probably more prevalent than is true in

Table 8.1 Filicide Perpetrators: 1980–2005 (N = 154)

Perpetrators	No. Cases	Percent Cases
Father	22	14
Mother	18	12
Stepfather	20	13
Boyfriend	63	41
Stepmother	3	2
Female babysitter	8	5
Male babysitter	5	3
Both parents	2	1
Girlfriend	5	3
Other	8	5

more developed societies. The murdering fathers were five Fiji Indians and one indigenous Fijian, all manual laborers. Collectively, they murdered 13 people in the period from 1982 to 1994. Many of the motives are similar to those in Western society: suspicion of wife's infidelity, rage at wife taken out on child, overzealous physical punishment, and inability to make an infant stop crying.

Death in these filicidal (and spousal, in two cases) cases was due to chopping or hacking (one family, $N = 5$), burning (one family, $N = 4$), strangulation, beating, starvation, and being thrown against a wall (each $N = 1$). Firearms are not available in Fiji, contrary to American experience, and mental illness was not evaluated in these cases, although one might hypothesize that it had a role in the two cases in which the wife and all children were murdered (Adinkrah, 2003). Although the sample is small, the cases are in accord "with previous literature in suggesting that couple violence and child maltreatment oftentimes coexist" (p. 566).

In Kuwait, a 36-year-old man forced his eight children to drink a poison-laced liquid, killing five of them, and then he drank the liquid. He survived, as did three of the children. Police were still investigating the motive for his filicides, although they appeared to be related to his wife walking out on the family (Agence France Presse, 2005). We have certainly seen this motive in the West, too.

In a report on "Family Homicide in Australia," the Australian Institute of Criminology found that there were an average of 25 child homicides each year in the country. Of these, biological mothers were responsible for 35% of the deaths; "stepfathers (or de factos) for 34 percent; and biological fathers for 29 percent" (Overington, 2005). As others have concluded as well, the mothers are more likely to be suffering from postpartum or other mental illness, while those in the father role have more often shaken or beaten the baby to death in a case of "discipline gone wrong."

Turning to the United States, we found different types of fathers who committed child homicide, although in most cases they shared a need to "control." In one case, Michael James Shukry, characterized as a "neat freak," had abundant "explanations" for the multiple injuries and ultimately the death of his girlfriend's 7-year-old son. Naturally, these were all "accidents" or the boy's fault, with 39 separate injuries found on him over time. Not long before the boy died, his aunt and a hospital social worker had contacted Child Protective Services in Sacramento (California) about possible child abuse, but the agency decided not to investigate. Shukry was convicted of child homicide and second-degree murder (Coronado, 2004).

Jerry Hobbs beat and stabbed his 8-year-old daughter and her 9-year-old friend because the daughter refused to come home with him after he had grounded her for taking $40 from her mother's purse (Ruethling, 2005; Wilgoren, 2005a). The mother had lifted the grounding. The youngster's friend was killed because she stood up for the daughter's refusal. Hobbs had been released from prison only a few weeks earlier after serving 2 years on an assault charge. His uncontrolled rage was evident in the 20 stab wounds on his daughter and 11 such wounds on her friend.

Marcus Wesson bred and dominated a large clan through incest. He was found guilty of murdering nine of his children in 2004. He also raped and molested seven of his minor daughters and nieces (Barbassa, 2005). He received the death penalty (Lopez, 2005).

In Wisconsin, William Bagneski was charged with murdering his 6-month-old son in November 1999 and his 8-month-old daughter in October 2001. Originally, the boy's death was attributed to SIDS (Kertscher, 2005). Charged and held in prison in 2004, Bagneski entered a plea bargain to first-degree reckless homicide at the opening of his trial in August 2005, but still could face up to 100 years in prison in lieu of the death penalty (Nelesen, 2005). He had been charged with child abuse against an older child in 1988 and had a young child with his second wife when indicted more recently.

Fathers who killed their children were more likely than mothers to kill their spouse as well as their children or to commit suicide after killing their spouse and children (Byard, Knight, James, & Gilbert, 1999). Some examples of such crimes, as well as those that follow, can be seen in appendix B. In some cases, both parents (or couples in these roles) are involved in the child homicide. Whether the female is equally at fault or "cooperates" out of fear of the male abusing or leaving her is often difficult to determine.

A particularly relevant study here is one by Brewster and colleagues from the U.S. Air Force and from Northern Illinois University (Brewster et al., 1998) in which the records of 32 infants, whose mean age at death was 4.92 months, were examined. The team reviewed five information sources (Air Force FAP Child/Spouse Abuse Incident Report, birth record of victim, medical record of victim, autopsy record of victim, and Air Force Office of Special Investigation's [OSI] Record of the Investigation [ROI], p. 94) and developed 58 variables concerning the victim, perpetrator, family, or incident.

The victims were 53% male and 37% female, 62% Caucasian and 38% African American; most were the first or only child; more than half were between the 36th and 39th percentiles in weight and length for their age; and 58% died of traumatic head injuries, while another 29% died of asphyxiation (Brewster et al., 1998, pp. 94–95). More than half of the babies had suffered abuse prior to the fatal incident. The mean, median, and modal times of day of the incident were all between 11 A.M. and 12:17 P.M.—approximately lunch time for the infant.

The perpetrator was most often the baby's father, mid-20s in age, more often in the Air Force than not (77%), and provoked in 58% of the incidents by the infant's crying (Brewster et al., 1998, p. 97). Unlike the perpetrators in many other studies, 97% of the parents in this study were married and living with spouse and child at the time of the infant's death. Several had been abused as children or had been seen clinically for spouse or child abuse. The fatal incident usually occurred "in the perpetrator's home (71%) when the perpetrator was left alone (86%) with the infant on the weekend (47%)" (p. 100).

The fact that the victim was the first and only child in most of these cases suggests that the parent–perpetrator knew too little about child development and so had unrealistic expectations regarding the infant's behavior, a circumstance noted in many infanticide cases. Brewster and colleagues mentioned, however, that the Air Force has a Family Advocacy First Time Parents Prevention Program (for which two of the families in the sample were eligible), a resource that probably should have its audience expanded. In many cases, the parent or other caretaker was reared in what would be considered today as an abusive home and so had no other model for handling the day-to-day problems of babies such as soiled diapers, crying, not "understanding" the word "no," and so on. This is doubtless true in many non-Air Force cases of fatal child abuse as well.

In September 2001, Juan Velasquez beat 20-month-old Liana Sandoval to death, tied her to an 18-pound block of cement, and held the weighted body on his lap while her mother, Virginia Venegas, drove to a canal in Phoenix. There, he sank the child's body in the water. Then, the couple called police and reported the child missing (Associated Press State and Local Newswire, 2004b). Velasquez was caught, tried, and, in October 2004, sentenced to death. Prosecutors also accused him of child abuse with Liana's 3-year-old sister. Venegas was tried and sentenced to 35 years to life (Kiefer, 2005).

On New Year's Day 2005, a young couple in Baltimore beat their 1-month-old infant to death and were charged with first-degree murder (Associated Press State and Local Newswire, 2005a). Two weeks later in Utah, Connie and Kevin Long, already under court-ordered supervision for alleged child endangerment, were arrested on child homicide and child abuse charges in the death of their 5-month-old son (Stewart, 2005). The couple had a history of drug abuse, were supposed to undergo daily drug testing and substance abuse counseling under a court order, and had already lost custody of their two older children because of their drug use. Each was given a sentence of 1 to 15 years.

An especially horrible case is that of two children deliberately placed in a bathroom with boiling water running, where they were scalded to death. On July 29, 2005, in Yonkers (New York), David Maldonado and his girlfriend, Luz Arroyo, placed his sons, David Jr., aged 20 months, and little David's half-brother, almost 3-year-old Elijaha Santana, in a bathtub filled with scalding water, where they were left for $2^1/_2$ hours. According to one report, "The temperature had gotten so hot that the porcelain of the sink and the tub and the toilet was over 120 degrees" (Solis, 2005). The alleged reason for placing them in the tub was that they were "sticky" from lollipops.

The older boy had apparently tried to save himself by standing on his toes (O'Connor, 2005). Their mother was intoxicated and asleep while the toddlers screamed and tried to escape the heat. She and the boys' father had been snorting heroin and smoking crack that evening (Bandler & Cohen, 2005). Maldonado was charged with two counts of second-degree manslaughter and Arroyo with two counts of criminally negligent homicide. At a hearing on September 6, 2005, Maldonado was charged with manslaughter, Arroyo with criminally negligent homicide, and both with endangering the welfare of a child (Bandler, 2005).

The county's Child Protective Services had a case file on the family, and a caseworker had visited them on June 1, 2005. The family was supposed to be visited every 2 weeks, but the caseworker had not seen them again and had not reported her inability to connect with them to her supervisor, as required. She was fired (Bandler, 2005).

Child Abuse

As we have seen, infanticide and filicide can result from child abuse, or Wilczynski's case of "discipline" (1997a), whether such abuse involves starvation, beatings, violent shaking, or neglect. Some of the cases that we documented in Appendix B, as well as many others that we did not track, resulted from a parent's frustration with the child's crying or other normal child behavior. Several of these have occurred even when a child is with a parent or with foster parents nominally under the supervision of social welfare agencies. Problems with that supervision will be discussed a bit later.

A number of common factors are related to child abuse, according to Gelles (1997). Among these are family factors, including the stresses that face a single parent rearing children alone; demographic factors, such as the age at which the mother first gave birth; economic factors that include poverty, occupation, or unemployment; stress, including too many children born too closely together, or the added burdens of handicapped or senile family members; social isolation; and the perpetrator's family history that may have featured spousal and child abuse. With respect to occupation, Gelles raises an interesting point: "Because blue-collar work requires following orders and deferring to authority, blue-collar workers tend to believe that their children should also follow orders and defer to authority" (1997, p. 61). Examined at another level, those who are employ*ers* may also expect others, including their children, to follow orders without question. If they were brought up this way (family history), the expectation is reinforced.

Educators, psychologists, physicians, and others have been required by state law since the mid-1960s to report suspected cases of child abuse to the police, and the social welfare agencies are then supposed to investigate the allegations and recommend whether or not the child should remain in the home. More than 1 million cases were substantiated in 1993, and additional cases were never reported (Gelles, 1997). Sometimes, the initial report is not made, for whatever reason the professional may give later. Too often, the welfare workers are given too many cases to assess, or they are too believing of what a parent tells them and simply check off another visit to the home. However, the reality is that the child *is* abused or neglected and they have not observed it. Many social workers and judges believe that the preservation of the family is more important than the alleged child abuse. The end result is too often the death of the child, with or without multiple fractures, brain damage, or malnutrition.

Legal Ramifications

Although the public is aghast at violence against very young children, cases of shaken baby syndrome (SBS) arouse mixed feelings. The realization that caretakers (parents or others) often face unending, difficult, exhausting, and frustrating duties strikes an empathetic chord: "That could be me!" This leads juries to reduce the guilt of the perpetrators (Colby, Sanders, & Wheeler, 2003). Moreover, shaking or suffocating a baby can be very difficult to prove. *Did* the baby suffer from an unfortunate accident? The result is that often the punishment meted out to the convicted is very light in view of the apparent circumstances (Phipps, 1999). The problem is further compounded by the difficulty of ascertaining the caretaker's motives in the abusive killing.

The best example of such attitudes is the notorious case of Louise Woodward, an *au pair* who was convicted of the murder of her charge, 8-month-old Matthew Eappen. The evidence indicated that the baby was shaken violently and also had a fracture at the base of the skull (suggesting impact). The trial judge ruled, however, that the murder conviction was a miscarriage of justice and reduced the conviction to involuntary manslaughter. Upon sentencing her to time served, he released her saying that there was no evidence of malice. Her behavior was characterized by confusion, inexperience, frustration, immaturity, and some anger, but not malice (in the legal sense), thus supporting a conviction for second-degree murder. "Frustrated by her inability to quiet the crying child, she was 'a little rough with him,' under circumstances where another, perhaps wiser, person would have sought to restrain the physical impulse" (*Commonwealth v. Woodward*, 1998, unpaged; cf. Phipps, 1999, p. 535).

An analysis of the many cases in the Westlaw database indicates this same attitude: convictions tend to be based on lesser counts and sentences vary in their punitive intensity. Because first-degree murder rests on proving premeditation, few prosecutors can obtain the necessary evidence to convince a jury. Courts, as we have shown, usually find that juvenile abuse is more reflective of uncontrolled anger or frustration. Prosecutors must establish the mental state or purpose at the moment of the offense. Terms that express these emotions include "intentionally, recklessly, negligently, knowingly, or purposefully," or "extreme indifference to human life" (Holmgren, 2001, p. 281). Without accompanying battering of the victim, shaken baby syndrome is difficult to determine and even more problematic in defining motive. The number of cases remanded or reversed by the appellate courts attests to this conundrum.

The Survivors

McKee and Shea (1998), in their study, mentioned the absence of research on sibling survivors of child homicide (in any of its forms). There is no question that the death of a sibling and subsequent incarceration of a parent for causing that death is traumatic for other children in the family. Are they placed in any kind of supportive relationship or left to flounder, perhaps to become mentally ill? Should they be placed in foster care? In some cases, they have been so placed, which can be yet another traumatic event.

Little attention, if any, has been given to other family members as well—parents of the homicidal parent, siblings of that parent. How do they deal with what the mother or father has done? Do they blame themselves for not foreseeing the tragedy, for not being alert to the individual's behaviors or feelings? Are *they* given any therapeutic support? It would seem that some kind of opportunity should be available for them to work out their interwoven feelings of anger, guilt, and depression. It may be that consideration of such therapeutic support should be included as one preventive measure of further child homicide—the subject of another chapter.

If These Are the Causes ...

It is readily apparent that the veracity of Wilczynski's list (1997a) of motives for child homicide can be demonstrated easily. What is less apparent is how to prevent motives from being acted upon, how to handle the perpetrators within the legal system, and how to support the survivors of these tragedies. Education about parenting and child development is one possible avenue for prevention, and certainly psychotherapy is an appropriate course to follow for the survivors. These matters will be dealt with in a later chapter. The interaction of child homicide and the legal system, the natural outcome of the crime, is the center of focus in the next chapter. As will be seen, it is not easy to balance the questionable state of mind of the perpetrator with what may be perceived as a gender-discriminatory legal system.

Neonaticide, Infanticide, Filicide, and the Law

9

When a parent commits infanticide or filicide, it is much easier to accuse him or her of murder (there is no denying that there was a living child) than it is to accuse the perpetrator of neonaticide, a crime that may not exist in a state's statutes or in the minds of legislators or jurists. However, what is murder? In many states, first-degree murder means that one person killed another willfully, deliberately, and with premeditation (Ford, 1996). In other states, there is a common-law definition of murder as "the killing of another with malice aforethought," as distinguished from manslaughter, which involves unlawful killing without malice (Ford, 1996, p. 531).

What we will deal with here is the interaction of neonaticide, infanticide, and filicide with the law. Such interaction raises many questions. What differences are there (or may there be) between those who commit neonaticide and those who abuse, neglect, or otherwise cause the death of a child older than 1 day? Is there a self-defense that is plausible? Does one charge fit all cases? In what ways should those who kill be punished if convicted of the crime? Some of these questions were explored briefly with reference to the Andrea Yates case, but will be discussed more fully here.

The Insanity Defense

In general, the insanity defense is based "on the belief that people who lack the ability to reason and exercise free choice should not be held criminally responsible for their conduct and that society is willing to excuse a person who is not culpable and did not make a meaningful choice" (Waldron, 1990, pp. 683–684). This does not mean that the act is condoned or seen as justified;

only that defendants may be excused because they did not know what they were doing and could not control their actions.

Although the ancient Romans recognized a state of *non compos mentis* or "no power of mind," it was not until 1843 that a statute was passed in England that acknowledged that sometimes a defendant really did not know what he or she was doing at the time of a crime. The M'Naghten rule stated that:

> at the time of the act, the accused was laboring under such defect of reason, from disease of the mind, as not to know the nature and quality of the act he was doing, or, if he did know it, that he did not know what he was doing was wrong. (Melton, Petrila, Poythress, & Slobogin, 1987, p. 115)

The concept of acting under an irresistible impulse was added in 1929. The M'Naghten rule was used as a defense in the United States as well until a new legal definition, the Durham rule, was enacted in 1954: "An accused is not criminally responsible if his unlawful act was the product of mental disease or mental defect." This was supplanted by the ALI/Brawner rule in the 1960s and 1972, which attempted to combine the earlier definitions, saying that a defendant is not responsible for his crime who " … as a result of mental disease or defect [Durham rule] lacked *substantial capacity* either to *appreciate* the criminality [wrongfulness—M'Naghten rule] of his conduct or to *conform his conduct* [irresistible impulse] to the requirements of the law."

Finally, in the United States, the Insanity Defense Reform Act of 1984 (IDRA of 1984) essentially returned to the M'Naghten rule by stating that "insanity may be used as a defense *only* if the defendant was unable to understand the nature and wrongfulness of his/her acts." (This would be true in federal cases, but not necessarily in those tried under state homicide statutes, which vary from state to state.) The American Psychiatric Association (1984) urged that the issue of mental capacity be retained as part of the insanity defense since those with severe mental defects could not *choose* to do wrong. However, the new law, which removed the volitional aspect of the earlier one, "placed the burden on the defendant to prove insanity by clear and convincing evidence rather than on the prosecution to disprove insanity" (Wrightsman, Nietzel, & Fortune, 1998, p. 310). The effect of having these different laws (and which law is in effect in which location) was seen in our earlier discussion of the Andrea Yates case. As Damme (1979) pointed out,

> What is unique in the insanity defence (*sic*) for infanticide is its radical departure from the normal criminal insanity defen[s]e—the McNaghten [*sic*] Rules of 1843 … the standards set

> by the McNaghten case could not have been met by any of the women acquitted of child-killing because of temporary insanity. (pp. 14–15)

It is difficult to believe that even a 14-year-old would not know that suffocating her newborn was wrong, *but* it could certainly be argued—and is argued in some cases—that she would be in such a state of panic and distress when delivering the baby that she could not *appreciate* the wrongfulness of what she was doing. This would be more difficult, but not impossible, to argue on behalf of a defendant who was already a mother. Although many of these cases appear to be similar on the surface, often unique circumstances outweigh rational thinking at the time of the baby's birth or death. Clearly, these should be considered in determining the charge as well as the sentence if the defendant is found guilty.

Postpartum Depression versus Postpartum Psychosis

Other defenses, for infanticide and filicide but not neonaticide, include postpartum depression and postpartum psychosis. Postpartum psychosis, as noted earlier, is a highly controversial topic and has sparked heated debate within the medical and legal communities. Women who have murdered their infants have used this defense, successfully in some cases.

There have been two different controversies about this presumption, however. Feminists criticized the notion of an exclusively female defense that will abet sexism. They further argue, therefore, that continued use of this defense would lessen opportunities that women have gained over the past few decades. Legal experts have been worried that attempts to write laws that would provide automatic treatment guidelines for women who kill their children under the influence of postpartum illness would provide ways for defense attorneys to use this as a means of exonerating murderers (whether they were mentally ill or not). Other attorneys have argued that present insanity or diminished capacity rules adequately protect sufferers of the condition (Schroeder, 1993). (These arguments preceded the IDRA of 1984, but still raise legitimate concerns.)

Crying for no reason when there *is* reason for smiles, feeling depressed, and behaving as if the world is entirely too much to cope with are all symptoms of postpartum depression, a condition that may arise anywhere from a few days postdelivery to a few months or even a year later. "The exact cause of postpartum psychiatric illness is not clear; however, some researchers believe it is a 'biopsychosocial' illness. This term implies that the illness is caused by the many bio-chemical, emotional, psychological, and social changes a woman experiences after childbirth" (Nelson, 1991, p. 5). "The widespread ignorance of postpartum disorders may be the reason why women suffering from postpartum disorders are not helped *before* an infanticide results. The lack of available medical attention for women suffering from postpartum disorders is a significant problem" (Reece, 1991, p. 748). (Such ignorance could and should be reduced by use of the Edinburgh scale and other tools introduced in an earlier chapter.)

In a Canadian study reported in 2005, the researchers compared postpartum depression in women in the provinces of Alberta and New Brunswick. They found that, even when services were available, half of their subjects did not use them. Many feared the shame and stigma they might have to face. In Alberta, every mother is screened for postpartum depression when she brings her baby in for immunizations; in New Brunswick, no such screening is done (Morris, 2005). They also found that the mothers suffering from postpartum depression wanted to be with mothers like themselves, in a support group as it were.

The condition is not listed separately in the *DSM-IV* or *DSM-IV-R* (American Psychiatric Association, 1994, 2000), as it has not been in any of the prior volumes of this series because of difficulties in developing an appropriate nosology; it is included under the heading of "Diagnostic Criteria for Psychotic Disorder Not Otherwise Specified" (298.9) (Nieland & Roger, 1997). It may be that conflicts within the mental health community as to what constitutes postpartum depression or even whether such a condition exists preclude any such inclusion.

A key point, however, is that those who support the existence of such a condition tend to agree that it does not occur until "a few days postdelivery." This would negate its use as a defense for neonaticide, although it has been used in cases of infanticide at the trial court level. Katkin (1992) asserted, "There are no appellate court decisions addressing the status of postpartum psychosis as a defense in infanticide cases" (p. 279), but that has changed in more recent years. On the other hand, if the symptoms interfere minimally with daily functioning and are not brought to a professional's attention, lack of treatment at a crucial moment could have tragic results (Schroeder, 1993).

Williamson (1993) provides the highlights of the differences of opinion, but appears to favor Dalton's (1989) four-facet characterization of the condition: "maternity blues," "postnatal exhaustion," "postnatal depression," and "puerperal psychosis." (As an interesting side note, Dalton suggests that some of the "maternity" or "baby blues" can be attributed to the lack of support the new mother has as a result of early discharge from the hospital after delivery. As managed care has become more common in the United States and hospitals discharge new mothers after 24 to 48 hours in most cases, the absence of professional support is more obvious. Even the visit of a well-baby nurse at home the next day after discharge may not assuage the anxieties and blues of a new mother, especially a first-time one. The presence of a doula, on the other hand, as noted in our comments on prevention in Chapter 11, might be more helpful.) "Maternity blues" occur just a few days to a few weeks after delivery and are highly transient; they can evoke sobs when the new mother is complimented on the name she chose for the infant, for example, or when the caller simply comments on "what a lovely day it is." The other conditions tend to have a later onset.

In a study comparing depression scores in postpartum and nonpostpartum subjects in Yorkshire, England, Nieland and Roger (1997) found that the postpartum group had higher "tension" and "low self-esteem" scores whether or not they scored high on the depression scale. They suggested, "Strategies aimed at bolstering or augmenting the self-esteem of women who are about to [give], or who have recently given birth, may therefore be effective in preventing or ameliorating post-partum symptoms" (p. 39). Whether there is a relationship between tension and self-esteem levels and hormonal imbalance was not part of the study.

On the other hand, postpartum psychosis, which occurs in about 1 to 4 women per 1,000 who give birth (Kaplan & Sadock, 1996; Morrison, 1995), is classified as a "brief psychotic disorder." Dalton (1989) called this "puerperal psychosis" and estimated its frequency at 1 in 500 women who have given birth—roughly the same proportion. Morrison says that it typically begins 4 weeks postdelivery and the patient exhibits "At least one of the following that is not a culturally sanctioned response: Delusions, Hallucinations, Speech that is markedly disorganized, behavior that is markedly disorganized or catatonic" (p. 237). (Kaplan and Sadock suggest that it begins 2 to 3 days postpartum [p. 94].) The patient exhibits the symptoms, which do *not* stem from a mood or schizophrenia-related disorder or from her general health or from intake of pharmacological substances, for 1 to 30 days and recovers completely. Whether this condition can serve to exculpate the new mother who has committed infanticide is arguable (and frequently argued). Rather than being a specific diagnosis, it is regarded as a mental illness that happens to occur after the birth of a child, although it does not fit the pattern of postpartum depression or postpartum psychosis.

The most severe (and rarest) form is psychosis, in which the woman does not know the difference between right and wrong; in many states, this must be present if the postpartum depression defense is to succeed (Lindsay, 1998b). Psychiatrist Doris Gunderson at the University of Colorado Health Sciences Center has described the patient as suddenly experiencing a marked drop in estrogen level, which can affect brain functioning, and possibly hearing voices that tell her to kill her child (Lindsay, 1998a, b).

British law recognizes that postpartum psychosis can contribute to infanticide and thus reduces the charge and the penalty accordingly. It specifically refers to the stresses of giving birth and to lactation as sources of postpartum psychosis if the child of this birth or breast-feeding is the victim. The *Infanticide Acts* of 1922 and 1938 reduced the charge from murder to manslaughter against the mother if she suffered from mental disturbance at the time (Kellet, 1992).

Dalton (1989), as noted earlier, asserted that the condition could arise immediately after delivery or within 2 weeks of the birth, and that the symptoms could last for 20 years in some cases (Williamson, 1993). One of the symptoms Dalton cited was "threats to injure" the baby, but not necessarily the fact of infanticide. These conflicts among psychiatrists make it small wonder that the courts are uncertain about the use of this defense. Indeed, the New South Wales Law Reform Commission (1997) stated:

> It seems now to be generally doubted that there is any medical basis for the notion of "lactational insanity." Inclusion of lactation as a ground of mental disturbance within the infanticide provisions appears to have been based primarily on a desire to provide a medical justification for extending infanticide beyond the first few weeks of birth. (p. 114)

There are other considerations here. In one type of situation, relevant to cases in which the mother harms or attempts to harm more than one child, Waldron (1990) suggested that a defense of postpartum psychosis can be appropriate the first time. However, if the woman becomes pregnant again, but fails to seek medical advice or to take any precaution against a recurrence of the illness, "she should be liable for reckless homicide for her omission in taking steps to avoid a substantial and unjustifiable risk of which she was aware" (p. 693).

Grossman (1990) pointed out that "women who suffer from postpartum psychosis once are at a significant risk of recurrence" (pp. 326–327). In one case that she cited, that of Sharon Comitz, medical records showed that she had a history of depression, particularly in association with the birth of her first child, but no one took precautions against her harming her next one (pp. 330–331; cf. Maier-Katkin, 1991). In Comitz's case, according to the appellate court record, she had suffered from postpartum depression following the birth of Nicole, was depressed during her pregnancy with Garrett (the 1-month-old she drowned), and had been ordered by her doctor to take medication for her depression after his birth (*Comm. of PA v. Sharon K. Comitz*, 1987). (After initially pleading not guilty to charges of first- and third-degree murder, she eventually pleaded guilty but mentally ill to the third-degree murder charge in 1985 and was sentenced to 8 to 20 years' imprisonment.)

Grossman (1990), Nelson (1991), and Waldron (1990) have each suggested, in one way or another, that not enough attention is paid to the mental health of women during pregnancy or in the postpartum period. Many young women need to learn about the work and responsibilities of motherhood as well as its joys, preferably before the baby arrives. Too often, postpartum depression or psychosis is handled as if it is a fairly common condition that is self-limiting and does not require special psychiatric or psychological care. Childbirth is a stressful, and usually joyful, life event, but additional emotional or social crises arising during or immediately after pregnancy may precipitate the development of postpartum illness. Often, experts note that there should be sociocommunal assistance for new mothers (Schroeder, 1993). There are not only medical treatments, but also support groups available for women with this condition, in addition to precautions that should be taken in the hospital and at home to avert harm to the infant. Grossman (1990) took the position that

> the psychiatric community must learn more about postpartum disorders. Only when the medical and the psychological communities accept the legitimacy of the postpartum illnesses should the legal community determine whether postpartum psychosis is deserving of a role as a legitimate criminal defense (p. 344).

Part of her argument is that no one seems to be concerned about the child victims of these women—their mothers—so something must be done to prevent further infanticides. Nelson (1991) added that the judiciary and the public should be educated about postpartum conditions and that research about causes and treatment of them should be encouraged.

Alternative Defenses

A related defense that has been applied to homicidal mothers is "extreme mental and emotional disorder" (EMED), which is included in the Model Penal Code (210.3(b) (American Law Institute, 1980). Typically, this is based on internal, usually long-standing stresses that lead the homicidal mother to some "reasonable excuse for the emotional disturbance" and subsequent homicide. This is a legal construct rather than a psychiatric or psychological one and is used in several states to reduce the charge or penalty. Ford (1996) asserted, "If provocation need not be external and immediate under the EMED doctrine, then the identification of such internal and long standing emotional stresses may be employed to invoke this partial defense for some mothers who kill their children" (p. 532). Such stresses might include dysfunctional or abusive families in the mother's childhood. For example, Susan Smith, who drowned her children, had experienced abandonment and sexual or emotional abuse repeatedly, ranging from her father's suicide when she was only 6 to sexual abuse by her stepfather and adultery by her husband. In addition, she had attempted suicide more than once (Zibart, 1996).

An alternative insanity defense could yield a verdict of "guilty but mentally ill" (GBMI), which generally requires that the defendant did commit the offense and was mentally ill at the time, but was not considered legally insane when the offense was committed (Shannon, 1981). These defendants are typically not perceived as threats to the community at large, as most murderers are. Thus, there have been two possible verdicts that can result from use of the insanity defense: "guilty but mentally ill" (GBMI) and "not guilty by reason of insanity" (NGRI).

In the first of these, the defendant is usually sent to a state or federal psychiatric hospital for treatment as well as incarceration. Should the individual recover from the mental illness, transfer to a regular prison would follow for the balance of the sentence. In the NGRI cases, many defendants simply walk out of the courtroom to freedom. Although both of these verdicts have been the outcome in what we might call "regular" murder cases, they can also be applied to neonaticide and infanticide cases, particularly the NGRI verdict. In both verdicts there is no way to deny that the mother killed her child, merely that she was not "responsible" when she did so.

What seems not to have been used adequately is a defense of "diminished capacity," which would avoid the claim of insanity in cases of neonaticide. It might also cause the charge to be reduced from murder to manslaughter. As Barton (1998) has suggested, moreover, "the idea of diminished capacity provides jurors and judges with a medium somewhere between guilt and innocence of the crime" (p. 618). Brusca (1990) has also expressed support for this defense when available evidence was insufficient to satisfy any of the standard insanity tests. It might even result in rehabilitative confinement rather than penal incarceration. Of all the defenses related to mental health (or illness), this would appear to be the one most closely fitting the rubric of therapeutic jurisprudence—that is, making a legal judgment with awareness of its mental health implications, problems of sentencing, and offender rehabilitation (Winick, 1997).

Munchausen syndrome by proxy (MSBP) is another defense that may be mounted. As noted earlier, a few notable cases thought to involve sudden infant death syndrome (SIDS) turned out to be MSBP cases. The parent has then attempted to offer some version of an insanity defense to what is an unusual and, in these cases, fatal form of child abuse. Although the parent, almost always a biological mother (Yorker, 1995), actively induces the child's symptoms or death by asphyxiation, injection of medications to cause a variety of symptoms, or introduction of poison or infectious agents into the child's system, the courts have apparently been unwilling to believe that the parent's acts can be lethal (Kinscherff & Famularo, 1991). The illness of the child is certainly premeditated because that is what meets the parent's needs; proving that in a homicide charge may be more difficult. Indeed, Brady (1994) has suggested that the varied factors in each MSBP case evoke so much complexity that the courts need to be creative in handling these matters.

In Defense of the Defendant

If postpartum depression, psychosis, or any similar defense is going to be undertaken on behalf of the homicidal mother, there are several items of information critical for the defense attorney to have. A mental health professional familiar with the nature of these conditions should be used to elicit information about the woman's personality before pregnancy and during it; should find out about her early history, family (and later) environment, personality traits, religious beliefs, and approach to problems; and should investigate her post-child-bearing behavior in detail (Hickman & LeVine, 1992).

A psychological or psychiatric examination that occurs weeks or months after the crime may or may not be productive in terms of understanding what was going on in the defendant's mind at the time of the crime. It can, however, bring to light disorganized or schizophrenic thinking, as well as other symptoms of mental illness that may have been a factor and that should be considered in court. A study of homicidal women in Finland, for example, found that all of those who had committed neonaticide had personality disorders and thus were judged not fully responsible for their acts (Putkonen, Collander, Honkasalo, & Lonnqvist, 1998).

The truth of the matter is that mothers who commit neonaticide face inconsistent charges across the country as well as inconsistent treatment if found guilty of a crime at any level. Rarely are they "sentenced" to psychiatric or psychological treatment, or to education about sex and pregnancy to prevent recurrences. In the case of Lisa, despite the fact that the court asked the commissioner of corrections to place her

> in the "least threatening" correctional facility available and where she could be provided with psychological therapy, Lisa spent almost 2 months in maximum security until space became available in a minimum security wing. Her therapy consisted of contact

> with a social worker for five minutes per week. (Atkins, Grimes, Joseph, & Liebman, 1999, p. 31)

So much for any realistic attempt to help a young woman who was anorexic, depressed, and suicidal, not to mention traumatized by her introduction to the criminal justice system.

There also appears to be inconsistent recognition of differences in the mother's mental state before and during the crime. This is said without implying that the crime is ever justified. However, the 15-year-old who has been in denial throughout the pregnancy and continues her denial by attempting initially to flush away the "thing" that has emerged from her body is far less a criminal than the 15- or 30-year-old who has told someone else of her pregnancy or who hides the newborn in a closet. *That* mother is aware of what is going on; although she, as much as the girl in the previous example, needs psychotherapeutic help, she may also need a custodial sentence to make it very clear to her that what she did was wrong. Each case needs to be evaluated in its context of the age, awareness of condition, and mental state of the accused. Stereotyped attribution of fault due to socioeconomic level, race, or educational level is inappropriate.

Mothers who commit infanticide *may* be suffering from postpartum depression or psychosis and merit similar rehabilitative sentencing, or they may be guilty of manslaughter or homicide in the more usual sense and deserve sentencing to a women's prison. As Barton (1998) concluded, "The same murder by the same mother could receive different treatment depending on the jurisdiction's laws, particular jury, or even the beliefs of a particular judge" (p. 509). On principle, such inequity should be impossible.

Variations in Penalties

Judges can influence sentencing and, indeed, many do so. Three cases in which these differences are most notable (since most neonaticides are similar) are those of three young girls who had no criminal records and whose prior behavior was adjudged to be exemplary:

1. Twenty-year-old Meshell Buffin, living at home, denied pregnancy and gave birth secretly in the bathroom of her parents' home. Her newborn, discovered in a trashcan, had severe head wounds and had been burned. She was indicted for second-degree murder, but in a plea bargain pleaded guilty to negligent homicide and was sentenced to 2 years.

2. Seventeen-year-old Rebecca Hopfer denied and concealed her pregnancy from her parents (though she did admit it to a girlfriend). She, too, gave birth in the bathroom alone and disposed of the baby in garbage bags in a trash can in the garage. She was indicted for first-degree murder and gross abuse of a corpse (although, unlike Buffin, she did not burn her baby), was convicted and sentenced to 15 years to life. It should be noted that psychiatric experts for the defense and the prosecution were in dispute. (*State v. Buffin*, 1987; *State v. Hopfer*, 1996)
3. Nineteen-year-old Barbara Jones gave birth alone in a bathroom and dropped her baby down an airshaft. She claimed that the baby was stillborn. She was convicted of murder and sentenced to 34 years in prison (although she, too, had no previous record as a teenager). The court of appeals denied a review of the evidence, but suggested that her sentence deserved a review and noted that she had already served 9 years. (*U.S. v Washington*, 1993)

There are also discrepancies among judges—not only in sentencing but also in evaluating the psychological factors in the mother's motivation. The result is that in similar cases some offenders are ordered into therapeutic care while others spend their time in prison. Andrea, a 17-year-old, disposed of her newborn in a plastic bag in the school yard. She was tried as an adult, pleaded guilty to criminally negligent homicide, and was sentenced to $1^1/_3$ to 4 years. When her case was appealed, the court granted her youthful offender status and remitted her case for resentencing. The evaluative psychiatric reports (state and defense agreed) led to a recommendation for appropriate therapeutic care not available in prison. The defendant's punishment was reduced to time served and 5 years' probation in which she would receive necessary treatment (*People v. Andrea*, 1992). The reasons for this decision were stated as follows:

> Because of the nature of the crime and the circumstances of its commission, we are persuaded that a period of probation with continued psychiatric counseling will be more helpful in rehabilitating this troubled young woman than will a return to incarceration. Because, as indicated in the presentence report, the much needed psychiatric care is not available to defendant in prison and it is conceded that she poses absolutely no threat to society, the only penal objectives to be served by imprisonment are retribution and deterrence. Here, the six months of prison time defendant has already served and the mental anguish visited upon her as a result of this tragic episode have had a markedly sobering effect.

> And, as society stands to gain so much from defendant, who is young, bright and has much to offer if her therapy is continued, and is in danger of losing so much if she is incarcerated, it is our view that a less restrictive deterrent is indicated than a return to incarceration.

Often, as we have seen, many of these perpetrators are young adolescents who are tried as adults, and that contributes to the variation of sentencing. The case of Sophia M. (age 14), who had ripped the baby's umbilical cord with her hands, then abandoned the live baby in a shoe box in a field, burying it a few days later, was tried in juvenile court. Expert testimony emphasized the defendant's immaturity. The judge, following the recommendations of the probation department, ordered that she stay in her mother's house, go to school and have therapy, and complete 100 hours of community service (*People v. Sophia M.*, 1987). In contrast, Diana Doss, age 15, whose case was discussed in Chapter 5, was sentenced to 20 years.

In several cases occurring in the 1990s, the charges ranged from a misdemeanor ("abuse of corpse") in a 1996 Texas case to 19 charges of manslaughter and at least 46 indictments for murder, variously designated as homicide, murder one, or murder two. Of 24 cases tracked in the first 5 years of the new century, there were ten charges of manslaughter, five of murder one, one of murder two, two criminally negligent homicides, and one misdemeanor, as well as (and sometimes combined with) two "child endangerment," and two "abuse of corpse." In some of these cases, there was no identified defendant and hence no charges were made.

> It is clear that the lenient impulse in neonaticidal cases is integrally related to the ambivalence evoked in us by the horror of these women's experiences in childbirth. To insist that these women's actions be regarded and judged "equally," in some abstract sense, to the actions of men is as absurd as it is impossible. (Oberman, 1996, p. 84)

Obviously this is a complex area and certainly one not usually taught in law school or necessarily in any traditional curriculum. In Marlow's opinion (1998), judges should be able to do their own research on psychological issues such as those relevant to these cases. That way, they are in a better position to understand expert testimony and defense claims and to determine the most effective sentence in terms of the particular circumstances. This view concurs with that of Wexler and Winick (1991), urging that the therapeutic impact of laws, if any, be considered.

In one article on neonaticide and infanticide (Hanson, 1997), it is interesting to note that in Texas, at least, there was a marked change in penalties for these crimes in the 1990s as compared with the mid-1980s. In 1985, according to Hanson, a mother who tried to kill all seven of her children and succeeded in drowning two of them received a sentence of 10 years' probation. In contrast, in four of five cases of neonaticide or infanticide tried between 1993 and January 1997, the murdering parent was given one or more life sentences (three cases) or 50 years in prison (one case). Further differences were discussed following the presentation of the Andrea Yates case earlier.

In Oberman's two samples (1996), it can be seen that prosecutors and the courts were sometimes quite punitive: 12 of 49 infanticide trials resulted in a sentence with a minimum of 5 years in prison and going up to a life sentence, while 6 of the 47 neonaticidal mothers received prison sentences ranging in duration from 1 to 20 years in prison. Similarly, Moss (1988) reported Katkin's summary of outcomes in 15 cases of infanticide over a 5-year period, where postpartum psychosis was the defense: "about half the women were found not guilty by reason of insanity, one fourth received light sentences, such as probation, and one fourth received long sentences" (p. 22).

By the time Grossman wrote (1990), Katkin had found a few more cases, but the pattern was very similar to the earlier one. Others have also reported about a 50% conviction rate on charges that vary from involuntary manslaughter to first-degree murder, with sentences ranging from suspended sentences to life imprisonment (Nelson, 1991; Waldron, 1990); however, there is some indication that all of these reports are based on the same cases.

Some states have responded to the puzzles posed by shaken baby syndrome (SBS)/shaking impact syndrome (S-IS) cases by adopting "homicide by abuse" laws to help prosecutors achieve more convictions (McMillan, 1995). As we have frequently demonstrated, states vary in their statutes and sentencing for these heinous crimes (Table 9.1). Some states require autopsies for all unnatural deaths of children; others have made physical abuse of children a felony (to be applied in a felony murder statute). Many still maintain traditional state laws for the crime of child murder, applying intent or recklessness or depraved indifference (Phipps, 1999).

Those states that have made child abuse a felony can, if death occurs as a result of violence, punish the perpetrator more harshly if he or she is found guilty. A case in North Carolina illustrates how proving malice and intent can influence the punishment meted out to abusers. Forty-four children died from SBS or blunt impact or a combination of the two from 1999 to 2003. Intent of malice is not always provable since most of the cases are the result of uncontrolled temper or frustration; thus, first-degree murder is untenable. Instead, charges are generally reduced to involuntary manslaughter and those convicted serve a few years in prison. Other factors mitigating stiffer

Table 9.1 Homicide Charges and Sentences

Examples of Sentences for Each Charge							
Capital murder	Death						
First-degree murder	Life/life w/o parole/death	Death	25 to Life	45 Years			
Second-degree murder	Life	30 Years	25 to Life	15 to Life	40 to 89	5 Years	12 Years
Unpremeditated murder	14 Years	$2\frac{1}{2}$ Years	15 Years	50 Years	21 Years		
Felony child abuse	15 to Life						
Involuntary manslaughter	20 to Life	8 to 15 Years	3 yrs probation	3 to 5 Years	7 Years	2 to 4 Years	3 Months
Reckless homicide	25 to Life						
First-degree assault	25 Years						
Felony injury	15 Years						
First-degree felony murder	10 Years						
Felony murder	Life without parole	Life	40 to 45 Years	Life			
Manslaughter	5 Years	6 Years	10 to 20 Years	27 Years	5 to 10 Years	Life	
Assault and battery	41 Months	1 Year	4 Years	21 Years	18 Months	25 Years	6 Years
Reckless endangerment	5 Years	10 Years					
Second-degree negligent homicide	6 Years	18 Years	6 Years	20 to 30 Years			
Second-degree manslaughter	7 Years						
Acute chronic abuse	1 to 10 Years						
Negligent homicide	2 Years; 5 probation	20 to 30 Years	$1\frac{1}{2}$ to 4 Years				
Aggravated child abuse	25 Years	12 Years					
Criminally negligent	14 Years						

Note: Based on appellate cases ($N = 500$).

sentences in most of these cases are that there are no witnesses and the evidence is mostly circumstantial.

Hence, in North Carolina in 18 cases of children's death, no one went to prison at all or at most were placed on probation (Locke, 2005). In other situations, the alleged perpetrators were convicted of felony murder and sentenced to 25 to 35 years in prison up to life without parole. If the prosecutors could not prove malice or intent, the appeals court invariably would remand the case and recommend a reduced sentence (cf. *State v. Blue*, 2000).

Sometimes the difficulty lies in a battle of expert witnesses. In the case of *William Baldwin v. North Carolina* (*News & Observer*, 2005), for example, paramedics rushed the 8-month-old child to a hospital where he died 2 days later. Baldwin, the father, had stated that the baby had rolled off the bed and hit the carpeted floor. The examining doctors were not called until a day after the baby was in the hospital. Attending physicians suspected shaken baby syndrome and the police charged the father with involuntary manslaughter. During the trial, the defense called four experts who testified that the baby had been hurt several days before, when the babysitter dropped him. They asserted that the second fall had triggered the trauma that led to the baby's death. They also attacked the validity of shaken baby syndrome. Baldwin was subsequently acquitted by the jury (*News & Observer*, 2005).

Another case in which there was conflicting testimony involved daycare provider Abigail Tuscareo, who had been accused of shaking a baby. The defense experts attempted to "debunk" the theory of SBS. Jan Leetsma (2005), a Chicago neuropathologist, claimed that shaking alone (i.e., without impact) cannot produce enough force to create brain trauma; the prosecution's doctor countered by saying that they do not know how much force is needed. Despite the arguments, Tuscareo was convicted of involuntary manslaughter and sentenced to 15 years. The appellate court remanded her conviction, and in her second trial she was declared innocent after new evidence from a pathology examination (not submitted at her first trial) revealed an old blood clot from a previous injury (Smart, 2005).

In *State v. Butts* (2004), the defendant was convicted of murder, involuntary manslaughter, and felonious assault of a 24-month-old child. The prosecution enlisted the testimony of three physicians and a coroner who testified that SBS was the cause of death. The defense called Plunkett, a well-known researcher, who testified that a child weighing 30 pounds could not have been killed by shaking alone, but did note that the child could suffer from an impact injury, perhaps a fall (cf. Plunkett, 2001). Butts was sentenced to 15 years to life.

As McKee and Shea (1998) pointed out, the crime is considered so terrible that sentences mandate prison or psychiatric hospitalization. This means the women receive their treatment in an institutional setting rather than within community-based programs. These women suffer difficulties adjusting to their families after conviction. There is less information available on the sentencing for fathers or other males or whether they have psychiatric hospitalization or psychotherapy.

This study also identified a group of victims who, like the filicidal women, also needed clinical services. "Seventy-eight percent of multichild families (24% in d'Orban's 1979 study) had sibling survivors who will likely require treatment for serious problems such as posttraumatic stress disorder or major depression" (McKee & Shea, 1998, p. 686). There is little available professional literature on the survivors, however. Actually, we found one report of a 9-year-old son of a homicidal mother who said he never wanted to see her again, but that is the only instance and certainly does not constitute "research." Another report, not involving a parental homicide, did reflect on the siblings of a 2-year-old killed by a stray bullet. The 4-year-old brother and younger sister apparently screamed all that night, asking for their brother repeatedly: "When is he coming home? Where is he?" (Gallahue, 2004). Their cries probably continued in the ensuing days and weeks because their capacity to comprehend the death of their brother would have been very limited.

Many of the cases that we have tracked in the past 10 to 15 years have yet to be resolved in the courts. In other cases, especially neonaticidal ones, the charge was reduced from murder to manslaughter and, when a trial had taken place, the women aged 21 and older were more likely to be imprisoned than those who were younger. Whether this was because it was felt they should have "known better" or been "more mature" is unclear, but it is possible that their acts were based more on biopsychosocial stresses than on hysterical denial, which may have influenced juries or judges. It has been suggested that because newborns may not be considered as real members of their families and communities, those who kill them often receive relatively lenient sentences from the legal system (Crittenden & Craig, 1990). However, as we have pointed out repeatedly, the outcome of a case in the United States may depend on who is defining "lenient," in contrast to more consistent approaches in Britain and other countries.

For example, Mackay (1993), reporting on 47 cases in Britain of which 21, or 44.7%, were neonaticide and an additional 24 were infanticide, found that the charge was generally reduced to manslaughter; most of the female defendants, if convicted, were placed on probation or referred for psychiatric help. Of the 13 male defendants, 12 of whom had previous criminal records, the 6 convicted of manslaughter were imprisoned or, in one case, hospitalized with restrictions. Several of the 47 cases, especially among the neonaticides, were dismissed because the director of public prosecution believed the cases did not serve the public interest or that the perpetrator was not legally responsible for the act. The prosecutor was more lenient with females than males, as the 1938 act criteria would favor such a bias, even though, as noted earlier, these alleged psychiatric outcomes of pregnancy and birth have been found unsound. On the other hand, the leniency may reflect a difference in victims—that is, the victims of males were more likely infants or older preschoolers than neonates and vice versa for the females.

Similarly, Wilczynski & Morris (1993)—also dealing with British cases, but in a range from neonaticide to filicide ($N = 395$) during the period from 1982 to 1989—found that of the persons convicted, "Mothers were less likely than fathers to be convicted of murder or to be sentenced to imprisonment and were more likely to be given probation and psychiatric dispositions" (p. 35).

The defense of infanticide or even great stress, they indicated, tended to evoke sympathy and efforts at support for the women, but not for the "wicked" men. The perception of mothers as nurturing and caring leads others to "assume that a 'normal' woman could surely not have acted in such a way. She must have been 'mad' to kill her own child" (p. 36). The same comment about gender-related leniency related to age of the victim suggested earlier may be relevant here.

Indeed, a later study by Wilczynski (1997b) is entitled "Mad or Bad?" She found that twice as many women as men used psychiatric pleas when accused of filicide. Of those found guilty, the men more frequently received longer and more custodial sentences than the women. They were also less likely to receive psychiatric treatment than the women, even when it was evident that they needed such help. Wilczynski found that filicidal women were more often viewed sympathetically than filicidal men, whose motives included retaliation against a spouse, jealousy, and discipline. She also found that the women were less likely to have committed violence prior to the case at hand or to have been abusive, whereas the male offenders were more likely to have exhibited such behaviors in their past. The question to be resolved in her paper was whether the males and females should be treated similarly under the law when they had committed the same crime (filicide). In her view, the men should be treated less harshly and given appropriate psychiatric treatment where warranted, although the women should not be treated more harshly.

Zingraff and Thomson (1984), on the other hand, cited research in which it had been suggested that the courts are more apt to sentence women harshly if their demeanors and behaviors do not conform to expected gender roles. Women who *do* fit female stereotypical patterns are treated more sympathetically. This explanation sheds some light on research findings, at least for misdemeanors. Child abandonment and assaults, however, "seem directly to contradict gender role expectations for females and the sentence lengths women receive for these two offenses do tend to be longer than those received by their male counterparts, although only the abandonment differential is statistically significant" (p. 410). This negative view of women convicted of a violent crime who deviate from the maternal stereotype is supported by Edwards' study in Great Britain (1986). Coughlin (1994) similarly reported a negative relationship between gender stereotype and sentencing.

Two American cases that reflect that negative relationship are those of Sheryl Ann Massip of Anaheim, California, and Jamie L. Goodrum of Wisconsin. On her 24th birthday in April 1987, Massip killed her 6-week-old son, Michael, by running over him with the family station wagon after an unsuccessful attempt to throw him, wrapped, in front of a passing car. That driver swerved and missed the "bundle." Massip was described as a "happy, healthy, nonviolent person who looked forward to motherhood" prior to Michael's birth. However, after the baby was born:

> she began feeling confused and worthless and during the next 6 weeks could neither sleep nor eat. She began having suicidal thoughts, such as jumping off a building or out of a window. She also experienced hallucinations; voices were telling her the baby was in pain. (*People v. Massip*, 1990)

Postpartum psychosis was used as a defense in this case, and a defense psychiatrist testified about her psychotic behavior. The jury did not agree and convicted her of second-degree murder. Subsequently, Massip filed for a new trial at which she was found to have been not guilty by reason of insanity at the time of the murder (suffering from postpartum psychosis) and was ordered to participate in an outpatient treatment program rather than be incarcerated. The case was subsequently appealed to the Supreme Court of California (*People v. Massip*, 1992).

In Goodrum's case (*People v. Goodrum*, 1989), she told police that her two sons, aged 14 months and 6 weeks, had been kidnapped and fabricated an elaborate story with a description of the car allegedly involved and of her being drugged by an assailant. Goodrum was on probation at the time. The police did not believe her story and called her probation agent, who ordered a probation hold. She was then picked up by the police. At first she maintained her story; later she confessed to killing the boys with a hammer. Goodrum was convicted on two counts of first-degree murder, with the jury finding that she was not suffering from a mental disease or defect. She appealed the decision based on a lack of the psychiatric testing recommended by an expert witness who testified on her behalf.

An Interesting Question

Most of the foregoing infanticide and filicide cases give rise to an interesting question. Where was the spouse or partner or parent of the mother who killed her children? How can a parent permit such abuse to be committed by his or her partner or mate without making some effort to safeguard the innocent child? As Pruett has written, substance abuse and other factors involved in child homicides "do not occur in a vacuum. Someone else must be absent or looking the other way at the wrong time for these deaths to occur" (2002, p. 354).

In most cases in our database and in the appellate cases we found, shaking by the parent, boyfriend, or babysitter occurred when the person was alone caring for the child. In those cases, there were no witnesses and little or no evidence of ongoing abuse; the passive parent was considered to be the innocent bystander.

The reason that the parent, especially the mother, does not defend the child even when there is a pattern of battering may stem from a number of domestic and psychological reasons. The parent may be so emotionally attached to the partner that he or she denies the obviously aberrant behavior. The parent may also be the victim of violence and thus be too cowed to interfere or protest. He or she may be overwhelmed by stress and social isolation and thus too frightened to assume parental responsibility. The parent may be too young and immature to assert authority. Although understandable, none of these factors relieves the passive bystander of his or her obligations to the helpless child.

Fugate (2001) raised much the same question but in reverse: why are women penalized under failure-to-protect laws when their male companion abuses or kills their child? "Failure to protect is a crime of omission where liability attaches for failure to act in certain situations where common law or statute has imposed upon a specific class of persons an affirmative responsibility for another's safety" (pp. 276–277). Whether it is the male or female partner who is the bystander, that individual has a duty to protect a child and may face criminal prosecution if the child is abused. Those laws fail to recognize that, in the case of mothers who fail to protect, the women may fear that *they* will be abused or killed.

Fugate found no men prosecuted for the same crime of omission and attributed this to prejudice based on gender stereotyping, citing one case in which "the court snidely described the mother's fear of her husband as a 'defense'" (p. 291), although she had been threatened by her husband. The mother knew, and presumably the court also knew, that the husband had murdered at least two women. At least one court has recognized that the legal system expects "perfection" of mothers and deems it inexcusable.

The state maintains legal responsibility for the welfare of its children and therefore legislates statutes that make parents liable for their failure to protect their children. Not all states have passed such laws, but those that have enacted them have enabled the state to prosecute passive parents for failure to protect their children and subjected them to criminal penalties (Rhein, 2003).

Indeed, New York State has a law extending the requirement to seek medical aid for seriously injured children to paid caretakers of children (see *People of the State of New York v. Eugene Wong*, 1993). Eugene and Mary Wong were paid to care for a 3-month-old baby, Kwok-Wei. In July 1988, the Wongs called Kwok-Wei's parents to inform them that the baby was dead and also called "911" requesting an ambulance for an unconscious child. At some point they claimed that their 3-year-old son had inadvertently shaken the baby hard enough to cause its death, but this was unlikely since Kwok-Wei was alive and crying from midnight to past 2 A.M. the night of his death.

The authorities could not determine which of the Wongs had caused the child's death and which of them had allowed it to happen, so both were charged with and convicted of first- and second-degree manslaughter and endangering the welfare of a child. The convictions were overturned by the court of appeals because no convincing evidence was presented at trial showing which party was the abuser and which the bystander (*People of the State of New York v. Eugene Wong* and *People of the State of New York v. Mary Wong*, 1993). Apparently, this was not the first time the Wongs had been accused of abusing a child for whom they were allegedly "caring." A social worker had interviewed them about the earlier incidents, but they were allowed to continue their babysitting service (Griffin, 2004).

The case of little 23-month-old Raven also illustrates the role of the passive parent effectively. Raven's stepfather abused and battered the small boy, who finally died from his injuries. The mother, Michelle Fuelling, aware of the maltreatment, nevertheless left the boy in his stepfather's care. After Raven's death, his stepfather was convicted of felony abuse and second-degree murder and sentenced to life imprisonment plus 390 years (*State v. Mendoza*, 2003). Fuelling was arrested and convicted of endangering the welfare of a child in the first degree and felony murder in the second degree because she knowingly acted in a manner that provided risk to the health and welfare of her son. She was sentenced to 5 years on the first charge and 10 on the second, to be served consecutively (*State of Missouri v. Fuelling*, 2004).

Are the Laws Antifemale?

The arguments about postpartum psychosis and other biologically based defenses for females remind us of the arguments against having a female president of the United States (or prime minister of England)—that is, her decisions would be subject to premenstrual or postmenopausal "whims." (Note: The British and others have overcome this argument in recent years.) Similarly, arguments about women murdering their babies that are based on lactation, the physical stress of childbirth, and similar causes are seen as gender biased.

In the absence of a federal law dealing with child homicide and in accord with the Tenth Amendment, we are confronted with at least 52 different sets of statutes dealing with such events (50 states and Puerto Rico and the District of Columbia). When a case arises, it also evokes arguments from antiabortionists versus pro-choice forces and from feminists of a variety of persuasions who perceive application of these laws as unfair, unreasonable, antifemale, or inadequate.

In the case of neonaticide, the antiabortionists see abortion and neonaticide as the same crime. Those who are pro-choice see no crime in abortion, generally permitted before the 24th week of pregnancy in most states. Infanticide, as we have previously noted, is a different crime, usually with motives different from those associated with neonaticide. Furthermore, infanticide may be committed by someone other than the biological mother—most frequently a male functioning in a parental role, whereas this is rarely true in cases of neonaticide. The recommendations of the New South Wales Law Reform Commission (1997) with respect to infanticide as a partial defense to murder provide helpful clarification of these questions.

The New South Wales Law Reform Commission (1997) acknowledged that the prosecution of women for the crime of infanticide as it has existed in the law has an unsound ideological basis, one with which many feminists would agree:

> Women are given special treatment by way of a gender-specific law based on the notion that they are naturally susceptible to mental instability as a result of giving birth. Arguably, this conveys a conception of women as inherently unstable because of their biology. (p. 116)

The commission also pointed out:

> No other crime is excused on the basis of social or economic necessity or adversity alone. To permit an exception to this general

> principle for women may benefit certain individuals but ultimately reinforces a view of women as especially weak and vulnerable because of their sex. (p. 123)

Furthermore, the commission voiced "concern that female offenders who do not fit easily into the stereotype of women as weak and frail victims of their biology may be condemned as 'bad mothers' and punished much more severely" (p. 117). A third consideration in the commission's recommendation was that the offense (and defense) of infanticide was limited to the natural mothers of victims aged less than 12 months, which left out other groups of offenders such as fathers, adoptive mothers, foster parents, and other caretakers of infants. In fact, they noted that a large percentage of children (other than neonates) were victims of men in abuse-type killings (pp. 118–119, n. 36), a fact frequently documented in daily U.S. newspapers.

Opponents of the Commission's recommendation took the position that "by abolishing a specific defen[s]e which relates solely to women, particular attention to the special problems which women face is reduced and the individual's mental state is emphasized, rather than the social factors which contributed to that state" (1997, pp. 122–123). As Lentz (1989) put it, since postpartum psychosis is an exclusively female defense, it might promote sexism; this is feared by many feminist groups because "regarding postpartum disorders as a defense will detract attention from other real events in women's lives and further the notion that women should not be accorded full responsibility for their actions" (p. 543). Similar arguments were advanced by Lansdowne (1990):

> The offen[s]e of infanticide … is a sex-specific offen[s]e, that can only be committed by women, in fact only by mothers, which is additional to the general defen[s]es of disturbed mental state, insanity and, in New South Wales and England, diminished responsibility. (p. 41)

Lansdowne further raised feminist objections to its status as a "specific homicide offen[s]e" in New South Wales, Victoria, and Tasmania. As we have seen, however, men as well as women can and do commit infanticide (and filicide); it is not a "sex specific offense," although neonaticide is (and may have been a more appropriate term for Lansdowne to have used).

Looking Back and Ahead

At this point, it is clear that children are endangered by their parents or caretakers for a variety of reasons that may or may not provide an adequate defense in court when child homicide occurs. It is also apparent that there are questions of gender discrimination involved in the law, at least in the United States, that have not only biological aspects but also political and other ramifications and implications. Those political and religious arguments will be discussed in the next chapter; their proponents (and opponents) can influence state and federal legislation that ultimately bears on the ways in which prevention measures, unwanted pregnancies, and prosecution of perpetrators are handled.

Choice and Reproduction: Political and Other Arguments

10

Among the alternative methods of preventing or dealing with unwanted and undesirable pregnancies have been the use of contraceptives and, if that failed, resort to an abortion. However, sex education is often needed to provide the information on how and when to use such alternatives, in addition to which contraception and abortion are practices that have provoked massive debate in our society. The disagreements involve not only moral and religious values, but also political issues and the status of women.

The rhetoric that has encompassed the controversy conceals a public discourse that is not necessarily based on logic, but rather on a series of firmly held beliefs. Many arguments have employed words such as homicide, murder, child killing, and infanticide or neonaticide as synonymous with abortion. Mary Glendon (1991) observed cogently that the way in which we name things and imagine them may be decisive for the way we feel and act with respect to them. If this is so, the dialogue over the issue of abortion reveals very passionate and powerful attitudes.

The language, symbol, analogy, and metaphor constantly evoked in various literary forms have also appeared in political verbiage and journalistic articles. The debates that have enveloped our communities, past and present, also used the lingual devices of infanticide to arouse emotional responses and reduce the level of rational discourse. The political divisiveness centered around the problems of neonaticide and infanticide encompass gender relationships, abortion, euthanasia, legal standards, and sex education. The rhetoric of abortion has often been heated and exaggerated as it concealed the hidden agenda of its proponents. Pro-life advocates regard those who disagree with them as "potential murderers"; pro-choice advocates view their opponents as violators of women's fundamental rights. The inability to arrive at any compromise or moral consensus in the dialogue on abortion has led instead to partisanship, fanaticism, and intolerance in language and even behavior.

At the heart of the debate is the answer to "What is a child?" When does life begin? Does personhood begin at conception? At the end of the first trimester? At birth? A week or a month or a year after birth? The boundary differs by culture, including religion, and disputes rage among biologists, philosophers, ethicists, pro-choice proponents, right-to-lifers, and others. Even if we could define the exact moment when life begins, the underlying issues and cultural disagreements would prevent compromise or any widespread acceptance of abortion.

> The politics of abortion have resulted in isolated rates for unborn children (twenty-six states have fetal homicide laws), while some legislators attempt to eliminate a pregnant woman's right to choose late-term abortion when her own life or health is at risk (the federal Partial Birth Abortion Act of 2003). (Barnes, 2005, p. 148) (Note: That act was declared unconstitutional in 2004 [Barnes, p. 162].)

The problem of defining when life begins did not exist in the past. Present-day technological and medical developments that allow the early identification of pregnancy and permit fetal viability earlier than ever have altered perceptions of pregnancy and abortion. Moreover, amniocentesis and other intrauterine testing have raised issues over the abortion or treatment of future babies found to be disabled.

The Abortion Controversy

Abortion was acceptable until the mid-19th century. Common law in the United States and Great Britain allowed abortion until "quickening" or the feeling of life. Before that, a woman was "irregular" in her menstrual cycle, and potions, herbs, vigorous exercise, and other strategies were used to bring on her period. Most abortions that occurred before then were helped by midwives practicing folklore methods that usually brought on spontaneous abortions, but no records were kept and thus we know very little about this. As the 19th century progressed, there was more knowledge about how abortion was accomplished and much evidence to indicate that it was practiced by the desperate poor and the well-to-do (Condit, 1990; Fuchs, 1992; Mohr, 1978).

Not until the middle of the 19th century, when medicine became the province of the male medical establishment, did abortion begin to acquire meaning, measurement, and state regulation. Physicians claimed that abortion and birth control were selfish actions that imperiled the family and the social order. Physicians did not seek to end abortion completely, only to control it. They wanted laws that permitted the doctor to decide whether the woman needed an abortion for health reasons. They were not concerned about the "personhood" of the fetus. "In classifying abortion as both a criminal offense and a health problem, pregnancy and its consequences were increasingly subject to state and medical intervention" (Ginsburg, 1989, p. 24).

Religious Views

One of the most ardent proponents of anti-abortion laws in the past and present has been the Catholic Church, which perceives life as beginning at the fertilization of the egg. However, in the distant past that was not always so. Christian thought under Augustine claimed that the soul was not present until quickening. By the 13th century, the church revised this point of view by adopting Aristotle's position: The presence of the soul did not appear until 40 days after conception for a male and 80 days after for a female. It was not until the end of the 17th century that the Catholic Church took its stand against abortion at any time (Rothman, 1989).

Abortion is now defined by the long held church commitment to the notion that the fetus is a full human person from the moment of fertilization, and therefore abortion is homicide. That means that even the possible death of the mother is insufficient reason to permit abortion. The only permissible exception is that of the unintended abortion that could happen if surgery is performed on the mother in life-threatening situations such as a cancerous uterus or an ectopic pregnancy (Noonan, 1979; Petchesky, 1981).

In contrast, the Jewish position, similar to the Protestant one, opposes "abortion on demand" as was noted earlier in Chapter 4. Jewish law declares that an existing human life must be protected over that of a potential life. For Jews, the fetus is not yet a human being, but has the potential for life. Therefore, if the mother's life or health is threatened, her needs are paramount and an abortion would be permitted.

The differing positions on abortion require a degree of tolerance that has not been forthcoming in political debates. The reasons often lie in the fact that the disputants have other agendas masked by strident rhetoric.

The old disputes about contraception were gradually resolved by growing concerns over unrestrained population growth, and by the appearance of the birth control pill in 1960. The 1965 Supreme Court decision, *Griswold v. Connecticut*, invoked the right of privacy that ended legal arguments over contraception and prepared the way for the pro-choice campaign for abortion rights that culminated in the *Roe v. Wade* decision in 1973 (Reagan, 1997; Tribe, 1990).

As earlier cultural demands for sexual freedom came to fruition during this period, social and religious conservatives became alarmed at what they perceived as pernicious changes in American behavior and morality. The Catholic Church had opposed contraception and abortion on religious grounds, but then Protestant evangelicals also embraced an anti-abortion position despite the fact that they had no prior history of such a position in their movement. Their leadership responded to feminism and the growing number of teenage pregnancies and abortions even within their own communities by sacralizing the abortion issue, equating it to sexual sinning in order to reemphasize Christian values of patriarchy, sacrificial motherhood, and sexual purity (Harding, 1990).

Language and Imagery

The pro-life faction has characterized abortion as neonaticide. This provocative imagery has selected two perceptions: one that abortion is indeed neonaticide and the other that it is as pernicious as the homicide of a newborn baby. By lumping the two perceptions together, the symbolism of the phraseology evokes a strong revulsion for abortion.

Visual aids used by pro-life propagandists enhance the impact of their arguments. The portrayal of actual fetuses evokes strong emotional reactions. "Any graphic depiction of an innocent sacrificial victim appeals to Christian themes deeply embedded in our culture" (Berger & Berger, 1984, p. 74). These pictures emphasize that the fetus is a developing child rather than its characterization by pro-choice people as just a piece of tissue (Wilson, 1994). Newman (1996) argues that in all of these representations the fetus is shown as intact, while the woman's body appears inert and fragmented:

> The effect is that the observer is encouraged to identify with the fetus rather than the woman who carries it—accepting the former as an autonomous and rights-bearing individual, while denying the latter any subjectivity, sympathy, and individuality, and hence any plausible claim to the rights of her own. (p. 8)

In contrast, pro-choice imagery is not as effective. Their pictures are symbols: the coat hanger to recall the risks of death in illegal abortion and the Statue of Liberty to symbolize the woman as downtrodden and threatened by those who would deny her reproductive freedom (Condit, 1990).

Pro-life advocates want to establish an environment that enhances the special and unique female characteristics of pregnancy and motherhood.

For some, abortion saps the vitality of the family and vitiates the father's obligation to sustain his family financially. Thus, hidden in some of the programs of the pro-life factions is also an agenda of banning sex education and contraception exclusive of sexual abstinence. Implicit in the pro-life dialogue is also a cultural code for the evils of our society: materialism. Therefore, according to the pro-life position, women who undergo pregnancy and delivery in the face of adversity and obstacles are heroic and truly feminine, and those who choose to abort are unnatural, weak, and unfeminine (not to mention selfish and immoral).

The use of this imagery in the partial birth abortion debate proved how effectively language can be used to garner support for a position by many who are pro-life. Further characterizing the procedure as murder akin to that of a living infant, one writer claimed that "doctors who performed this procedure (whatever their motive) are the American successors to Mengele, who performed medical experiments in Nazi Germany and who was an abortionist" (Bethell, 1988, pp. 22–23). Pro-life literature that shows photographs of the discarded bodies of concentration camp victims and then, next to those, photographs of fetuses stuffed into plastic garbage bags for disposal has offended many.

Metaphoric allusions that compare abortion to the Holocaust have been cited by the religious Right in their arguments (Isser, 1997). Numerous individuals perceive the equating of abortion with the victims of the Nazi Holocaust as unseemly and a distortion of the debates. It seems very wrong to them to appropriate Jewish suffering for the propagation of views about abortion. They raise the question: Does not comparing "abortions with the horror of the Holocaust deprive Nazism of moral significance and debase Jewish history by exploiting it for sectarian Christian goals" (Mensch & Freeman, 1991, p. 935)?

However, pro-choice proponents have used language in a similar fashion. The word *abortion* has been used in two ways. There are induced abortions and spontaneous abortions. One is caused by medical intervention and the other is a consequence of a bad pregnancy. Is the spontaneous abortion then an act of murder? Is it, too, neonaticide? Since spontaneous abortions occur very frequently, is nature a murderer?

Modern medical research has shown that a newly fertilized egg has a small chance of coming to term. Pro-choice proponents stress that since the egg can be so easily destroyed by nature, it can be replaced by another one. The importance of the zygote (as they label the developing egg to distinguish it from the more developed fetus) rests upon proper care that can bring it to full development. "The responsibility is to a fetus that will become one's child but not necessarily to this particular fetus. The use of similar language in both instances distorts and devalues the basic arguments and makes a middle ground more difficult to achieve" (Greenwood, 1994, p. 499). The use of ultrasound pictures early in the first trimester, a technique unknown more than 40 years ago, only reinforces their belief. Such pictures would have been helpful in the case of Sherri Finkbine.

The case of Sherri Finkbine, a woman pregnant with a fetus disabled by the drug thalidomide, has been particularly emphasized in connection with these arguments (Condit, 1990). In 1962 Finkbine was known as "Miss Sherri" of the television show *Romper Room*. While in Europe with her husband, she had taken some medication to relieve pain she was having from a minor medical problem. The medication was thalidomide. What was not widely known at the time was that taking the drug between the 26th and 60th days after conception could result in severe damage to the fetus' arms or legs. When it came to her attention, Finkbine scheduled a legal abortion in Phoenix. When that became known through the media, the outcry was tremendous and the abortion was canceled. She subsequently flew to Sweden, had the abortion, and found that her baby would have been born missing three of four limbs. The negative reaction to her abortion, even with this outcome, was such that she lost her job and her local physician; her husband, a teacher, also encountered many protests. They later had two daughters. Finkbine's case, however, played an important role in the ultimate ruling of *Roe v. Wade* in 1973.

In addition to the possibility of a seriously damaged fetus, feminist women see their bodies as a part of their individuality, and they deny what they perceive as subjection to the decisions and regulations of others, including their male partners. They see any regulation as an infringement of liberty and individuality—a cardinal belief in our American society. Control over the womb is central to the notion of female identity and the woman's role in American society. Thus, the arguments over abortion can be applied as well to the issues of contraception, amniocentesis, surrogate motherhood, and *in vitro* fertilization. These issues become very significant for young women who face unwanted pregnancies or when they seek help for avoidance of motherhood or for fertility assistance. As they turn to counseling or proposals that could bring comfort and aid, they discover that the agencies are involved in acrimonious controversies over gender roles and how they should behave in their unhappy circumstances.

On the other hand, for people who are strongly pro-choice, the imagery of the language equating neonaticide and abortion produces a different perception. Since the proponents of choice conceive of the fetus as potentially capable of human life but not yet a person, to them the equating of the life of an infant and that of a fetus is immoral. They see such language and judgment of homicide as a denial of the baby's humanity and a lessened respect for human life. In this case, the vivid imagery produced by pro-life adherents has widened the chasm between the two groups.

Part of the early struggles of the women's suffrage movement in America was to use the vote in order to have more control over their private lives:

> The constitutional claim of choice in the personal, private world is thus even more important to women than the claim to equal citizenship. Male power over women's sexuality and maternity has restricted women to a passive role, permitting them to control conception and childbirth only through a strategy of denial. (Karst, 1984, p. 452)

Furthermore, these women envision the intensity of the pro-life language as proof of their opponents' desire to maintain a continuing control of women. By resisting laws that permit women to take charge of their own bodies, especially laws with emphasis on their control of reproductive rights, pro-life positions are deemed destructive to equality and autonomy for women (Hernandez-Truyol, 1997). Ginsburg (1989) argued that "both symbolically and experientially the definition of female gender identity and the domestic domain have focused more and more on questions regarding reproduction and its relationship to nurturance" (p. 213).

Pro-choice opponents also view legal, safe abortion as an essential aspect of protecting women from the problems associated with child-bearing. This is an option that heterosexually active women have, allowing them to determine with whom, or whether, they will have children (Ginsburg, 1989).

At the moment, controversy also swirls over the use of the so-called "morning after" pill. Opponents declare that it is an abortifacient agent and the use of the pill would encourage promiscuity; others insist that it is a valuable contraceptive, especially for those who fear an unexpected pregnancy (as in cases of rape). Women, even when armed with a prescription, have found some pharmacists unwilling to sell the drug. Presently, the FDA has denied the right to purchase the pill without a doctor's prescription, thereby limiting its use. This issue, too, is inherently part of the political and cultural wars over conception.

In the Courts

After much protest and agitation, pro-choice forces were able to achieve the victory of *Roe v. Wade* (1973), which permitted abortion in the first trimester. Subsequently, state courts have wrestled with permitting abortion in later trimesters to save the mother's health and also with the question of whether teenagers can have abortions without parental consent (Harris, 1977). Restrictions, such as a waiting period or notification of a parent (or judicial approval in lieu of such notification), have been required in some states, such as Pennsylvania, Missouri, and New Hampshire.

> Of the first 1,300 Massachusetts abortion cases involving petitions to bypass parental consent, courts found the adolescent to be mature in 90% of all cases and in all but five of the remaining cases, held that abortion was in her best interest. (Rhode, 1992, p. 125)

In New Jersey, the ACLU filed suit against a law due to be effective in September 1999 that would require doctors to notify a minor's parent 48 hours before performing an abortion or obtain a "judicial bypass" (Martello, 1999). The parental notification legislation was held unconstitutional because the law "imposes no corresponding limitation on minors who seek medical and surgical care otherwise related to her pregnancy or child." The law violated the state constitution's equal protection provisions (*Planned Parenthood of Central New Jersey v. Farmer*, 2000). A similar law in New Hampshire was brought before the Supreme Court in the 2005–2006 term.

The arguments over such regulations rest in part on when life begins (or indeed, what is considered "life") and when the fetus is viable. The *Casey* decisions of the U.S. Supreme Court (*Planned Parenthood of Southeastern Pennsylvania, et al. v. Robert P. Casey, et al.*, 1992) rejected the trimester framework of *Roe*; reaffirmed the state's legitimate interest in "the protection of potential life," and explicitly held that even though a woman alone must choose whether to abort before the fetus is viable, the state is not prohibited "from taking steps to ensure that this choice is thoughtful and informed" (Wilson, 1994, p. 22).

In *Doe v. Bolton* (1973), the Supreme Court ruled that Georgia's requirement of approval of an abortion by a hospital medical committee or other physician violated the privacy of the doctor and patient. However, in *Webster v. Reproductive Health Services* (1989), the Court upheld a Missouri law that (1) prohibited performance of abortions by public employees and in state-financed facilities; and (2) upheld a provision that required physicians to determine whether an unborn child is viable, if the physician has reason to believe its gestational age is 20 weeks or more (Cleary, 1991, p. 54). Note that the wording is unborn *child*.

A bare majority of the justices reaffirmed *Roe* but changed its meaning and application. Speaking through Justice Sandra Day O'Connor, the Supreme Court reasserted that a woman has a "constitutional liberty" to "some freedom to terminate her pregnancy." However, the state could now place restrictions on this right, even when the fetus is not yet viable, provided those restrictions do not impose an "undue burden" on its exercise. The *Casey* decision had acknowledged that the state could exercise some degree of regulation of abortion (Poland, 1997).

The Court's reasoning for these decisions also reflected a new philosophic leaning. The original *Roe* ruling had been based on the right to privacy, but feminist jurisprudence began to attack this concept, insisting that abortion rights should be based on a criterion of sexual equality. They claimed that, in the past, contraception and abortion restrictions were enacted for the explicit purpose of enforcing separate spheres of behavior for the sexes and to engender subordination of women. Mackinnon (1989) argued that "giving women control over sexual access to their bodies and adequate support of pregnancies and care of children extends sex equality. In other words, forced maternity is a practice of sex inequality" (p. 117). The U.S. Supreme Court has begun to move in this direction. In the rulings in the *Casey* decision, the Court narrowly upheld privacy rights, but also went on to declare that the state had

> to respect a pregnant woman's decision about abortion because her suffering is too intimate and personal for the State to insist ... upon its own version of the woman's role, however dominant that role has been in the course of our history and our culture .... (Allen, 1992, p. 686)

Does Fetus = Person?

These issues have continued to cause disagreement and difficulties in interpretation and legislation. For instance, a key problem that arises from the rhetorical arguments of abortion is the one of "the fetus is a person" ideology. If that concept is legally adopted, then the next step is to protect the fetus even *in utero* (Tribe, 1990).

The woman's autonomy is then challenged in the workplace, clinics, and courts (Rhoden, 1988). The employer could legally and morally ban women from jobs where there may be a hazard to her present or future reproductivity. The Pregnancy Discrimination Act of 1978 provided only minimal protection (Wilson, 2005). The excuse of hazards to the fetus gives employers the right to exclude women from equal employment opportunity, but also allows employers to ignore harmful agents in the workplace that may hurt the male's potential for fertility (Becker, 1986). For example, the case of *International Union v. Johnson Controls* (1991) centered about a ruling of the company that banned women of childbearing age from certain jobs, contending that they were too risky for future pregnancies. The court rejected that ruling, calling the order gender biased and saying that the same jobs could injure male fertility as well. In medicine, the fetus could be the patient and the pregnant woman simply its "environment." In legal cases, the husband or male partner could assert that these issues are paramount in debates over women's rights and her quest for equality.

Amazing technological and medical developments have enabled physicians to treat and cure fetal defects *in utero*. This power may help parents who desire a healthy baby, but do the procedures then become the entering wedge for the medical profession and social workers to impose their programs of prenatal care, to stop abortions, or to supervise the lifestyle of prospective mothers under the rubric of avoiding child abuse (Bowes & Selegstad, 1981)? What can and does happen is that, depending upon the ideology of the medical personnel, doctors can discredit or annul the woman's right of decision in medical treatment. If the woman is merely a "vessel" for the unborn, then the rights of the fetus can prevail over her health and wishes. "Women are put into an impossible dilemma. If the damaged fetus can be treated, does that mean it must be" (Petchesky, 1990, p. 358)? The dilemma is between denying her autonomy if she accedes to treatment and being guilty of neglect if she refuses.

In matters of equal decision over abortion, do male partners have certain rights over the pregnancy? If the relationship is loving, caring, intimate, and based on mutual trust, the male should share, especially if he is supportive of the female. In contrast, paternal rights claims can also rest on the premise that the fetus has independent rights, and the father has a traditional proprietary right in the partner's body and its progeny. (Wives and children have not been viewed as *property* in family law for more than 50 years. This does not mean, however, that the practice necessarily follows in step.)

The nature of laws, therefore, that involve the status of family, the role of society and welfare, and, indeed, the regulation of women's lives becomes a part of passionate political debate. If the fetus is a separate being, the government may define how a woman lives and how she cares for herself. Her life can be rigidly regulated. Petchesky (1990) claims that "men have reduced the pregnant woman to the status of maternal environment, a passive spectator in her own pregnancy" (p. 240). In addition, this view, according to Sunstein (1992), "is often closely identified with the understanding … that sexual activity should be exclusively for the purposes of reproduction" (p. 30).

Some pro-lifers allege that the easy availability of abortion would encourage sexual promiscuity and activity for nonreproductive purposes. Their opponents believe, on the contrary, that sexual freedom is important for men and women and that this freedom includes the right to have an abortion as well as to engage in nonreproductive sexuality. Indeed, a large part of Sunstein's argument rests on the issue of sex-role stereotyping and sexual discrimination: Forcing a woman to continue her pregnancy by law, it is argued, dictates roles that differ for men and women and makes women second-class citizens, which is unconstitutional and against several laws passed in recent decades.

As the issue is debated in the press and other media, it has also entered the legal and political arenas. Various states have enacted legislation, or the courts have ruled in appellate decisions, on the question of whether a fetus is a child. In South Carolina, for example, Cornelia Whitner was accused of child abuse because she took drugs during her pregnancy. In 1992, she pled guilty to criminal child neglect because her baby was born with cocaine metabolites in its system as a result of her ingestion of crack cocaine during her pregnancy. Subsequent appeals brought the case to the South Carolina Supreme Court in 1997, where her conviction was upheld. This court ruled that provisions about child abuse and endangerment in the 1985 South Carolina Children's Code applied to a fetus, for, they wrote, "We hold the word 'child' as used in that statute includes viable fetuses" (*Whitner v. State*, 1997, p. 27). In a second case in South Carolina, Talitha Renee Garrick was also found guilty of killing her unborn fetus and sentenced to a prison term, subsequently changed to probation (Copeland, 1997). "South Carolina is the only state where a pregnant woman can be sent to prison for potentially harming a viable fetus" (Anon., 1998, p. 24). (Note: South Carolina was joined by Wisconsin later in 1998.)

The *Whitner* case is one of several conflicting decisions cited by the Supreme Court of Wisconsin, which was also wrestling with the question of what was meant by the word "child" in the state's CHIPS (*Ch*ild *I*n Need of *P*rotection or *S*ervices) statute. In the instant case, Angela M. W. was pregnant and using cocaine. Lower courts had ruled that the "child"—that is, the fetus—was in need of protective custody because of the mother's drug use, and the petitioner argued that if the child was placed in protective custody that would violate her (the mother's) rights to equal protection and due process (*Angela M. W. v. Kruzicki*, 1995). The Wisconsin Supreme Court, in a divided decision, reversed the lower courts and ruled that a fetus was not a child under the relevant statute. However, that would not have been the decision if the case had been heard in mid-1998 instead of 3 years earlier because a bill was passed by the Wisconsin legislature in 1998 that defined a fetus as a human being from the moment of fertilization (Herbert, 1998). Relevant to the problem of drug-addicted pregnant women is a call to the several states to enact legislation that would oblige the woman to complete a drug rehabilitation program or lose her parental rights (Zitella, 1996).

The Florida State Supreme Court ruled that a pregnant woman could not be charged with murder or manslaughter for shooting herself in the abdomen to kill her fetus (News in Brief, 1997). The 19-year-old woman charged had been turned away from an abortion clinic for lack of funds. She was single, unemployed, and already the mother of a toddler. (Note: The Hyde Amendment [1976] excluded abortion from "the healthcare coverage provided for low-income women through Medicaid, except when a woman's life is in danger" or, as amended later, in cases of rape or incest [Barnes, 2005, p. 155].) The Florida court "pointed out that American and English common law confers immunity on pregnant women who cause injury or death to their fetuses, although a third party may be prosecuted" (Anonymous, 1998, p. 24).

For a third view, the Pennsylvania legislature passed a fetal homicide bill in 1997 that would make it a crime "to kill an unborn child through an assault on the mother." The bill in no way affected the state's abortion laws (Capital Report, 1997, p. 9). This would appear to parallel the Florida law rather than the South Carolina law. However, in a case involving an accident caused by a drunken driver, a Pennsylvania superior court "ruled that a viable fetus is considered a person under the state's criminal code and that criminal actions that injure or kill a fetus can be prosecuted" (Henson, 1999).

Feminists have found in this issue questions that relate to their functions and roles in society. This discussion had its roots in the feminist movement at the end of the 19th century. The key factors in the feminists' search for autonomy rested on the conflicts between personhood and the societal requirement that the female could be fulfilled only in marriage and motherhood. As literature and history have taught us, neonaticide, infanticide, filicide, and abandonment have been persistent problems plaguing governments, although they were perceived largely as female crimes. The issue for feminists has been not only that women have been stereotyped and pushed by community mores into subordinate and defined roles, but also that the policies of legislators (mostly male) can legally bind and control women, making their lives rigidly regulated.

The ongoing quarrels also involve "morning after" pills, birth control, and RU-486 (Leland, 2005). Pro-life advocates claim that these are the "slippery slope" to infant euthanasia, teen illegitimacy, and. in general, moral debauchery. On the other side, pro-choice groups characterize any attempt at regulation or limits on education as the "slippery slope" to denial of civil rights, invasion of privacy, and the restoration of patriarchy (Roberts, 1993). The majority of Americans have embraced *Roe v. Wade* because they desire to have the option of abortion, but at the same time they want it only as a last resort and thus are willing to permit some regulations upon the procedure. In practice, the American public has adopted a workable compromise, but to the ardent believers on both sides of the issue, these pragmatic methods of handling a sensitive moral cause are seen as dangerous precedent. The vitriolic language and the deep cleavages of cultural and moral beliefs have poisoned the ability to solve the many social problems attached to family planning and adolescent development. In so doing, there is a high risk of rhetoric overriding reason.

Proponents of anti-abortion or "right-to-life" legislation are entitled to their views. They overstep the boundaries of church–state separation in the Constitution and respect for the rights of others, however, when they seek to impose their views on everyone else. As we have already indicated, most religions are opposed to abortion, but some permit it on a limited range of grounds such as rape, incest, or danger to the physical or mental health of the mother. If a member of one of the latter faiths, or an atheist for that matter, seeks an abortion on such a legitimate basis, it is not the business or the right of pro-lifers to prohibit it through legislation. Furthermore, if the right to an abortion exists "in rape or incest cases, the only realistic way to protect that right seems to be to create a general right to abortion" (Sunstein, 1992, p. 40).

Euthanasia and Infanticide

Medical science, through the test of amniocentesis and the use of ultrasound, can provide women with information about whether they will have a baby with serious defects. This raises new issues: women who learn that their fetus is defective may elect to have an abortion, as in the Finkbine case, and pro-life advocates characterize those abortions as "fetal euthanasia" (Ramsey, 1970). The latter found an ally among those who see these abortions as an expression of dislike of and prejudice against the disabled.

In contrast, doctors and patients who support early testing and the consequent decisions of the parents have done so because they feel that the family should decide whether they are willing to accept the commitment for the care of such children. Calmer voices that have been drowned in the polemical outrage of both sides have suggested that perhaps abortion in these cases should be restricted only to those conditions incompatible with life, such as Tay-Sachs disease, or, perhaps, that women who are prepared to act on the basis of the tests' results must at least learn more about what is involved in caring for children with disabilities before they are allowed to end their pregnancies (Rhoden, 1988).

To Treat or Not to Treat

Many newborns whose congenital abnormalities are horrific are not treated so as to spare them and their families the hardships of continuing therapies, pain, disability, and emotional havoc (Zajac, 1989). If and when a child is born with terrible illness and incurable defects that would hamper any normal development, what should be the policy of the parents? The issue is fraught with the same indeterminacy of language and the same distortions observed in the abortion debates. Is the denial of medical or surgical procedures infanticide, as claimed by those who believe that all measures should be employed to save every infant (Koop, 1989)? In the past, midwives often did let severely impaired infants die; in many places, these babies were destroyed (Hontela & Reddon, 1996).

Death for sick infants, accompanied by parental participation, can be accomplished by withdrawing or withholding medical treatment or by administering lethal overdosage for eugenic or humanitarian reasons. This is a more common problem than has generally been believed. Until fairly recently, children would have died because nothing could be done for them, but now they survive, especially if they are treated at a hospital with specialized intensive care units (Lund, 1985; Rhoden, 1988).

The cases of many newborns are complex, with few available answers. For instance, some babies are born alive, but have such massive problems that they will die no matter what is done for them. In those cases, there may be less argument that they should be left untreated. In other cases, babies born with minor problems should certainly be treated and kept alive. Cases that are more difficult to assess, such as extremely premature birth, Down's syndrome, and spina bifida, lead to questioning of parents' and physicians' judgments.

In 1973, a study in a New Haven hospital revealed that, in an 18-month period, 14% of the 299 infant deaths were related to withholding treatment. As more knowledge of these practices occurred, more objections were raised to what had been considered a private matter to be decided between the parents and physician (Maciejczyk, 1983). The debate gained momentum with the publicity arising from the "Baby Doe" case in 1982. A Down syndrome infant, known only as "Infant Doe," needed surgery to correct a blocked esophagus and thereby allow food to reach her stomach. The parents refused consent to the surgery and also withheld food and water from the child. The infant died 6 days later.

National media attention touched off debate about decisions made in neonatal intensive care cases. The widespread public interest caused the Department of Health and Human Services to issue regulations designed to require hospitals to provide medically indicated treatment to handicapped infants. The rulings were immediately challenged in the courts. Several states then enacted legislation concerning withholding treatment from defective infants. Before the Baby Doe case, the practice of withholding treatment had received little or no publicity; afterward, more and more cases were heard in the courts. When judges were confronted with these medical decisions, they found competing rights and interests, with some courts granting *a priori* parental rights and others granting priority to the defective infant's right to life (Maciejczyk, 1983).

Federal laws concerning prevention of child abuse, emergency medical treatment, and guidelines for health care providers give some guidance in life support versus life termination for newborns and infants with especially complex medical problems, but may also be in conflict in specific cases. "As a philosophical approach, the 'quality of life' view, like the 'sanctity of life' position, recognizes human life as a value" (Fine, 2000, p. 350). Current federal policy, which mandates treatment in almost all cases in which the newborn's death is not imminent, focuses more on the "sanctity of life" position rather than on the burdens the physical problems impose on the infant and his or her prospective quality of life—that is, how much suffering the infant must endure.

In the Netherlands, on the other hand, the "Groningen Protocol for Euthanasia in Newborns" focuses on the "quality of life," averring that "To keep alive an infant whose short life expectancy will be dominated by pain—pain that it can neither bear nor comprehend—is … to do that infant a continuous injury" (Holt, 2005, p. 14). The American Academy of Pediatrics believes that the ultimate decision should be made by the parents, in consultation with physicians, clergy, and other family members (Fine, 2000). Inconsistencies between state and federal constitutional law, however, frequently result in "too much deference to parents in some situations and too little deference in others" (Rosato, 2000, p. 3). Rosato has proposed a bioethical approach to a resolution of such conflicts, focusing on the rights of the child and deciding these cases outside the child abuse/neglect context (p. 50).

Conjoined Twins

A more complex problem arises in the case of the live birth of conjoined twins. "Conjoined twins occur once in every 50,000 to 60,000 live births, according to the Children's Hospital of Philadelphia … . About 70% of conjoined twins are female. Many are stillborn. Only 35% survive the first day" (Johnston, 2003). (Another source says that conjoined twins are born approximately once in every 40,000 births, but only once in every *200,000 live* births, with only 65% surviving past the first day. Such births are more likely to occur in India or Africa, possibly influenced there by environmental conditions [http://zygote.swarthmore.edu/cleave3a.html].) The most common joining of the bodies is an anterior union of the upper half of the trunk of the body—approximately 35% of such cases.

In several cases, however, separation of conjoined twins may mean that one child must die so that the other may live. This obviously causes much agony and many challenges to parents and doctors and involves legal, religious, moral, and ethical controversies in the decision making. The choice to be made is always difficult. If the parents opt to sacrifice one twin so that the other might live, some might accuse them of neonaticide or infanticide, depending on when the surgical severance occurs in the twins' young lives. Each case of conjoined twins, however, is unique because *where* and *how* they are joined dictate whether or not they can be separated with both children surviving (as well as the quality of life), only one of the two surviving, or both dying. A further consideration is the availability of medical skill and technology to perform the necessary surgery.

The most famous conjoined twins were Eng and Chang Bunker, born in 1811 in Siam; they were joined at the chest and known as "the Siamese twins." They lived until 1874 and became well-known as they toured with P. T. Barnum. Within more recent years, we have witnessed on television news programs the seemingly miraculous, and certainly delicate, surgery to separate Philippine-born twins Carl and Clarence Aguirre, joined at the head when they were born in 2002. In this case, both survived, although they will require additional surgery as they grow older (Fitzgerald, 2005). On September 25, 2005, they were shown taking their first steps alone ("Dateline NBC").

In England, Mary and Jodie were born in 2000 joined at the lower abdomen and with a fused spine; Mary depended on Jodie for life, literally sucking life from her sister through the bloodstream. The doctors believed that the twins should be separated, with only Jodie surviving, or both would die within 3 to 6 months. The parents refused, on religious grounds, to permit the operation. The physicians took the case to court and through appeals to the Supreme Court of Judicature in the Court of Appeals. Ultimately, this court ruled that the surgery should be done so that Jodie might live. It was performed shortly thereafter, with the result that Jodie is developing normally (Park, 2002). The controversy continues in law review articles, with some arguing that killing one twin to save the other is immoral (Lugosi, 2001).

Before birth, it was known that Natasha and Courtney Smith were joined with a single heart and a single liver. Some doctors at the Honolulu hospital where they were to be born determined that the heart should go to Natasha, which would mean that Courtney would die, but other doctors disagreed. Those who favored the operation argued that Courtney could have a heart transplant, although its feasibility was unknown. In this case, the parents assented to the surgery. The twins were born on April 29, 2002, but they lived only 19 days (Park, 2002).

In yet another case, twin girls in San Antonio were connected "from chest to belly, ... were face to face, with their arms draped around each other. The girls shared a heart, liver, diaphragm and parts of their intestines" (Associated Press State and Local Newswire, 2004a). They were placed on ventilators, but, after their parents consulted with their doctors, were taken off their respirators at age 6 months as their condition continued to deteriorate.

Legislative and Judicial Responses

The problem of what to do has continued, however, because the issues are so complex, ambiguous, and difficult to define that neither state nor federal legislation has responded to the challenges of ill babies, and court rulings in individual cases have been contradictory and sometimes misleading. The controversy remains heated but unresolved. Parents and physicians who decided whether or not to treat the infants were not consistent in their judgments, and the ethical or moral beliefs were not universally acceptable. Indeed, there was dissension about what laws were even applicable (Evans, 1989).

The state always makes the value of life a basic, integral concept and therefore the common law concept of *parens patriae* vests the state with guardianship power over disabled individuals that allows intervention to preserve their physical and mental well-being. In the case of sickly infants, the state must also consider the allocation of scarce medical resources. The state's *parens patriae* power has frequently been invoked to limit parental freedom and authority in matters affecting a child's welfare (Maciejczyk, 1983). But parents also have intrinsic rights and interests because they bear the ultimate responsibility for the care and treatment of their children; traditionally, they have the authority to make decisions concerning their children's welfare. In the case of "Baby K" in 1994, for example, the courts ruled that the treatment of an encephalic infant at the parents' request must be honored by the hospital despite the futility of such help (Poland, 1997).

Eugenics, Mercy-Killing, and Euthanasia

Modern debates over abortion and the right to (let) die are not new and are not the result of new technologies. Eugenics played a large role in American debates in the past, often encompassing race, immigration, and health policies, including who was fit to live (Pernick, 1996). However, the Nazi programs of racial purity during the 1930s and 1940s made the issue totally unsavory, for the Nazis did not practice mercy-killing, but rather a form of mass annihilation of infants, children, and adults whom they considered physically and mentally ill or inferior. Such eugenics became ever more unacceptable, although there have been recurrences in parts of Africa in the past several years.

Recall the primitive form of eugenics that was practiced in primitive societies, Greece, and Rome by exposing or killing deformed or so-called "weak" babies, and the shift to no justification for killing as Jewish, and then Christian, practices became more widespread. The controversy has been intensified by debates over Dutch legislation and Dr. Kevorkian's campaign to permit assisted suicides, or mercy killing as in Oregon's proposed legislation. In contrast, there are those who declare that "the deliberate killing—because that is what it is—of a newborn whether by act of omission or a deliberate procedure that deprives the child of life is infanticide" (Koop, 1989, p. 101).

Debates in the medical and bioethical establishments keep re-emerging: How aggressive should the treatment be for such babies? Do we just let them die? Do we give them some treatment to ease the pain, but let them die, etc.? Some physicians feel that their decision made with the parents' consent should be private and should be respected. Most of the cases of ill newborns are complex, and doctors are often motivated by what they consider to be the need to relieve the parents and the infant's siblings from seemingly crushing burdens (Koop, 1989).

The most acrimonious debates have occurred over the views of Peter Singer, a widely respected philosopher, notably on "animal rights" and on the necessity of the affluent peoples of the Earth to help the starving. Basing his ethical conceptions upon utilitarian philosophical principles rather than traditional morality, he has aroused emotional responses to his views that advocate abortion and euthanasia. Singer's reputation stems from his book, *Animal Liberation* (1975), in which he argued that humans were not special or essentially different from animals and, therefore, should not enjoy special rights. He asserted that newborns are not yet self-conscious beings aware of themselves as distinct entities. A day-old infant has no desires or feelings in Singer's view. In his view, if it is morally right to shoot a badly injured or sick animal if it is in pain and has no hope of recovery, then it is equally right to kill an incurably sick infant. It is only our misplaced respect for the doctrine of the sanctity of human life that prevents us from seeing that what obviously is wrong to do to a horse is equally wrong to do to a defective infant (Singer, 1979).

Singer's view provoked opposition because it seemed to many an excursion into moral relativity and a denial of the Christian–Judaic tradition of the sanctity of life (Jamieson, 1999). To others, the arguments were reminiscent of those used in Nazi Germany to justify mass killings (Burleigh, 1994).

The Parental Positions

People who object to abortion motivated by knowledge that the fetus would be born with a severe disability maintain that this type of abortion, unlike most others, is not a private event. Therefore, many pro-life proponents advocate restricting access to the diagnostic technologies that provide women with information about their fetuses. That raises new issues. Children need to be wanted, desired, and cherished. The family undertakes the unending chores and demands of children: feeding, support, love, and discipline. Parents cannot relinquish their decision to raise a child when he or she has colic or an extreme case of the "terrible two's" or becomes a rotten adolescent. (Note: There are cases, as we have already seen, in which parents *do* abandon or harm children in these circumstances, often with disastrous consequences.)

Opponents of criminalization of abortion believe that the fetus is not a person or, at least, is not yet a member of the family. The family should be able to decide when they want a baby and accept their commitment once the child is conceived (Greenwood, 1994). Whatever their reasons for abortion or withholding care, they are attempting to say that they could not handle this problem and that the child might suffer in their care. (To say that they should surrender the child for adoption by others who could care for the child is not only easier said than done, but rarely solves the problem because such children may languish in foster care or be moved from one placement to another with negative effects on their emotional well-being.) They passionately believe that a child should be a commitment of love undertaken by the family.

The family that assumes responsibility for an infant with disabilities undertakes a potentially monumental task. The demands on the mother may be overwhelming, the emotional drain on the marriage and the other siblings in a family may be heavy, and the financial costs may be staggering. There is little community support in this situation, especially for poorer families. These are only some of the reasons given to avoid the birth of a baby with disabilities, and people who make such decisions should not be judged by one criterion, according to those who hold this point of view (Buchanan, 1996).

On the other hand, others are even more passionate about caring for the infant no matter what his or her condition may be. Koop expressed the belief that infant patients should receive the same thoughtful and thorough care as adult patients. As he wrote, "Just because he is small, just because he cannot speak for himself, this is no reason to regard him as expendable" (1989, p. 101). Some affirm that, if euthanasia were permitted, parents would be denied the rewards and satisfaction of working for the rehabilitation of their children. In their view, this care could only lead to the growth of the family in compassion, character, deeper understanding, and stronger affectionate bonds (Evans, 1989).

Despite the belief by some that suffering and care for children strengthens character and the family, evidence indicates that many family members do suffer chronic anxieties, guilt, and depression (Fost, 1981; Gustafson, 1973; Stinson & Stinson, 1981). The decision to withhold treatment, reduce care, or do everything possible necessitates agreements by the family and the physicians. To achieve this is sometimes difficult. Physicians play a central role in the diagnosis of baby defects, and they may question individual cases of parental refusal to authorize medical care by referring the case to state child welfare agencies as a form of child neglect. Strong disagreements can develop between the common law right of family autonomy and medical personnel insistence on enforcement of state child neglect laws (Knepper, 1994), as we noted in the previous chapter.

Proponents of the primacy of parental decision-making with respect to treatment decisions often do not take into account that many families are incapable of assuming such responsibility. The parents of impaired infants may be teenagers. They may be unmarried, raising questions about parenthood—particularly if the father wishes to enforce his rights—maybe even financially as well as legally. Some families may be dysfunctional: have a single mother, be a blended family, be unmarried cohabitors, or be drug addicted, illiterate, or abusive. That complicates the situation; if care is to be provided for these babies, who in such a family will assume the responsibility for a sickly infant who requires more care, more love, and more financial resources than these dysfunctional parents can provide?

Stop a moment and put yourself in the shoes of a parent with such a sick infant. What would *you* do?

Closing Thoughts

Despite the diverse opinions presented here, most people are uncomfortable with the actual murder of sick infants. The withholding of treatment, on the other hand, is complicated and requires more analysis than that of ideology. Certainly communities need to be empathetic when parents desire to withhold care for infants with severe and ultimately totally debilitating disabilities because there is little support for the parents or the disabled (except in rare cases). But even if we could accept infant euthanasia, we should never forget that infants are full human beings and should not be considered as expendable or having lesser value than others who are older. There is an intrinsic moral principle that all human life is sacred; therefore, mercy killing should never be acceptable. Treatment for the very defective infant is another matter; there are some cases in which it might be permissible, even in the infant's best interests, to withdraw or withhold care (Post, 1990).

Just as the abortion issue has been concerned with morality, theology, and differing cultural values and traditions, the topic of sex education as one of the methods of dealing with teenage pregnancies has become the center of heated political controversies. The pertinence, utility, and need for such programs will be discussed in the next chapter.

Child Homicide: Preventive Measures

11

As enlightened as we may think we are at the beginning of the 21st century, a society that focuses on punishment rather than prevention has learned little from the past. One of the purposes of punishment is allegedly deterrence of future crimes, and it is clear that function has had little success. It is doubtful that we will ever eradicate the abuse and murder of children totally, but we have a moral and professional obligation to do what we can to prevent these crimes.

As we have shown, children are killed most often because of the problems of people who are supposedly adult enough to know better. Our emphasis in prior chapters has been on the negative—that is, child homicide; our emphasis here is on the prevention of such crimes. Infanticide and filicide have frequently been the outcome of child abuse, which may come in the form of outright neglect as well as physical assaults. The U.S. Advisory Board on Child Abuse and Neglect noted an increase in the reported cases during the period from 1985 to 1993 (Berthea, 1999). The National Child Abuse and Neglect Data System reported continuing increases in child abuse and neglect fatalities "from 1.84 per 100,000 children in 2000 to 1.96 in 2001 and 1.98 in 2002" (National Clearinghouse, 2004). (They acknowledge that some of the increase may simply reflect better reporting.) Many agencies and groups have called for, and are still calling for, more extensive and intensive efforts at primary prevention of child abuse on the familial and societal levels. Primary prevention involves, among other ingredients, a healthy injection of education.

Prevention of Neonaticide

There are two major approaches to combating the problem of neonaticide. One is to prevent pregnancy, especially among girls in their teens. A strong voice for this option is that of Oberman (1996), as noted earlier. As the National Center for Health Statistics has reported, the birth rate for teenagers has been declining steadily since 1995 (Ventura, Mathews, & Curtin, 1999b). Whether we are addressing teens or older women, however, prevention of pregnancy is a major key to reducing the number of births of unwanted babies. The other possible approach is to ensure prenatal care when pregnancy does occur, so the prospective mother and the fetus not only have appropriate medical care, but also the social and psychological support that eliminates denial and makes her aware of her options. To Crittenden and Craig (1990), such programs are critical for every pregnant mother, as well as having medical and other personnel alert to the dangers of postpartum depression.

Programs aimed at preventing pregnancy are termed *primary*; those working with teens (or older women) who are already pregnant or parenting are considered to be *secondary* programs. There will probably always be a problem about prenatal care and continuing support when the woman is in a state of denial about being pregnant, but the proposed programs can at least reduce the number of cases in that category. According to available federal statistics, in 1997, first trimester prenatal care improved for the eighth consecutive year (Ventura, Martin, Curtin, & Mathews, 1999a).

In many cases that we found, the girl or young woman had had medical attention while pregnant, but *not* for the pregnancy, because she denied the pregnancy to herself and described any symptoms to her doctor as menstrual "irregularities." Wissow (1998) has suggested that doctors be more careful in their examinations and use tactful questioning and pregnancy tests to detect pregnancy. (Note: In this era of managed care, there may be more need for justification of pregnancy tests than mere suspicion on the doctor's part if the cost of the test is to be reimbursed.) They can refer the patient, if pregnant, for appropriate prenatal care and support services. They may also need to reassure some of their patients of confidentiality—that is, that they will not tell the girl's parents of her pregnancy unless she agrees. (This flies in the face of legislation that has been passed in several states that requires parents to be notified if their underage daughter seeks an abortion, but even some of those laws permit exceptions or alternatives when such notification may endanger the girl.)

Sex Education

Confronted by changing sexual mores, teen pregnancies, and more never-married mothers, society seeks ways to influence the prevalent youth culture. One of the ways suggested is to increase sexual education for the whole community, but make it particularly directed toward the young and available in the public schools. The issue is whether there should be sex education in the schools at all and, if there should be, what it should include.

Liberals have wanted to develop curricula that would include contraception information that would encourage young people to take proper precautions to avoid possible pregnancy, as well as to prevent the growing menaces of venereal disease and AIDS. Conservative Christian groups have opposed sex education that promoted knowledge of contraception and gave information on homosexuality. They fear that the full discussion of sexual information would encourage premarital sexual relationships. Many, however, do advocate the teaching of abstinence only.

Although debate over programs to influence teen behavior remains passionate, many state legislators seem to favor some kind of sex education in schools. Most states have provided a basic form of instruction on disease prevention and contraception as well as stressing abstinence education. In 1996, 22 bills were introduced on school-based sex education. Half would have increased parental involvement or insisted on emphasizing abstinence until marriage; the other half would expand existing programs.

In Florida, AIDS education activities were supported, with details of the programs specified. Massachusetts law insisted that students have parental permission to attend sex education classes, while Rhode Island passed laws that allowed parental review of curricula and materials and also permitted parents to remove their children from these classes (Sollum, 1997). In Colorado in 1996, conservatives attempted, but failed, to amend the state constitution by a law that would have given parents the right "to direct and control the upbringing, education, values and discipline of their children" (Donovan, 1997, p. 187). Polls reported in 1999 and 2000, however, indicated that an overwhelming percentage of Americans (76 to 90%, depending on the item) believed that youths should receive information about contraception and prevention of STDs and how to avoid unwanted pregnancies (Parker, 2001).

A large number of parents have expressed concerns that schools cannot present sex without including values and since teachers could not be neutral, the curriculum should center on biology rather than attempt to regulate teen behavior. They claim that parents, churches, and other community groups should assume the responsibility of educating children in more morally directed teenage pregnancy prevention. What should be emphasized, they assert, is that premarital sex is wrong and abstinence is the only permissible behavior. As one writer suggested, “Unless sex education addresses values, ethics, morality, deferment of gratification, and goals, it is incomplete and potentially dangerous” (MacDonald, 1987, p. 384).

Data reported from the Youth Risk Behavior Survey at the turn of this century indicate that half of all high school students have engaged in sexual intercourse at some point in their lives, and percentages rise with increasing grade level. Oral and anal intercourse was also found to be common. Not only were 9% of females aged 15 to 19 years becoming pregnant each year, but about three million adolescents *each year* were also acquiring a sexually transmitted disease. These numbers are despite the offering of required sex education classes from elementary school (57%) to high school (82%) (Parker, 2001).

These figures have led to research on how effective such teaching is, whatever its content. As in the case of arguments over what should be taught, debates range widely. One of the proposed solutions to reducing the number of unwanted pregnancies has been to introduce sex education and contraception information into the curriculum starting in the junior high school (although, as noted earlier, this has changed to beginning in elementary school). Evidence available to Stout and Rivara (1989) indicated that the traditional sex education programs in junior and senior high schools had little or no impact upon adolescent sexual activity. On the other hand, most studies emphasize the lack of evidence that “sex education classes, condom distribution programs or exposure to pregnant and parenting classmates promotes sexual activity … ” (Stevens-Simon & Kaplan, 1998, p. 1206).

Yet, impelled by ideological bias, many studies report more or less success depending upon their point of view. One excellent study is an example of these inconsistencies. The authors reflected the commonly held opinion that the effect of sex education at best was problematical, citing test reports that demonstrated less change than hoped. Then another author continued by noting that most Americans feel that sex education should begin at home, but also believe it should be taught at school and that the programs should stress sexual restraint and promote family values such as fidelity and commitment in marriage. They concluded that “it appears that sex education programs that promote abstinence can be effective in producing a positive attitude change toward abstinence” (Olsen, Weed, Ritz, & Jensen, 1991, p. 640).

In contrast, in an equally valid study, the authors claimed that “abstinence only” education, though seemingly successful, had major drawbacks. They found that studies show that convincing, strong inculcation of the necessity of sexual abstinence before marriage inhibited conversation about safe sex. It created “an atmosphere in which teenagers are emotionally incapable of using the knowledge they acquire in the classroom to make the kinds of conscious decisions about their behavior to avoid pregnancy" (Stevens-Simon & Kaplan, 1998, p. 1206).

Mauldon and Luker (1996) claimed that contraceptive education was successful. If contraceptive education occurs in the same year that a teenager becomes sexually active, the odds of any method or condom use are increased by 70 to 80%, and the odds of pill use are more than doubled (p. 19). In direct contradiction, Maynard and Rangarajan (1994) said that enhanced family planning information and counseling for first-time teen mothers did little or nothing to stop subsequent pregnancies.

Other reports adopted a more dispassionate view. One cited 23 studies that discussed the most successful of these programs. They noted:

> Not all sex and AIDS education programs had significant effects on adolescent sexual risk-taking behavior, but specific programs did delay the initiation of intercourse, reduce the frequency of intercourse, reduce the number of sexual partners, or increase the use of condoms or other contraceptives. (Kirby et al., 1994, p. 339)

Later research from California (Kirby, Korpi, Barth, & Capampang, 1997) echoed these sentiments, and a condom distribution program in Philadelphia also produced results that showed no increase in the level of sexual activity among young people (Furstenberg, Geitz, Teitler, & Weiss, 1997). Both studies indicated, however, that there was not a statistically significant increased use of contraceptives either. The Centers for Disease Control and Prevention (CDC) found a number of programs successful, including "Reducing the Risk," "Safer Choices," "Becoming a Responsible Teen (BART)," "Making a Difference: An Abstinence Approach to STD," and others (Kirby, 2001). The Seattle Social Development Project, aimed at students in high-crime area elementary schools, included teacher training, parenting classes, and child social skills training (Lonczak, Abbott, Hawkins, Kosterman, & Catalano, 2002). Details of the program are discussed later.

What has been shown in these studies is that some programs are more effective than others, and effort is needed to discover, distill, and use the more effective curricula. As long as the debates are mired in ideological and cultural conflicts, however, the necessary pursuit of the best means to teach our children more careful and more meaningful sexual behavior will not take place. Moreover, all of these educational efforts must compete with blatant examples of women in the public eye having babies out of wedlock, commercials promoting sexual prowess, and information available in the media and on computers of how to look and be "sexier." Unless youths are rigorously home-schooled and isolated from their peers, there is no way that they can avoid the contra-education efforts.

Pregnancy Prevention

Prevention of pregnancy begins with information. Vance (1985) urged sex education, in a family context, from kindergarten through grade 12, using precise language to avoid misconceptions. For those who think kindergarten is too early to mention such concepts, it might be informative to observe the television programs that these little ones watch and see what sexual content is conveyed in them. In one study (Ward, 1995), it was found that more than one in four interactions in primetime programs watched by young viewers had statements related to sexuality, with more such content in the programs aimed at adolescents than young children (which does not mean that younger children do not see these programs). Hogue (1997) pointed out that while explicit sexuality is on television and film screens, contraceptive ads are not allowed and the consequences of unprotected sex are rarely presented. This is an inappropriate imbalance.

One example of Vance's approach is seen in a long-term study in Seattle. A 12-year study conducted in Seattle's most crime-ridden neighborhoods worked with children in grades 1 through 6 and sought to "foster an interest in school and learning among children and to enhance their self-esteem … " (Brody, 1999). The findings at follow-up when the subjects were age 18 showed that, compared to peers who had not been in the intervention program, the subjects were "13 percent less likely to engage in sexual intercourse, 19 percent less likely to have had multiple sex partners and 35 percent less likely to have caused a pregnancy or to have become pregnant" (Brody, 1999).

The youngsters were taught problem-solving skills beginning in first grade, and they were also taught how to say "no" and still retain their friends. In addition, parenting programs were offered and more than 40% of parents of the subjects participated in this aspect of the intervention project. With the resulting enhanced self-esteem, improved parenting at home, and strengthened skills, there was apparently less need on the part of many of the participating youngsters to find "love" or acceptance through sexual activity.

The programs sponsored by the 1996 Welfare Reform bill were principally of the primary type, but were based on an "abstinence-only" philosophy and were not permitted to provide information about contraception (Wurf, 1997). Similarly, in 1998, an amendment to the Health and Human Services bill then in Congress would have mandated that all Title X clinics (established in 1970 to reduce unintended pregnancy among low-income women) require minors to obtain parental consent before receiving contraceptives or abortion-related services (Russell, 1998).

Although such an approach may mirror some religious and idealistic views, it does not conform to other religious (and nonreligious) practices or to contemporary reality. Some parents (and others) allege that if contraceptive information is included, this is tantamount to telling adolescents that their sexual activity is expected and approved. Similarly, anti-abortionists are loudly opposed to abortion even being mentioned as part of sex education. For the youths, the necessary admission of sexual activity needed to gain the consent may be more than they are willing to do; they would rather risk pregnancy than tell their parents what they do. Indeed, it is taking this risk that has too often resulted in neonaticide.

Participants in the 1999 Teen Pregnancy Prevention Conference held at Pennsylvania State University in November 1999 discussed education programs that began as early as age 9 and that involved boys and girls (not necessarily together) and their parents. (Note: Age 9 is *not* too early to begin this instruction. The National Vital Statistics Report lists the number of babies born to mothers aged 10 to 14 years [Martin, Smith, Mathews, & Ventura, 1999], although the figures reported on decreases in adolescent pregnancies refer to the 15- to 19-year age group and do not mention the younger girls.)

Some of the programs offered in Pennsylvania involve working with diverse communities and encouraging community support for pregnancy prevention programs. At least one middle school program stresses training in parenting, although others include only facets of parenting skills. Abstinence is a principal focus of several programs, but others explore the pleasurable as well as the painful aspects of sexual feelings. This means that self-respect as well as respect for others is also taught in some of the workshops.

Several abstinence programs are described by Napier (1997), who is obviously against sex education programs that include contraceptive information with its implication that "teens will be teens." One such program, sponsored by To Our Children's Future With Health, Inc., a Philadelphia group, provides a variety of programs to preteens, teenagers, and parents. Supported by state and federal funds, the program pays stipends to the preadolescent participants; for some, that is sufficient reason to attend (Raghavan, 1998).

However, another Philadelphia study reported in the *Journal of the American Medical Association* divided 6th- and 7th-graders into three groups, each of which received 8 hours of health education. "One focused on abstinence; one concentrated on condom use; and a control group addressed avoiding nonsexual diseases" (Jemmott, Jemmott, & Fong, 1998). The researchers found that after 6 months and again after 12 months, more of the abstinence group students were having sex than condom-group students, and more of them were having unprotected sex. An Institute of Medicine study found that abstinence-only sex education did not delay the onset of sexual intercourse (Hogue, 1997).

On the other hand, Weckerle and Wolfe (1998) cited programs introduced at the elementary and middle school levels that try to teach relationship skills and provide information about dating. As they commented, "It is disturbing that teenagers appear to be poorly informed concerning what constitutes normative dating behavior" (p. 355) and also appear to be at risk for dating violence. Their program tries to identify (and ultimately to reduce) the risk factors, which include family background, psychological adjustment, and personal resources.

A handbook addressed to adolescent girls and written in language that they can understand, together with its discussion guide (Mathes & Irby, 1993), provides an informative basis for pregnant teens in terms of what is happening within their bodies, what care they need, and what happens at delivery. It also has several very useful chapters on the baby's development during pregnancy and postnatally so that the young mother knows what to expect. Perhaps tucked *between* these two sections deliberately, two chapters focus on (1) choices to be made with respect to becoming or remaining pregnant; and (2) sexually transmitted diseases. The chapter on choices includes information ranging from abstinence to prescriptions, but opens with a concept too often overlooked: "Thinking ahead." The chapter on diseases brings to the fore risks in this aspect of sexual activity that adolescents too often ignore, much to their later distress.

Pathway/Senderos, a neighborhood-based teen pregnancy prevention program in New Britain, Connecticut (Pearlman & Bilodeau, 1999), is a replication of a very successful youth development/teen pregnancy prevention program begun in Harlem (New York) in the 1980s (Carrera & Dempsey, 1988). Participants are recruited during the 6th grade and they remain in the 5-days-per-week program throughout high school (as long as they do not become pregnant). "However, if a female participant does become pregnant, or a male participant impregnates anyone, she or he is then referred to the appropriate community agency for young parents" (Pearlman & Bilodeau, p. 93).

Collaboration between academic psychologists and the community-based workers seeks to intervene in the poverty/school dropout/teen parenting cycle prevalent in a "deteriorating Spanish-speaking area" in New Britain. The program, which uses a case management approach, is based on an approach that "connects academic failure and continuing poverty to teen pregnancy, and academic success, including college, to a vision of future opportunity" (Pearlman & Bilodeau, 1999, p. 93). The doctoral students and their professors who are involved contribute information, resources, and time to the program while also learning of real community needs and problems involved in working with these disadvantaged youths.

In another program that used slightly older peers to provide education about safe sex practices, young medical students in Australia were sent back to their former schools to teach adolescents before they became sexually active (Short, 1998). The program, begun in 1992, was so successful that its sponsors in Melbourne were invited by the Chinese Ministry of Health to work with medical schools in Beijing and Shanghai to try to develop something similar in those cities.

Just looking at the issue of sex education from the standpoint of providing adequate and appropriate information to young people, it is apparent that this is not being done in enough schools. Indeed, it is not being provided adequately even at home. The result is that adolescents, and children even younger, are surrounded by sexual stimuli but lack adequate information to deal with it. For example, how many mothers tell their preteen daughters much about their maturing bodies beyond the details of menstruation? How many say to a daughter, "It's *your* body. *You* are responsible for its care. It is up to *you* to see that it is not violated"? There is at least one magazine, addressed to and written by teenagers, *Teen Voices,* that has published a series of articles on teen pregnancy containing the thoughts of pregnant teenagers ("So you're going to be a mother ... " 1999). How effectively it reaches the appropriate target audience is unknown.

Stoiber, Anderson, and Schowalter (1998) have indicated several items of misinformation held by adolescents relevant to sexuality, and urge the use of small group-counseling types of programs to provide correct information as well as support to teenagers in this area. They also point out that the best prevention programs reach youngsters *before* they become sexually active. Such programs promote abstinence, provide information about sexually transmitted diseases, and improve decision-making skills, among other themes. "It should be noted that frank discussions about sex often do not occur in classroom settings or occur too late, after adolescents have already become sexually active" (p. 285).

Planned Parenthood's TIPS (Teen Information and Peer Services) Program trains teens to be resources for their high school peers. They can discuss pregnancy as well as birth control, sexually transmitted diseases, and abstaining from sex (Brown, 1997; Minton, 1998). The Girls, Inc. organization, which seeks to help girls reach their potential, also sponsors a number of programs to provide this type of information to young girls.

Not only girls need to be taught. A Mother–Son Health Promotion Project was conducted in several Philadelphia public housing projects and had as one of its goals educating mothers so that they could teach their sons about and influence their sexual behavior (Dubin, 1998). Emphasis in this area is on STDs and the use of condoms. On the other hand, when adolescent boys have already become fathers, they also need intervention programs.

Stoiber, Anderson, & Schowalter found four goals of intervention groups for adolescent fathers "supported in the literature: (1) social support; (2) vocational/career development; (3) parent/child relationship; and (4) prevention of subsequent conceptions" (1998, p. 295).

Corcoran, Franklin, and Bell (1997) asked 105 teenagers participating in adolescent pregnancy education programs in Texas what they thought should be included in the programs. These males (22%) and females (78%), ranging in age from 11 to 22 years (86% aged 14 to 18), and largely from lower income families, answered a variety of questions, often with embarrassment. Questions concerning the use or avoidance of birth control led to some answers that indicated that young people rejected birth control because of the lack of spontaneity, embarrassment at buying birth control materials, fear of parents finding out, anxiety about side effects of medical methods, or belief that pregnancy would not happen to them (invincibility). Youngsters' responses to why they had babies indicated that they desired or needed love, or they wished to keep the male partner. For some, babies were "accidents," while others wanted attention from or popularity with peers.

When queried on "all the reasons you can think of for teens becoming pregnant *when they don't want to be*," young people cited the lack of knowledge about or misuse of contraceptives or peer pressure. Then they were asked, in view of their knowledge, what advice they would give to a teen who did not want to become pregnant. The teens had a variety of suggestions to offer peers to reduce their vulnerability to pressures to have sex and to increase sources of information available.

Other questions were asked of teens already pregnant or parenting, beginning with "How many of you had planned to get pregnant when you did?" (Corcoran, Franklin, & Bell, 1997, p. 373). Many commented that they had not been prepared for the rigors of pregnancy or the lack of sleep and isolation from others once the baby arrived. These comments demonstrate the need for information such as that contained in the Mathes and Irby handbook (1993) referred to earlier.

Secondary Prevention

In a study of 70 patients delivered at a Cleveland hospital in 1978 who had no prenatal care, 20 of 43 cited internal barriers for not having prenatal care: depression, denial of pregnancy, fear of doctors, unplanned pregnancy; 10 of 43 cited external barriers: financial problems, no transportation, no child care, inability to obtain clinic appointment, clinic wait too long; and 13 of 43 said they had no problems with the pregnancy or no special reason for not seeking prenatal care (Joyce, Diffenbacher, Greene, & Sorokin, 1983). These researchers concluded that while hospitalized women received good prenatal care and were prepared for future pregnancies, those women who denied their pregnancies or did not seek care remained at risk for the future. "In order to reduce the incidence of 'no care' deliveries, community outreach and marketing strategies to reach the patient population who do not seek care are necessary in addition to hospital-based approaches" (pp. 94–95).

Other studies that cite barriers to prenatal care included long waits at clinics, short time with the medical personnel, and communications difficulties, especially for non-English-speaking patients (Oropesa, Landale, Inkley, & Gorman, 1999). Oropesa and colleagues also found, in their study of 1255 mothers from the Puerto Rican Maternal and Infant Health Survey, that prenatal care was less likely when the pregnancy was an unwanted one.

In Baltimore, the city school system established the Paquin School in 1966 to make a positive change in the lives of childbearing adolescents (Boyer-Patrick, 1999). A magnet school that draws from beyond the city limits, Paquin also has a school-based clinic providing counseling services from clinical social workers and psychiatrists. In addition to academic (grades 6 to 12) and counseling services, the school also has a small on-site day care facility, vocational, and back-to-school re-entry programs, and a program aimed at young fathers.

Boyer-Patrick found, in the responses to his survey (answered anonymously), that only 4% of the sample ($N = 110$) felt that they would not be able to complete high school due to parenting responsibilities. More than a third of the group believed that they would be able to complete college, and almost one quarter thought that they would be able to complete an advanced professional degree. These figures, as Boyer-Patrick noted, were seen despite the fact that many of the girls lived in homes where their parents had not completed high school, let alone college. Perhaps more important was his finding that they did not stay in therapy unless they had previously been willing to discuss their pregnancy with close friends or significant adults. He concluded that an atmosphere of trust had to be developed if the professional counseling was going to be effective—an important point if special programs are truly going to help these adolescents.

Needless to say, not all prospective mothers are adolescents and not all of them are substance abusers of one kind or another. Those women who *are* drug addicts, however, place the babies they carry at considerable risk of brain damage, organ damage, seizures, respiratory disorder, and behavioral symptoms. The Medical University of South Carolina in Charleston established a program in which pregnant women who tested positive for cocaine use were given a choice: They could enter a rehabilitation program at the hospital to become drug free or they might be arrested and serve jail time (Zitella, 1996). Hospital personnel did extensive drug counseling, as well as urging the pregnant patients to participate in the rehabilitation program for their benefit (no arrest) and so that they would give birth to a healthy baby.

There were successes with this approach, but it was stopped because the federal government perceived it as discriminatory (most of the participants were poor nonwhites) and threatened to withdraw funding from the medical school (Zitella, 1996). Zitella's proposal that cocaine-addicted mothers participate in such a program or lose parental rights may be perceived in the same way, but she does have a valid point—if parents do not take responsibility for their children's well-being, then government is forced to care for them—at great expense socially as well as financially.

Finally, a group of programs begin during pregnancy, especially with adolescents and very young adult mothers-to-be, and continue through the early postnatal period. These programs provide the kind of support that used to be common in remote villages and ancient communities, a support that teaches the mother-to-be about becoming and then being a mother and enhances her pleasure in her baby. The principal support figure is often a "doula"—a woman who is not a midwife (although she may well be present at the time of delivery) but who is a mentor, a hand-holder, a coach, and a source of support for the mother-to-be before and after birth (Behnke & Hans, 2002; Wilgoren, 2005b). In a program that provided social support to pregnant low-income, largely Latina (65%) women in early pregnancy, the women had easier deliveries, healthier babies, and less postpartum depression than might have been expected from their life circumstances (Collins, Dunkel-Schetter, Lobel, & Scrimshaw, 1993). Had a support program such as "Baby Boot Camp" (Schachman, Lee, & Lederman, 2004) existed in Hawaii several years ago, as well as at other military facilities, maybe Renee Beth Smith would not have killed her 9-week-old infant in 1997 for lack of anyone to support her (see Chapter 8 and Appendix A).

In yet another program, a doula was assigned to pregnant incarcerated women in an effort to benefit the baby as well as the mother-to-be. Apparently this did help the women to refocus their thinking in a more rational direction, as well as make delivery a more positive experience than was the norm in jail (Schroeder & Bell, 2005). This type of support program can clearly help mothers as they move from pregnancy to parenting and possibly reduce the risks of neonaticide and infanticide.

Preventing Infanticide and Filicide

In the cases of infanticide and filicide, clearly there needs to be prevention as well. Parents, especially fathers or those in that role, must be shown the value and effectiveness of alternative disciplinary strategies to shaking and beating children. Classes for parents *and* school children in behavior management and adult–child communication should be available at no charge as a community service; the media as well should contribute information and samples of appropriate disciplinary techniques (Crittenden & Craig, 1990).

Parenting education—that is, the realities of infant and child development among other matters, is critical for adolescent parents, perhaps especially the fathers, but is also important for chronologically, if not emotionally, more mature parents. There might then be fewer abusive overreactions to wet diapers, infant cries, and similar normal situations that too often result in homicide. These classes, too, might begin and be required at 4th or 5th grade level, emphasizing the 24-hour responsibility of parenting, the total commitment needed by babies, and the fact that parents "give" more to babies than they "get" in return, at least for many months or even years. This is also important for babysitters, which is another reason why it should be taught so early. Other needs for adolescent parents typically include taking control of their sexual activity, learning how to set goals and to move toward their attainment, and how to follow through on their plans and commitments.

One program for adolescent mother groups is outlined in terms of session-by-session objectives, with samples of specific activities, for which only the session titles are cited here (Stoiber et al., 1998, pp. 299–300):

Session One: Memories as Motivation for Being the Best Possible Parent
Session Two: Communication Competence
Session Three: Exploring Communication Patterns
Session Four: Sexual Refusal and Pregnancy Prevention
Session Five: Reflective Decision Making Applied to Sexual Situations and Parent Situations
Session Six: Feeling Nurtured
Session Seven: Understanding Love, Friendship, and Sexuality
Session Eight: Goal Setting and Future Planning
Session Nine: Constructing Career Pathways
Session Ten: Staying on Track

Another type of program, involving home visits by nurses and even trained non-nurses, has been found to be very helpful to young (usually under age 19) or unmarried single mothers in terms of avoiding welfare dependence, child abuse, involvement with drugs, or trouble with the law (Olds et al., 1998). The support begins when a female is pregnant with her first child and continues until the child is 2 years old; it includes advice on child-rearing and life skills as well as medical matters. Not only did the women function better as mothers, but they were also less likely to mistreat their children and had less sexual activity. For a program that cost less than $3,000 per year per mother, the results, followed for 15 years, seem highly cost effective in their positive results for the families involved and in savings for welfare programs.

In some communities, such as Burlington, Vermont, and Glenside, Pennsylvania, there have been residential "family centers" for young mothers where parenting, life skills, and therapeutic classes were offered in addition to regular high school education. The combination of support, instruction, and therapy provided benefits to the mother, the child, and thereby to society in social and economic costs (Berman, 1999).

Confirmation of the value of intensive care in infancy and early childhood comes from the follow-up of programs such as High/Scope at Perry Preschool in Ypsilanti, Michigan (almost 30 years of follow-up studies) and the Frank Porter Graham Child Development Center at the University of North Carolina at Chapel Hill, where more than 100 subjects first seen as toddlers were evaluated at age 21 (Waggoner, 1999). Benefits to the mothers as well as the children were found in terms of education and employment status. A cost-benefit analysis of the High/Scope program "showed that for every $1 spent on child care, taxpayers saved $7, mainly from costs to crime victims" (Waggoner, 1999). In addition, one might expect savings from the lack of need for welfare payments, extended medical care to babies born to drug-addicted or malnourished mothers, and extended schooling in the form of repeated grades.

New parents can be taught the dangers of shaking the baby via an inexpensive (less than $10 per infant) and very short video program designed by Dr. Mark Dias, a pediatric neurosurgeon at Penn State (Pennsylvania State University, 2005; cf. Semuels, 2005). In a study by Dias that tracked babies born in Buffalo, New York, area hospitals over a 6-year period whose mothers were exposed to the program, he found that cases of abusive head injuries per 100,000 births were cut almost in half. Given that the medical care for babies suffering from shaken baby syndrome can run from $300,000 to $1 million for 3 years *per child* (Semuels, 2005) and the possible long-term damage to the child's development, widespread use of Dias' program seems highly appropriate.

A different approach—video-guided group sessions—was used with parents of children aged 3 to 8 years who had been diagnosed with oppositional defiant disorder or conduct disorder (Webster-Stratton & Reid, 2003). The group sessions taught the parents positive parenting skills and behavior management skills. The result was improved parent–child interaction, reduced criticism of the children by the parents, reduced violent discipline, and reduced child conduct problems.

Apart from the risk of child homicide stemming from parental lack of knowledge, lack of resources, and lack of commitment, there are risks also when the children have disabilities such as severe cerebral palsy, moderate or severe mental retardation, or autism. Their parents believe that they have altruistic motives in killing them—that they are ending the child's suffering. Autism is a neuropsychiatric syndrome that appears early in the child's life and is more prevalent in boys, occurring as often as six cases per 1,000 children (Palermo, 2003). It "is characterized by a disturbance in interpersonal behaviors; abnormal language; limited, abnormal, or absent emotional reciprocity; and repetitive and stereotyped behaviors" (Palermo, p. 49).

Given these problems, it is difficult for parents to bond with these children as well as stressful for them to witness the children's difficulties and the stigma that becomes attached to them by others. There are no known physical causes for autism, nor are there very many effective therapies. Having the parents as part of a "treatment team" in whatever treatment is available, thus relieving *their* stress and possible feelings of "blame" for some unknown contribution to their children's condition, is important if they are not to become so depressed and guilt ridden that they decide to put the child out of his or her "misery." This must be part of the interaction that physicians and health care professionals have with the parents (and other family members).

Other Alternatives

If the girl or young woman can admit her pregnancy to herself and to someone who can help her, then she need not be placed in the position of feeling that there is no alternative to neonaticide. If she and her boyfriend or husband can admit that they do not know how to parent and seek help, then infanticide and filicide might also be reduced. In the case of pregnancy, adoption is a very constructive alternative. To avert child abuse or neglect, the foster care system *may* be helpful to the child, at least until the parents learn how to parent effectively and if social caseworkers are available to provide sufficient support.

Adoption

Historically, adoption was a largely satisfactory alternative to teenage or unmarried motherhood and certainly to neonaticide and infanticide. Whether the neonate was left where he or she was certain to be found and cared for, as in the contemporary "Safe Haven" program, or the pregnant woman was cared for in a Salvation Army residence or other program and the newborn placed for adoption from that situation, the new baby had a fighting chance at a good life. In some other cases, especially when the mother was quite young and had little support, she might turn to adoption when she found infant care overwhelming. The benefits to the child and to the receiving caretakers who thereby attained their much-desired status as parents were generally strongly positive.

There are potential problems today, however, that were less common than in the past. One is obviously substance abuse before or during pregnancy and its effect on the fetus/baby. Another is exposure to unhealthy factors in the environment and to diseases such as HIV and AIDS that were unknown decades ago. The possibility of a girl or young woman reneging on her decision for placement (or the father not agreeing to it) or of her becoming too intrusive in an "open adoption" situation also plays a role in domestic neonatal adoption today (Schwartz, 2006). Having heard of one too many upset adoptions in this country or being faced with a years-long wait for a placement via a social services agency, many prospective adoptive parents are looking elsewhere. Overseas adoptions have their parental problems as well, though, including the difficulty of adopting a very young and healthy baby (Schwartz, 2000; Schwartz & Kaslow, 2003).

Foster Home Placement

A major function of welfare agencies across the United States is the protection of children from abuse. When, as the result of someone's call, it finds actual abuse or child endangerment, the agency typically removes the child from the home and places the youngster in a foster home. This can prevent infanticide or filicide as long as the child is in a safe foster setting. Meanwhile, at least in theory, the potentially abusive/homicidal parent can be helped with psychotherapy and parenting education. A parent sensitive to his or her emotional difficulties might even request the temporary foster placement while seeking to straighten out life's difficulties. There is concern today, however, that some foster home placements continue too long for the welfare of the children involved, and a number of states have moved to make such placements permanent via adoption if the parents have not been rehabilitated within a 2- or 3-year period. In addition, social workers with too heavy a caseload may not be effective in their supervisory visits to homes where there has been a history of abuse or neglect (Schwartz, 2006).

Summarizing the Alternatives

It is important for people in our society to recognize that we cannot solve all problems regarding neonaticide, infanticide, and filicide and that we cannot prevent teenage pregnancy completely. It is also important to recognize that there are certain realities that cannot be ignored: youths and adults alike will engage in sexual relations without being aware of, or of ignoring if they are aware, the possible consequences or the preventive alternatives to these consequences. There is no reason why parents cannot teach abstinence at home while the school conveys information available in the larger society such as the use of contraceptive measures to avoid pregnancy and sexually transmitted diseases. Therefore, a rapprochement needs to be reached in terms of what is included in sex education because prevention is far less costly to human lives as well as in dollars than paying for the welfare, psychotherapy, and penal bills after the fact. There is also no reason why parents and schools cannot teach child development as well as parent responsibilities so that fewer children's lives are lost to abuse and neglect.

12 Concluding Thoughts and Recommendations

> Society is often only concerned with treating, or prosecuting, the mother after she has hurt or killed her child; what is more important is protecting her before she has a chance to do so. The key to preventing such tragedies is education of both the general public and medical professionals. (Schroeder, 1993, p. 292) (This applies as well to fathers and father figures.)

Reviewing the historical, literary, and multicultural aspects of neonaticide, infanticide, and filicide, as has been done here, provides a context for crimes that some people may think are new bases for today's headlines. Clearly, this is not the case. Motives have not changed appreciably over the centuries, although we may be more aware of their variety today. What *has* changed in some jurisdictions is the way in which the perpetrators of these crimes, especially neonaticide, are regarded by the law. There is also greater awareness, in some quarters, of the need for changing society's perspective as Schroeder, quoted here, has suggested, although we would add lawyers, legislators, and judges to his target audience.

Provide Information

It is already evident that a focus on preventing unwanted pregnancy is needed, especially among teenagers, although women in their 20s and older may also be in need of appropriate information. This should be made available through multiple outlets, from medical offices to schools to recreation centers. Public service announcements on radio and television, around the clock, should make women aware of where they can get help and information. In addition, factual information about the joys and irritants of infant and child development needs to be available to all who interact with children of any age. Education should therefore have a very high position on the priority list of eliminating, or at least reducing, crimes against children.

That not everyone will be reached or, if reached, will pay attention to this information is a given. There will still be neonaticides, infanticides, and filicides, but if *one* child's life is saved, if *one* adult is kept from committing child homicide and another intervenes to prevent fatal child abuse, the effort will be worthwhile. Ultimately, the ripple effect will occur and more children and adults will be spared tragic ends.

Therapeutic Rehabilitation

In the present, however, we are confronted with hundreds of child homicides each year. The uneven treatment across the United States of mothers who commit neonaticide, with an emphasis on punishment, needs to be restructured. That the young woman has committed a crime is not disputed; the circumstances under which she acted and the ways in which she "pays" for her act must be re-evaluated. Great Britain and other sectors of the United Kingdom recognize that these women are typically not "threats to society" who need punishment in prison, but rather that they need mental health therapy and rehabilitative education as well. They can be confined, if necessary, and receive treatment in a psychiatric hospital instead of a prison. They can participate in community service projects as part of their sentence—perhaps teaching younger girls how to prevent pregnancy or, if pregnant, how important it is to have prenatal care, the alternatives to neonaticide, or how to be a good mother if that is the choice.

Providing adequate mental health care for women who have committed neonaticide or killed an infant or toddler while in the throes of postpartum depression or psychosis, whether on an in-patient or out-patient basis, is a problem. Resources are even less available if these women are in prison. If the woman committed infanticide or filicide for other reasons (convenience, revenge, in anger), however, that should be treated as a crime.

As Spinelli (2004) and others have pointed out, most Western countries focus on prevention and rehabilitation with regard to maternal infanticide. The United States does not; it emphasizes punishment. Women who suffer from postpartum psychosis do not need punishment. Therapy and, possibly, appropriate medication will deter them from killing again. Most countries distinguish between such cases and those resulting from other causes. (One difficulty is that postpartum psychosis does not have a clear diagnostic category in the APA's *DSM-IV*, as noted earlier.) Whatever the cause of the crime, many of these women "have been judged not only in terms of what they allegedly did, but also their compliance (or lack of it) with stereotypical female behavior" (Schwartz & Isser, 2001, p. 707).

For mothers who commit any form of child homicide, there is a great need to bring together the efforts of those who work in the fields of psychology, law, and public policy in the interdisciplinary arena known as "therapeutic jurisprudence." This approach goes beyond mental health law *per se* and "seeks to focus attention on an often neglected ingredient in the calculus necessary for performing a sensible policy analysis of mental health law and practice—the therapeutic dimension … " (Wexler & Winick, 1991, p. 979).

Of the three broad categories of child homicide with which we have been concerned, neonaticide appears to be the one for which therapeutic rehabilitation should be introduced first as a major component of any sentence determined by the court. Fazio and Comito (1999) have asserted that those who have committed neonaticide, especially teenagers in this group, are the criminal offenders most amenable to rehabilitation. Furthermore, they typically are not repeat offenders and do not pose a threat to society. In the view of these lawyers, neonaticide is not perceived as a premeditated homicide; "it is a compulsive and rash act that occurs immediately after birth when the girl confronts what she has denied for nine months" (p. 3167).

We would not say that the crime occurred as a result of physiological changes in the female during pregnancy or immediately following delivery; that creates an inferiority in females that is untrue. More appropriately in most of the neonaticide cases, we would say that the new mother suffered from "diminished capacity" to appreciate the wrongfulness of what she was doing because of a host of other sources of emotional upset at the time of delivery and immediately following. She is rarely a threat to society in the way in which a child abuser or those guilty of other violent crimes are, so she should be helped to understand *what* she did and *why* she did it in order to prevent a recurrence. This would ultimately benefit society more than the typical incarceration in which rehabilitation is a minor concern, if it is offered at all.

When mothers become aware of their imprudent actions and sincerely regret their behavior, their remorse for years to come will be punishment enough. If she will berate herself for decades to come, Ford asks whether the state needs to impose very severe or very long penalties as well. "Generally, society considers random, repeated, and cold-blooded killers as the most dangerous to society. How much does a murdering mother's profile conform to this description?" (Ford, 1996, p. 529)

Some neonaticides (more than one third of those we located) were committed by women aged 21 years and older. Assuming that these women were of at least average intelligence, they should certainly have been conscious of their pregnancy, been aware that prenatal care was needed for themselves if not for the baby to come, and also have been aware of the fact that there were alternatives to raising the child that did not involve murder. Although these "older" women should have known better than the adolescents, they may well have had some of the same emotional conflicts and psychological problems that the younger women had, and they may be equally in need of psychotherapy if they are to be restored to society as contributors rather than as parasites or pariahs.

It is tragic that a mother feels that she cannot afford (economically) to have another child, but then she has to think ahead about consequences if she has sexual relations without using contraceptive measures, whatever her reason for so doing may be. Indeed, teaching that there may be multiple options that require making a choice among them and that decision-making has consequences should be an integral part of elementary, middle, and senior high school education. It would most likely have positive effects in many areas of life, not just in this one.

Infanticide and filicide are crimes quite different from neonaticide in motive as well as method. Fathers or father figures are significantly more often involved in these crimes than in neonaticide. There is no argument that they should be handled somewhat differently at the time of sentencing because their motives and emotional state are usually quite different from those of the mothers. In some cases, impatience with normal infant or child behavior, such as crying or soiling, is involved.

What is very much needed here as a preventive is parenting education—that is, knowledge of the realities of infant and child development and behavior. As recommended for pregnancy prevention, this should begin for boys and girls in the early school years, because the age of becoming a parent (or a babysitter) seems to occur earlier as the years pass. It should certainly be available in women's prisons and ideally in men's as well, even though this is after the fact. It may prevent a recurrence if the prisoner is ever released.

In other cases, malice is at the root of the crime, whether anger and a desire for revenge with respect to the other parent or some other reason. In an ideal world, becoming mature would include learning how to handle disappointments and anger in constructive ways; unfortunately, we cannot reach everyone in our real world. When some form of malice is the motive, clearly punishment is appropriate; therapy could be rehabilitative in some cases. Some homicidal parents may be sociopathic and are more dangerous to society than other perpetrators of the same crime. Whether they can be helped by counseling or therapy varies with the specific nature of their mental illness.

A third source of child homicide is Munchausen syndrome by proxy, which, like neonaticide, calls for psychotherapy as part of the sentence. A study by a professor of psychiatry at Johns Hopkins University has indicated that almost 300,000 prisoners across the country who have committed violence are mentally ill and in need of psychotherapy (Butterfield, 1999). Many of these have been guilty of child homicide.

Homicidal mothers are generally at the bottom of the pecking order in a women's prison (Coulombis, 1998), and this may be true for homicidal fathers as well. Apart from any physical harm that might befall them as a result of this, the emotional impact of so much negative attention can only create more psychological problems than they had when they committed the crime. These may lead to suicide attempts, self-hatred that immobilizes them in nonprison relationships, or full-blown psychosis. Support groups for homicidal mothers have been founded in some prisons (France, 1997; Kaplan, 1988), attempting to reduce the most negative feelings and foster more positive aspects of their beings. Whether men would respond to support group efforts is unknown, but there is no harm in trying to reach them.

The Role of Therapeutic Jurisprudence

"*Therapeutic jurisprudence* is the study of the role of the law as a therapeutic agent" (Wexler, 1997, p. 233; Winick, 1997, p. 185). It is an interdisciplinary approach that focuses on applying existing law in a way that will enhance the psychological well-being of those to whom the law is applied. However, too often the variations in laws and their interpretation in the more than 50 state-level jurisdictions in this country do not "permit jurisprudence to function either in a therapeutic manner or prudently in terms of what is best for the individual and for society" (Schwartz & Isser, 2001, p. 713). It would be helpful if legislators learned about the ways in which neonaticide, infanticide, and filicide can differ from more "traditional" homicides and then enacted statutes that recognized these differences from the prosecutorial and punitive perspectives.

Judges should be aware of the mental health views regarding the stresses of pregnancy, postpartum depression, and even the changes that impending parenthood bring. As we have noted earlier, Marlow (1998), among others, has argued that judges should be able to undertake their own research in an effort to better understand the complex issues with which they are confronted rather than depending on the arguments presented at the bar. Indeed, Wexler (1997) has proposed a subfield of *comparative* therapeutic jurisprudence that would actually encourage judges to learn how other countries deal with a particular offense; this might be particularly beneficial when dealing with neonaticide, as well as infanticide and filicide. If members of the judiciary were more aware of the mental health aspects of these crimes and of the ways in which they are handled in various countries, their instructions to juries as well as their application of sentencing guidelines might be more constructive to the prisoner's future.

The goal of sentencing should also be considered. Philosophically, we might ask what is accomplished by prolonged incarceration. Is sentencing to be primarily, perhaps solely, punitive? Is it to be retribution by a vengeful society? Is it to be a deterrent to others? Or is the aim to return the individual to society as a contributor rather than as a threat to the community? Obviously, the answers depend on the crime, the motive, and the nature of the perpetrator. "Incarcerating one girl for this act [neonaticide] will not result in deterring another girl from committing neonaticide; if one does not plan for an act to occur, one cannot be deterred from such [an] act" (Fazio & Comito, 1999, p. 3167).

The therapeutic/rehabilitative goal, particularly with neonaticidal mothers and some of those who commit infanticide, benefits the community ultimately in that the individuals will no longer represent a danger to themselves or others. In the long term, this may mean that fewer prisons need to be built. In the case of infanticides and filicides that have motives less related to intense and irrational emotionality, there should certainly be incarceration of the guilty in most cases. However, there should also be mandatory rehabilitative counseling or psychotherapy of the perpetrators as a condition of probation, parole, or ultimate release from prison. If the individual has learned only how to cope with prison and fellow prisoners, nothing has been accomplished in terms of teaching him or her how to be a better person in the family and in society.

In addition to considering the benefits of applying therapeutic jurisprudence, the importance and value of teaching many life skills from early childhood on is critical. These skills should include the facts that choices are to be made and that they have consequences; knowledge about sex, pregnancy, and parenting should be apparent. Virtually everyone agrees that one must learn how to drive before obtaining a driver's license, for example, but we have no such mandate for the far more important role as a parent. Perhaps it is time that we did.

Appendix A

Neonaticide Cases

No.	Case	Age	Date	State	Charges and Dispositions[a]
1	Diane O'Dell	20s	1982/1983/ 1985	NY	Killed three newborns in 1980s. Convicted of three counts of murder 2 in Dec. 2003; sentenced to 25 yrs.–life (see also Appendix B).
2	Elizabeth Ehlert	30	8/1990	IL	Charged/convicted of murder 1; sentenced to 58 yrs. Conviction reversed (1995); retrial on appeal (12/98), found guilty and sentenced to 30 years. Retrial (11/02) and conviction reversed.
3	Stephanie Wernick	20	12/1990	NY	Charged/convicted criminally negligent homicide. Sentenced to 1–1$^{3}/_{4}$ yrs.; case decided in Dec. 1996 after appeal; plea: "neonaticide syndrome."
4	Tina Brosius	18	5/1994	PA	Murder 1, life sentence.
5	Melissa McManus	17	1994	PA	Drowned newborn, life sentence.
6	Rebecca Hopfer	17	8/1994	OH	Murder, 15 yrs.–life
7	Caroline Beale	23?	9/1994	NY	Mans., 8 mos. + 5 yrs. probation with psychotherapy (to be served in England).
8	Tracie Ribitch	17	1994	MI	Pled guilty to involun. mans. in 1997, 5 yrs. probation + 2000 hrs. comm. service (talking about risks and consequences of unprotected sex); in 2/99, question of whether she was fulfilling comm. service requirement.
9	Lorie Ann McGuire	21	2/1995	WV	Volun. mans. 3–15 yrs.; also had 14-month-old daughter.
10	Jeana Hill	32	2/1995	LA	Charged with murder 1, pled to mans. Sentenced to 45 yrs.

Neonaticide Cases (Continued)

No.	Case	Age	Date	State	Charges and Dispositions[a]
11	Mariafelisa Smith	27	4/1995	CA	Murder 1, 15 yrs.–life.
12	Tracy Rowland	17	4/1995	AK	Murder 1.
13	Shantelle Renee Harrison	17	2/1995	LA	Murder 2, found guilty 7/30/98; mandatory life sent.
14	Mona Ballard	17	4/1995	OK	"Alford" plea to murder 2, 10 yrs. + 10 yrs. suspended sent. with mandatory pregnancy test every 30 days.
15	Lisa Murphy; Billy Stockwell	17; 22	5/1995	TN	Murphy: murder 1 charge: facilitating murder, 10 yrs. Stockwell: murder 1 for burying baby alive, life.
16	Lori Pinkerton	24	5/1995	PA	3rd degr. murder.
17	Talitha R. Garrick	25	6/1995	SC	Involun. mans., 3 yrs.; later suspended to 3 yrs. probation.
18	Jackie Lee Anderson	36	8/1995	CA	Murder 2, 15 yrs.–life. Therapy recommended in prison.
19	Germaine Hovland	34	10/1995	IL	Found guilty of 1st degr. murder, 18 yrs.
20	Amanda Beckett	>18	11/1995	CT	Mans., 18 months.
21	Elizabeth Nelson	18	2/1996	MI	Murder 2.
22	Kelli Moye	15	2/1996	IL	1st degr. murder. Allegedly admitted crime in Oct. 1999, 4 yrs. (IQ c. 85); to be released c. 9/5/01.
23	Teresa Sanchez	21	3/1996	CA	Murder 2, 25 yrs.–life.
24	Connie Lombardi	40	6/1996	IL	Murder 2; pled guilty, 15 yrs.–life.
25	Juanita Laredo	24	7/1996	TX	Misdemeanor: abuse of corpse, 1 yr.?
26	Jodi Jean Feldmann	19	7/1996	IL	Murder, insanity defense. Guilty of involun. mans.; 4 yrs.
27	Janet Walters	40	9/1996	CO	Held on suspicion of murder 1; 5 yrs.
28	Tracy Cardwell	31	10/1996	NJ	Pled guilty to mans. (8/29/98); 7 yrs.
29	Amy Grossberg; Brian Peterson	18; 18	11/1996	DE	Grossberg: murder 1. Pled to mans. (7/9/98); $2^1/_2$ yrs. prison + $1^1/_2$ yrs. home confinement + 5 yrs. probation. Peterson: pled to mans.; 2 yrs. prison + 6 yrs. probation. Both: 300 hrs. comm. service.
30	Karlie DiTripani	19	12/1996	NY	Murder 2 > manslaughter 2; 5 yrs. probation + comm. service. Psych. program.
31	Jannifer Butler	23/24	12/1996	FL	Murder 1 + aggrav. child abuse. Pled *nolo contendere* to murder 2; 21 yrs. without parole.

Neonaticide Cases (Continued)

No.	Case	Age	Date	State	Charges and Dispositions[a]
32	Summer McKee	19	12/1996	IL	Murder 1, pled guilty to involun. mans. and concealment of a homicide. 30 mos. probation + psychotherapy + 500 hrs. comm. service and full-time school or work.
33	Jennifer A. Pyles	24	1996/1997	OH	Involun. mans.; 2 yrs.
34	Racquel Phifer	20	1/1997	NC	Charged with murder 1. Pled guilty to murder 2; 10 yrs.
35	Carole Bowe	31	2/1997	IA	Murder 1 (two counts—earlier death of newborn in 1992). Pled guilty to two counts of "killing a viable fetus aborted live"; sentenced to two consecutive 25-yr. terms.
36	Melissa Strawbridge	21	3/1997	NY	Murder 2; 9/98: free on bail.
37	Leonor Banuelos	29	5/1997	IL	Murder 1.
38	Audrey Iacona	17	5/1997	OH	Charged with murder; found guilty of involun. mans. + abuse of a corpse; 8 yrs. Appeal 1/19/99 in comm. college. Retrial 2/8/99 did not occur then; 4/16/99: retrial denied 1/10/01.
39	Glendi Mendes	18	5/1997	MA	Murder 1; 5 yr. sent.; illegal immigrant.
40	Melissa Seaner	17	5/1997	PA	Pled to mans., 4 yrs. Paroled after 10 mos. (9/98).
41	Linda Chu	20	5/1997	CA	Murder 1. Pled no contest to felony child abuse; 10 yrs., with minimum of 5 yrs. to be served.
42	Melissa Drexler ("Prom Mom")	18	6/1997	NJ	Indicted for murder, pled not guilty. Pled to aggrav. mans.; 15 yrs. (10/29/98). Paroled 11/26/01.
43	Jennifer Garcia	19	6/1997	CA	Killed newborn daughter and dumped body in a garbage can; charged with murder.
44	Paula Bailey	20	7/1997	IL	Charged with murder 1 (pled guilty to involun. mans., but judge rejected plea). $1^1/_2$–$2^1/_2$ yrs., intensive probation + counseling + comm. service.
45	Diane Capobianco	38	7/1997	NY	Murder.
46	Tanya Hudson	24	9/1997	FL	Murder 1; sentenced to 15 yrs.; on appeal.

Neonaticide Cases (Continued)

No.	Case	Age	Date	State	Charges and Dispositions[a]
47	Miriam Guerrero	22	9/1997	CA	Suspicion of murder. Pled to involun. mans., 14 yrs.
48	Patricia Leal	20	10/1997	CA	Murder 1 + assault of a minor. Convicted of murder 2, 25 yrs.–life.
49	Samantha Pearson	18	10/1997	TX	Charged with murder, 10 yrs. + 10 yrs. probation.
50	Judith Martinez	15	10/1997	NY	Allowed newborn daughter to drown in toilet; charged with murder.
51	Tammy Dube	17	11/1997	CO	Murder 1 and child abuse. Criminally negligent child abuse, 2 yrs. (mildly retarded).
52	Helen Sim	16	11/1997	NJ	Aggrav. mans.; not guilty (by judge, 5/29/98).
53	Shantela Smith	19	11/1997	MS	Allowed newborn daughter to drown in toilet; charged with murder. Put on probation (4/11/99).
54	Marianne Biancuzzo	19	11/1997	AZ	Charged with murder (12/6/97), convicted of negligent homicide (11/21/98). 1 yr. in prison (out during day to work) + 3 yrs. probation + 500 hrs. comm. service.
55	Amy T. Diver	26	11/1997	OR	Murder by abuse (Klamath Falls, OR).
56	Dineen DiLeo	27	12/1997	CT	Charged with murder/capital felony. Mother of two
57	Kathryn E. Burton	24	1997	OH	15 yrs.–life.
58	Anonymous	15	1/1998	NY	Unlawful disposal of body.
59	Heidi Sonnenberg	22	1/1998	UT	3rd degr. felony child abuse—homicide. Defense was *prehnexia*; 1 yr. in treatment program.
60	Marie Adams	18	2/1998	NV	Murder 2 and child abuse.
61	Nicole Coleman	UK	2/1998	CT	Pled not guilty to murder and capital felony charges; trial set for 2/1999. "Alford" plea, 15 yrs. (6/28/00).
62	Dyneaka L. Hall	16	2/1998	MD	Pled guilty to murder 2 and child abuse. Sentenced to 20 yrs., but judge suspended all but 8 yrs.
63	Jimi Lee	22	3/1998	CA	Charged with murder 2. Convicted of involun. mans., 4 yrs.
64	Anonymous	14	4/1998	CO	Charges not filed as of 4/11/98.

Neonaticide Cases (Continued)

No.	Case	Age	Date	State	Charges and Dispositions[a]
65	Kristin Matheny	22	4/1998	IL	Charged with not notifying coroner of a death. 90 days in jail + 2 yrs. "intense" probation + 90 hrs. comm. service + counseling.
66	Tremaine Ingram	19	6/1998	AK	Pled guilty to negligent homicide and abuse of corpse. Prosecutor asked for 6 yr. sentence.
67	Lee Vang	13	6/1998	WI	Charged with murder 1 and hiding a corpse; had been raped. Found guilty in juvenile court of 1st degr. reckless homicide; 3 yrs. in juvenile facility.
68	Yudit Rosales	20	6/1998	CA	Murder.
69	Anonymous	16	6/1998	NJ	Aggrav. mans.
70	Leslie Allen	32	6/1998	NJ	Tampering with evidence, possibly murder. Baby was stillborn; charges dropped.
71	Theresa R. Turner	32	6/1998	MD	2nd degr. mans. possible; charges withdrawn.
72	Anonymous	>18	7/1998	OH	Involun. mans.; probably less than 2 yrs. in youth prison.
73	Linda Huynh	14	9/1998	TX	Capital murder; pled guilty to charge of injury to a child. 3 yrs. in juvenile correctional facility; brother and mother also charged.
74	Stephanie Major	28	10/1998	KY	Charged with murder, abuse of corpse, tampering with evidence in death of infant; 25 yrs.
75	Sharon Denise Walker	30	10/1998	WI	Pled guilty to homicide; 30 yrs.
76	Maria Gabriel	33	11/1998	IL	Charged with 1st degr. murder.
77	Noemi Munoz	17	11/1998	TX	Allowed newborn son to bleed to death by not cutting umbilical cord (seen as omission rather than intent). Charged with injury to child.
78	Kanika S. Wells	19	12/1998	CA	Murder; suffocation of newborn.
79	Anonymous	16	12/1998	OH	Newborn buried alive. Charges: delinquency by reason murder and child endangerment; gross abuse of corpse. Pled guilty (4/10/99) to delinquency by involun. mans.
80	Heidi Davis	19	12/1998	WA	Murder 2; suffocation of newborn.
81	Angela Maria Garza	17	1/1999	TX	Under investigation; may not be charged.
82	Anonymous	17	1/1999	MN	No charges as of 1/13/99.

Neonaticide Cases (Continued)

No.	Case	Age	Date	State	Charges and Dispositions[a]
83	Charley Cobb (f)	17	1/1999	NH	Negligent homicide, $3^1/_2$–7 yrs. Suspended sentence.
84	Anonymous	16	1/1999	MA	Grand jury called.
85	Anonymous	16	1/1999	FL	Decomposing body of newborn boy found in backpack; "mother" being questioned.
86	Theresa Harris	22	2/1999	NM	Charged with child abuse resulting in death and tampering with evidence 6/2/99. Child died of asphyxia.
87	Karine G. Epailly	25	3/1999	VA	Charged with involun. mans. and felony child neglect in death of daughter. Faced 10-yr. sentence; charge suspended.
88	Brigitte Green	20	3/1999	GA	No charges as of 4/1/99.
89	Kizzi Wallace	20	4/1999	NY	Probable charge of murder 2.
90	Danielle Hill	18	4/1999	PA	4/17: charged with criminal homicide. Accidental death plea rejected. 8/4/00; 5–10 yrs. for murder 3. Pled no contest and volunteered for tubal ligation (at state expense).
91	Andrea Sprague	Unkown	4/1999	NJ	Pled guilty to aggrav. mans.
92	Nicole Boyer	13	4/1999	PA	Suffocated newborn daughter, buried her in a cabinet drawer. Charged with criminal homicide as an adult; revised 12/28/99 to trial as a juvenile.
93	Tracee Austin	24	5/1999	VA	Charged with murder of her newborn girl.
94	Lisa Callhan	20+	6/1999	NY	Homicide or miscarriage?
95	Carin Madden	20	8/1999	OH	"Neonaticide syndrome" plea. Pled guilty to aggrav. murder and gross abuse of corpse; 20 yrs.–life.
96	Michele Nicole Huey	17	10/1999	CA	Homicide.
97	Abigail V. Caliboso; Jose E. Ocampo	20; 19	3/2000	DE	Baby abandoned on floor of portable toilet; died before being found. Pled guilty to mans. 12/5/01. Both sentenced to 8 yrs. in prison, but with probation after 4 yrs. Each fined $12,500; each ordered to perform 300 hrs. comm. service; also must undergo mental health evaluation.
98	Darvell Thomas	16	12/2000	NY	Charged with manslaughter.

Neonaticide Cases (Continued)

No.	Case	Age	Date	State	Charges and Dispositions[a]
99	Sylvia Hernandez	18	1/2001	NY	Baby smothered. Pled guilty to manslaughter; 7 yrs. (8/21/01).
100	Lisa Small	16	3/2001	NY	Baby smothered and fed to family's rotweiler. Charges: manslaughter, criminally negligent homicide.
101	Jane Labenecki	c. 19	3/2001	PA	Baby apparently born alive and smothered (alleged e-mail to roommate). Charge: "concealing baby born out of wedlock" (6/29/01). Pled guilty to misdemeanor: concealing death of a child born out of wedlock; 5 yrs. probation with continued psychological treatment.
102	Unknown	14	12/2001	NY	Baby born into toilet and drowned; charged with manslaughter.
103	Kathleen E. Brown	24	12/2001	NY	Smothered newborn son in bedroom while relatives ate Christmas dinner. Found guilty of murder 2 in May 2003; sentenced to 18 yrs.–life (thrown out; to be reheard 2/18/04). May also have given birth to full-term boy in April 2001 or earlier (*NYT* 1/20/04). Pled guilty to murder 2 on 6/7/04; sentenced to 18 yrs.–life (9/16/04); pregnant when sentenced.
104	Karen D. Mako	20	10/2002	PA	Delivered son in shower, wrapped him in paper towels and duffel bag; bag found atop trash bin at Clarion Univ. Charged with criminal homicide; pled guilty to felony involun. mans., 9 mos.–2 yrs.
105	Unknown; Boyfriend	**17**; 20	12/2002	CT	Baby buried in boyfriend's backyard. Girl went to hospital for postnatal complications; had hidden pregnancy from her parents.
106	Unknown	14	3/2003	NJ	Suffocated newborn son; discovered when she was taken to hospital complaining of abdominal pains (postpartum problems). Will not be tried as an adult, but faces up to 20 yrs. if found guilty (*Inquirer*, 5/2/03). Pled guilty to endangering welfare of child and concealing human remains (10/29/03); given 6 yrs. probation and outpatient counseling (4/15/04).

Neonaticide Cases (Continued)

No.	Case	Age	Date	State	Charges and Dispositions[a]
107	Chante Bass	19	11/2003	PA	Suffocated newborn son; charged with murder and abuse of corpse.
108	Unknown	Unknown	11/2003	NY	Dead newborn found outside church door.
109	Kristen Cleaver	18	11/2003	WI	Left newborn face down in bathtub; placed baby in bag and hid her in bedroom. Charged with homicide and could face "life" in prison. 11/25/05: *Miranda* rights were violated, acc. to Wisc. Ct. Appeals.
110	Unknown	Unknown	12/2003	PA	Infant girl born alive found in a barrel outside an Amish school near Strasbourg 3/9/04.
111	Nicole Coleman	Unknown	1/2004	PA	Baby girl suffocated and placed in duffel bag, which was then hung outside window. Mother and grandmother called 911 re: miscarriage. Charged with homicide (May 2004), then with involun. mans.; 60 weekend days in jail + 6 mos. house arrest + therapy.
112	Ana Rodriguez	34	1/2004	NY	Baby boy asphyxiated, hidden in bucket under kitchen sink. Charged with murder 2; convicted of criminally negligent homicide and manslaughter, sentencing 6/21/05. Lives with boyfriend and daughters ages 8, 10, 14.
113	Amy Detior	20	Spring 2004	OH	Gave birth to live boy who, she said, would not suckle; bathed herself, did laundry, drove 25 mi. to her parents' home, by which time he had died. Put him in plastic garbage bag and dropped him off bridge. Convicted May 2004 of reckless homicide, abuse of corpse, and child endangerment; sentenced to 5 yrs. (June 2004).
114	Unknown	15	6/2004	MI	Hid newborn in plastic shopping bag in her room; criminal charges likely.
115	Bernardita Gomez-Coronado	Teen	6/2004	MI	Smothered newborn son after giving birth alone; no prenatal care, hospital or social support. Charged with murder 1, sentenced to 1 yr. + deportation to Guatemala (6/10/05).

Neonaticide Cases (Continued)

No.	Case	Age	Date	State	Charges and Dispositions[a]
116	Alainer Warren	25	6/2004	GA	Gave birth to identical premature twins and apparently drowned them in toilet. Claimed she did not know she was pregnant; charged with murder.
117	Unknown	13	1/2005	NY	Gave birth to son; could not quiet his cries, so threw him out window. Boyfriend (baby's father, age 15) arrived 14 hrs. later, wrapped newborn in towels, and left him on nearby church stoop.
118	Unknown	17	1/2005	NY	Gave birth to baby alone, which fell into toilet. She cut off umbilical cord, washed it, wrapped it in her pajamas, and put it in closet until morning. Went to hospital because of bleeding, showed nurse baby in bag, and only wanted to go to school.
119	Nicole Cherise Batiste	19	10/2005	FL	Gave birth to baby boy; left him on floor to die, then wrapped him in towel, placed him in plastic container, and hid body in her truck's toolbox. Went to local ER saying she had suffered a miscarriage. Had not told baby's father or her mother that she was pregnant; baby's father was also 19—son of sheriff. Charged with aggravated manslaughter (1st degr. felony). Could face 30 years unless tried as youthful offender (4 yrs.+ 2 yrs. supervision).
120	Danielle Eboni Riley	21	10/2005	MD	Gave birth in bathroom at college dorm; put baby's body in plastic bag and then into storm drain. Admitted birth to her mother the next day; 11/30/05: charged with 1st degr. murder.

[a] In some cases, it was impossible to discover the ultimate outcome.

Appendix B

Infanticide and Filicide Cases

No.	Name	Age	Date	State	Charges and Dispositions[a]
1	Marie Noe	20–40	1949–1968	PA	Accused of suffocating eight of ten children (Munchausen by proxy); other two children died of natural causes. Arrested 8/98 and accused of murders; sentenced (1999) to 5 yrs. house arrest + psychological evaluations + 20 yrs. probation 9/20/01. Diagnosed as having "mixed personality disorder"—no MSBP.
2	Waneta Hoyt	Unknown	1965–1971	NY	Five children allegedly died of SIDS; prosecuted in 1994, 75 yrs.–life.
3	Mary Beth Tinning	20+	1972–1985	NY	Suspected in deaths of her eight children (beg. 1972); all died before age 5. Smothered $3^1/_2$-mo.-old daughter in 1985; serving 20 yrs. in prison.
4	Diane O'Dell	20s	1980s	NY	Allegedly killed (and carried around with her the bodies of) three or four infants for about 10 yrs.; put three of the bodies in storage locker in Arizona in the 1990s. Has eight living children, ages 7–25; serving 25 yrs.–life (see also Appendix A).
5	Stephen C. Johnson, Jr.	Unknown	12/1983	MD	Took PCP and 2 or 3 days later decapitated 13-mo.-old son with butcher knife; claimed that under drug influence he believed son was Jesus and had to die for his sins. Sentenced to life in prison, reduced in 2003 to 30 yrs. because of ineffective counsel at original trial. Scheduled for release 12/6/05.

Infanticide and Filicide Cases (Continued)

No.	Name	Age	Date	State	Charges and Dispositions[a]
6	Diane Lumbrera	20+	1976–1990	TX	Six children + niece died in her care; convicted of suffocating 4-mo.-old son in KS in 1990. Pled "no contest" to charge of killing another infant son in TX; given two life sentences, imprisoned in KS.
7	Sharon K. Comitz	Unknown	1/1985	PA	Drowned month-old son; pled and found guilty of GBMI. Appealed sentence, but denied by PA Sup. Ct., 1987.
8	Claudette Kibble	Teen	1986–1990	TX	Confessed in 1995 to drowning two babies, attempting to suffocate one (of five others). Pled guilty in exchange for three consecutive life sentences.
9	Sheryl Lynn Massip	24	1987	CA	Ran over 6-wk-old son; may have had postpartum depression. Pled NGRI. Originally found guilty of murder 2, then found NGRI and ordered to participate in outpatient treatment program.
10	Paula J. Sims	20s	1989	IL	Gave birth to Loralei in 1986, a son in 1988, and Heather in 1989. Suffocated each daughter a few weeks after birth, alleging a madman murdered them. Husband suspected but never charged. 1990: tried, pled not guilty, but jury said guilty. Sentenced to life imprisonment. Subsequently learned about insanity defenses and in 1994 filed *pro se* petition alleging defense counsel had been ineffective for not exploring possibility she suffered from postpartum depression. 2001: appeal denied by Appellate Ct. of Ill., 5th D.

Infanticide and Filicide Cases (Continued)

No.	Name	Age	Date	State	Charges and Dispositions[a]
11	Dawn March	17	9/1989	CT	Threw her 6-mo.-old daughter into the Housatonic River ("voices" told her to). Acquitted on grounds of postpartum psychosis (1st in CT for this) but remanded to state Psychiatric Security Review Board for 20 years. Released from supervision 5/14/05; must continue in psychotherapy.
12	Teresa Torres	23	1/1994	NJ	Killed 4-mo.-old daughter during bout of depression; charged with aggravated manslaughter. Trial 7/1–7/2/98: Acquitted.
13	Susan Smith	23	11/1994	SC	Drowned two sons in her car—they interfered with her new romance. Found guilty of murder; sentenced to life.
14	Selina Anderson	Unknown	1995	LA	Smothered 17-mo.-old daughter; accused of murder 2. Trial: 12/1/98; outcome unknown. May have killed 4-mo.-old in 1992 and 19-day-old in 1994.
15	Elizabeth Rosa	25	11/1996	NJ	Suffocated "fussy" $3^1/_2$-mo.-old son. Mother smoked crack cocaine that a.m. Pled guilty to aggrav. mans.; could get 40 yrs. Sentence unknown.
16	Andrea Blue, R.N.; Donald Ford, M.D.	35	3/1997	PA	Fed 4-mo.-old son formula laced with cocaine. Charged with murder, conspiracy, and drug violations (9/98).
17	Charlene Wise	36	8/1997	PA	Starved 5-yr.-old daughter to death in basement; also endangered 8-yr.-old son—both as punishment. Found guilty of 3rd degr. murder, child endangerment, and concealing a corpse. Sentenced to maximum of 28–56 years; blamed drugs.

Infanticide and Filicide Cases (Continued)

No.	Name	Age	Date	State	Charges and Dispositions[a]
18	Renee Beth Smith	20	9/1997	HI	Suffocated 9-wk-old daughter; husband in the Navy left for 14-wk course in Texas day after baby's birth. Charged with murder 1 (federal court), pled guilty to murder (to avoid "incarceration without possibilities"); sentenced to life. May have some therapy in sentence.
19	Susan Mitchell; Billy G. Mitchell	37	10/1997	KY	Starved 2-yr.-old son, but had paid-up insurance on three children @ $60K each; all malnourished. Charged with murder.
20	Nancy J. Montealbano	45	10/1997	PA	Beat 3-yr.-old adopted daughter to death for knocking over potty. Charged with 3rd degr. murder/aggravated assault/endangering welfare of a child. Pled GBMI to manslaughter; sentence: 4–14 yrs.
21	Carla Lockwood	34	10/1997	NY	Starvation death of 4-yr.-old daughter. Pled guilty to murder 2; sentenced to 15 yrs. Mother of 10, including 7-mo.-old twins; 7/22/02: children's father convicted of murder 2 for "depraved indifference" to child's life. Faced sentence of 15–25 years.
22	Barbara Brown; Ricky Brown; Janette Ables	Unknown	12/1997	WV	Arson death of five children to collect on homeowner's ins. policy. Charged with arson and maybe murder.
23	Jason LeeRoy Hunt; Tina Reinmann	25; 22	3/1998	OK	Slapped, choked, and threw 3-yr.-old daughter of his live-in girlfriend because child wet her diaper. Both charged with murder 1 (mother aware he was abusive).
24	Bethe Feltman	32	4/1998	CO	Strangled 3-yr.-old son and suffocated 3-mo.old daughter; charged with murder. Defense was postpartum depression (hospitalized prior to murders); 7/01: hospitalized.

Infanticide and Filicide Cases (Continued)

No.	Name	Age	Date	State	Charges and Dispositions[a]
25	Sharon Alley	29	5/1998	VA	Killed 8-mo.-old daughter. Charged with murder 1; pled NGRI: postpartum depression/psychosis, under treatment. Pled guilty to murder 2 and felony child abuse 1/24/99. Sentenced to 36 yrs; 9-yr.-old son never wants to see her again.
26	Louise Lee Davis	25	5/1999	NC	Shook 5-mo.-old daughter to death. Served 1 yr. + 11 months.
27	Khoua Her	24	9/1998	MN	Strangled her six children; charged with murder 2. Tried to commit suicide; evaluated for competency. Sentenced to 50 yrs. (Hmong refugee; domestic violence involved).
28	James H. Proctor, Jr.	23	11/1998	PA	Killed 10-wk-old daughter for crying too long. Charged with murder 1; death penalty sought.
29	Daywaren Stewart	23	12/1998	GA	Murder and cruelty to children in shaking death of his 2-mo.-old daughter.
30	Heidi Anfinson	38	1998	IA	Mother walked away from 2-wk-old son in his bathtub and he drowned. Sank his body with 25 lbs. of rocks in nearby lake. Mistrial in 1999; convicted of murder 2 in 2000. Sentenced to 50 yrs.; 2005: appeal on grounds that her lawyer should have used an insanity defense of postpartum psychosis. 12/24/05: appeal denied.
31	Dina Abdelhaq	34	1/1999	IL	Suffocated 7-wk-old daughter to collect $200K life ins. to support gambling. Convicted of ins. fraud in federal court; sentenced to 21 yrs.
32	Marilyn Lemak	41	3/1999	IL	Poisoned and suffocated three children and attempted suicide; reason: anger and jealousy at husband who was seeing another woman. Had been depressed since birth of youngest 3 yrs. earlier; in midst of a divorce. Court-appointed psychiatrist declared her unfit to stand trial on murder 1. 12/19/01: Found guilty 4/8/02; life imprisonment without parole.

Infanticide and Filicide Cases (Continued)

No.	Name	Age	Date	State	Charges and Dispositions[a]
33	Alejandro DeJesus	50	3/1999	PA	Estranged husband, denied custody of 6-yr.-old. Shot daughter and 22-yr.-old son + two other boys; committed suicide. Wife had restraining order; she escaped shooting.
34	Martita Gonzalez	17	2000	NJ	Threw 15-mo.old son into Passaic River because she had date and could not find babysitter. Confessed next day; 1/03: pled guilty to aggravated manslaughter; 2/25/03: sentenced to 18 yrs.
35	Brenda Matthey; Robert Matthey	Unknown	10/2000	NJ	Adopted 7-yr.-old son (from Siberia) died after months of harsh treatment—locked in unheated basement room, bruised. Also had four biological sons. Couple charged with aggravated manslaughter, child endangerment, witness tampering (5/9/04); 7/23/04: Sentenced to 10 yrs. each.
36	Maria deLourdes Nieves	Unknown	3/2001	AZ	Charged with death of 9-mo.-old Michelle.
37	Rei Fujii	23	6/2001	Calgary, Canada	Neglect of 15-mo.-old son and drowning of 3-mo.-old daughter; both died after being left alone for 10 days while she went to parties. Overwhelmed by maternal responsibilities; 1/11/02: court approved two charges of murder 2; 4/1/02: will plead guilty at trial in July '02; 6/3/04: denied parole.

Infanticide and Filicide Cases (Continued)

No.	Name	Age	Date	State	Charges and Dispositions[a]
38	Andrea Yates	36	6/2001	TX	Drowned her five children, ages 6 mo. to 7 yrs. Had postpartum depression/psychosis after fourth child was born; on medication; recurred after birth of fifth child; hospitalized. Off medication 2 weeks before drownings. 9/20/01: question of competence to stand trial; DA seeking death penalty; 2/19/02: defense was NGRI; 3/12/02: found guilty of murder of three children; 3/15/02: life sentence – min. of 40 yrs.; 3/21/02: placed in psychiatric prison; 1/6/05: new trial ordered because of false testimony by Dr. Park Dietz; 11/9/05: appellate court upheld new trial or plea bargain. 2/06: moved to mental health facility pending new trial.
39	Robin Parker	33	6/2001	NC	Murder–suicide: CO poisoning of three children and herself. Accused of crime by her employer; if third conviction, would have faced 10+ yrs. in prison.
40	Juan Velasquez; Virginia Venegas	Unknown	9/2001	AZ	Assaulted and drowned girlfriend's 20-mo.-old daughter; 3-yr.-old sister had also been beaten severely. Mother drove to canal while Velasquez held the baby. 10/8/04: Velasquez sentenced to death; Venegas sentenced to 35 yrs.– life. Arizona Supreme Court awarded \$5M to surviving older sister; \$2.5M to her father.
41	Henry C. Hohberger, III	40	11/2001	PA	Fatally beat and shook 7-wk-old daughter; allegedly had asked girlfriend four times to abort baby. Allegedly wanted a son and wanted to avoid paying child support. Charged with murder 1; 6/10/03: $17^1/_2$ –35 yrs.

Infanticide and Filicide Cases (Continued)

No.	Name	Age	Date	State	Charges and Dispositions[a]
42	Christian Longo	27	12/2001	OR	Accused of murdering his wife and three children (ages 2, 3, 4). Flew to Mexico; captured 1/13/02. 4/7/03: charged with four counts of murder and convicted; 4/16/03: death penalty. Described as "connoisseur of wine and cars who killed his family so he could enjoy a more uninhibited lifestyle" (*NY Times*).
43	Heather Lindorff; James Lindorff	37; 52	12/2001	NJ	Charges: 1st degr. murder, endangering welfare of a child; child abuse in killing of 5-yr.-old adopted son (Russian). Acquitted of murder charge; 3/30/04: sentenced to 6 yrs. Husband convicted of child abuse; serving 4 yrs. on probation. Couple had adopted five other Russian children who were placed with Heather 's mother.
44	Stephanie Fitzgerald	16	1/2002	NJ	Smothered 8-mo.-old daughter; had been hospitalized three times for emotional problems. Pled guilty to aggravated manslaughter 8/21/02: sentenced to 12 yrs. Judge considered her psychological problems as "mitigating" but not a defense.
45	Ellen Feinberg	43	3/2002	IL	Pediatrician stabbed her 10-yr.-old son to death and wounded his younger brother; called police. Charged with murder and attempted murder; placed in mental health facility; 12/3/02: declared NGRI.
46	Michael W. Fisher	Unknown	5/2002	PA	Allegedly tortured 2-yr.-old boy in his care, who died as a result. Accused of 1st degr. murder
47	Christopher Deming	29	8/2002	WI	4-mo.-old daughter died in his care; "battered child syndrome"; had been left on waterbed unattended. Pled guilty to neglecting a child, leading to death; 8/05: sentenced to 10 yrs. in prison + 5 yrs. "extended supervision."

Infanticide and Filicide Cases (Continued)

No.	Name	Age	Date	State	Charges and Dispositions[a]
48	Keith Walker	29	9/2002	PA	Charged with 3rd degr. murder of 2-wk-old son; also involun. mans.—severe beatings.
49	Chinyere Onuba; Tyrrell Minerva	23; 28	12/2002	NJ	Allowed infant son to starve to death at 5 mos. June 2003: both pled guilty to reckless manslaughter; she was given 9 yrs. in prison.
50	Michael J. Shukry	22	12/2002	CA	Convicted of child homicide and murder 2; 2/21/04: sentences of 15–life and 25–life
51	Merry Long	Unknown	2/2003	PA	Grandmother laced baby's formula with salt to get back at son and his girlfriend. Warrant filed in July '03 for her arrest. Baby's body could not compensate for overdose of salt. 8/12/03: captured in Minnesota; 8/05: died of cancer.
52	Jennifer P. O'Connor	40	4/2003	CT	Shot 7-yr.-old daughter because of frustration with child's learning disabilities and behavior. History of psychiatric/emotional problems; 4/16/03: charged with murder, pled innocent; 7/1/03: placed in mental health treatment at East Lyme Correctional Institute. Divorced from child's father.
53	Robin Edwards (M)	37	4/2003	VA	Shot three sons (ages 5, 7, 9), then committed suicide. Estranged from wife, although she wanted him to have interaction with boys.
54	Deanna Laury	38	5/2004	TX	Called police to say she had just killed her older sons (6 and 8); 13-mo.-old son found in crib with pillow over his head and massive head injuries. Charged with capital murder and aggravated assault; 4/5/04: NGRI.
55	Tracie Kitchen	30	6/2003	MI	Smothered 21-mo.-old son, then buried him in backyard. Charged with murder 1.

Infanticide and Filicide Cases (Continued)

No.	Name	Age	Date	State	Charges and Dispositions[a]
56	Naomi Gaines	24	7/2003	MN	Pushed 14-mo.-old twin sons over a bridge into Mississippi River (one rescued), then jumped off bridge herself; rescued. Charged with murder 2; sentenced to 18 yrs. + 9 mos. after plea agreement. Has other children.
57	Mine An Ener	38	8/2003	MN	Villanova history professor killed 6-mo.-old "sickly" daughter (Down syndrome). Confessed to police in an "emotionless" interview. Was on medication for postpartum depression; 8/30/03: committed suicide in prison.
58	Janet Crawford; James Tatar	Unknown	8/2003	PA	Convicted of starving 4-yr.-old Kristen Tatar to death so she would be free of Tatar's inhuman treatment of daughter. Both convicted of 1st degr. murder and serving life terms; 11/11/05: Crawford appealed for reversal.
59	Amanda Hamm; Maurice LaGrone, Jr.	27; 28	9/2003	IL	Both accused of drowning her three children (in back seat of her car) in Clinton Lake. Each charged with nine counts of murder; prosecutor seeking death penalty. 4/06: LaGrone sentenced to life.
60	Lisa Diaz	33	9/2003	TX	Drowned 6- and 3-yr.-old daughters. Aug. 2004: Found to have been insane at time of the crime; Sept. 2004: acquitted by NGRI.
61	Omar Guzman	20	2/2004	CT	Shook 2-mo.-old son to death because of his crying while waiting for boy's mother; 2/24/04: 1st degr. assault + murder charge. 1/8/05: sentenced to 17 yrs. Took responsibility.
62	Victor Fuentes	19	3/2004	NY	Shook 3-mo.-old son to death to stop him from crying. Nov.11, 2005: pled guilty to manslaughter; sentence: 14 yrs. in prison.

Infanticide and Filicide Cases (Continued)

No.	Name	Age	Date	State	Charges and Dispositions[a]
63	Marcus Wesson	57	3/2004	CA	Murdered nine of his children (in clan he devised and dominated). Found guilty; 7/27/05: death penalty. Patriarch of a clan he bred through incest.
64	Robert Morris, Jr.	27	4/2004	PA	Charged with murdering his four children, ages 24 days to 18 mo. over a period of 8 yrs. 2/16/06: NG of deaths of 2 children in 1995; guilty of 3rd degr. murder in deaths of 2 other children. Life sentences will be sought.
65	William Bagneski	35	5/2004	WI	Charged with murdering 6-mo.-old Joel on Nov. 2, 1999; originally death thought to be from SIDS. Charged with murdering 8-mo.-old Kelby Oct. 17, 2001—head injuries. 8/15/05: plea bargain to 1st degr. reckless homicide; 10/19/05: sentencing—possibly 100 yrs. Had been charged with child abuse in 1988; has 2-yr.-old with second wife.
66	Ryan W. Workman	25	8/2004	PA	Shook 3-mo.-old Alexis multiple times to stop her crying. Found guilty of 3rd degr. homicide; 11/2/05: sentenced to 9–18 years.
67	Andrea Labbe	26	12/2004	Toronto	Killed husband (age 47), 3-yr.-old daughter, and herself; wounded 2-yr.-old daughter; also had 7-mo.-old daughter. Postpartum depress/psychosis?
68	Steven Walczak	23	12/2004	PA	Strangled 4-yr.-old daughter; may have killed 9-mo.-old son in April 2004 (allegedly died of SIDS/asphyxia). Waived preliminary hearing; hearing scheduled for 3/9/05. 10/5/05: pled guilty to both murders; will be sentenced to life without parole plus 20–40 years.
69	Tanea Bullock; Lawrence Watson	20; 25	1/2005	MD	Beat 1-mo.-old son to death. Both charged with murder 1, child abuse, assault.

Infanticide and Filicide Cases (Continued)

No.	Name	Age	Date	State	Charges and Dispositions[a]
70	Connie Long; Kevin Long	Unknown	1/2005	UT	Both charged with 1st degr. felony child homicide and 2nd degr. felony child abuse in death of their 5-mo.-old son. Both were drug users and had previously lost custody of their other children because of drug use. Were ordered to have daily drug testing; caseworker had last visited home on 1/3/05. 5/16/05: Kevin sentenced to 1–15 yr. term; 7/11/05: Connie sentenced to up to 15 years.
71	Helen Kirk	33	3/2005	MA	Strangled 3-yr.-old son believing he was the devil; had been treated for mental illness. In 2002, her husband accused her of being "crazy" and like Andrea Yates. 5/27/05: not competent to stand trial; being held in state hospital.
72	Thuy Dang	37	3/2005	PA	Mother killed her two children (6 and 10) and then committed suicide. Had apparently been on medication until a year before. 13-yr.-old son heard brother's screams, but could not save any of the three.
73	Tonya Vasilev	34	4/2005	IL	Stabbed son (age 9) and daughter (age 3) more than 200 times. Charged with murder 1. 3-mo.-old child had died in 2002 in a house fire. Case reopened, but no foul play found. History of depression, possibly mental illness. Under heavy medication in psychiatric ward of Chicago hospital.
74	Jerry Hobbs	34	5/2005	IL	Stabbed daughter, age 9 (20 times), and her girlfriend, age 9 (11 times), to death because daughter would not accompany him home when he told her to. Long history of violent rages; 29 arrests/10 convictions. 6/1/05: charged with murder 1; 6/9/05: pled not guilty.

Infanticide and Filicide Cases (Continued)

No.	Name	Age	Date	State	Charges and Dispositions[a]
75	Luz Arroyo; David Maldonado	25; 31	7/2005	NY	Two sons, ages 2 and 20 mo., died of burns from scalding after being locked in the bathroom with steaming water turned on. Both parents had gone to bed in drug-induced stupor. Arroyo charged with two counts of criminally negligent homicide; could get up to 4 yrs. Maldonado charged with two counts of 2nd degr. mans.; could get up to 7 yrs. Registered with Child Services Protection Agency; caseworker fired for infrequent visits and reports. 1/25/06: both parents pled guilty — he to 2nd degr. mans. (5–15 yrs.) and she to criminally negligent homicide (1–4 yrs); drug charges dropped.
76	Matthew Carovillno	19	7/20/2005	OH	Raped and beat his girlfriend's 18-mo.-old daughter (Kaylee Schnurr) to death. Charged with aggravated murder, murder, child endangerment, and rape. Could be sentenced to death if convicted.
77	Ian Wilson	26	9/6/2005	CA	Charged with (and pled not guilty to) charges of murder and child abuse in death of 19-day-old baby. Infant died of blunt-force trauma to head. Preliminary hearing 10/5/05. If convicted, could serve 15 yrs.– life.
78	Charles Finley	19	9/21/2005	OH	Beat girlfriend's 1-yr.-old son (Christopher Beck) to death. Charged with aggravated murder, murder, and felonious assault. Could get death sentence if convicted.
79	Darius Myrick	32	10/6/2005	OH	Grabbed his daughter (Aliyah) from her mother's house and ran away with her. Child's body was found the next day. Charged with aggravated murder; could get death sentence if convicted.

Infanticide and Filicide Cases (Continued)

No.	Name	Age	Date	State	Charges and Dispositions[a]
80	Lashaun Harris	23	10/2005	CA	Threw her three children—ages 16 mos., $2^1/_2$, and 6 yrs.—into San Francisco Bay (heard voices telling her to do this). Diagnosed schizophrenic; had not been taking her medication; could not gain admission to a mental health facility because she had no ins. Charged with murder and assault; pled not guilty.
81	Victor Henriquez	17	10/2005	CN	Shook girlfriend's 5-mo.-old son, resulting in his death from blunt head trauma. Initially charged with 1st-degr. assault.
82	Gordon Franklin	39	10/2005	OH	Beat 13-yr.-old daughter to death with a golf club. Charged with aggravated murder; could get life sent.
83	Tracina Vaughan	25	11/6/2005	NY	Mother left 1-yr.-old boy in bathtub with 3-yr.-old half-brother—found unconscious and then died. She was playing CDs for 40 min. at the time. Mother charged with reckless endangerment and endangering welfare of a child (two cts. each). Had pled guilty 6 mos. earlier to endangering the welfare of the older boy (drug abuse involved); Children's Services involved. Her life "a mess" from early years (*NYT*-11/12/05).

[a] In some cases, it was impossible to discover the ultimate outcome.

References

ABC News (1997, July 7). ABC *Good Morning America*, Transcript #97070711-j01.

ABC News (2006, March 20). Judge delays Andrea Yates retrial. Accessed April 10, 2006 from http://www.wjla.com/news/stories/0306/311874.html.

ACOG (American College of Obstetricians and Gynecologists), 2002. Downloaded June 6, 2005.

Accused baby killer avoids death penalty. (1998, May 20). *Honolulu Star-Bulletin*, p.1.

Adinkrah, M. (2003). Men who kill their own children: paternal filicide incidents in contemporary Fiji. *Child Abuse & Neglect, 27*, 557–568.

Adler, N. E. (1984). Contraception and unwanted pregnancies. *Behavioral Medicine Update, 3*(4), 28–34.

Adler, N. E. (1992). Unwanted pregnancy and abortion: definitional and research issues. *Journal of Social Issues, 48*, 19–35.

Adler, N. E., Smith, L. B., & Tschann, J. M. (1998). Abortion among adolescents. In *The new civil war: The psychology, culture, and politics of abortion*, L. J. Beckman, & S. M. Harvey (Eds.). Washington, D.C.: American Psychological Association, pp. 285–298.

Adoption of Keefe, 733 N.E. 2d 1075 (Mass. 2000).

Agence France Presse (2005, April 21). Kuwaiti father poisons children, killing five. Downloaded June 21, 2005 from LexisNexis.

Alexander, R., Sato, Y., Smith, W., & Bennett, T. (1990). Incidence of impact trauma with cranial injuries ascribed to shaking. *American Journal of Diseases of Childhood, 144*, 93–106.

Alexander, R. D. (1987). *The Biology of Moral Systems*. Hawthorne, NY: A. de Gruyter.

Allen, A. L. (1992). Autonomy's magic wand: Abortion and constitutional interpretation. *Boston University Law Review, 72*, 683–698.

Allen, H. (1993). George Eliot and the ambiguity of murder. *Studies in the Novel, 25*(1), 59–75.

American Academy of Pediatrics Committee on Child Abuse and Neglect (2001a). Distinguishing sudden infant death syndrome from child abuse fatalities. *Pediatrics, 107*(2), 437–444.

American Academy of Pediatrics Committee on Child Abuse and Neglect (2001b). Shaken baby syndrome: Rotational cranial injuries. Technical report. *Pediatrics, 108*(1), 206–210.

American Law Institute (1980). *Model penal code and commentaries: Official draft and revised comments.* Philadelphia: American Law Institute.

American Psychiatric Association (1980). *Diagnostic and statistical manual of mental disorders* (3rd ed.). Washington, D.C.: The Association.

American Psychiatric Association (1984). *Issues in forensic psychiatry.* Washington, D.C.: The Association.

American Psychiatric Association (1987). *Diagnostic and statistical manual of mental disorders* (3rd ed.). Rev. Washington, D.C.: The Association.

American Psychiatric Association (1994). *Diagnostic and statistical manual of mental disorders* (4th ed.). Washington, D.C.: The Association.

American Psychiatric Association (2000). *Diagnostic and statistical manual of mental disorders*, (4th ed.) Text revision. Washington, D.C.: The Association.

Amighi, J. K. (1990). Some thoughts on the cross-cultural study of maternal warmth and detachment. *Pre- and Peri-Natal Psychology, 5*(2), 131–146.

Anderegg, D. (2003). *Worried all the time: Overparenting in an age of anxiety and how to stop it.* New York: Free Press.

Andrea Pia Yates, Appellant v. The State of Texas, Appellee (2005, January 6). In the Court of Appeals for the First District of Texas, Nos. 01-02-00462-CR and 01-02-00463-CR.

Angela M. W. v. Kruzicki, WI 95-2480 W (1995).

Annie Cordes v. State, 54 Tex. Crim. 204, 112 S. W. 943 (1908).

Anonymous (1998, January 10). Abortion: When a fetus is a person. *The Economist, 246*, 24.

Anonymous (2001, March 5). Couple appeals faith-healing convictions to U.S. Supreme Court. *The Legal Intelligencer*, p. 5.

Arnoldi, K. (1999). *The amazing "true" story of a teen-age single mom.* New York: Hyperion.

Artingstall, K. (1998). *Practical aspects of Munchausen by proxy and Munchausen syndrome investigation.* Boca Raton, FL: CRC Press.

Ashe, M. (1992). The "bad mother" in law and literature: a problem of representation. *Hastings Law Journal, 43*, 1017–1037.

Asher, R. (1951). Munchausen syndrome. *Lancet*, 1(6), 339–341.

Asser, S. M., & Swan, R. (2000). Child fatalities from religion-motivated medical neglect. *Cultic Studies Journal, 17*, 1–14.

Associated Press (1997a, May 18). Newborn is found alive in shallow grave. *The New York Times*, p. A15.

Associated Press (1997b, October 22). Baby is left in box; mother is 12, note says. *The New York Times*, p. A16.

Associated Press (1998, December 8). Teen hopes to avoid deportation in rape. *Ann Arbor* (MI) *News.*

Associated Press (2005a, July 2). FDA reiterates warning on adult antidepressants. *The Philadelphia Inquirer*, p. A16.

Associated Press (2005b, July 24). Convicted couple doesn't regret turning down medical care for child. LousivilleChannel.com. Downloaded July 26, 2005.

Associated Press State and Local Newswire (2004a, January 31). Conjoined twins die in San Antonio. Downloaded July 6, 2005.

Associated Press State and Local Newswire (2004b, October 8). Man sentenced to death in child homicide case. Downloaded March 16, 2005 from Lexis–Nexis.

Associated Press State and Local Newswire (2005a, January 3). Parents held in apparent beating death of city infant. Downloaded March 16, 2005 from Lexis–Nexis.

Associated Press State and Local Newswire (2005b, March 3). Mother sentenced on charges of contaminating toddler daughter's IV. Downloaded from Lexis–Nexis April 2, 2005.

Associated Press State and Local Newswire (2005c, July 6). Yates lawyers say conviction should remain overturned. Quincy, MA: *The Patriot Ledger*, p. 1.

Associated Press State and Local Newswire (2005d, August 12). Couple sentenced in death of newborn daughter. Franklin, IN. Downloaded from Lexis–Nexis Sept. 8, 2005.

Atkins, E. L., Grimes, J. P., Joseph, G. W., & Liebman, J. (1999). Denial of pregnancy and neonaticide during adolescence: Forensic and clinical issues. *American Journal of Forensic Psychology, 17*(1), 5–33.

Atwal, G. S., Rutty, G. N., Carter, N., & Green, M. A. (1998). Bruising in nonaccidental head injured children: a retrospective study of the prevalence, distribution and pathological associations in 24 cases. *Forensic Science International, 96*(2–3), 215–230.

Ball, H. L. & Hill, C. M. (1996). Reevaluating "twin infanticide." *Current Anthropology, 37*(5), 856–863.

Bandler, J. (2005, September 14). Child Protective Services probed punishment of scalded Yonkers boys. *The Journal News* (Yonkers, NY). Downloaded Nov. 25, 2005.

Bandler, J., & Cohen, S. (2005, October 7). Parents of scalded boys shared drugs, trouble. *The Journal News* (Yonkers, NY). Downloaded Nov. 25, 2005.

Barbassa, J. (2005, June 18). Father guilty in killing of 9 children. *The Philadelphia Inquirer*, p. A14.

Barber, M. A., & Davis, P. M. (2002). Fits, fancy or fatal fantasy? Fabricated seizures and child abuse. *Archives of Disease in Childhood, 86*, 230–233.

Bard, J. S. (2005). Rearranging deck chairs on the Titanic: Why the incarceration of individuals with serious mental illness violates public health, ethical, and constitutional principles and therefore cannot be made right by piecemeal changes to the insanity defense. *Houston Journal of Health Law and Policy, 5*, 1–73.

Barker, L. H., & Howell, R. J. (1994). Munchausen syndrome by proxy in false allegations of child sexual abuse: Legal implications. *Bulletin of the American Academy of Psychiatry & Law,* 22, 499–510.

Barlow, S. A. (1989). Stereotype and reversal in Euripedes' *Medea. Greece and Rome, 36*(2), 158–171.

Barlow, S. H., & Clayton, C. J. (1996). When mothers murder: understanding infanticide by females. In H. V. Hall (Ed.), *Lethal violence 2000: A sourcebook on fatal domestic, acquaintance and stranger aggression* (pp. 203–229). Kamuela, HI: Pacific Institute for the Study of Conflict and Aggression.

Barnes, A. (2005). Update on abortion law. In A. Barnes (Ed.), *The handbook of women, psychology, and the law* (pp. 147–177). New York: John Wiley & Sons.

Barton, B. (1998). Comment: When murdering hands rock the cradle: An overview of America's incoherent treatment of infanticidal mothers. *Southern Methodist University Law Review, 51*, 591–619.

Becker, M. E. (1986). From *Muller v. Oregon* to fetal vulnerability practices. *University of Chicago Law Review, 53*, 1219–1273.

Behlmer, G. K. (1979). Deadly motherhood: infanticide and medical opinion in mid-Victorian England. *Journal of the History of Medicine, 34*, 403–427.

Behnke, E. F., & Hans, S. L. (2002). Becoming a doula. *Zero to Three, 23*(2), 9–13.

Bell, E., & Robins, E. (1901; reprint 1991). *Alan's wife.* In Fitzsimmons, L., & Gardner, V. (Eds.), *New woman plays* (pp. 9–25). Portsmouth, NH: Methuen Drama.

Bendix, R., & Zumwalt, R. L. (1995). *Folklore interpreted: Essays in honor of Dundes.* New York: Garland Publishing.

Bennett, H. (1922). The exposure of infants in Ancient Rome. *The Classical Journal, 23*, 341–351.

Benoit, M. B. (1997). The role of psychological factors on teenagers who become parents out of wedlock. *Children and Youth Services Review, 19*, 401–413.

Berger, P., & Berger, B. (1984). *The War over the family: Capturing the middle ground.* Garden City, NY: Anchor Press.

Berman, N. (1999). Personal communication.

Berthea, L. (1999). Primary prevention of child abuse. *American Family Physician, 59*, 1577–1585.

Bethell, T. (1988). A heinous procedure. *The American Spectator, 31*(4), 20–24.

Bienstock, S. L. (2003). Mothers who kill their children and postpartum psychosis. *Southwestern University Law Review, 32*, 451–499.

Bluestein, D., & Rutledge, C. M. (1992). Determinants of delayed pregnancy testing among adolescents. *Journal of Family Practice, 35,* 406–410.

Bond, E. (1966). *Saved.* New York: Hill & Wang (1st American edition).

Bonnet, C. (1995). Adoption at birth: Prevention against abandonment or neonaticide. *Child Abuse and Neglect, 17,* 401–513.

Bookwalter, B. E. (1998). Note: Throwing the bath water out with the baby: Wrongful exclusion of expert testimony on neonaticide syndrome. *Boston University Law Review, 78,* 1185–1210.

Boswell, J. (1988). *The kindness of strangers: The abandonment of children in Western Europe from late antiquity to the Renaissance.* New York: Pantheon.

Bourget, D., & Bradford, J. M. W. (1990). Homicidal parents. *Canadian Journal of Psychiatry, 35,* 233–238.

Bourget, D., & Labelle, A. (1992). Homicide, infanticide, filicide. *Psychiatric Clinics of North America, 15*(3), 661–673.

Bowes, W. A., & Selegstad, B., Jr. (1981). Fetal versus maternal rights: Medical and legal perspectives. *Obstetrics and Gynecology, 58,* 209–214.

Boyer-Patrick, J. (1999). Use of counseling by pregnant or postpartum teens. *Psychiatric Times, 16*(9).

Brady, M. M. (1994). Munchausen syndrome by proxy: How should we weigh our options? *Law and Psychology Review, 18,* 361–375.

Brenton, H. (1996). Can you refuse the bargain of a lifetime? *New Statesman, 9*(420), 38–39.

Brewer, C. (1994, August 29). With sex and kids, men get off the hook. *Dayton Daily News,* p. 6A.

Brewster, A. L., Nelson, J. P., Hymel, K. P., Colby, D. R., Lucas, D. R., McCanne, T. R., & Milner, J. S. (1998). Victim, perpetrator, family, and incident characteristics of 32 infant maltreatment deaths in the United States Air Force. *Child Abuse and Neglect, 22*(2), 91–101.

Brezinka, C., Huter, O., Biebl, W., & Kinzl, J. (1994). Denial of pregnancy: Obstetrical aspects. *Journal of Psychosomatic Obstetrics and Gynecology,* 15, 1–8.

Bridis, T. (1997, October 3). Kentucky parents are charged in toddler's starvation death. *The Philadelphia Inquirer,* p. A3.

Brienza, J. (1997). When the bough breaks: Can justice be served in neonaticide cases? *Trial, 33*(12), 13–17.

Brockington, I. (2004). Diagnosis and management of postpartum disorders: a review. *World Psychiatry, 3*(2), 89–95.

Broder, S. (1988). Child care or child neglect? Baby farming in late nineteenth-century Philadelphia. *Gender and Society, 2*(2), 128–148.

Brody, J. E. (1998, February 10). Genetic ties may be factor in violence in stepfamilies. *The New York Times,* pp. F1, F4.

Brody, J. E. (1999, March 15). Earlier work with children steers them from crime. *The New York Times*, p. A16.

Brown, P. (1997, November 5). Hidden pregnancies: Girls bearing bad secrets. *Newsday* (New York), p. A50.

Brozovsky, M., & Falit, H. (1971). Neonaticide: Clinical and psychodynamic considerations. *Journal of the American Academy of Child Psychiatry, 10*, 673–683.

Brusca, A. D. (1990). Postpartum psychosis: A way out for murderous moms? *Hofstra Law Review, 18*, 1133–1170.

Bryant, T. L. (1990). Oya-ko Shinju: Death at the center of the heart. *UCLA Pacific Basin Law Journal, 8*(1), 1–31.

Buchanan, A. (1996). Choosing who will be disabled: Genetic intervention and the morality of inclusion. *Social Philosophy and Policy, 13*, 18–46.

Burden of Proof (1998, July 9). CNN Television.

Burke, B. (1984). Infanticide: Why does it happen in monkeys, mice, and men? *Science, 5*, 26–31.

Burleigh, M. (1994). Return to the planet of the apes? Peter Singer controversy in Germany. *History Today, 44*(10), 6–10.

Burling, S. (2005, April 18). Preempting postpartum depression. *The Philadelphia Inquirer*, pp. F1, F12.

Burling, S. (2005, May 11). Bill targets pregnancy, depression. *The Philadelphia Inquirer*, pp. B1, B6.

Buss, M. (1999). *Evolutionary psychology: The new science.* Boston: Allyn and Bacon.

Butterfield, F. (1999, July 12). Prisons brim with mentally ill, study finds. *The New York Times*, p. A10.

Byard, R. W., Knight, D., James, R.A., & Gilbert, J. (1999). Murder–suicides involving children: A 29-year study. *American Journal of Forensic Medicine and Pathology, 20*, 323–327.

Caffey, J. (1972). On the theory and practice of shaking infants: Its potential residual effects of permanent brain damage and mental retardation. *American Journal of Diseases of Children, 124*, 161–169.

Caffey, J. (1974). The whiplash shaken infant syndrome: Manual shaking by the extremities with whiplash-induced intracranial and intraocular bleeding, linked with residual permanent brain damage and mental retardation. *Pediatrics, 54*, 369–403.

Callahan, R. (1999, June 28). Father says he suffocated son in revenge. *The Philadelphia Inquirer*, p. A2.

Campion, J. F., Cravens, J. M., & Covan, F. (1988). A study of filicidal men. *American Journal of Psychiatry, 145*, 1141–1144.

Capital Report (1997, September 29). *Pennsylvania Law Weekly*, p. 9.

Carr, C. (1991). *The angel of darkness.* New York: Random House.

Carr-Saunders, A. M. (1922). *The population problem: A study in human evolution.* Oxford, England: Clarendon Press.

Carrera, M. (1997). My secret life: PACT, an adoption alliance. Pact Press, 28–30.

Carrera, M., & Dempsey, P. (1988, January–February). Restructuring public policies' priorities on teen pregnancy: A holistic approach to teen development and teen services, *SIECUS Reports*, 6–9.

Castaneda, R. (2005, October 24). Parents get $1 million in false abuse case. *Washington Post*, p. B2.

Cavaliere, F. (1995, August). Parents killing kids: a nation's shame. *APA Monitor*, p. 34.

CBS News (2005, July 15). Mom injected child with feces. Accessed July 17, 2005 from http://CBS3/kyw.com.

Chandra, A., Abma, J., Maza, P., & Bachrach, C. (1999). Adoption, adoption seeking, and relinquishment for adoption in the United States. *Advance Data from Vital and Health Statistics*, 306. Hyattsville, MD: National Center for Health Statistics.

Chase, J. (1999, January 27). Accused mom stole jewelry, witness says theft, baby's death linked to gambling. *Chicago Tribune*, p. 4.

Chen, D. (1998, June 18). Insanity defense may be used in retrial of Palatine woman. *Chicago Tribune*, p. 7A.

Christoffel, K. K. (1984). Homicide in childhood: a public health problem in need of attention. *American Journal of Public Health, 74*, 68–70.

Cleary, M. F. (1991). From *Roe* to *Webster*: Psychiatric, legal, and social aspects of abortion. *American Journal of Forensic Psychology, 9*(1), 51–63.

CNN.com (2005a, October 21). Mother pleads not guilty. Downloaded October 25, 2005.

CNN.com (2005b, November 9). Prosecutor: New trial for Andrea Yates. Downloaded November 9, 2005.

Cohen, M. (1993). Empowering the sister: female rescue and authorial resistance in *The Heart of Midlothian. College Literature, 20*(2), 58–69.

Colby, C., Sanders, T., & Wheeler, P. (2003, February). Prosecuting cases of suspected "shaken baby syndrome": A review of current issues. *Criminal Law Review*, 93–106.

Cole, J. (1996). A sudden and terrible revelation: motherhood and infant mortality in France, 1858–1874. *Journal of Family History, 21*(4), 410–445.

Coley, R. L., & Chase-Lansdale, P. L. (1998). Adolescent pregnancy and parenthood: Recent evidence and future directions. *American Psychologist, 53*, 152–166.

Collins, N. L., Dunkel-Schetter, C., Lobel, M., & Scrimshaw, S. C. M. (1993). Social support in pregnancy: Psychosocial correlates of birth outcomes and postpartum depression. *Journal of Personality and Social Psychology, 65*, 1243–1258.

Combs, C. (1997, April 22). Religious parents didn't intend daughter's death, lawyer says. *The Legal; Intelligencer*, p. 3.

Commonwealth of Pennsylvania v. Brian Smith, 675 A.2d 1221 (1996).

Commonwealth v. Campbell, 580 A2d 868 (PA. Super. Ct. 1990). *Juvenile and Family Law Digest*, 116–118.

Commonwealth v. Comitz, 365 Pa.Super. 599, 530 A.2d 473 (1987).

Commonwealth v. Louise Woodward, 427 Mass. 659, 694 N.E. 2d 1277 (1998).

Commonwealth v. Nixon 1998.

Commonwealth v. Robinson, Mass. App. Ct. 62, 565 N.E. 2d 1229 (1991).

Commonwealth v. Velasquez S.E.2d, 2004 WL1773647 Va. App. 2004.

Condit, C. M. (1990). *Decoding abortion rhetoric*. Urbana: University of Illinois Press.

Corcoran, J. (1998). Consequences of adolescent pregnancy/parenting: A review of the literature. *Social Work in Health Care, 27*(2), 49–67.

Corcoran, J., Franklin, C., & Bell, H. (1997). Pregnancy prevention from the teen perspective. *Child and Adolescent Social Work Journal, 14*, 365-382.

Cordes v. State, 54 Tex. Crim. 204, 112 S.W. 943 (1908).

Cornell, L. L. (1996). Infanticide in early modern Japan? Demography, culture, and population growth. *Journal of Asian Studies, 55*(1), 22–50.

Coronado, R. (2004, February 21). Child's killing draws two life terms. *Sacramento Bee*, p. B3.

Costen, J. (1995). *Sleep, my child, forever.* New York: Penguin Books.

Coughlin, A. M. (1994). Excusing women. *California Law Review, 82*, 1–93.

Coulombis, A. (1998, November 23). Bearing weight of a scarlet letter. *The Philadelphia Inquirer*, pp. 1, 5.

Cox, J. L., Holden, J. M., & Sagovsky, R. (1987). Edinburgh postnatal depression scale. *British Journal of Psychiatry, 150*, 782–786.

Crimmins, S., Langley, S., Brownstein, H. H., & Spunt, B. J. (1997). Convicted women who have killed children: a self-psychology perspective. *Journal of Interpersonal Violence, 12*(1), 49–69.

Crittenden, P. M., & Craig, S. E. (1990). Developmental trends in the nature of child homicide. *Journal of Interpersonal Violence, 5*, 202–216.

Crouch, S. (1987). Aunt Medea. *New Republic, 197*, 1538–1543.

Cummings, P., Theis, M. K., Mueller, B. A., & Rivera, F. P. (1994). Infant injury death in Washington State: 1981 through 1990. *Archives of Pediatric and Adolescent Medicine, 148*, 1021–1026.

Cushman, L. F., Kalmuss, D., & Nemerow, P. B. (1993). Placing an infant for adoption: The experiences of young birthmothers. *Social Work, 38*, 264–272.

Cutrona, C. E., Hessling, R. M., Bacon, P. L., & Russell, D. W. (1998). Predictors and correlates of continuing involvement with the baby's father among adolescent mothers. *Journal of Family Psychology, 12*, 369–387.

Dahir, V. B., Richardson, J. T., Ginsburg, G. P., Gatowski, S. I., Dobbin, S. A., & Merlino, M. L. (2005). Judicial application of *Daubert* to psychological syndrome and profile evidence: A research note. *Psychology, Public Policy and the Law, 11*, 62–79.

Dalton, K. (1989). *Depression after childbirth*. New York: Oxford University Press.

Daly, M., & Wilson, M. (1984). A sociobiological analysis of human infanticide. In G. Hausfater, & S. B. Hrdy (Eds.), *Infanticide: Comparative and evolutionary perspectives* (pp. 487–502). New York: Aldine.

Daly, M., & Wilson, M. (1988). Evolutionary social psychology and family homicide. *Science, 242*, 510–524.

Daly, M., & Wilson, L. M. (1994). Some differential attributes of lethal assault on small children by stepfathers versus genetic fathers. *Etiology and Sociobiology, 15*, 207–217.

Daly, M., & Wilson, L. M. (2001). An assessment of some proposed exceptions to the phenomenon of nepotistic discrimination against stepchildren. *Annales Zoologici Fennici, 38*, 287–296.

D'Amico, S. (2001). Inherently female cases of child abuse and neglect: A gender-neutral analysis. *Fordham Urban Law Journal, 28*, 866–880.

Damme, C. (1978). Infanticide: The worth of an infant under the law. *Medical History, 22*, 1–24.

Darnton, R. (1985). *The great cat massacre and other episodes in French cultural history.* New York: Vintage Books.

Daubert vs. Merrill Dow Pharmaceuticals, Inc. 509 U.S. 579 (1993).

David, H. P. (1992). Born unwanted: long-term developmental effects of denied abortion. *Journal of Social Issues, 48*(3), 163–181.

Davies, W. H., & Garwood, M. M. (2001). Who are the perpetrators and why do they do it? *Journal of Aggression, Maltreatment & Trauma, 5*(1), 41–54.

Dawkins, R. (1976). *The selfish gene.* New York: Oxford University Press.

Demb, J. (1991). Abortion in inner-city adolescents. *Family Systems in Medicine, 9*, 93–102.

Denno, D. W. (2003). Who is Andrea Yates? A short story about insanity. *Duke Journal of Gender Law & Policy, 10*, 1–60.

DePalma, A. (1997, December 1). Father's killing of Canadian girl: Mercy or murder? *The New York Times*, p. A3.

Dickemann, M. (1975). Demographic consequences of infanticide in man. *Annual Review of Ecology and Systems, 6*, 1007–1037.

Dickemann, M. (1979). Female infanticide, reproductive strategies and social stratification: A preliminary model. In Chagnon, N. A., & Irons, W. L. (Eds.), *Evolutionary biology and human behavior: An anthropological perspective* (pp. 321–368). North Scituate, MA: Duxbury Press.

Dobson, V., & Sales, B. (2000). The science of infanticide and mental illness. *Psychology, Public Policy, and Law, 6*, 1098–1112.

Doe v. Bolton, 410 U.S. 179 (1973).

Doege, D. (1998, November 19). Mother pleads guilty in newborn's death; charge reduced to reckless homicide. *Milwaukee Journal Sentinel*, p. 3.

Donohoe, M. (2003). Evidence-based medicine and shaken baby syndrome: Part 1 literature review, 1996–1998. *American Journal of Forensic Medicine and Pathology, 25*(2), 239–242.

Donovan, P. (1997). The Colorado parental rights amendment and how and why it failed. *Family Planning Perspectives, 29*(4), 187–190.

Donsky, P. (1997, May 23). Prosecutors mull lesser charges against mother in baby's burial. *The Tennessean*, p. 2B.

Donzelot, J. (1979). *The policing of families* (Hurley, R., transl.). New York: Pantheon Books.

d'Orban, P. T. (1979). Women who kill their children. *British Journal of Psychiatry, 134*, 560–571.

Dribben, M. (1998, July 16). Sexism slanted Del. baby case. *The Philadelphia Inquirer*, p. R1.

Dubin, M. (1998, May 11). Serious mother–son talk. *The Philadelphia Inquirer*, pp. F1, F4.

Duhaime, A-C., Christian, C. W., Rorke, L. B., & Zimmerman, R. A. (1998, June 18). Nonaccidental head injury in infants—the "shaken baby syndrome." *New England Journal of Medicine, 338*, 1822–1829.

Durham, W. H. (1990). Advances in evolutionary cultural theory. *Annual Review of Anthropology, 19*, 187–210.

Easton, P. (2005a, March 17). Russell Yates finalizes divorce from Andrea Yates. Associated Press State and Local Newswire. Downloaded from LexisNexis, March 17, 2005.

Easton, P. (2005b, May 3). Prosecutors appeal decision to overturn Yates convictions. Associated Press State and Local Newswire. Downloaded from LexisNexis, May 25, 2005.

Eau Claire teen admits reckless homicide charge in baby's death. (1998, September 26). *Star Tribune* (Minneapolis), p. 3B.

Ebrahim, A. F. M. (1991). *Abortion, birth control and surrogate parenting: An Islamic perspective*. Indianapolis, IN: American Trust Co.

Editorial (1998, February 26). Side arguments obscure appeal for Hopfer. *Dayton Daily News*, p. 1A.

Editorial Roundup (1998, June 15). *Idaho Statesman*, p. 7A.

Edwards, S. (1981). *Female sexuality and the law*. Oxford, England: Martin Robertson.

Edwards, S. S. M. (1986). Neither bad nor mad: The female violent offender reassessed. *Women's Studies International Forum, 9*(91), 79–87.

Efrati, A. (2004, August 2). SIDS research focuses on possible genetic risk. *The Deseret Morning News* (Salt Lake City, UT). Downloaded Sept. 29, 2005

Ehrenreich, B. (1998, January). Where have all the babies gone? *Life, 21*, 68–76.

Eliot, G. (1859; reprint 1981). *Adam Bede.* New York: Signet Books.

Emerick, S. J., Foster, L. R., & Campbell, D. T. (1986). Risk factors for traumatic infant death in Oregon, 1973 to 1982. *Pediatrics, 77*, 518–522.

Erikson, E. H. (1950). *Childhood and society.* New York: W. W. Norton.

Eshbacher, K. S. (2005, March 11). Incomprehensible: Killer parents not as rare as people think. *The Patriot Ledger* (Quincy, MA), p. 1.

Euripedes (431 B.C.; reprint 1938). *Medea* (Coleridge, E. P., transl.). In W. J. Oates, & E. O'Neill, Jr. (Eds.), *The complete Greek drama*, vol. I, (pp. 723–762). New York: Random House.

Evans, D. (1989). The psychological impact of disability and illness on medical treatment decisionmaking. *Issues in Law and Medicine, 5*(3), 277–299.

Fazio, C., & Comito, J. L. (1999). Note: Rethinking the tough sentencing of teenage neonaticide in the United States. *Fordham Law Review, 67*, 3109–3168.

Feldman, M. D. & Ford, C. V., with Reinhold, T. (1994). *Patient or pretender: Inside the strange world of factitious disorders.* New York: John Wiley & Sons.

Fimbres, G. (1998, September 22). Living hell: a local psychiatrist will show the differences between heartless baby-killers and girls who don't understand they are having a baby. *Tucson Citizen*, p. 1B.

Fine, D. K. (2000). Government as God: An update on federal intervention in the treatment of critically ill newborns. *New England Law Review, 34*, 343–362.

Finkel, N. J., Burke, J. E., & Chavez, L. J. (2000). Commonsense judgments of infanticide: Murder, manslaughter, madness, or miscellaneous? *Psychology, Public Policy, and Law, 6*, 1113–1137.

Finnegan, P., McKinstry, E., & Robinson, G. E. (1982). Denial of pregnancy and childbirth. *Canadian Journal of Psychiatry, 27*, 672–674.

Fitzgerald, K. (2005, April 22). Former conjoined twins still catching up. Associated Press. Downloaded July 6, 2005.

Fitzsimmons, L., & Gardner, V. (1991). *New woman plays.* Portsmouth, NH: Methuen Drama.

Flannery, M. T. (1998). First do no harm: The use of covert video surveillance to detect Munchausen syndrome by proxy—an unethical means of "preventing" child abuse. *University of Michigan Journal of Law Reform, 35*, 105–118.

Folkenburg, J. (1985, May). Teen pregnancy: who opts for adoption? *Psychology Today*, 16.

Forbes, T. R. (1986). Deadly parents: child homicide in eighteenth- and nineteenth-century England, *Journal of the History of Medicine, 41*, 175–199.

Ford, J. (1996). Note: Susan Smith and other homicidal mothers—in search of the punishment that fits the crime. *Cardozo Women's Law Journal, 3*, 521–548.

Fost, N. (1981). Counseling families who have a child with severe congenital anomalies. *Pediatrics, 67*, 321–324.

Fox-Genovese, E. (1988). *Within the plantation household: Black and white women of the old south*. Chapel Hill, NC: University of North Carolina Press.

France, D. (1997). Why was disposal the only thought that occurred to them? *New Woman, 27*(9), 124–125, 144–145.

Francus, M. (1997). Monstrous mothers, monstrous societies: Infanticide and the rule of law in restoration and eighteenth-century England. *Eighteenth-Century Life, 21*(2), 133–156.

Friedman, L. M. (1991). Crimes of mobility. *Stanford Law Review, 43*, 637–658.

Friedman, S. H., Horwitz, S. M., & Resnick, P. J. (2005). Child murder by mothers: A critical analysis of the current state of knowledge and a research agenda. *American Journal of Psychiatry, 162*, 1578–1587.

Frye v. United States, 54 App. D.C. 46 (1923), 293 F. 1013.

Fuchs, R. (1984). *Abandoned children: Foundlings and child welfare in nineteenth-century France*. Albany, NY: State University of New York Press.

Fuchs, R. (1992). *Poor and pregnant in Paris: Strategies for survival in the nineteenth century*. New Brunswick, NJ: Rutgers University Press.

Fugate, J. A. (2001). Who's failing whom? A critical look at failure-to-protect laws. *New York University Law Review, 76*, 272–308.

Furstenberg, F. F., Geitz, L. M., Teitler, J. O., & Weiss, C. C. (1997). Does condom availability make a difference? An evaluation of Philadelphia's Health Resource Centers. *Family Planning Perspectives, 19*(3), 123–127.

Gallahue, P. (2004, April 2). Tot-slay agony; sibling survivors still scream in despair, *The New York Post*, p. 11.

Gartner, R. (1991). Family structure, welfare spending, and child homicide in developed democracies. *Journal of Marriage and the Family*, 53, 231–240.

Gavitt, P. (1994). Perche non avea chi la ghovernasse: cultural values, family resources abandonment in the Florence of Lorenzo d'Medici, 1467–1485. In J. Henderson, & R. Wall. (Eds.), *Poor women and children in the European past* (pp. 65–94). New York: Routledge.

Geddes, J. F., Taskert, R. C., Hackshaw, A. K., Nickols, C. D., Adams, G. G., Whitewall, H. L., & Scheimberg, I. (2003). Dual hemorrhages in nontraumatic infants' deaths: Does it explain the bleeding in shaken baby syndrome? *Neuropathology and Applied Neurobiology, 29*, 14–22.

Gelles, R. J. (1995). *The book of David: How preserving families can cost children's lives*. New York: Basic Books.

Gelles, R. J. (1997). *Intimate violence in families* (3rd ed.). Thousand Oaks, CA: Sage.

Geraghty, M. (1997, September 12). Hidden pregnancies and babies' deaths raise painful questions for college. *The Chronicle of Higher Education, 44*, A49–A50.

Geronimus, A. T. (1987). On teenage childrearing and neonatal mortality in the United States. *Population and Development Review, 13*, 245–280.

Gillis, J. R. (1983). Servants, sexual relations and the risks of illegitimacy in London, 1801–1900. In J. L. Newton (Ed.), *Sex and class in women's history* (pp. 114–146). London: Routledge and Kegan Paul.

Ginsburg, F. D. (1989). *Contested lives: The abortion debate in an American community*. Berkeley, CA: University of California Press.

Glendon, M. A. (1991). *Rights talk*. New York: Free Press.

Goethe, J. W. Von (1808; reprint 1950) (Taylor, B., transl.). *Faust*. New York: Modern Library.

Goldenberg, C. L. (1999). Sudden infant death syndrome as a mask for murder: Investigating and prosecuting homicide. *Southwestern University Law Review, 28*, 599–611.

Goldman, L. H., & Yorker, N. C. (1999). Mommie dearest? Prosecuting cases of Munchausen syndrome by proxy. *Criminal Justice, 13*(4), 26–33.

Goodnough, A., & Weber, B. (1997, July 2). The picture of ordinary. *The New York Times*, pp. B1, B6.

Gordan, S. (1998). Mothers who kill their children. *Buffalo Women's Law Journal, 6*, 86–103.

Gottlieb, C. N. (1996). Filicide: A strategic approach. *Psychology—A Journal of Human Behavior, 33*(3), 40–42.

Gould, S. J. (1980). Sociobiology and human nature: A post-Panglossian vision. In A. E. Montague (Ed.), *Sociobiology examined* (pp. 283–290). New York: Oxford University Press.

Granzberg, G. (1973). Twin infanticide—a cross-cultural test of a materialistic explanation. *Ethos, 1*(4), 405–412.

Graves, R. (1988). *The Greek myths*. Mt. Kisco, NY: Moyer Bell, Ltd.

Green, C. M. (1990). Neonaticide and hysterical denial of pregnancy. *Obstetric and Gynecological Survey, 45*(8), 534–535.

Green, C. M., & Manohar, S. V. (1990). Neonaticide and hysterical denial of pregnancy. *British Journal of Psychiatry, 156*, 121–123.

Green, E. C. (1999). Infanticide and infant abandonment in the new South: Richmond, Virginia, 1865–1915. *Journal of Family History, 24*(2), 187–211.

Greenwood, D. J. H. (1994). Review essay: Beyond Dworkin's dominions: Investments, memberships, the tree of life and abortion. *Texas Law Review, 72*, 471–630.

Griffin, L. (2004). "Which one of you did it?" Criminal liability for "causing or allowing" the death of a child. *Indiana International & Comparative Law Review, 15*, 89–114.

Griffin, M. R., Ray, W. A., Livengood, J. R., & Schaffner, W. (1988). Risk of sudden infant death syndrome after immunization with the diphtheria–tetanus–pertussis vaccine. *New England Journal of Medicine, 319*(10), 618–623.

Grim, W. E. (1988). *The Faust legend in music and literature.* Lewiston, NY: The Edwin Mellen Press.

Griswold v. Connecticut, 381 U.S. 479 (1965).

Grossman, J. L. (1990). Postpartum psychosis—a defense to criminal responsibility or just another gimmick?, *University of Detroit Law Review, 67*, 311–344.

Group for the Advancement of Psychiatry Committee on Psychiatry and Law (1969). The right to abortion: a psychiatric view. *GAP Reports, 7*(74), 197–227.

Gunter, M. (1998). Induction, identification or *folie a deux*? Psychodynamics and genesis of Munchausen syndrome by proxy and false allegations of sexual abuse in adolescents. *Medicine and Law, 17*, 359–376.

Gustafson, J. M. (1973). Mongolism, parental desires, and the right to life, *Perspectives in Biology and Medicine, 16*, 529–557.

Guterman, N. B., & Lee, Y. (2005). The role of fathers in risk for physical child abuse and neglect: Possible pathways and unanswered questions. *Child Maltreatment, 10*(2), 136–149.

Hall, D., Eubank, L., Meyyazhagen, S., Kenney, R. D., & Johnson, S. C. (2000). Evaluation of covert video surveillance in the diagnosis of Munchausen syndrome by proxy: Lessons from 41 cases. *Pediatrics, 105*, 1305–1312.

Hall, H. V. (1999). Personal communication.

Hanley, R. (1997, June 25). New Jersey charges woman, 18, with killing baby born at prom. *The New York Times*, pp. A1, B4.

Hanley, S. B. (1983). A high standard of living in nineteenth-century Japan. *Journal of Economic History, 43*(1), 183–192.

Hanson, E. (1997, January 30). Infanticide cases still evoke shock, horror in jaded public. *Houston Chronicle*, p. A21.

Harding, B., Risdon, R. B., & Krous, H. F. (2004). Shaken baby syndrome. *British Medical Journal, 328*, 720–721.

Harding, S. (1990). If I should die before I wake: Jerry Falwell's pro-life gospel. In F. Ginsberg, & A. Tsing (Eds.), *Uncertain terms: Negotiating gender in American culture* (pp. 76–98). Boston: Beacon Press.

Harris, M. (1977). *Cannibals and kings: The origin of cultures.* New York: Random House.

Hatina, J. D. (1998). Shaken baby syndrome: Who are the true experts? *Cleveland State Law Review, 46*, 557–583.

Hay, M., & Roberts, P. (1980). *Bond: A study of his plays.* London: Eyre Methuen.

Haywood-Brown, H. (2003). Munchausen syndrome by proxy: Some medico-legal issues. *Judicial Officers Bulletin, 16*, 33–34, 40.

Hennes, H., Kini, N., & Palusci, V. J. (2001). The epidemiology, clinical characteristics and public health implications of shaken baby syndrome. In S. Lazoritz & V. Palusci (Eds.), *The shaken baby syndrome: A multidisciplinary approach* (pp. 19–41). Binghamton, NY: Haworth Maltreatment and Trauma Press.

Henriques, U. R. Q. (1967, July). Bastardy and the new *Poor Law. Past and Present, 37*, 103–129.

Henshaw, S. K. (1997). Teenage abortion and pregnancy statistics by state, 1992. *Family Planning Perspectives, 29*(3), 115–122.

Henson, R. (1999, April 9). Pa. court rules fetus is a person. *The Philadelphia Inquirer*, pp. B1, B6.

Herbert, B. (1998, June 14). In America: Hidden agendas. *The Philadelphia Inquirer*, p. WK15.

Herman-Giddens, M. E., Brown, G., Verbiest, S., Carlson, P., Hooten, E. G., & Butts, J. B. (1999). Under-ascertainment of child-abuse mortality in the United States. *Journal of the American Medical Association (JAMA), 282*(5), 463–467.

Hernandez-Truyol, B. E. (1997). Conceptualizing violence: Present and future developments in international law: Panel 1: Human rights and civil wrongs at home and abroad; old problems and new paradigms; sex, culture, and rights: a reconceptualization of violence for the twenty-first century. *Albany Law Review, 60*, 607–634.

Herz, E. K. (1992). Prediction, recognition, and prevention. In J. A. Hamilton, P. N. Harberger (Eds.), *Postpartum psychiatric illness: A picture puzzle* (pp. 73–75). Philadelphia: University of Pennsylvania Press.

Hesketh, T., & Zhu, W. X. (1997). The one child family policy: the good, the bad, and the ugly; health in China, part 3. *British Medical Journal, 314*, 1685–1692.

Hickman, S. A., & LeVine, D. L. (1992). Postpartum disorders and the law. In J. A. Hamilton, & P. N. Harberger (Eds.), *Postpartum psychiatric illness: A picture puzzle* (282–295). Philadelphia: University of Pennsylvania Press.

Higginbotham, A. R. (1989). Sin of the age: infanticide and illegitimacy in Victorian London. *Victorian Studies, 32*(3), 319–337.

Hoffer, P. C., & Hull, N. E. H. (1981). *Murdering mothers: Infanticide in England and New England 1558–1803*. New York: New York University Press.

Hofferth, S. L., & Anderson, K. G. (2003). Are all dads equal? Biology versus marriage as a basis for paternal investment. *Journal of Marriage and Family, 65*, 213–232.

Hogue, C. J. R. (1997). Missing the boat on pregnancy prevention. *Issues in Science and Technology, 13*(4), 41–46.

Holden, C. E., Burland, A. S., & Lemmen, C. A. (1996). Insanity and filicide: Women who murder their children. *New Directions for Mental Health Services, 69*, 25–34.

Holmgren, B. K. (2001). Prosecuting the shaken infant case. *Journal of Aggression, Maltreatment & Trauma, 5*(1), 275–339.

Holt, J. (2005, July 10). Euthanasia for babies? *The New York Times Magazine*, pp. 11–14.

Hontela, S., & Reddon, J. R. (1996). Infanticide of defective newborns: An old midwife's story. *Psychological Reports, 79*(3, Part 2), 1275–1278.

Hornblower, S. (1983). *The Greek World, 479–323 B.C.* London: Methuen.

Houston Chronicle News Service (2001, July 1). Not without precedent. www.HoustonChronicle.com.

Hoyert, D. L., Kung, H-C., & Smith, B. L. (2005, February 28). National Vital Statistics Reports: Deaths: Preliminary data for 2003. Washington, D.C.: U.S. Department of Health and Human Services, Table 7.

Hrdy, S. B. (1984). When the bough breaks: there may be method in the madness of infanticide. *Sciences, 24*(2), 45–50.

Hrdy, S. B. (1992). Fitness tradeoffs in the history and evolution of delegated mothering with special reference to wet-nursing, abandonment, and infanticide. *Ethology and Sociobiology, 13*, 409–442.

Hufton, O. H. (1974). *The poor of eighteenth-century France, 1750–1789.* Oxford, England: Clarendon Press.

Hughes, J. (1987). *The fatal shore: A history of transportation of convicts to Australia, 1787–1868.* London: Harvill Press.

Hughes, R. A. (1990). Psychological perspectives on infanticide in a faith healing sect. *Psychotherapy, 27*(1), 107–115.

Hull, T. H. (1990). Recent trends in sex ratios at birth in China. *Population and Development Review, 16*(1), 63–83.

Hunt, C. E. (2001). Sudden infant death syndrome and other causes of infant mortality: Diagnosis, mechanisms, and risk for recurrence in siblings. *American Journal of Respiratory and Critical Care Medicine*, 164, 346–357.

Hyde Amendment, Department of Labor Appropriations Act (Sect. 509), 1994, 107 Stat. 1082.

Iffy, L., & Jakobovits, A. (1992). Infanticide: new medical considerations. *Medicine and Law, 11*, 269–274.

Illick, J. E. (1974). Child-rearing in seventeenth-century England and America. In L. DeMause (Ed.), *A history of childhood* (pp. 303–351). New York: Psychohistory Press.

Illinois Report (1998, August 8). *State Journal Register* (Springfield, IL), p. 7.

In re Haviland. Court of Appeals Minnesota: Matter of child Deedra and Timothy Haviland, Parents. No. C0-02-`1822 (29 April 2003).

Insanity Defense Reform Act of 1984, Pub. L. No. 98-473, 18 U. S. C. β 17.

International Union U. A. W. v. Johnson Controls. 111 S. Ct. 1196 (1991).

Isser, E. R. (1997). *Stages of annihilation.* Cranbury, NJ: Associated University Presses.

Isser, N. K., & Schwartz, L. L. (2006). Shaken baby syndrome. *Journal of Psychiatry and Law, 34*(3).

Jackson, M. (1996). *New-born child murder: Women, illegitimacy, and the courts in eighteenth-century England.* Manchester, England: Manchester University Press.

Jamieson, D. (Ed.) (1999). *Singer and his critics.* Malden, MA: Blackwell.

Jemmott, J. B., III, Jemmott, L. S., & Fong, G. T. (1998). Abstinence and safer sex: HIV risk-reduction interventions for African-American adolescents: A randomized controlled trial. *Journal of the American Medical Association, 279*, 1529–1536.

Jimmerson, J. (1990). Female infanticide in China: an examination of cultural and legal norms. *UCLA Pacific Law Basin Journal, 8*, 47–79.

Johansson, S., & Nygren, O. (1991). The missing girls of China: a new demographic account. *Population and Development Review, 17*(1), 35–51.

John Josef v. State, 34 Tex. Crim. 446 (1895).

Johnston, S. (2003, November 17). Decisions involve the heart and mind: Risky medical operations separating conjoined twins make headlines. *The Toronto Sun*, p. 35.

Jones, C. M. (1993). *Sula* and *Beloved:* Images of Cain in the novels of Toni Morrison. *African American Review, 27*, 615–626.

Jones, M. (2005, July 15). Leading doctor struck off over dead baby case. Reuters, U.K. Downloaded July 15, 2005.

Jones, O. D. (1997). Evolutionary analysis in law: an introduction and application to child abuse. *North Carolina Law Review, 75*, 1117–1180.

Joyce, K., Diffenbacher, G., Greene, J., & Sorokin, Y. (1983). Internal and external barriers to obtaining prenatal care. *Social Work in Health Care, 9*(2), 89–96.

Kadish, S. H., & Schulhofer, S. J. (1995). *Criminal law and its processes, cases and materials* (6th ed.). Englewood Cliffs, NJ: Aspen Law and Business.

Kahan, B., & Yorker, B. C. (1991). Munchausen syndrome by proxy: Clinical review and legal issues. *Behavioral Sciences and the Law, 9*, 73–83.

Kalmuss, D., Namerow, P. B., & Cushman, L. F. (1991). Adoption versus parenting among young pregnant women. *Family Planning Perspectives, 23*, 17–23.

Kansas v. Lumbrera, 257 Kan. 144, 891 P 2d 1096; 1995 Kan. LEXIS 40.

Kaplan, H. I., & Sadock, B. J. (1996). *Pocket handbook of clinical psychiatry* (2nd ed.). Baltimore, MD: Williams and Wilkins.

Kaplan, M. F. (1988). A peer support group for women in prison for the death of a child. *Journal of Offender Counseling, Services, and Rehabilitation, 13*(1), 5–13.

Karst, K. L. (1984). Woman's constitution. *Duke Law Journal, 3*, 447–508.

Kasule, O. H. (2003). Social and religious dimensions of unwanted pregnancy: An Islamic perspective. *Medical Journal of Malaysia, 58*(Suppl. A), 49–60.

Katkin, D. M. (1992). Postpartum psychosis, infanticide, and criminal justice. In J. A. Hamilton, & P. N. Harshberger (Eds.), *Postpartum psychiatric illness: A picture puzzle* (pp. 275–281). Philadelphia: University of Pennsylvania Press.

Kaye, N. S., Borenstein, N. M., & Donnelly, S. M. (1990). Families, murder, and insanity: psychiatric review of paternal neonaticide. *Journal of Forensic Science, 35*(1), 133–139.

Kellet, R. J. (1992). Infant and child destruction—the historical, legal and pathological aspects. *Forensic Science International, 53*, 1–18.

Kellum, B. A. (1973). Infanticide in England in the later Middle Ages. *History of Childhood Quarterly, 1*(3), 367–388.

Kelly, C. (2002). The legacy of too little, too late: The inconsistent treatment of postpartum psychosis as a defense to infanticide. *Journal of Contemporary Health Law and Policy*, 19, 247–277.

Kemme, S. (2000, March 24). Mom gets life for killing newborn. *The Cincinnati Enquirer*. Downloaded from <enquirer.com> June 26, 2005.

Kemp, A. M. (2002). Investigating subdural hemorrhage in infants. *Archives of Disease in Childhood, 86*, 98–102.

Kertscher, T. (2005, July 16). Green Bay man heads to trial in deaths of 2 of his children. <JSOnline>. Downloaded July 18, 2005.

Kertzer, D. I. (1993). *Sacrificed for honor: Italian infant abandonment and the politics of reproductive control*. New York: Beacon Press.

Kiefer, M. (2005, June 12). Prosecutor refuses to give bad guys a break. <AZcentral.com> Downloaded June 17, 2005.

Kim, N. S. (1997). The cultural defense and the problem of cultural preemption: A framework for analysis. *New Mexico Law Review, 17*, 101–139.

Kingston, M. H. (1989). *Woman warrior: Memoirs of a girlhood among ghosts*. New York: Vintage Books.

Kinscherff, R., & Famulario, R. (1991). Extreme Munchausen syndrome by proxy: The case for termination of parental rights. *Juvenile and Family Court Journal, 40*, 41–49.

Kirby, D. (2001). Emerging answers: Research findings on programs to reduce teen pregnancy. Washington, D.C.: National Campaign to Prevent Teen Pregnancy. <www.teenage pregnancy.org>.

Kirby, D., Korpi, M., Barth, R. P., & Capampang, H. H. (1997). Impact of postponing sexual involvement curriculum among youth in California. *Family Planning Perspectives, 29*(3), 100–108.

Kirby, D., Short, L., Collins, J., Rugg, D., Kolbe, L., Howard, M., Miller, B., Sonenstein, F. A., & Zabin, L. S. (1994). School-based programs to reduce sexual risk behaviors: A review of effectiveness. *Public Health Reports, 109*, 339–360.

Kirwin, B. (1997, September). The coed baby killer. *Cosmopolitan*, 272–275.

Knelman, J. (1998). Women murderers in Victorian Britain; popular press portrayal of women murderers during the Victorian era. *History Today, 48* (8), 9–14.

Knepper, K. (1994). Withholding medical treatment from infants: When is it child neglect? *University of Louisville Journal of Family Law, 33*, 1–53.

Kobbé, C. W. (1919; reprint 1987). *The definitive Kobbé opera book*, Earl of Harewood (Ed.). New York: Putnam.

Koop, C. E. (1989). Life and death and the handicapped. *Issues in Law and Medicine, 5*, 101–107.

Korbin, J. E. (1986). Childhood histories of women imprisoned for fatal child maltreatment. *Child Abuse and Neglect, 10*, 331–338.

Kord, S. (1993). Women as children, women as childkillers: infanticide in eighteenth-century Germany. *Eighteenth Century Studies, 26*(3), 449–466.

Kouno, A., & Johnson, C. F. (1995). Child abuse and neglect in Japan: coin-operated locker babies. *Child Abuse and Neglect, 19*(1), 25–31.

Kovera, M. B. (2002). The effects of general pretrial publicity on juror decisions: An examination of moderators and mediating mechanisms. *Law and Human Behavior, 26*, 43–72.

Krous, H. F., Nadeau, J. M., Silva, P. D., & Blackstone, B. D. (2003). A comparison of respiratory symptoms and inflammation in sudden infant death syndrome and in accidental or inflicted infant death. *American Journal of Forensic Medicine and Pathology, 24*(1), 1–8.

Kunst, J. L., & Reed, M. (1999). Cross-cultural issues in infanticide: A case study. *Cultural Diversity and Ethnic Minority Psychology, 6*(2), 147–155.

Kunz, J., & Bahr, S. J. (1996). A profile of parental homicide against children. *Journal of Family Violence, 11*, 347–362.

Kuturah Aldridge v. Comm. of Va (2004), 44 Va. App 618, 606 S.E. 2dd 539.

Lagaipa, S. J. (1990). Suffer the little children: the ancient practice of infanticide as a modern moral dilemma. *Issues in Comprehensive Pediatric Nursing, 13*, 241–251.

Lane, R. (1986). *Roots of violence in black Philadelphia, 1860–1900.* Cambridge, MA: Harvard University Press.

Lane v. Commonwealth, 248, S. E. Va. (1978).

Langer, W. L. (1974). Infanticide: a historical survey. *History of Childhood Quarterly, 1*, 353–366.

Lansdowne, R. (1990). Infanticide: psychiatrists in the plea bargaining process. *Monash University Law Review, 16*(1), 41–64.

Latine Marie Gordon Davidson v. State of Indiana, 558 N.E.2d, 1077, 1990.

Lavilla, S. (1998, September 17). Why her? *Asian Week.* World Wide Web <www.asianweek.com/098/coverstory.html> retrieved October 18, 2001 from source.

Lazoritz, S., & Paulsci, V. J. (Eds.). (2001). *The shaken baby syndrome: A multidisciplinary approach.* New York: Haworth Maltreatment & Trauma Press.

Leboutte, R. (1991). Offense against family order: infanticide in Belgium from the fifteenth through the early twentieth centuries. *Journal of the History of Sexuality, 2*(2), 159–185.

Ledwon, L. (1996). Maternity as a legal fiction: infanticide and Sir Walter Scott's *The Heart of Midlothian*. *Women's Rights Law Reports, 18*(1), 1–16.

Lee, A. K. (1994). Attitudes and prejudices toward infanticide: Carthage, Rome and today. *Archaeological Review from Cambridge, 13*(2), 65–79.

Leetsma, J. F. (2005). Case analysis of brain-injured admittedly shaken infants: 54 cases, 1969–2001. *American Journal of Forensic Medicine and Pathology, 26*(3), 199–212.

Leland, J. (2005, October 2). Abortion might outgrow its need for *Roe v. Wade*. *The New York Times*, Sect. 4, p. 14.

Lentz, M. E. (1989). A postmortem of the post partum psychosis defense. *Capitol University Law Review, 18*, 525–544.

Lester, D. (1986). The relation of twin infanticide to status of women, societal aggression, and material well-being. *Journal of Social Psychology, 126*(1), 57–59.

Leung, A. K. C. (1995). Relief institutions for children in nineteenth-century China. In A. B. Kinney (Ed.), *Chinese views of childhood* (pp. 251–279). Honolulu: University of Hawaii Press.

Levene, A. (1998, September 6). Italian dustbins bear a warning: "not for babies." *Chicago Tribune*, p. 8.

Levene, S., & Bacon, C. J. (2004). Sudden unexpected death and covert homicide in infancy. *Archives of Disease in Childhood*, 89, 443–447.

Lewin, T. (1998, October 15). Youth pregnancy rate falls, report says. *The New York Times*, p. A27.

Lewis, C. F., & Bunce, S. C. (2003). Filicidal mothers and the impact of psychosis on maternal filicide. *Journal of the American Academy of Psychiatry and Law, 31*, 459–470.

Lewis, C. F., Baranoski, M. V., Buchanan, J. A., & Benedek, E. P. (1998). Factors associated with weapon use in maternal filicide. *Journal of Forensic Science, 43*, 613–618.

Li, L. (1991). Life and death in a Chinese famine: Infanticide as a demographic consequence of the 1935 Yellow River flood. *Comparative Studies in Sociology and History, 33*(3), 466–510.

Liang, B. A., & Macfarlane, W. (1999). Murder by omission: Child abuse and the passive parent. *Harvard Journal of Legislation, 36*, 397–450.

Liddle, R. (2005, June 26). Mumbo-jumbo syndrome. (London) *Sunday Times*, p. 15.

Light, M. J., & Sheridan, M. S. (1990). Munchausen syndrome by proxy and apnea (MBPA): A survey of apnea programs. *Clinical Pediatrics, 29*, 162–168.

Lindsay, S. (1998a, April 26). Depression exceeds "baby blues," "voices" may tell mom she must kill children. (Denver) *Rocky Mountain News*, p. 32A.

Lindsay, S. (1998b, April 26). Mom accused of killing kids may attempt rare defense, postpartum depression is central to legal claim. (Denver) *Rocky Mountain News*, p. 5A.

Litchfield, R. B., & Gordon, D. (1980). Closing the "tour." *Journal of Social History, 13*, 458–472.

Liu, S. M. S. (2002). Postpartum psychosis: A legitimate defense for negotiating criminal Responsibility. *The Scholar: St. Mary's Law Review on Minority Issues, 4*, 339–404.

Locke, M. (2005, September 18). A moment of violence, a child's life destroyed. Raleigh, NC: *News & Observer.* Downloaded September 18, 2005.

Loggins, K. (1998, November 7). Appeals court affirms guilty verdict of father in murder of newborn son. *The Tennessean*, p. 6B.

Lonczak, H. S., Abbott, R. D., Hawkins, J. D., Kosterman, R., & Catalano, R. F. (2002). Effects of the Seattle Social Development Project on sexual behavior, pregnancy, birth, and sexually transmitted disease outcomes by age 21 years. *Archives of Pediatrics and Adolescent Medicine, 156*, 438–447.

Long v. Texas, 586 S.W.2d, 1979 Tex. Crim. App.: Lexis 1640.

Lopez, P. (2005, June 30). Jury recommends death for Wesson. *The Fresno Bee* (CA), p. A1.

Loyd, L. (1998, August 6). Mother, now 69, charged with suffocating 8 babies. *The Philadelphia Inquirer*, pp. A1, A18.

Loyd, L. (1999, March 20). Jury convicts mother who starved child. *The Philadelphia Inquirer*, p. R1.

Lugosi, C. I. (2001). Playing God: Mary must die so Jodie may live longer. *Issues in Law and Medicine, 17*, 123–165.

Lumsden, C. J., & Wilson, E. O. (1983). *Promethean fire: Reflections on the origin of mind.* Cambridge, MA: Harvard University Press.

Lund, N. (1985). Infanticide, physicians, and the law: The "Baby Doe" amendments to the *Child Abuse Prevention and Treatment Act. American Journal of Law and Medicine, 11*, 1–29.

Lyons, G. (2003). Shaken baby syndrome: A questionable scientific syndrome and a dangerous legal concept. *Utah Law Review*, 1109–1132.

MacDoman, M. F., & Atkinson, J. O. (1999). Infant mortality statistics from the 1997 period linked birth/infant death data set. *National Vital Statistics Report, 47*(23). Hyattsville, MD: National Center for Health Statistics.

MacDonald, D. I. (1987). An approach to the problem of teen pregnancy. *Public Health Reports, 102*, 377–385.

Maciejczyk, J. M. (1983). Withholding treatment from defective infants. *Notre Dame Law Review, 59*, 21–30.

Mackay, R. D. (1993, January). The consequences of killing very young children. *Criminal Law Review*, 21–30.

Mackinnon, C. A. (1989). *Toward a feminist theory of the state.* Cambridge, MA: Harvard University Press.

Mahler, K. (1997). Young mothers who choose adoption may be regretful, but not usually depressed. *Family Planning Perspectives, 29*(3), 146–147.

Maier-Katkin, D. (1991). Postpartum psychosis, infanticide and the law. *Crime, Law, and Social Change, 15*, 109–123.

Manchester, J. (2003). Beyond accommodation: Reconstructing the insanity defense to provide an adequate remedy for postpartum psychotic women. *Journal of Criminal Law and Criminology, 93*, 713–752.

Mapanga, K. G. (1997). The perils of adolescent pregnancy. *World Health, 50*(2), 16–17.

Marks, M. N., & Kumar, R. (1993). Infanticide in England and Wales. *Medicine, Science, and the Law, 33*(3), 329–339.

Marks, M. N., & Kumar, R. (1996). Infanticide in Scotland. *Medicine, Science, and the Law, 36*, 299–305.

Marleau, J. D., Poulin, B., Webanck, T., Roy, R., & Laporte, L. (1999). Paternal filicide: a study of 10 men. *Canadian Journal of Psychiatry, 44*, 57–63.

Marlow, J. D. (1998). From black robes to white lab coats: the ethical implications of a judge's *sua sponte, ex parte* acquisition of social and other scientific evidence during the decision-making process. *St. John's Law Review, 72*, 291–335.

Marshall, C. (2005, October 21). Woman charged in deaths of her 3 children. *The New York Times*, p. A 22.

Martello, T. (1999, September 14). ACLU sues to block N.J. abortion law. *The Philadelphia Inquirer*, p. R5.

Martin, J. A., Hamilton, B. E., Sutton, P. D., Ventura, S. J., Menacker, F., & Munson, M. L. (2005). Births: Final data for 2003. *National Vital Statistics Reports, 54*(2). Hyattsville, MD: National Center for Health Statistics.

Martin, J. A., Smith, B. L., Mathews, T. J., & Ventura, S. J. (1999). Births and deaths: Preliminary data for 1998. *National Vital Statistics Report*, 47 (25). Hyattsville, MD: National Center for Health Statistics.

Mary Harris v. State, 30 Tex. Ct. App. 549; 17 S. W. 1110 (1891).

Mason, J. D. (2004). Munchausen syndrome by proxy. Downloaded March 15, 2005 from www.emedicine.com/emerg/ropic8.30htm.

Massaro, T. M. (1997). The meanings of shame: Implications for legal reform. *Psychology, Public Policy, and the Law, 3*, 645–704.

Mathes, P. G., & Irby, B. J. (1993). *Teen pregnancy and parenting handbook*. Champaign, IL: Research Press.

Mathis, D. (1997, December 22). Rape in Brazil leads to ultimate child-abuse case. *The Orlando Sentinel*, p. A21.

Matsumoto, A. (1995). A place for consideration of culture in the American criminal justice system: Japanese law and the Kimura case. *D.C. Law Journal of International Law & Practice, 4*, 507.

Matsuoka, A. (1997, November 7). Grand jury indicts mom for first-degree murder. *Honolulu Star-Bulletin*, p. 4.

Matter of Aaron S., 625 N.Y.S. 2d 786, 787 (Fam. Ct. 1993).

Mauldon, J., & Luker, K. (1996). The effects of contraceptive education on method use at first intercourse. *Family Planning Perspectives, 28*(1), 19–24, 41.

Maynard, R., & Rangarajan, A. (1994). Contraceptive use and repeat pregnancies among welfare-dependent teenage mothers. *Family Planning Perspectives, 26*(5), 198–205.

Mays, S. (1993). Infanticide in Roman Britain. *Antiquity, 67*(257), 883–888.

McBride, T. M. (1976). *The domestic revolution: The modernization of household services in England and France (1820–1920)*. New York: Holmes and Meier.

McCullogh, M. (1998, March 6). Amy Grossberg passed polygraph tests, lawyers say. *The Philadelphia Inquirer,* pp. B1, B4.

McGee, J. (2005, May 25). Lawyer: Killer mom is insane or great actress. *The Patriot Ledger* (Quincy, MA), p. 1.

McKee, G. R. (2006). *Why women kill.* New York: Oxford University Press.

McKee, G. R., & Shea, S. J. (1998). Maternal filicide: a cross-national comparison. *Journal of Clinical Psychology, 54*, 679–687.

McKee, L. (1984). Sex differentials in survivorship and the customary treatment of infants and children. *Medical Anthropology, 8*(2), 91–108.

McMillan, J. P. (1995). Prosecuting child abuse: Homicides in Iowa. *Drake Law Review, 44*, 129–160.

McQuaide, S., & Ehrenreich, J. H. (1998). Women in prison: approaches to understanding the lives of a forgotten population. *Affilia, 13*, 233–246.

Meadow, R. (1977). Munchausen syndrome by proxy: the hinterland of child abuse. *Lancet, 2*, 343–345.

Meadow, R. (1998). Munchausen syndrome by proxy abuse perpetrated by men. *Archives of Disease in Childhood, 78*(3), 210–216.

Meadow, R. (2002). Different interpretations of Munchausen syndrome by proxy. *Child Abuse and Neglect, 27*(4) 353–355.

Melton, G. B., Petrila, J., Poythress, N. G., & Slobogin, C. (1987). *Psychological evaluations for the courts: A handbook for mental health professionals.* New York: Guilford.

Mendlowicz, M. V., Rapaport, M. H., Mecler, K., Golshand, S., & Moraes, T. M. (1998). A case-control study on the sociodemographic characteristics of 53 neonaticidal mothers. *International Journal of Law and Psychiatry, 21*, 209–219.

Mensch, E., & Freeman, A. (1991). The politics of virtue: animals, theology, and abortion. *Georgia Law Review, 25*, 923–982.

Meyer, P., & Oberman, M. (2001). *Mothers who kill their children: Understanding the acts of moms from Susan Smith to the "prom mom."* New York: New York University Press.

Michalopoulos, C. (2003). Fill in the holes of the insanity defense: The Andrea Yates case and the need for a new prong. *Virginia Journal of Social Policy & the Law, 10*, 383–409.

Michaud, M. (2001). Guilty but not responsible: The need for a criminal duty to mitigate injuries. *Suffolk University Law Review, 34*, 629–647.

Milden, R., Rosenthal, M., Winegardner, J., & Smith, D. (1985). Denial of pregnancy: an exploratory investigation. *Journal of Psychosomatic Obstetrics and Gynecology, 4*, 255–261.

Miller, L. (1990). Psychotic denial of pregnancy: phenomenology and clinical management. *Hospital and Community Psychiatry, 41*, 1233–1237.

Minton, L. (1998, June 14). "Oh, no, I can't get pregnant": Teen parents talk about what they've learned. *Parade*, 16–17.

Mitchell, E. K., & Davis, J. H. (1984). Spontaneous births into toilets. *Journal of Forensic Science, 29*(2), 591–596.

Mochow, S. P. (1997). Munchausen syndrome by proxy: A subtle form of child abuse and a potential due-process nightmare. *Journal of Juvenile Law, 18*, 167–185.

Mohr, J. C. (1978). *Abortion in America: The origins and evolution of national policy, 1800–1900.* New York: Oxford University Press.

Montague, A. E. (1980). Introduction. In A. E. Montague (Ed.), *Sociobiology examined* (pp. 3–15). New York: Oxford University Press.

Morgan, C. (1995). Psychosocial variables associated with teenage pregnancy. *Adolescence, 30*, 277–289.

Morris, C. (2005, October 6). New study finds stigma and fear haunt moms suffering postpartum depression. http://Canada.com/News. Accessed October 6, 2005.

Morris, E. G. (2004, April 12). Civil commitment vs. life in prison: what Andrea Yates got that Deanna Laney didn't. *Texas Lawyer, 20*(6), p. 27.

Morrison, J. (1995). DSM-IV *made easy: A clinician's guide to diagnosis.* New York: Guilford.

Morrison, T. (1988). *Beloved.* New York: Plume.

Moss, D. C. (1988, August 1). Postpartum psychosis defense. *ABA Journal*, p. 22.

Most, D. (1999). *Always in our hearts: The story of Amy Grossberg, Brian Peterson, and the baby they didn't want.* Hackensack, NJ: Record Books.

Munoz, R. A. (1985). Postpartum psychosis as a discrete entity. *Journal of Clinical Psychiatry, 46*, 182–184.

Murphy, P. (1994). Scott's disappointments: reading *The Heart of Midlothian. Modern Philology, 92*(2), 179–198.

Myers v. Commonwealth. No. 1780-92-1, 1994 WL389 748, Va Ct. App. July 26, 1994.

Nadeau, M. (1997). Parents killing children: A revised typology of filicide. Paper presented at the Annual Meeting of the American Psychological Association, Chicago, IL.

Napier, K. (1997). Chastity programs shatter sex-ed myths. *Policy Review, 83*, 12–15.

National Child Abuse Defense and Resource Center (2004). Accessed February 3, 2004 from http://www. falseallegations.org

National Clearinghouse on Child Abuse and Neglect Information (2004). Child abuse and neglect fatalities: Statistics and interventions. Downloaded September 15, 2005.

National Institute of Neurological Diseases and Stroke (n.d.). NINDS Shaken baby syndrome information page. Downloaded June 29, 2005.

Neal, O. R. (1995). National issues: myths and moms: images of women and termination of parental rights. *Kansas Journal of Law and Public Policy, 5*, 61–71.

Nelesen, A. (2005). Bagneski faces trial in kids' deaths. *Green Bay Press-Gazette* (WI). Accessed August 5, 2005 from http://www.greenbaypress gazette.com

Nelson, A. L. (1991). Postpartum psychosis: a new defense? *Dickinson Law Review, 95*, 625–650.

New South Wales Law Reform Commission (1997). *Partial defences to murder: Provocation and infanticide.* Sydney, Australia: The Commission.

Newman, K. (1996). *Fetal positions, individualism, science, visuality.* Stanford, CA: Stanford University Press.

News in Brief (1997, October 31). *The Philadelphia Inquirer*, p. A4.

News & Observer (2005). Baby deaths challenge prosecutors. September 16, 2005. Accessed from www.newsobserver.com

Nieland, M. N. S., & Roger, D. (1997). Symptoms in postpartum and nonpostpartum samples: Implications for postnatal depression. *Journal of Reproductive and Infant Psychology, 15*, 31–42.

Nixon v. PA 533 U.S. 924, 121 S.Ct. 2541, 2001.

Noonan, J. (1970). An almost absolute value in history. In Noonan, J. (Ed.), *The morality of abortion*, (pp. 55–63). Cambridge, MA: Harvard University Press.

Oberman, M. (1996). Mothers who kill: coming to terms with modern American infanticide. *American Criminal Law Review, 34*(1), 1–110.

O'Connor, A. (2005, September 7). Yonkers: Parents charged in sons' deaths. *The New York Times*, p. 4.

O'Donovan, K. (1984). The medicalization of infanticide. *Criminal Law Review*, 259–264.

Ogle, R. S., Maier-Katkin, D., & Bernard, T. J. (1995). A theory of homicidal behavior among women. *Criminology, 33*(2), 173–193.

O'Hare, P. (2006). Andrea Yates case: Prosecutors on the defense. Accessed February 25, 2006 from http://www.HoustonChronicle.com

Ohio v. Hopfer, 112 OH App. 3d 521 (1996).

Olds, D., Henderson, C. R., Jr., Cole, R., Eckenrode, J., Kitzman, H., Luckey, D., Pettitt, L., Sidora, K., Morris, P., & Powers, J. (1998). Long-term effects of nurse home visitation on children's criminal and antisocial behavior: 15-year follow-up of a randomized controlled trial. *Journal of the American Medical Association, 280,* 1238–144.

OLPA (Office of Legislative Policy and Analysis). Legislative updates. Downloaded March 15, 2005.

Olsen, J. A., Weed, S. E., Ritz, G. M., & Jensen, L. C. (1991). The effects of three abstinence sex education programs on student attitudes toward sexual activity. *Adolescence, 26,* 631–641.

O'Malley, S. (2004). *"Are you there alone?" The unspeakable crime of Andrea Yates.* New York: Simon and Schuster.

Oropesa, R. S., Landale, N. S., Inkley, M., & Gorman, B. K. (1999). Prenatal care among Puerto Ricans on the U.S. Mainland. Paper presented at the Annual Meeting of the American Sociological Association, Chicago, IL.

Overington, C. (2005, September 22). Eyes on the child. *The Australian.* Downloaded 9/22/05 from www.theaustralian.news.com.au/common/story.

Overpeck, M. D., Brenner, R. A., Trumble, A. C., Tripletti, L. B., & Berendes, H. W. (1998). Risk factors for infant homicide in the United States. *New England Journal of Medicine, 339,* 1211–1216.

Owens, D. (2005, June 15). Mom who killed infant freed from state care. *The Hartford Courant* (Northwest Connecticut edition), p. 87.

Pact, an Adoption Alliance (1996). Overview of Pact, an Adoption Alliance, with questions and answers on adoption. *Is Adoption for You?* 1–11.

Palermo, G. B. (2002). Murderous parents. *International Journal of Offender Therapy and Comparative Criminology, 46*(2), 123–143.

Palermo, M. T. (2003). Preventing filicide in families with autistic children. *International Journal of Offender Therapy and Comparative Criminology, 47*(1), 47–57.

Park, S. K. (2002). Severing the bond of life: When conflicts of interest fail to recognize the value of two lives. *University of Hawaii Law Review, 25,* 157–198.

Parker, J. T. (2001). School-based sex education: A new millennium update, ERIC Digest. Washington, D.C.: ERIC Clearinghouse on Teaching and Teacher Education.

Parness, J. A. (1993). Pregnant dads: the crimes and other misconduct of expectant fathers. *Oregon Law Review, 72,* 901–918.

Pearlman, S. F., & Bilodeau, R. (1999). Academic-community collaboration in teen pregnancy prevention: New roles for professional psychologists. *Professional Psychology, 30,* 92–98.

Pennsylvania State University (2005, May 7). Study shows education program reduces shaken-baby-syndrome incidents. *Law & Health Weekly,* p. 323.

People of the State of New York v. Eugene Wong and People of the State of New York v. Mary Wong, 81 NY 2d 600, 619 M.E. 2d 377, 601 NYS 2d 440 (July 8, 1993).

People v. Andrea, FF 586, NYS 2d, LexisNexis 9333.423, NY App. Div. (1992).

People v. Apodaca, 76 CA App. 3rd 479; 1978 Cal. App. LEXIS 1145; 142 Cal Reptr.830.

People v. Avery, 88 IL App. 3rd 771; 410 NW 2d 1093 (1980).

People v. Campbell, 159 IL 9; 42 NE 123 (1895).

People v. Coulter, 697 NYS 2d 498 (Dist. Ct. 1st Dist. NY 1999).

People v. Doss, 214 IL App. 3rd 1051; 574 NE 2d 806 (1991).

People v. Ehlert, 1-93-1518 274 IL App. 3rd 1026 (1990).

People v. Goodrum, 152 WI 2d 540, 449 NW 2d 41 (WI App. 1989).

People v. Keeler, 2 al. ed 610' 470 P. 2d 617 (1970), CA Reptr. 481; 40 LR 3rd 520.

People v. Kirby, 223 MI 440; 194 NW (1923).

People v. Massip, 274 CA Reptr. 369, 798 2d 1212 (1990).

People v. Massip, 824 P. 2d 568, 4 Cal. Rptr. 2d 762 (1992).

People v. Philips, 122 Cal. App. 3s 69, 76 (Cal. Ct. App. 1981).

People v. Sims, 244 Ill. App. 3d 966, 184 Ill. Dec. 135 (2001).

People v. Sophia M., 234 CA Reptr. 698 (CA Ct. App. 1987).

People v. Wernick, 89 NY 2d 111; 674 NE 2d 322 (1996); 651 NYS 2d 392.

People v. Westfall, 198 CA App.; 18 CA Reptr. 3561 (1961).

Perlman, C. M. (1998). Diagnosing the truth: Determining physician liability in cases involving Munchausen syndrome by proxy. *Washington University Journal of Urban and Contemporary Law, 54*, 267–290.

Pernick, M. S. (1996). *The black stork: Eugenics and the death of "defective" babies in American medicine and motion pictures since 1915*. New York: Oxford University Press.

Petchesky, R. P. (1981). Antiabortion, antifeminism, and the rise of the New Right. *Feminist Studies, 7*, 206–246.

Petchesky, R. P. (1990). *Abortion and woman's choice: The state, sexuality, and reproductive freedom*. Boston: Northeastern University Press.

Phipps, C. A. (1999). Responding to child homicide: A statutory proposal. *Journal of Criminal Law and Criminology, 89*, 535–593.

Piers, M. W. (1978). *Infanticide*. New York: Norton.

Pinker, S. (1997a, November 2). Why they kill their newborns. *The New York Times Magazine*, pp. 52–54.

Pinker, S. (1997b). *How the mind works*. New York: Norton.

Pipher, M. (1994). *Reviving Ophelia: Saving the selves of adolescent girls*. New York: Ballantine Books.

Planned Parenthood of Central New Jersey v. Farmer, 165 NJ 609, 762 A. 2d 620 (2000).

Planned Parenthood of Southeastern Pennsylvania, et al. v. Robert P. Casey, et al., 505 U.S. 833; 112 S. Ct. 2791 (1992).

Plunkett, J. (2001). Fatal pediatric head injuries caused by short-distance falls. *American Journal of Forensic Medical Pathology, 22*(1), 1–12.

Poland, S. C. (1997) Landmark legal cases in bioethics. *Kennedy Institute of Ethics Journal, 7*(2), 191–209.

Pomeroy, S. B. (1993). Infanticide in Hellenistic Greece. In A. Cameron, & A. Kugrt, (Eds.), *Images of women in antiquity* (pp. 207–219). Detroit: Wayne State University Press.

Posner, R. (1998). Lecture: Oliver Wendell Holmes lectures. The problematics of moral and legal theory. *Harvard Law Review, 111*, 1637–1709.

Post, S. G. (1990). Infanticide and geronticide. *Ageing and Society, 10*, 317–328.

Prentice, M. A. (2001). Prosecuting mothers who maim and kill: The profile of Munchausen by proxy litigation in the late 1990s. *American Journal of Criminal Law, 28*, 373–412.

Prince v. Commonwealth of Massachusetts, 321 U.S. at 155 (1944).

Pruett, M. K. (2002). Commentary: Pushing a new classification schema for perpetrators of maternal filicide one step further. *Journal of the American Academy of Psychiatry & Law, 30*, 352–354.

Puit, G. (1998, March 16). Experts offer reasons why teens kill their babies. *Las Vegas Review-Journal*, p. 1A.

Putkonen, H., Collander, J., Honkasalo, M. L., & Lonnqvist, J. (1998). Finnish female homicide offenders, 1982–1992. *Journal of Forensic Psychiatry, 9*, 672–684.

Quadagno, J. S. (1979). Paradigms in evolutionary theory: the sociobiological model of natural selection. *American Sociological Review, 44*, 100–109.

Quinlan, C. (2003/2004). Postpartum psychosis and the United States criminal justice system. *Buffalo Women's Law Journal, 12*, 17–23.

Raghavan, S. (1998, May 31). Seminar tells teens in Phila. why to say no to sex. *The Philadelphia Inquirer*, p. B2.

Ramsey, P. (1970). Reference points in deciding about abortion. In J. Noonan (Ed.), *The morality of abortion* (pp. 60–89). Cambridge, MA: Harvard University Press.

Ransel, D. L. (1988). *Mothers of misery: Child abandonment in Russia*. Princeton, NJ: Princeton University Press.

Ratner, R. A. (1985). A case of child abandonment—reflections on criminal responsibility in adolescence. *Bulletin of the American Academy of Psychiatry and Law, 13*, 291–301.

Re Austynn, App. Ct. 4d ed Cal. 2004.

Reagan, L. J. (1997). *When abortion was a crime: Women, medicine, and the law in the United States, 1867–1973*. Berkeley: University of California Press.

Reece, L. E. (1991). Mothers who kill: postpartum disorders and criminal infanticide. *UCLA Law Review, 38*, 699–757.

Reid, M. C. (1997). The case of *Medea*—a view of fetal–maternal conflict. *Journal of Medical Ethics, 23*(91), 19–25.

Reid v. State, 964 S. W. 2d 723; 1998 Tex. App. LEXIS 1122 (February 29, 1998).

Resnick, P. (1969). Child murder by parents: A psychiatric review of filicide. *American Journal of Psychiatry, 126*(3), 73–82.

Resnick, P. (1970). Murder of the newborn: a psychiatric review of neonaticide. *American Journal of Psychiatry, 126*, 1414–1420.

Reuters (1997, December 14). Girl, 11, asks judge for abortion. *The Philadelphia Inquirer*, p. A20.

Rhein, R. (2003). Assessing criminal liability for the passive parent: Why New York should hold the passive parent criminally liable. *Cardozo Women's Law Journal, 9*, 627–657.

Rhode, D. L. (1992). Politics and pregnancy: adolescent mothers and public policy. *Southern California Review of Law and Women's Studies, 1*, 99–132.

Rhoden, N. K. (1988). Litigating life and death. *Harvard Law Review, 102*, 375–442.

Richter, J. S. (1998). Infanticide, child abandonment, and abortion in Imperial Germany. *Journal of Interdisciplinary History, 28*(4), 511–551.

Riet, D. (1986). Infanticide et société au XVIII siècle: Bruits publics et rumeurs dans la Communauté. *Ethnologie Française Nouvelle Serie, 18*(4), 402–406.

Roberts, D. E. (1993). Motherhood and crime. *Iowa Law Review, 79*, 95–141.

Robinson, B. E. (1988). Teenage pregnancy from the father's perspective. *American Journal of Orthopsychiatry, 58*(91), 46–51.

Roe v. Wade, 410 U.S. S. Ct. 113 (1973).

Rosato, J. L. (2000). Using bioethics discourse to determine when parents should make health care decisions for their children: Is deference justified? *Temple Law Review, 73*, 1–68.

Rose, L. (1986). *The massacre of the innocents: Infanticide in Britain 1800–1939.* London: Routledge and Kegan Paul.

Rosenberg, D. A. (1997). Munchausen syndrome by proxy: Currency in counterfeit illness (5th ed.). In M. E. Helfer, R. S. Kempe, & R. D. Krugman (Eds.), *The battered child* (pp. 413–30). Chicago: University of Chicago Press.

Rothman, B. K. (1989). *Recreating motherhood: Ideology and technology in a patriarchal society.* New York: Norton.

Rothstein, M. (1998, May 2). Now a warm welcome instead of a cold bath for a Harvard biologist. *The New York Times*, pp. B9, B11.

Rowe, G. S. (1991). Infanticide, its judicial resolution and criminal code revision in early Pennsylvania. *Proceedings of the American Philosophical Society, 135*(2), 200–232.

Ruble, R. (1999, February 21). Number of abandoned babies rise. *Tulsa World*, p. 25.

Rue, V. M. (1985). Death by design of handicapped newborns: the family's role and response. *Issues in Law and Medicine, 1*(3), 201–225.

Ruethling, G. (2005, May 11). Father of slain 8-year-old is accused of murdering her and best friend, 9. *The New York Times,* p. A15.

Ruggiero, K. (1992). Honor, maternity, and the disciplining of women: Infanticide in late nineteenth-century Buenos Aires. *Hispanic American Historical Review, 72*(3), 353–373.

Rush, B. L. (2005). Letter to the editor: New moms with depression need help; jail time and wearing blinders do not solve the problem. *Chicago Sun-Times*, p. 56.

Russell, E. (1998, October 14). Fox, Planned Parenthood at odds over vote on Title X amendment. *Jenkintown Times-Chronicle — Glenside News* (PA), p. 19.

Ryan, J. (1998, December 6). Freedom of choice. *San Francisco Chronicle,* p. 1.

Sadoff, R. L. (1995). Mothers who kill their children. *Psychiatric Annals, 25,* 601–605.

Saternus, K., Kernbach-Wighton, G., & Oehmichen, M. (2000). The shaking trauma in infants—kinetic chains. *Forensic Science International, 109*(3), 203–213.

Sauer, R. (1974). Attitudes to abortion in America, 1800–1973. *Population Studies: American Journal of Demography, 28*(1), 53–67.

Sauer, R. (1978). Infanticide and abortion in nineteenth-century Britain. *Population Studies: American Journal of Demography, 32*(1), 81–93.

Saunders, E. (1989). Neonaticides following "secret" pregnancies in seven case reports. *Public Health Reports, 104*(4), 368–372.

Schachman, K. A., Lee, R. K., & Lederman, R. P. (2004). Baby boot camp: Facilitating maternal role adaptation among military wives. *Nursing Research, 53*(2), 107–115.

Scheibner, V. (2001). Shaken baby diagnosis on shaky ground. *Journal of Australasian College of Nutritional and Environmental Medicine, 20*(2), 5–8.

Scheier, R. (2005, July 27). Postpartum depression fight begins; state launches campaign to help mothers. *Herald News* (Passaic County, NJ), p. B01.

Scheper-Hughes, N. (1989, October). The human strategy: death without weeping. *Natural History,* 8–16.

Schnitzer, P. G., & Ewigman, B. G. (2005). Child deaths resulting from inflicted injuries: Household risk factors and perpetrator characteristics. *Pediatrics, 116*, 687–693.

Schreier, H. A., & Libow, J. A. (1993). *Hurting for love: Munchausen by proxy syndrome.* New York: Guilford Press.

Schroeder, C., & Bell, J. (2005). Labor support for incarcerated pregnant women: The doula project. *The Prison Journal, 85*, 311–328.

Schroeder, T. L. (1993). Postpartum psychosis as a defense for murder? *Western State University Law Review, 21*, 267–293.

Schulte, R. (1984). Infanticide in rural Bavaria in the nineteenth century. In H. Medick, & W. Sabean (Eds.), *Interest and emotion: Essays in the study of family and kinship* (pp. 77–102). Cambridge, England: Cambridge University Press.

Schultz, M. (1991). The blood libel: a motif in the history of childhood. In A. Dundes (Ed.), *The blood libel legend, a casebook in anti-Semitic folklore* (pp. 273–303). Madison: University of Wisconsin Press.

Schwartz, L. L. (2000). Adoption: Parents who choose children and their options. In F. W. Kaslow (Ed.), *Handbook of couple and family forensics* (pp. 23–42). New York: John Wiley & Sons.

Schwartz, L. L. (2006). *When adoptions go wrong: Family psychology and legal issues.* Binghamton, NY: Haworth Press.

Schwartz, L. L., & Isser, N. (2001). Neonaticide: An appropriate application for therapeutic jurisprudence? *Behavioral Sciences and the Law, 19*, 703–718.

Schwartz, L. L., & Kaslow, F. W. (Eds.) (2003). *Welcome home: An international and nontraditional adoption reader.* Binghamton, NY: Haworth Press.

Scott, P. D. (1973). Parents who kill their children. *Medicine, Science, and the Law, 13*, 120–126.

Scott, W. (1830; reprint 1994). *The heart of Midlothian.* New York: Penguin Books.

Scrimshaw, S. C. M. (1978). Infant mortality and behavior in the regulation of family size. *Population and Development Review, 4*(3), 383–403.

Semuels, A. (2005, April 27). Shaken baby syndrome. *Pittsburgh Post-Gazette,* p. D-1.

Shedd v. State, 178 GA 653 173 SE 847 GA (1934).

Sheridan, M. S. (2003). The deceit continues: an updated literature review of Munchausen syndrome by proxy. *Child Abuse and Neglect, 27*, 431–451.

Short, R. (1998). Teaching safe sex in school. *International Journal of Gynecology and Obstetrics, 63*, S147–S150.

Shorter, E. (1975). *The making of the modern family.* New York: Basic Books.

Showalter, E. (1980). Victorian women and insanity. *Victorian Studies, 23*, 157–180.

Siegel, C. D., Graves, P., Maloney, K., Norris, J. M., Calonge, B. N., & Lezotte, D. (1996). Mortality from intentional and unintentional injury among infants of young mothers in Colorado, 1986–1992. *Archives of Pediatric and Adolescent Medicine, 150*, 1077–1083.

Silva, J. A., Leong, G. B., Dassori, A., Ferrari, M. M., Weinstock, R., & Yamamoto, J. (1998). A comprehensive typology for the biopsychosciocultural evaluation of child-killing behavior. *Journal of Forensic Science, 43*, 1112–1118.

Silverman, R., A., & Kennedy, L. W. (1988). Women who kill their children. *Violence and Victims, 3*(92), 113–127.

Simpson, C. (1999, February 12). Woman guilty of killing baby for insurance. *Chicago Sun-Times*, p. 9.

Singer, P. (1975). *Animal liberation: A new ethic for our treatment of animals.* New York: Random House.

Singer, P. (1979). *Practical ethics.* Cambridge, MA: Cambridge University Press.

Singer, P. (1981). *The expanding circle: Ethics and sociobiology.* New York: Farrar, Straus, and Giroux.

Singleton v. State, 33 AL App. 536; 35 So 2d 375 (1948).

Smart, C. (2005, October 2). No proof on either side of the shaken baby debate. *Salt Lake* (Utah) *Tribune.* Retrieved October 20, 2005.

Smith, J. M. (2003). *A potent spell: Mother love and the power of fear.* Boston: Houghton Mifflin.

Smithey, M. (1998). Infant homicide: victim/offender relationship and causes of death. *Journal of Family Violence, 13,* 285–297.

So you're going to be a mother (1999). *Teen Voices, 8*(91), 23–29.

Sobol, M. P., & Daly, K. J. (1992). The adoption alternative for pregnant adolescents: decision making, consequences, and policy implications. *Journal of Social Issues, 48,* 143–161.

Solinger, R. (1990). The girl nobody loved: psychological explanations for White single pregnancy in the pre-*Roe v. Wade v. Thomas* era, 1945–1965. *Frontiers, 11*(2/3), 45–54.

Solinger, R. (1992). Race and "value": Black and White illegitimate babies in the U.S.A., 1945–1965. *Gender and History, 4,* 343–363.

Solis, M. (2005). Child services worker fired after boys' scalding deaths. Accessed August 1, 2005 from http://www.abclocal.go.com/wabc/news/print.Wabc180105yonkersparentsts/M.html

Sollum, T. (1997). State actions in reproductive health issues in 1996. *Family Planning Perspectives, 29*(91), 35–40.

Southall, D., Plunkett, M., Banks, M., Fakov, A., & Semuels, M. (1997). Covert video recordings of life-threatening child abuse: Lessons for child protection. *Pediatrics, 100,* 735–760.

Spielvogel, A. M. & Hohenor, H. C. (1995). Denial of pregnancy: a review and case reports. *Birth, 22,* 220–226. Courtesy of Blackwell Science. With permission.

Spinelli, M. G. (2004). Maternal infanticide associated with mental illness: Prevention and the promise of saved lives. *American Journal of Psychiatry, 161,* 1548–1557.

Stanfield, J. (2000). Current public law and policy issue: Faith healing and religious treatment exemptions to child-endangerment laws: Should parents be allowed to refuse necessary medical treatment for their children based on their religious beliefs? *Hamline Journal of Public Policy and Law, 22,* 45–86.

Starling, S. P., Holden, J. R., & Jenny, C. (1995). Abusive head trauma: The relationship of perpetrators to their victims. *Pediatrics, 95,* 259–262.

State of Missouri v. Michelle Rene Fuelling, No. WD 62493 (Oct. 26, 2004).

State of New Jersey v. Steven Anthony Galloway, 628 A. 2d 735 (1993).

State v. Blue, 138 N.C. App. 404, 531 S.E. 2d 267, N.C. App. (June 20, 2000).

State v. Buffin, 511 So. 2d LA Ct. App. (1987).

State v. Butts, N.E. 2004 WL 449245-2005-Ohio 1136, Ohio App. 10 Dist. (Mar. 11, 2004).

State v. Doyle, 287 NW 2d NE (1978).

State v. Eugene Wong and *State v. Mary Wong*, 81 NY 2d 600, 619 N.E. 2d 377, 601 NYS 2d 440.

State v. Hopfer, 679 NE 2d, 328 OH Ct. App. (1996).

State v. Maurico, Supreme Ct. AL 523 So. 2d 87 (1987).

State v. McGuire, 200 W. VA 823; 490 SE 2d 912 (1997).

State v. McKown, 475 NW 2d 63 (MN 1991) (see *Juvenile and Family Law Digest*, February 1992, 79-80).

State v. Mendoza, 1125 S.W. 3d 873, Mo. App. WD 2003 (October 7, 2003).

Steelman, E. S. (2002). Note: A question of revenge: Munchausen syndrome by proxy and a proposed diminished-capacity defense for homicidal mothers. *Cardozo Women's Law Journal, 8*, 261–312.

Stevens-Simon, C., & Kaplan, D. (1998). Teen childbearing trends: Which tide turned when and why? *Pediatrics, 102*, 1205–1207.

Stevens-Simon, C., & Mcanarney, E. R. (1994). Childhood victimization: relationship to adolescent pregnancy outcome. *Child Abuse and Neglect, 18*, 569–575.

Stewart, K. (2005, January 15). "Suspicious overtones" in death of baby in Tooele. *The Salt Lake Tribune* (UT), p. B2.

Stinson, R., & Stinson, P. (1981). On the death of a baby. *Journal of Medical Ethics, 8*, 5–18.

Stoiber, K. C., Anderson, A. J., & Schowalter, D. S. (1998). Group prevention and intervention with pregnant and parenting adolescents. In K. C. Stoiber, & T. R. Kratchowill (Eds.), *Handbook of group intervention for children and families* (pp. 280–306). Boston: Allyn & Bacon.

Stout, J. W., & Rivara, F. P. (1989). Schools and education: Does it work? *Pediatrics, 83*, 375–379.

Straight, S. (1998, January 25). Very first person: The secret of motherhood: Birth may come naturally, sometimes unexpectedly, but nurturing must be learned. *Los Angeles Times*, p. 14.

Stuttaford, T. (2005, June 13). Syndrome is one of the most difficult to identify. Accessed December 3, 2005 from www.Timesonline.uk.

Sunstein, C. R. (1992). Neutrality in constitutional law (with special reference to pornography, abortion, and surrogacy). *Columbia Law Review, 92*, 1–52.

Sussman, G. D. (1975). Wet-nursing business in the nineteenth century. *French Historical Studies, 9*(2), 304–328.

Swendsen, J. D., & Mazure, C. M. (2000). Life stress as a risk factor for postpartum depression: current research and methodological issues. *Clinical Psychology: Science and Practice, 7*, 17–31.

Symonds, D. A. (1997). *Weep not for me: Women and ballads and infanticide in early modern Scotland.* University Park, PA: Pennsylvania State University Press.

Tappin, D., Ecob, R., & Brooke, H. (2005). Bedsharing, roomsharing, and sudden infant death syndrome in Scotland: A case-control study. *Journal of Pediatrics, 147*, 32–37.

Thane, P. (1979). Women and the poor law in Victorian and Edwardian England. *History Workshop Journal, 6*, 29–51.

Thompson, K. R. (1998). Comment: The putative father's right to notice of adoption proceedings: Has Georgia finally solved the adoption equation? *Emory Law Journal, 47*, 1475–1509.

Tilly, L. A., Scott, J. W., & Cohen, M. (1976). Women's work and European fertility patterns. *Journal of Interdisciplinary History, 6*, 447–476.

Tobin, E. (1993). Law and literature imagining the mother's text: Toni Morrison's *Beloved* and contemporary law. *Harvard Women's Law Journal, 15*, 233–273.

Trachtenberg, J. (1943). *The devil and the Jews: The medieval conception of the Jew and its relation to modern anti-Semitism.* New Haven: Yale University Press.

Trexler, R. (1973). The foundlings of Florence, 1395–1455. *History of Childhood Quarterly, 1*(4) 259–275.

Tribe, L. (1990). *Abortion: The clash of absolutes.* New York: W. W. Norton.

U.S. v. Washington, ex rel. Jones v. Washington, 836 F. Supp. 502 (ND IL 1993).

U.S. v. Welch, U.S. App. No. 93-4043 (September 19, 1994).

Uscinski, R. (2002). Shaken baby syndrome: fundamental questions. *British Journal of Neurosurgery, 16*(3), 217–219.

Vaillant, D. (2000). The prosecution of Christian Scientists: A needed protection for children or insult added to injury? *Cleveland State Law Review, 48*, 479–502.

Valverde, L. (1994). Illegitimacy and the abandonment of children in the Basque country, 1550–1800. In J. Henderson, & R. Wall (Eds.), *Poor women and children in the European past* (pp. 51–64). London: Routledge.

Van Biema, D. (1998, August 31). Faith or healing? Why the law can't do a thing about the infant mortality of an Oregon cult. *Time*, 68–69.

Vance, P. C. (1985). Love and sex: can we talk about that in school? *Childhood education, 61*, 272–276.

Vasillopoulos, C. (1994). *Medea* and the transformation of the tragic politic. *Social Sciences Journal, 31*, 435–461.

Ventura, S. J. (1984). Trends in teenage childbearing, United States, 1970-81. *Vital and Health Statistics*, Series 21, No. 41, DHHS Pub. No. (PHS) 84-1919, Public Health Service. Washington, D.C.: U.S. Government Printing Office.

Ventura, S. J., Hamilton, R. E., & Sutton, P. D. (2003). Revised birth and fertility rates for the United States, 2000 and 2001. *National Vital Statistics Reports, 51*(4). Hyattsville, MD: National Center for Health Statistics.

Ventura, S. J., Martin, J. A., Curtin, S. C., & Mathews, T. J. (1999a). Births: Final data for 1997. *National Vital Statistics Report.* Hyattsville, MD: National Center for Health Statistics.

Ventura, S. J., Mathews, T. J., & Curtin, S. C. (1999b). Declines in teenage birth rates, 1991–98: update of national and state trends. *National Vital Statistics Report.* Hyattsville, MD: National Center for Health Statistics.

Waggoner, M. (1999, October 22). Good child care pays years later, study finds. *The Philadelphia Inquirer,* p. A3.

Waldron, K. (1990). Postpartum psychosis as an insanity defense: underneath a controversial defense lies a garden variety insanity defense complicated by unique circumstances for recognizing culpability in causing. *Rutgers Law Review, 21*, 559–597.

Waltner, A. (1995). Infanticide and dowry in Ming and Early Qing China. In A. B. Kinney (Ed.), *Chinese views of childhood* (pp. 193–219). Honolulu: University of Hawaii Press.

Ward, L. M. (1995). Talking about sex: Common themes about sexuality in the prime-time television programs children and adolescents view most. *Journal of Youth and* Adolescence, *24*, 595–615.

Weaver v. State, 24 Ala. App. 208, 132. So. 706 (Mar. 03, 1931).

Webster-Stratton, C., & Reid, M. J. (2003). The Incredible Years parent, teachers, and children training series: A multifaceted treatment approach for young children with conduct problems. In A. E. Kazdin & J. R. Weisz (Eds.), *Evidence-based psychotherapies for children and adolescents* (pp. 224–240). New York: Guilford Press.

Webster v. Reproductive Health Services, 109 S. Ct. 3040 (1989).

Weckerle, C., & Wolfe, D. A. (1998). Windows for preventing child and partner abuse: Early childhood and adolescence. In P. K. Trickett, & C. J. Schellenbach (Eds.), *Violence against children in the family and the community* (pp. 339–369). Washington, D.C.: American Psychological Association.

Weekes-Shackelford, V. A., & Shackelford, T. K. (2004). Methods of filicide: Step parents and genetic parents kill differently. *Violence and Victims, 19*, 75–81.

Weisenburger, S. (1998). *Modern Medea: A family history of slavery and child murder from the Old South.* New York: Hill and Wang.

Welch v. United States, 513 U.S. 1169, 115 S.Ct. 1142, No. 94-7385 (February 21, 1995).

Welner, M. (1997, January 1). "Neonaticide syndrome" barred from insanity defense: insufficient foundation without *Frye* hearing. *The Forensic Echo, 1*(3), 1–3.

Werblowsky, R. J. Z., & Wigoder, G. (Eds.) (1965). *The encyclopedia of the Jewish religion.* New York: Holt, Rinehart, and Winston.

Werner, O. H. (1917; reprint 1960). *The unmarried mother in German literature with special reference to the period 1770–1800.* New York: AMS Press.

Wexler, D. B. (1997). Therapeutic jurisprudence in a comparative law context. *Behavioral Sciences and the Law, 15*, 233–246.

Wexler, D. B., & Winick, B. J. (1991). Therapeutic jurisprudence as a new approach to mental health law policy analysis and research. *University of Miami Law Review, 45*, 979–1004.

Wheeler, K. H. (1997). Infanticide in nineteenth-century Ohio. *Journal of Social History, 31*, 407–418.

Wheelwright, J. (1998, July 27). Women: a life given … and taken. How can a woman manage to conceal her pregnancy for nine long months, then kill her newborn baby? Julie Wheelwright reports. *The Manchester Guardian*, p. T4.

Whitley, G. (2005, January 20). Psycho mom. *Dallas Observer.* Downloaded from dallasobserver.com., November 28, 2005.

Whitner v. State of South Carolina, Opinion No. 24468 (1997).

Wilczynski, A. (1991). Images of women who kill their infants: the mad and the bad. *Women and Criminal Justice, 2*(2), 71–88.

Wilczynski, A. (1997a). *Child homicide.* London: Greenwich Medical Media, Ltd.

Wilczynski, A. (1997b). Mad or bad? *British Journal of Criminology, 37*, 417–436.

Wilczynski, A., & Morris, A. (1993, January). Parents who kill their children. *Criminal Law Review*, 31–36.

Wiley, C. (1990). Staging infanticide: the refusal of representation in Elizabeth Robin's *Alan's wife. Theatre Journal, 42*, 432–446.

Wilgoren, J. (2005a, May 12). Ex-convict stabbed girls to death over $40, officials say. *The New York Times*, p. A17.

Wilgoren, J. (2005b, September 25). "Mothering the Mother" during childbirth and after. *The New York Times*, p. A14/

Wilkey, I., Pearn, J., Petrie, G., & Nixon, J. (1982). Neonaticide, infanticide, and child homicide. *Medicine, Science, and the Law, 22*, 31–34.

Williams, B. J. (1981). A critical review of models in sociology. *Annual Review of Anthropology, 10*, 163–192.

Williamson, G. L. (1993). Postpartum depression syndrome as a defense to criminal behavior. *Journal of Family Violence, 8*, 151–165.

Williamson, L. (1978). Infanticide: an anthropological analysis. In M. Kohl (Ed.), *Infanticide and the value of life* (pp. 61–73). Buffalo, NY: Prometheus Books.

Wills, A. D. (2004). Neonaticide: The necessity of syndrome evidence when safe haven legislation falls short. *Temple Law Review, 77*, 1001–1038.

Wilson, E. O. (1980). *Sociobiology* (abridged ed.). Cambridge, MA: Belnap Press of Harvard University Press.

Wilson, E. O. (1988). *Consilience: The unity of knowledge.* New York: Knopf.

Wilson, J. Q. (1994). On abortion. *Commentary, 97*(91), 21–37.

Wilson, L. (2005). Pregnancy discrimination in the workplace. In A. Barnes (Ed.), *The handbook of women, psychology, and the law* (pp. 124–146). New York: John Wiley & Sons.

Wilson, S. (1988). Infanticide, child abandonment, and female honor in nineteenth-century Corsica. *Comparative Studies in Sociology and History, 30*, 762–783.

Winick, B. J. (1997). The jurisprudence of therapeutic jurisprudence. *Psychology, Public Policy, and the Law, 3*, 184–206.

Winpisinger, K. A., Hopkins, R. S., Indian, R. W., & Hostetler, J. R. (1991). Risk factors for childhood homicides in Ohio: a birth certificate-based case-control study. *American Journal of Public Health, 81*, 1052–1054.

Wisner, K. L., Gracious, B. L., Piontek, C. M., Peindl, K., & Percl, J. M. (2003). Postpartum disorders: Phenomenology, treatment approaches, and relationship to infanticide. In M. Spinelli (Ed.), *Infanticide: Psychosocial and legal perspectives on mothers who kill* (pp. 35–60). Washington, D.C.: American Psychiatric Publishing.

Wissow, L. S. (1998). Editorial: Infanticide. *New England Journal of Medicine, 339*, 1239.

Wolman, B. B. (Ed.) (1965). *Handbook of clinical psychology.* New York: McGraw-Hill.

Wright, R. (1994). *The moral animal: Evolutionary psychology and everyday life.* New York: Pantheon Books.

Wrightsman, L. S., Nietzel, M. T, & Fortune, W. H. (1998). *Psychology and the legal system* (4th ed.). Pacific Grove, CA: Brooks/Cole.

Wrightson, K. (1982). Infanticide in European history. *Criminal Justice History, 3*, 1–20.

Wurf, M. K. (1997, Summer). Welfare Reform Bill tackles teen pregnancy. *Girls Ink*, p. 3. Accessed from http://www2.hawaii.edu/~heiby/overheads classification.html.

Yorker, B. C. (1995). Current topics in biomedical ethics: Covert video surveillance of Munchausen syndrome by proxy: the exigent circumstances exception. *Health Matrix: Journal of Law–Medicine, 5*, 325–345.

Zajac, B. M. (1989). Legal issues in neonatal intensive care. *Hospital and Health Sciences Administration, 34*, 578–587.

Zibart, E. (1996, August). The *Medea* syndrome: Women who murder their young. *Cosmopolitan*, 176–179.

Zimmer, C. (1996). First, kill the babies: evolutionary explanations for infanticide. *Discover, 17*(9), 72–81.

Zingraff, M., & Thomson, R. (1984). Differential sentencing of women and men in the U.S.A. *International Journal of the Sociology of Law, 12*, 401–413

Zitella, J. J. (1996). Note: Protecting our children: A call to reform state policies to hold pregnant drug addicts accountable. *John Marshall Law Review, 29*, 765–798.

Zurzola, A. (1998, June 10). Dad weeps for mom who vanished, left baby in toilet. *The Bergen County Record* (NJ), p. a3.

Index

A

B

C

D

E

F

G

J

K

L

M

N

O

P

R

S

T

U

V

W

Y